Cooking For Dummies,® 2nd Edition

Cheat Sheet

The Ten Commandments of Cooking

- **Taste. Taste. Taste.** That's the only way to know whether your dish is coming out right.

- **Be patient.** Don't blow hot breath over a pot to make it boil faster. Just cover it with a lid.

- **Be flexible.** If something looks terrific in the market (or something you planned to buy *doesn't*), be willing to modify your meal plans.

- **Be thrifty.** Don't throw away anything unless it's spoiled. Use bones and peelings for stocks, leftovers for next-day dishes, stale bread for croutons, and so on.

- **Be organized.** Do all preparation (rinsing, chopping, measuring, and so on) before you begin cooking.

- **Develop a memory bank for flavors and how they work together, particularly herbs and spices.**

- **Don't be a slave to recipes, even if you're a beginner.** Feel free to modify something if the change suits your tastes.

- **Make sure that your knives are sharp and your equipment is in good working order.** You could easily cut yourself with a dull blade, because it requires you to use more force.

- **Use only the freshest ingredients.**

- **Remember that no dish, no matter how botched or burned, is a failure.** Try it out on unsuspecting kids or the dog.

Timesaving Tips

- Precook pieces of chicken, meat, or vegetables in your microwave before finishing them on the grill.

- Take steaks and other meats out of the refrigerator about 15 minutes before cooking so that they warm to room temperature. They'll cook faster and more evenly.

- Line the broiler pan with aluminum foil to ease cleanup when broiling hamburgers, fish, steaks, and chops.

- Make salad dressings that contain onion, garlic, fresh herbs, and the like in a food processor or blender to save chopping time.

- Place a garlic clove on a cutting board and whack it with the flat side of a heavy knife or a cleaver to make removing the skin easier. The skin should split right off.

- Roll a lemon or orange under the palm of your hand on the countertop to make extracting the juice easier.

Common Conversions

Liquid volume equivalents

1 cup = 8 fluid ounces

2 cups = 1 pint or 16 fluid ounces

2 pints = 1 quart or 32 fluid ounces

4 quarts = 1 gallon

$\frac{1}{2}$ tablespoon = $1\frac{1}{2}$ teaspoons

1 tablespoon = 3 teaspoons

2 tablespoons = 1 fluid ounce

Dry equivalents

$\frac{1}{4}$ cup = 4 tablespoons

$\frac{1}{3}$ cup = 5 tablespoons plus 1 teaspoon

$\frac{1}{2}$ cup = 8 tablespoons or 4 ounces

$\frac{3}{4}$ cup = 12 tablespoons

1 cup = 16 tablespoons

2 cups = 1 pint

4 cups = 1 quart

Baking equivalents

1 cup sifted cake flour = 1 cup minus 2 tablespoons sifted all-purpose flour

1 cup sifted all-purpose flour = 1 cup plus 2 tablespoons sifted cake flour

1 teaspoon double-acting baking powder = $\frac{1}{4}$ teaspoon baking soda plus $\frac{1}{2}$ teaspoon cream of tartar

Miscellaneous equivalents

1 tablespoon prepared mustard = 1 teaspoon dried mustard

1 cup stock or broth = 1 bouillon cube dissolved in 1 cup boiling water

1 square (1 ounce) baking unsweetened chocolate = 3 tablespoons cocoa powder plus 1 tablespoon butter

1 ounce semisweet chocolate = 3 tablespoons cocoa powder plus 2 tablespoons butter plus 3 tablespoons sugar

Food equivalents

2 slices bread = 1 cup fresh bread crumbs

1 stick butter = 8 tablespoons butter

1 pound butter = 4 sticks butter

1 pound confectioners' sugar = about $4\frac{1}{2}$ cups confectioners' sugar, sifted

1 pound granulated sugar = 2 cups granulated sugar

$\frac{1}{2}$ pound hard cheese = about 2 cups grated cheese

1 cup heavy whipping cream = 2 cups whipped cream

(continued)

(continued)

1 medium lemon = about 3 tablespoons lemon juice or 2 to 3 teaspoons grated peel

1 pound apples = about 3 apples

1 large onion = about 1 cup chopped onion

1 cup raw converted rice = 4 cups cooked rice

1 large tomato = about ¾ cup chopped tomato

1 pound all-purpose flour = about 4 cups sifted flour

(For additional listings, see Appendix B.)

Recipe-Reading Checklist

- ✔ Read through the recipe at least twice to make sure that you understand the directions.
- ✔ Make sure that you can perform all the techniques.
- ✔ Check that you have all the necessary equipment and ingredients.
- ✔ Make sure that you have enough time before serving to prepare and cook the recipe.
- ✔ Check whether you can (or need to) make any part of the recipe ahead of time.
- ✔ Read through the ingredients to see whether you like them all (sea slugs anyone?), as well as whether the recipe has too much fat, sugar, or salt for your dietary needs.
- ✔ Check whether you need to use an ingredient, such as butter or oil, at different stages in the recipe so that you don't make the mistake of using that ingredient all at once.
- ✔ Find out whether you need to preheat the oven.
- ✔ Check the yield of the recipe.

Cooking For Dummies, 2nd Edition

Cheat Sheet

First Aid for Cooking Blunders

Bread, burned: Scrape off the black part with a grater.

Butter, blackened in pan: Pour off and discard the burned butter and wipe the pan. Use equal amounts of butter and vegetable oil, which don't burn as easily.

Cake, burned bottom: Cut away the black part and fill any holes with frosting. Scrape surface burns with a grater.

Cake, sticks to pan: Let sit for 5 minutes and then try again.

Chicken, browning too fast: Cover the browned parts with foil, shiny side out; continue roasting until all the chicken is cooked.

Eggshells, crack while hard-cooking: Add a teaspoon of salt or a few drops of lemon juice to the cooking liquid to prevent the white from running out of the shell.

Egg whites, won't whip: Try again with whites at room temperature. Use a copper bowl or add a pinch of cream of tartar before whipping.

Fat, splattering in pan: Add pinch of salt or cornstarch to the hot fat. Pour off the fat as soon as possible — or cover the pan.

Fruits, discolored: If cut fruits such as bananas and apples start turning brown, sprinkle them with lemon juice and cover with plastic wrap.

Gravy, lumpy: Whisk vigorously or whirl in a food processor.

Gravy, too thin: Raise heat and reduce, whisking until the gravy thickens. Or add a creamy paste of 1½ teaspoons cornstarch mixed with ½ cup stock or water for every 1 cup of gravy. Stir and cook for about 2 minutes over medium heat.

Gravy, too salty: Add a little brown sugar or currant jelly.

Puddings, thick skin forms on top: Let cool to room temperature, cover with plastic wrap, and refrigerate.

Rice, crunchy: Add a little water and continue cooking.

Soufflé, won't rise: Salvage as an alternative dessert (fallen soufflés are very chic in restaurants) by placing it as attractively as you can on a serving dish. Garnish with ice cream and a sprig of mint.

Soup, too salty: Add water. Or add slices of potato, which soak up salt. Just be sure to remove the potato slices before serving.

Soup, too thin: Make beurre manié (a 1 to 1 ratio of softened butter and flour mashed into a paste). Add to soup and stir well over medium heat until it thickens. Arrowroot and cornstarch are other thickeners. Blend with a little water before serving soup.

Soup or stew, lacks flavor: Add freshly grated lemon peel. Also try adding salt, fresh or dried herbs, or a pinch of sugar.

Vegetables, overcooked: Puree in a blender, adding a little cream (or half-and-half) and seasonings to taste.

For Dummies: Bestselling Book Series for Beginners

Praise for Cooking For Dummies

"Cooking — like anything — must be fun and should not be taken too seriously. Seasoned with Bryan Miller's hilarious sense of humor, *Cooking For Dummies* helps us do just that."

> — Ferdinand Metz, President, The Culinary Institute of America

"Always a dummy, but with *Cooking For Dummies,* an enlightened one!"

> — Paul C.P. McIlhenny, Executive Vice President, McIlhenny Co. (Tabasco Brands Products)

"Most of all, cooking should be an adventure, and it should be fun. *Cooking For Dummies* is seriously informative with a big dash of humor."

> — Wolfgang Puck, Chef and Owner of Spago Restaurant

"No 'dummy' — the person who adds *Cooking For Dummies* to his or her cookbook collection. Come to think of it, so encyclopedic, practical, and unintimidating . . . *Cooking For Dummies* could be the first and only book in your kitchen."

> — William Rice, food and wine columnist, *The Chicago Tribune* and author of *The Steak Lover's Cookbook*

"Too often cookbooks are sanctimonious, but in *Cooking For Dummies,* the table is a fun place. It will nourish your tummy as well as your humor."

> — Jacques Pépin, Chef and Author

"The recipes for 'dummies' are so delicious I felt compelled to eat the book."

> — Robert Klein, Actor and Comedian

"Applause to Bryan Miller for dishing humor up with the serious subject of cooking."

> — Molly Chappelet, Proprietor, Chappelet Vineyards, Napa Valley

"Simple to use and full of helpful hints and tips, *Cooking For Dummies* is sure to become a must have for 'dummies' and experienced chefs alike."

— Joachin Splichal, Chef/Owner, Patina and Pinot Restaurants

Praise for Marie Rama

"The main thing I look for in a guest on my TV show — or in a cookbook author — is the ability to teach. I'm always delighted to interview — or read! — Marie Rama, who's one of the great teaching foodies."

— David Rosengarten, Star of the Television Food Network's *Taste* and Cookbook Author

"Talk show hosts are always looking for the perfect guest. I found one in Marie Rama. Beyond professional, she is focused, gives great information, and is truly entertaining. Maybe she should host her own program?"

— Mark Summers, former talk show host of *Biggers and Summers* and *Double Dare*

"I've had the opportunity to have Marie Rama as a guest on *Creative Living* several times through the years, and always looked forward to working with her. Her professionalism as a food expert, as well as her delightful personality, make her the consummate guest."

— Sheryl Bordon, Producer/Host, *Creative Living*

"Marie has visited our TV kitchen on a number of occasions. She's shown us her with her talent and expertise that she's no 'dummy' when it comes to cooking."

— David Smith, host, *The Exchange,* Connecticut

"Marie's a delight, and as at home in the kitchen as a banana in a bowl of pudding! Our viewers thought so too, and let us know that they want to see more of her, and soon."

— Marietta Hoover Caudill, Associate Producer, *Wave 3 News Sunrise,* Louisville

Praise for Bryan Miller

"... the most influential food critic in the world. ..."

— Nicholas Lander, *Financial Times,* London

"Everybody in the food business, and a lot who aren't, know Bryan Miller. ..."

— Jim Quinn, *Town & Country* magazine

"Miller's lively writing style ... is one of *The Times'* sparkiest features. ..."

— James Reginato, *W Magazine*

"The most famous gastronomic critic in the world. ..."

— Luis Bettonica, El Pipiripao, Barcelona

™

BESTSELLING BOOK SERIES

References for the Rest of Us!®

Do you find that traditional reference books are overloaded with technical details and advice you'll never use? Do you postpone important life decisions because you just don't want to deal with them? Then our *For Dummies*® business and general reference book series is for you.

For Dummies business and general reference books are written for those frustrated and hard-working souls who know they aren't dumb, but find that the myriad of personal and business issues and the accompanying horror stories make them feel helpless. *For Dummies* books use a lighthearted approach, a down-to-earth style, and even cartoons and humorous icons to dispel fears and build confidence. Lighthearted but not lightweight, these books are perfect survival guides to solve your everyday personal and business problems.

"More than a publishing phenomenon, 'Dummies' is a sign of the times."

— The New York Times

"A world of detailed and authoritative information is packed into them..."

— U.S. News and World Report

"...you won't go wrong buying them."

— Walter Mossberg, Wall Street Journal, on For Dummies books

Already, millions of satisfied readers agree. They have made For Dummies the #1 introductory level computer book series and a best-selling business book series. They have written asking for more. So, if you're looking for the best and easiest way to learn about business and other general reference topics, look to *For Dummies* to give you a helping hand.

Hungry Minds™

1/01

Cooking FOR DUMMIES®

2ND EDITION

by Bryan Miller and Marie Rama

Foreword by Wolfgang Puck

Hungry Minds™

Best-Selling Books • Digital Downloads • e-Books • Answer Networks • e-Newsletters • Branded Web Sites • e-Learning

New York, NY ◆ Cleveland, OH ◆ Indianapolis, IN

Cooking For Dummies®, 2nd Edition

Published by
Hungry Minds, Inc.
909 Third Avenue
New York, NY 10022
www.hungryminds.com
www.dummies.com (Dummies Press Web site)

Library of Congress Catalog Card No.: 99-69712

ISBN: 0-7645-5250-3

Printed in the United States of America

10 9 8 7 6 5 4 3 2

2O/SW/QW/QR/IN

Distributed in the United States by Hungry Minds, Inc.

Distributed by CDG Books Canada Inc. for Canada; by Transworld Publishers Limited in the United Kingdom; by IDG Norge Books for Norway; by IDG Sweden Books for Sweden; by IDG Books Australia Publishing Corporation Pty. Ltd. for Australia and New Zealand; by TransQuest Publishers Pte Ltd. for Singapore, Malaysia, Thailand, Indonesia, and Hong Kong; by Gotop Information Inc. for Taiwan; by ICG Muse, Inc. for Japan; by Intersoft for South Africa; by Eyrolles for France; by International Thomson Publishing for Germany, Austria and Switzerland; by Distribuidora Cuspide for Argentina; by LR International for Brazil; by Galileo Libros for Chile; by Ediciones ZETA S.C.R. Ltda. for Peru; by WS Computer Publishing Corporation, Inc., for the Philippines; by Contemporanea de Ediciones for Venezuela; by Express Computer Distributors for the Caribbean and West Indies; by Micronesia Media Distributor, Inc. for Micronesia; by Chips Computadoras S.A. de C.V. for Mexico; by Editorial Norma de Panama S.A. for Panama; by American Bookshops for Finland.

For general information on Hungry Minds' products and services please contact our Customer Care Department within the U.S. at 800-762-2974, outside the U.S. at 317-572-3993 or fax 317-572-4002.

For sales inquiries and reseller information, including discounts, premium and bulk quantity sales, and foreign-language translations, please contact our Customer Care Department at 800-434-3422, fax 317-572-4002, or write to Hungry Minds, Inc., Attn: Customer Care Department, 10475 Crosspoint Boulevard, Indianapolis, IN 46256.

For information on licensing foreign or domestic rights, please contact our Sub-Rights Customer Care Department at 212-884-5000.

For information on using Hungry Minds' products and services in the classroom or for ordering examination copies, please contact our Educational Sales Department at 800-434-2086 or fax 317-572-4005.

Please contact our Public Relations Department at 212-884-5163 for press review copies or 212-884-5000 for author interviews and other publicity information or fax 212-884-5400.

For authorization to photocopy items for corporate, personal, or educational use, please contact Copyright Clearance Center, 222 Rosewood Drive, Danvers, MA 01923, or fax 978-750-4470.

Hungry Minds™ is a trademark of Hungry Minds, Inc.

About the Authors

Bryan Miller is a former restaurant critic and feature writer for *The New York Times,* who also wrote *Desserts For Dummies* (with Bill Yosses), published by Hungry Minds, Inc. He also has written nine other books, including three cookbooks with Pierre Franey *(Cuisine Rapide; The Seafood Cookbook — Classic to Contemporary;* and *A Chef's Tale,* also with Richard Flaste) and four editions of *The New York Times Guide to Restaurants.* Mr. Miller also collaborated for 13 years with Pierre Franey on the syndicated "60-Minute Gourmet" column, which appeared weekly in *The New York Times.* His eleventh book, *Cooking with the 60-Minute Gourmet,* was published in September 1999. He is the recipient of the "James Beard Who's Who Food and Beverage Award," which recognizes outstanding achievement in the field of food and wine. Mr. Miller currently serves as a culinary consultant and instructor at The Culinary Institute of America in Hyde Park, New York.

Marie Rama is an independent food, beverage, and media consultant, who also wrote *Grilling For Dummies* (with John Mariani), published by Hungry Minds. She has worked as a professional pastry chef and as a recipe developer for several food companies and associations, including the McIlhenny Company and the United Fresh Fruit and Vegetable Association. Ms. Rama has served as the Director of Weddings, Romance, and Entertaining for Korbel Champagne and as the "Lemon Lady" for Sunkist Growers, appearing on hundreds of television and radio shows around the United States and Canada. Ms. Rama lives in Bronxville, New York, with her husband, Mark Reiter, and their two sons, Nicholas and William.

Authors' Acknowledgments

There are many people we would like to thank for helping and supporting us with this second edition of *Cooking For Dummies*.

We would like to thank and acknowledge again the excellent, and uniquely creative work of our illustrator Elizabeth Kurtzman and Hungry Minds cartoonist Rich Tennant.

Special thanks also to Laura Pensiero, who helped with recipe testing and tasting, and to our technical editor, Cynthia Nims, who tirelessly reviewed every word that was printed here. And kudos to photographer Ellen Silverman, food stylist Sally Schneider, prop stylist Robyn Glaser, and cover stylist Roscoe Betsill, along with Sally O'Brien, for their artistic contributions.

The following experts, companies, and associations provided us with invaluable information: Susan Lamb Parenti and the National Cattlemen's Beef Association; Robin Kline and the National Pork Producers Council; Sherry Weaver and the National Turkey Federation; and the Sunkist Growers, Inc.

We also thank Elizabeth Kuball, our Project Editor at Hungry Minds, for her enthusiastic spirit, consummate editorial skills, and complete devotion to every detail of this project. Others at Hungry Minds who have our thanks and appreciation include Hungry Minds Acquisitions Editors Holly McGuire and Linda Ingroia.

Once again a special thanks to our IMG agent, Mark Reiter, who came up with the brilliant idea of writing a second edition that was larger and more comprehensive than the first, and to Kathy Welton, Vice President and Publisher at Hungry Minds, who gave us the green light to go ahead and get it done.

Publisher's Acknowledgments

We're proud of this book; please register your comments through our Online Registration Form located at www.dummies.com.

Some of the people who helped bring this book to market include the following:

Acquisitions, Editorial, and Media Development

Project Editor: Elizabeth Netedu Kuball
  (Previous Edition: Pamela Mourouzis)

Acquisitions Editors: Holly McGuire and Linda Ingroia

Technical Editor: Cynthia Nims

Recipe Tester: Laura Pensiero

Editorial Coordinator: Heather Prince

Editorial Director: Kristin A. Cocks

Production

Project Coordinator: Emily Perkins

Layout and Graphics: Karl Brandt, Brian Drumm, Barry Offringa, Jill Piscitelli, Brent Savage, Brian Torwelle, Dan Whetstine, Erin Zeltner

Special Art: Elizabeth Kurtzman

Proofreaders: Laura Albert, Corey Bowen, John Greenough, Christine Pingleton, Marianne Santy, Charles Spencer

Indexer: Sherry Massey

Special Help
  Michelle Hacker, Amanda M. Foxworth, Beth Parlon

General and Administrative

Hungry Minds, Inc.: John Kilcullen, CEO; Bill Barry, President and COO; John Ball, Executive VP, Operations & Administration; John Harris, CFO

Hungry Minds Consumer Reference Group

  Business: Kathleen A. Welton, Vice President and Publisher; Kevin Thornton, Acquisitions Manager

  Cooking/Gardening: Jennifer Feldman, Associate Vice President and Publisher

  Education/Reference: Diane Graves Steele, Vice President and Publisher

  Lifestyles: Kathleen Nebenhaus, Vice President and Publisher; Tracy Boggier, Managing Editor

  Pets: Dominique De Vito, Associate Vice President and Publisher; Tracy Boggier, Managing Editor

  Travel: Michael Spring, Vice President and Publisher; Suzanne Jannetta, Editorial Director; Brice Gosnell, Publishing Director

Hungry Minds Consumer Editorial Services: Kathleen Nebenhaus, Vice President and Publisher; Kristin A. Cocks, Editorial Director; Cindy Kitchel, Editorial Director

Hungry Minds Consumer Production: Debbie Stailey, Production Director

◆

The publisher would like to give special thanks to Patrick J. McGovern, without whom this book would not have been possible.

◆

Recipes at a Glance

Meat and Poultry

Fish and Shellfish

Meatless Main Dishes

Vegetables and Side Dishes

Sauces and Garnishes

Desserts

Beverages

Contents at a Glance

Cartoons at a Glance

By Rich Tennant

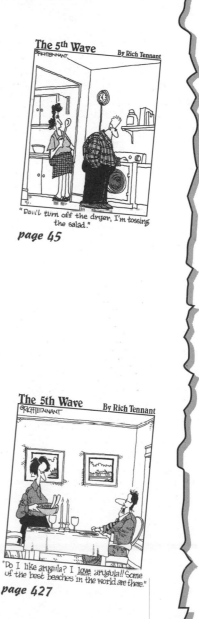

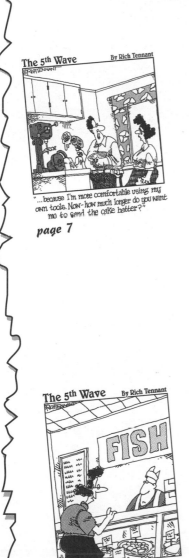

Fax: 978-546-7747
E-mail: richtennant@the5thwave.com
World Wide Web: www.the5thwave.com

Table of Contents

Foreword

· ·

*C*ooking For Dummies may seem at first glance to be just a lighthearted romp through the culinary meadow, but in fact, beneath all the fun it is a solid learning tool that introduces readers to an impressively wide range of skills. Wonderful ingredients and good technique are what good food is all about, and because knowing how to bring out the best in food is what makes a meal memorable, technique is the foundation of all good cooking, professional or amateur. Every great chef starts somewhere, and *Cooking For Dummies* shows you where.

At one of my restaurants, Spago in Los Angeles, we focus on grilling. Sure, we get our famous results partly by having a great staff and a professional kitchen, but *Cooking For Dummies* shows the home cook that superior grilling (as opposed to the average wham-bam backyard fare) lies in a number of easy-to-master techniques. Step-by-step recipes and illustrations walk you through different levels of sophistication, so you can see how all great food has the same beginnings.

Cooking is also about making wonderful food to share with family and friends, and *Cooking For Dummies* lets you do just that. Think of this book as a set of training wheels that prop you up as you learn all the twists and turns of the kitchen. Not only will you come away with plenty of exciting dishes, but you will also eventually take off the training wheels and set off on your own.

Cooking should be an adventure, a series of small discoveries that lead to a lifetime of great meals. *Cooking For Dummies* gives you all the information and direction you need to set out on that adventure, confident and ready to cook great food!

—Wolfgang Puck

Introduction

● ●

*W*hether you fancy yourself a hotshot home cook or someone who wouldn't know a whisk from a weimaraner, *Cooking For Dummies,* 2nd Edition, can help you. For the novice, our technique-oriented approach teaches you the "whys" of cooking and not just the "whats" found in traditional recipe books. That way, you can eventually throw away your training wheels (but not this book!) and create dishes all on your own.

More-experienced cooks may want to hone their basic skills, and the more than 200 recipes in this book offer plenty of food for thought.

Unlike most cookbooks, this one is more than a compilation of tasty recipes. We also focus on cooking techniques like broiling, steaming, braising, and roasting. After you learn these techniques, you are no longer a slave to recipes. Once again, you can cook with imagination and creativity — and that's the sign of a skilled cook.

The best part about discovering how to cook this way is that, while you are practicing your techniques, you have all kinds of delightful food to eat. Sure beats trumpet lessons.

Furthermore, this book is structured around the way you live. For example, it includes information about cooking for guests when you have only one hour, cooking economically, and making a delicious meal when you don't even have time to get to the market.

Most of all, you'll actually have fun as you explore the endless pleasures of cooking. And that, after all, is what food is all about.

The Good News

In the past decade, the food revolution has made available to home cooks products that they had never dreamed of: truffles, flavored vinegar, exotic seafood, frozen stocks, goat cheese, and countless types of olive oil, to name just a few. At the same time, the technology of cooking equipment has narrowed the gap between home and professional kitchens.

The Real News

Of course, new products and technology don't make a good cook. The requirements of a refined cook have not changed since the seventeenth century: a sensitive palate, an understanding of cooking techniques and products, strong knife skills, and patience. These are skills we want to help you develop.

How to Use This Book

We start at the very beginning: your kitchen and your equipment. What basic tools do you need? How do you use these things? Then we move on to cooking techniques to get you up and running as soon as possible. Doing simple things well offers great personal satisfaction, as you will see.

Depending on your needs and cooking skills, you can start at the beginning of the book and work your way through, go straight to the chapters that interest you most, or read the book Arab-style, from the back to the front.

How This Book Is Organized

This book is organized around cooking techniques and real-life situations. Major sections are called *parts*. Within each part are chapters that address specific subjects. Following is a rundown of each part and what you can read about there.

Part I: Go On In — It's Only the Kitchen

What is this strange room? It's the most popular room in the house, where friends hang out as they help themselves to your food and drinks; parties inevitably gravitate; and couples have their best arguments. This part is designed to help you get over your fear of cooking. It touches on kitchen design and organization, helping you to arrange your appliances, kitchen space, counters, and cabinets for maximum efficiency. It also covers in detail necessary equipment like pots, pans, knives, and all kinds of gadgets. Plus, we get you cooking right away in this part, with simple yet delicious recipies that will whet your appetite to cook even more.

Part II: Know Your Techniques

Part II is where the fun begins. Each chapter includes recipes that illustrate an essential cooking technique: braising, sautéing, roasting, grilling, and more. From that starting point, we take you through a number of recipe variations that show you how to improvise with confidence and skill.

Part III: Expand Your Repertoire

Part III looks at pasta, eggs, and larger categories of dishes like soups, salads, desserts, and one-pot meals. Here, you can read about how to make the perfect omelet, how to mix a balanced vinaigrette, and how to make a pretty soup garnish. Also included are illustrations and charts — like the one identifying different types of pastas (so that you know tagliatelle from linguine) — and, of course, dozens of delicious recipes.

Part IV: Now You're Cooking! Real Menus for Real Life

Part IV injects another dose of reality into the cooking experience. Most glossy cookbooks assume that you have all the time in the world to prepare a dish. Some books also assume that price is no object — "now take that loin of veal and sprinkle it with black truffles" — and that everybody lives next door to a gourmet market. In the real world, you have 45 minutes, if you're lucky, to prepare dinner while a 2-year-old is clinging to your leg and the cat is coughing up hair balls. At the same time, the local supermarket may be closing in 5 minutes. Now that's real-life cooking. And that's what these chapters are all about.

Part V: Special Occasions

Part V offers some great menus for popular special occasions. We give you everything you need to make your Fourth of July party a hit. We also cover Super Bowl parties, from the kickoff to the two-minute warning. And we provide a fantastic menu for a Thanksgiving dinner. If a holiday or special occasion is quickly approaching and you have no idea what to cook, turn to these chapters for some complete menus.

Part VI: The Part of Tens

Just when you thought that we had covered everything, we give you more! These quick lists include sundry observations about cooking, a few important reminders, plus a list of classic cookbooks you should know about.

Part VII: Appendixes

This straightforward reference section gives you useful lists and charts, as well as a glossary. Here, you can find the meaning of more than 100 common cooking terms. We also provide common equivalents and substitutions for those emergency situations when you discover at the last minute that you don't have the ingredient you need.

Icons Used in This Book

Icons are those nifty little pictures in the margin of this book. They each grab your attention for a different reason, and we explain those reasons here:

When there's an easier way to do something, a step you can take to save money, or a shortcut you can take to get yourself to the dinner table faster, we let you know by marking the tip with this icon.

The kitchen can be a dangerous place. This icon, like a flashing yellow light, steers you clear of potentially dangerous mishaps.

We hope that you remember *every* valuable piece of information in this book, but if your brain can hold only so much, make sure that you hang on to the tidbits marked by this icon.

We show you skills all along, but some skills are more important than others. This icon highlights fundamental skills and techniques that you should practice. Some are easy, such as zesting an orange. Others, like carving ham, require more concentration.

This chef's toque, a symbol of culinary excellence, alerts you to the advice and secrets of some of the world's greatest chefs.

We anticipate possible problems with a recipe — you ran out of cooking liquid in the rice, the soufflé didn't rise, and so on — and, in paragraphs marked by this icon, we offer solutions.

In many cases, we give you a recipe, say meat loaf, and then describe easy variations that use different ingredients, various sauces, and so on.

A Few Guidelines before You Begin

Before charging ahead to make any of the recipes in this book, you should know a few things about the ingredients we choose to use:

- **Milk is always whole.** You can substitute low-fat or skim milk, but these give soups and sauces a thinner, less creamy consistency.

- **Use unsalted butter so that you can control the amount of salt in a dish.** We don't recommend substituting margarine, which has just as many calories per tablespoon (100) as butter. Margarine's flavor is inferior to butter as well.

- **Unless otherwise noted, all eggs are large.**

- **All dry ingredient measurements are level.** Brown sugar is measured firmly packed.

- **All salt is common table salt and pepper is freshly ground.** We seldom specify measured amounts of salt and pepper because every cook has a different palate. Sample the recipe several times during preparation to taste for seasoning, and add salt and pepper to taste when we instruct you to do so.

And keep the following general tips in mind:

- Read through each recipe at least once to make sure that you have all the necessary ingredients and utensils, understand all the steps, and have enough preparation time. (We begin each recipe by listing the cooking utensils you need as well as the preparation and cooking times.)

- Be sure to use the proper size pan when a measurement is given.

- Preheat ovens, broilers, and grills at least 15 minutes before cooking begins. Place all food on the middle rack of the oven unless the recipe says otherwise.

- Most of the recipes in this book are written to serve four. You can reduce by half or double many of them to satisfy two or eight people.

- If you're looking for vegetarian recipes, you can easily find them in the Recipes in This Chapter list, located at the beginning of every chapter. Vegetarian recipes are marked by a veggie bullet, instead of the usual triangle.

Part I
Go On In — It's Only the Kitchen

The 5th Wave   By Rich Tennant

"...because I'm more comfortable using my own tools. Now-how much longer do you want me to sand the cake batter?"

In this part . . .

There's no doubt about it: If you want to learn to cook, you have to go into the kitchen. If this idea seems frightening, try looking at photographs of your kitchen for a few weeks until you feel better; stand just outside the kitchen until your nerves subside. Then make the final assault.

After you're inside, we can help you make it an enjoyable and efficient room in which to prepare all kinds of wonderful food. In this part, you'll find everything from kitchen design to cooking equipment, from lighting your cooking area to seating party guests on the kitchen counter when they insist on watching you work. You'll even try your hand at a couple of recipes sure to please your family and friends.

Chapter 1

Warming Up to Your Kitchen

In This Chapter

▶ How the kitchen has become the soul of the home

▶ Why the kitchen should be more like a tunnel of love than a chamber of terror

▶ Setting up a great work space

▶ Making your kitchen safe and user-friendly

From morning till night, sounds drift from the kitchen, most of them familiar and comforting, some of them surprising and worth investigating. On days when warmth is the most important need of the human heart, the kitchen is the place you can find it; it dries the wet sock, it cools the hot little brain.

— E. B. White

*W*hether you have a cramped apartment kitchen with counter space the size of a cereal box, or a sprawling country kitchen with a commercial stove and a work island, this chapter can help you become a more productive cook. To be sure, space is great. But knowing how to use what you have efficiently is the real key. You would be surprised to see how small some restaurant kitchens are; they work, however, because everything is in its place and is easily accessible. Have you ever ricocheted around the kitchen desperately searching for a spatula while your omelet burned on the range? We want to ensure that you're never in that situation again.

Aside from discussing smart kitchen design, in this chapter we look briefly at large appliances — refrigerators, stoves, microwaves, and such — just so you'll be armed with knowledge if you have to buy or replace anything in your kitchen.

And forgive us if we get a bit mushy about kitchens being the soul of the home, where happy memories are made along with roasted chickens and golden apple pies. It just happens to be true.

To get started, here are seven good reasons why everyone should learn to cook:

✔ When you dine in restaurants, you can complain with authority that particular dishes are not made the way you make them at home.

✔ You get to use all kinds of amusing implements — and actually know what to do with them.

✔ You can control your diet rather than depend on the dubious victuals churned out by carryout places or frozen food purveyors.

✔ At home, seconds and thirds are permissible.

✔ Feeding friends and loved ones is inherently more intimate than going to a restaurant.

✔ Establishing a connection with the food chain allows you to distinguish quality food from what's second rate. Who knows, you may even be inspired to plant a vegetable garden next spring.

✔ You start hanging around the cookbook section in bookstores, fertile terrain for opposite-sex encounters.

The Evolution of the Modern Kitchen

In the 1950s, domestic architecture hid the kitchen from the rest of the house — remember Rob and Laura Petrie's suburban digs in the 1960s television sitcom *The Dick Van Dyke Show*? A swinging door concealed their kitchen. This setup allowed Rob endless opportunities for pratfalls, but it also made a statement about the home kitchen: It was a place you went only when you had to, a utilitarian room with no more allure than the garage.

Today, kitchens are often the most "designy" rooms in the house, complete with colorful Italian wall tiles, antique tables, terra-cotta floors, work islands, skylights, and professional stoves. The Petries' swinging door (and maybe a wall as well) has been knocked down to open the kitchen to the living area. Food as theater! Cooking as camaraderie! Friends interact in the kitchen; strangers are greeted in the living room.

Today's more casual, personal style of entertaining allows what once would have been considered barbaric: watching food being prepared! However, today's near obsession with food has made the kitchen the most interesting — not to mention the most fun — room in the house.

Guests who offer to work save on labor costs. Don't discourage them.

Do You Need a Big Kitchen?

You don't need a fabulous kitchen to prepare fabulous food. But a well-designed workplace sure makes cooking easier and more pleasurable. Catherine Beecher, an ardent feminist and cookbook author in the late nineteenth century, decried the cavernous Victorian kitchens of the day. She wrote that sprinting around a vast room was not only fatiguing but also inefficient. Beecher looked for models of a workable kitchen and found it in, of all places, a railroad dining car (this was before the days of Amtrak).

In the early twentieth century, architects took Beecher's message and started designing spaces that required minimal movement to cook a meal. Ideally, you could be at the range and in a few steps reach over to the icebox, the bread box, and the produce bin.

In the 1980s, the pendulum began to swing back toward large, lavish kitchens with islands, skylights, and more chrome than a Chevrolet factory. Some of these rooms are highly functional; others are pure vanity.

Kitchens of the new millennium are characterized (frequently, but not always) by a cook's need for ease and efficiency, as kitchen designers recoil at the "stadium" styles of the past.

From Chaos to Confidence: Setting Up Your Cooking Space

Catherine Beecher had a good point. If you want to run, join a health club. Although nothing is wrong with a large, eat-in kitchen, the design of the cooking area should be practical.

You should be able to move from your working counter space to the stove and the refrigerator in a smooth, unobstructed fashion. This working space actually has a name: the *kitchen triangle* (see Figure 1-1). If a table, plant, or small child is blocking the way, move it.

Countertops

Counter space is the single most overlooked item in many kitchens. The counter is where you set out and prepare food (often on a cutting board), stack plates, put kitchen machines, and lose car keys amid the clutter. Try to keep your counters neat and clean. So many kitchen counters are cluttered with paraphernalia that they become nearly useless. Place only your most frequently used appliances on top of your counters — the coffee machine, toaster, and blender, for example. Put away all other appliances that consume precious work space. What's more, a kitchen counter is not a magazine rack, plant holder, wine bin, or phone book shelf, so try not to use it for these purposes.

You can place a ripping hot pot or roasting pan on a slab of granite or on a countertop made of ceramic tile. But when you place hot pots and pans on most other countertops, including those made of expensive Corian (a synthetic, solid-surface material), they can scorch. As a general rule, set hot pots and pans on your stovetop or on a heat-resistant ceramic or metal trivet.

Lighting

It goes without saying that kitchens should be well lit — the stove and work spaces most of all. If you have a combination kitchen/dining area, you may want to put the lights on a dimmer. That way, you can keep the kitchen bright while the dining area is dim.

Another option is to have special lighting for the cooking area, either inset into overhead cabinets or in the ceiling. Nothing is worse than trying to check your food in a dimly lit area. If your kitchen is poorly lit over the cooking area, the least expensive solution is a wall-mounted supplementary light.

Figure 1-1:
An efficient kitchen triangle.

TIP

Countertop materials

If you are thinking of changing your countertops, consider these choices:

- **Hardwood** is attractive and functional. However, varnish seals tend to break down with use, and little cracks and crevices can catch food particles. That's why it's important to wash wood counters often with soap and water (and occasionally with ammonia or bleach).

- **Marble** is cool, making it ideal for preparing pastry, which is less likely to stick to it. It's also beautiful but, on the downside, marble is very expensive and can stain.

- **Stainless steel** is ideal in many ways, although somewhat harsh and industrial looking. Stainless steel does not break, rust, or tarnish, which is also why it is a good material for sinks.

- **Tile** is beautiful, rich looking, and functional as long as the surface is flat and seamless. However, tile tends to chip and wear away, especially if you place hot pots and pans on it.

- **Synthetic surfaces** of all kinds are highly functional. Corian is a synthetic material that has a deep opalescent quality. It can be cut and shaped in every which way without showing a seam. It is very hard and durable (but not scorch-proof) — and very expensive.

- **Plastic lamination,** such as Formica, has many advantages for the home kitchen. It is durable and relatively inexpensive, comes in various colors, and can be molded around edges. It should not be used as a cutting surface, however, or as a resting place for hot pots and pans.

Storage

You can't have too much storage space in your kitchen. Of course, most of us have to make do by being creative with what we have.

Dry storage

Dry storage refers to anything that is not refrigerated or frozen. Many ingenious kitchen cabinets are on the market, such as those that have storage shelves on the swing-out doors as well as inside. If your cabinets don't have this feature, you can improvise by mounting racks on the inside of the doors. Roll-out cabinets under counters are also convenient options.

You can store dried beans, pasta, flour, tea, coffee, and the like in large glass jars and place them on a shelf. Store the items you use every day closest to your stove or workstation. Look around your kitchen for any wall space where you can mount a shelf. Use the vertical space in your kitchen, too. Don't overlook the space above your cabinets for storage.

Store your knives in a butcher block or on magnetic wall strips far from a child's reach. Keeping knives in a drawer not only ties up space but also dulls their blades quickly.

Kitchen islands are extremely efficient in that they can have considerable storage space below. Moreover, they can double as a kitchen table. If you don't have an island (and you have the space), consider buying a butcher block table with shelving underneath.

Wet storage

You don't have much room to experiment when it comes to refrigeration. A refrigerator/freezer should be within steps of your work space. You can store a stand-alone freezer, however, in another room off the kitchen or even in the basement.

Exhaust

Adequate exhaust is crucial to the comfort of a kitchen. Many exhaust systems for home ranges and microwaves are inadequate if you do a lot of cooking, especially sautéing and roasting. A separate exhaust system that has a grease filter and a pipe that vents smoke outside is a smart investment. Some units retract into the wall when not in use. Some cooks prefer downdraft exhaust systems — those that pull air down into the unit — because they save space. However, such units must fight warm air's tendency to rise, limiting their effectiveness.

Major Appliances

In this section, we discuss the various types of appliances available to home cooks today. Chances are that you are not in a position to make major changes in your appliances and will have to make do with what you already have. Knowing each appliance's relative strengths and weaknesses, however, can help you do so.

Ovens and stovetops

Kitchen technology is giving professional cooks space-age ovens and stoves — induction cooking based on a magnetic principle, gadgets that whip up ice cream to order, induction and steam ovens, to name a few. All these inventions will likely filter down to the home before long, and some of them already have.

How does this thing cook?

Every microwave has an energy box called a *magnetron,* which produces microwaves (from electricity). The microwaves pass through materials like glass, paper, china, and plastic and convert to heat when they come in contact with food molecules. The microwaves cause the water molecules in the food to rotate so rapidly that they vibrate, creating friction and heat.

A major misconception is that microwaves cook from the inside out. They do not. Microwaves penetrate primarily the surface and no farther than 2 inches into the food. The heat spreads by conduction to the rest of the food.

Following is a rundown on basic home stoves and ovens and what you should know about them.

Cooking with gas

Most serious cooks prefer gas stoves. You can turn a gas flame up and down quickly, which is important in sautéing and sauce-making. Commercial gas ranges are extremely powerful and can cut your cooking time by as much as one-fourth, but simple home ranges work just fine for most purposes.

A gas range built within the last ten years should not smell of gas from flaming pilots. Newer models no longer have standing pilots. They ignite electronically; therefore, gas does not flow through the system unless the range is turned on. If you do smell gas, you have a leak in your system. This situation is dangerous — call your gas company immediately. Do not use the stove or any other electrical appliances, even your lights, because doing so can spark an explosion.

Electric heat

Electric ranges became all the rage after World War II. They were considered clean, easy to use, and modern. The drawback to electric ranges is their slow response time. Reducing heat from high to low can take a minute; gas can do it in seconds. However, electric ovens are preferred by many professional chefs, especially for baking, because they are very accurate and consistent. Today's gas and electric ovens generally hold and maintain oven temperature within a variance of about 5 degrees.

Induction

Induction is a new form of kitchen heat. Some professional chefs are so impressed with it that they predict it will replace all other systems in ten years.

Whether that is true, induction cooking is impressive to watch. Basically, it works on a magnetic transfer principle — heat passes via magnetic force from the burner to the pan. If you place a paper towel between the burner and the pan, the towel does not get hot. A 2-quart pot of water comes to a boil in about a minute. However, an induction cooktop uses only selected metal pans to which a magnet adheres, such as stainless steel. Copper and glass cookware, for example, do not work. An induction cooktop is expensive, priced at over $800 for four burners.

Convection ovens

Chefs have used convection ovens for years. If we were to recommend an addition to your kitchen, a convection oven might be the one. A small fan in the rear of the oven circulates air all around the food to cook it rapidly and evenly. Cooking times and temperature settings are reduced by about 25 percent, so most manufacturers suggest that you reduce the cooking temperature given in the recipe by 25 degrees when baking. Some oven manufacturers offer both regular and convection cooking at the flick of a switch.

If a convection wall oven is over your budget, consider the smaller, less expensive convection toaster oven, especially if you're cooking for one or two. It can toast, bake a cake, broil a burger, and roast a small chicken. And cooking times are shorter than in conventional ovens.

Microwave ovens

Microwave cooking is unlike all kinds of conventional cooking. You must follow a different set of cooking rules. Although over 90 percent of American kitchens have a microwave, most people use the microwave only as a reheating and defrosting device. If this is your intention, purchase a simple unit with only one or two power levels. If you're short on counter or wall space, consider a microwave-convection oven combination that allows you to cook by using either method.

Microwaves cannot pass through metal, so you cannot cook with traditional metal cookware. You can, however, use flameproof glass, some plastics, porcelain, paper, ceramic, and plastic cooking bags. Some microwaves permit you to use aluminum foil to cover dishes, as long as the foil doesn't touch the oven walls or the temperature probe. Check your operating manual to see whether your appliance allows using foil in this way. Cookware placed in the microwave should not get hot. If it does, it's probably not microwavable.

A microwave is not a replacement for conventional cooking of grilled meats, baked breads, cakes and cookies, and other foods that need browning — unless it has a browning unit. Use your microwave for what it does best in combination with other appliances. For example, you can precook chicken in minutes in the microwave and finish it under the broiler or on an outdoor grill. Following are some other microwave tips:

✔ Recipes that require a lot of water, such as pasta, don't work as well in a microwave and probably cook in less time on your stovetop.

✔ Foods must be arranged properly to cook evenly. Face the thickest parts, like broccoli stalks, outward toward the oven walls. Arrange foods of the same size and shape, such as potatoes, in a circle or square with space between them and no item in the center.

✔ Covering dishes eliminates splattering, but it also cuts down on cooking time. Frequently stirring, turning, and rotating foods ensures an even distribution of heat.

✔ As with conventional cooking, cutting foods into smaller pieces shortens cooking time.

✔ Before cooking, pierce with a fork foods that have skins, like potatoes, hot dogs, and sausages. This releases steam that can lead to sudden popping and splattering.

✔ A number of variables, including the type of microwave, can affect a recipe's cooking time, so check for doneness after the minimum cooking time. You can always cook food longer. Also, always observe the recipe's "standing" time, because microwaved food continues to cook after you remove it from the oven.

✔ Be sure to use the defrost power setting (30 to 40 percent of full power) when thawing food to ensure slow and even defrosting; otherwise, the outside of the food may start to cook before the inside is thoroughly thawed.

Read your microwave manual carefully before using it. One woman we know ruined her microwave oven because she used it as a kitchen timer, not realizing that you should never run an empty microwave, a warning found in just about every manual.

Most major appliance companies, including General Electric (800-626-2000), Amana (800-843-0304), and KitchenAid (800-422-1230) have toll-free information numbers with appliance experts on hand to answer questions about using and caring for your microwave.

The refrigerator

Refrigerators are the black holes of the kitchen — objects drift in and are never seen again, at least until the next thorough cleaning. At that time, your leftovers may resemble compost. And what's in this little ball of aluminum foil? *Do not open!*

Refrigerators come in many sizes and shapes. A family of four needs a minimum of 16 cubic feet and should probably buy one that's at least 18 cubic feet (unless you have a teenage boy, in which case you need a second refrigerator). If you use the freezer a great deal, having the freezer compartment on the top, rather than the bottom, is more convenient. Make sure that the doors open in the most convenient way for your kitchen. Also check the door compartments to see whether there is space to place a bottle upright. The door should not be cluttered with little compartments that just eat up space.

Try not to pack the refrigerator too densely. This way, the cold air has sufficient space to circulate around and cool the food. Store foods in the same spot so that you don't have to search for that little jar of mustard or jelly every time you open the door.

The bottom drawers are usually the coldest and should be used for storing meat, poultry, and fish. Fresh vegetables are usually stored in the "crisper" drawer, which is often located just above the meat bin. Salad greens and leafy herbs can be washed, thoroughly dried, and wrapped in paper towels to extend their storage life. Other vegetables, like broccoli and cauliflower, should be washed just before serving. Excess water on any vegetable in storage can hasten its deterioration.

Liberate old food from the refrigerator every two weeks or so, and give the fridge a good soap-and-water bath every few months. Invite your friends to the event, if you like. An open box of baking soda at the back of a shelf soaks up odors. Remember to replace the baking soda every few months.

Kitchen Safety 101

You may think that the biggest danger in the kitchen is serving a meal that has guests roaring hysterically with laughter on their way home. As humiliating as that can be, home cooks should be aware of other perils as well.

Do you remember Dan Akroyd's classic skit on *Saturday Night Live,* in which he impersonates Julia Child? In the middle of his cooking demonstration, he pretends to accidentally cut off his fingers: "Just a flesh wound," he warbles and continues cooking. Then he severs his wrist, his hand falling to the ground. Blood spurts everywhere. Pretty funny, huh?

That wildly exaggerated scene carries a cautionary note about razor-sharp knives: Always pay attention to what you're doing because one slip can cause great pain. (Keep in mind that dull knives can be dangerous, too, because they force you to apply more pressure, and your hand may slip while doing this.) Other rules of safety include the following:

✔ Store knives in a wooden block or on a magnetic bar, not in a kitchen drawer.

✔ Never cook in loose-hanging clothes that may catch fire.

✔ Never cook while wearing loose-hanging jewelry that can get tangled around pot handles.

✔ Professional chefs have hands of asbestos from years of grabbing hot pots and pans. You do not. Keep pot holders nearby and use them.

✔ Turn pot handles away from the front of the stove, where children may grab them and adults can bump into them.

✔ Don't let temperature-sensitive foods sit out in your kitchen, especially in warm weather. Raw meat, fish, and certain dairy products can spoil quickly, so refrigerate or freeze them right away.

✔ Wipe up spills immediately so that no one slips and falls.

✔ Don't try to cook if your mind is elsewhere, because your fingers may wind up elsewhere as well.

✔ Separate raw meat, especially poultry, from produce and other items in your refrigerator to avoid cross-contamination of harmful bacteria from one food to another.

✔ Wash your hands before handling food. Hands can be a virtual freight train of bacteria, depending, of course, on what you do during the day. Also wash thoroughly after handling meat or poultry.

✔ To avoid panic-stricken searches, always return utensils to the proper place. Always return a knife to its holder when you're finished with it.

✔ Clean up as you work. Obvious, no? Then why doesn't everyone do it? We know people who can make a tuna fish sandwich and leave the kitchen looking as if they had just served a lunch to the Dallas Cowboys. Put away dirty knives, wipe down counters, and return food to the refrigerator between steps in a recipe — doing so keeps you thinking clearly and discourages household pets from jumping onto countertops. Plus, cleaning up as you go frees up that spatula or whisk for the next step of the recipe.

✔ Every kitchen needs a fire extinguisher. It is inexpensive (about $15), easy to use, and mounts on the wall. This device may not do much for your cherries jubilee, but it can avert a disaster.

✔ The old wives' tale "Oil and water do not mix" happens to be true. Throwing water on a grease fire makes it worse by spreading it around. If the fire is contained in a pot or pan, cover it with a lid. For a fire in your oven or one that has spread to the floor, a few handfuls of baking soda or salt should cut off its oxygen supply while you grab the fire extinguisher.

Chapter 2

The Cook's Tools

In This Chapter

▶ Deciding which items you really need

▶ Hot, hot, hot: Cookware materials from copper to stainless

▶ Choosing knives and using them properly

▶ Blenders, bakers' tools, and some other stuff you don't need

▶ Caring for your new tools

▶ Getting started with two easy recipes

Recipes in This Chapter

↻ Scrambled Eggs

▶ Tuscan Bread Salad

🍴 🥚 🍶 🌶 🥬 🌿

Kitchen equipment is sort of like a car. When you first get your driver's license, a dented ten-year-old Honda Civic is nirvana. But as you become a more experienced driver, you start dreaming of a better car, maybe a new Ford Explorer. When you enter the wonderful world of cooking, you really can do fine with just a few basic tools — the ride may not be as luxurious as a new Ford Explorer, but you'll still get to the prom on time.

This chapter is all about understanding and using kitchen equipment. Learning how to use kitchen equipment properly — say, a chef's knife — is time well spent.

If you are just getting started or are on a tight budget, here are some essential tools. As you become more proficient, you may want to expand your repertoire — and, for that reason, we let you know about more luxurious equipment, too.

First, we list the bare-bones-all-I-can-spend-now kitchen equipment (you can find more detailed descriptions of these items later in this chapter):

✔ **10-inch chef's knife:** You can perform more than 80 percent of all cutting and slicing chores with this knife.

✔ **Paring knife:** For peeling, coring, and carving garnishes from vegetables and fruits.

✔ **10-inch nonstick frying pan:** The all-around pan for sautéing, making egg dishes, braising small quantities of food, and more.

- ✔ **3-quart saucepan:** For cooking vegetables, rice, soups, sauces, and small quantities of pasta.

- ✔ **Expandable steamer attachment (to fit the 3-quart saucepan):** For steaming vegetables, fish, and shellfish.

- ✔ **10-quart stock pot with lid:** For making stocks or large quantities of soup, pasta, and vegetables. You'll be surprised by how often you use this pot.

- ✔ **Electric blender:** This machine does not slice and chop like a food processor, but it's terrific for making quick, healthful sauces (see Chapter 7), soups, purees, and drinks.

- ✔ **Heavy-duty roasting pan:** For all kinds of roasting.

- ✔ **Liquid and dry measuring cups:** So you don't botch up recipes by using too much or too little of something.

- ✔ **Strainer:** Essential for certain sauces, pastas, salads, and soups.

- ✔ **Meat thermometer:** Why guess?

- ✔ **Vegetable peeler, pepper mill, hand cheese grater, rubber spatula, and wooden spoons:** Don't go off the deep end buying little kitchen gizmos; these tools are all you need to get started.

In this chapter, we describe many items generically, occasionally mentioning well-known brands with good reputations. We also offer advice on which materials to look for — stainless steel, copper, aluminum, and so on — and what size of appliance to consider, as well as how to judge whether the equipment is well made. Bone up on the precise definitions and names of these items, especially if you plan to order equipment by mail.

Don't Get Skewered in Kitchen Shops

First, a word about price and availability. Listing specific prices is difficult because retail markups on kitchenware vary greatly from store to store, generally ranging from 50 to 100 percent of the wholesale price. For example, a quality, heavy-gauge, 10-inch, stainless steel skillet with a base of sandwiched aluminum (or copper) can cost $100 or more at a major department store or kitchenware shop, but the same item may cost 20 to 30 percent less in a well-known discount house. Because you can find such variation in price, our best advice is to shop around, including on the Internet.

A Rose Is a Rose, but a Pot Is Not a Pan: Cookware

If it has two opposite-set handles and a lid, it's classified as a *pot. Pans* have one long handle and come with or without lids. This section gives a rundown of important pots and pans and how to evaluate them.

Among major brands of retail cookware are All-Clad, Berndes, Borgeat, Calphalon, Chantal, Cuisinart, Demeyere, Farberware, Le Creuset, Mauviel, Paderno, Revereware, Sitram, and T-Fal. Most major companies offer limited lifetime warranties and will replace a pot, pan, or other piece of equipment if a problem arises from normal wear and tear.

Here are some things to keep in mind when buying cookware:

- **Examine how you cook and how you will use equipment.** For example, if you do a lot of fat-free and low-fat cooking, you'll want to invest in several nonstick pieces.

- **Think twice about buying whole sets, even if they are on sale, unless you can use every piece.** Sets are limited to one type of material and one style, whereas you may be better off with various styles and materials.

- **Grasp the handle of the pan in the store.** It should sit comfortably in your hand. Ask yourself whether having a heat-resistant handle is important, or whether you always remember to cook with a pot holder.

- **Consider the appearance of your cookware.** Appearance is especially important if you decide to hang your pots and pans for decoration. Stainless steel and copper look great.

- **Buy the best equipment you can afford.** It's the same philosophy you use when buying a man's suit: One quality, durable suit is far preferable to two cheesy getups. Cheap, flimsy pots and pans need to be replaced after a few years of normal use.

Pots and pans have handles with varying degrees of heat resistance. Many pans with metal handles are made to withstand extreme temperatures. Sometimes cooking starts on top of the stove and finishes in the oven or under the broiler. Just to be sure, assume that every handle is roaring hot, no matter how well made; never grab one without a *real* pot holder. Don't use a cotton dish towel as a substitute for a pot holder; not only could a dish towel catch on fire, but it's also too thin to provide proper protection from a hot handle.

Heavy-gauge cast-iron skillet

The cast-iron skillet, shown in Figure 2-1, has been a standard in American and European kitchens for hundreds of years and still outperforms contemporary cookware in some respects (for example, browning, blackening, and searing). Better yet, a cast-iron skillet is one of the most inexpensive pans you can find, and it will outlast most other skillets as well. Tag sales and antique shops are loaded with them.

Figure 2-1: You use a cast-iron skillet for browning, searing, and more.

cast-iron skillet

Before using a cast-iron skillet for the first time, season it by wiping it with vegetable oil and then heating it on the range on a medium setting for about 2 minutes. In addition, you must thoroughly wipe the skillet dry after washing it to prevent rust. Clean the skillet gently with soap and water; never scour with metal pads. (Plastic pads are fine.) Look for a skillet with a spout for pouring off fat.

Pancake griddle

If you have hungry children around the house, this flat, nonstick griddle is well suited for pancakes, grilled cheese sandwaches, bacon, and the like.

Omelet pan or skillet

A 10-inch omelet pan with curved sides, shown in Figure 2-2, is handy to have around. Contrary to what manufacturers say, reserving the omelet pan exclusively for eggs is not necessary. An omelet pan is also excellent for sautéing potatoes and other vegetables. (See Chapter 4 for more information about sautéing.) But if you keep the pan (whether nonstick or untreated metal) in pristine condition and grease it well before cooking, you can make picture-perfect omelets.

If you're eager to make something with the equipment you have, try your hand at this quick and easy recipe for scrambled eggs. Perfect for the beginner, and loved by all, these eggs are sure to please and impress your family and friends.

TIP

Keep this tip in mind if you want to make excellent scrambled eggs: Don't overbeat the eggs before you cook them.

Figure 2-2:
Omelet pans
are great for
making
scrambled
eggs,
fried eggs,
frittatas, and
more.

10" omelet pan

Some scrambled egg recipes call for cream, which adds a nice smoothness to the eggs; others call for water, which increases the volume by stimulating the whites to foam. You can use either ingredient for the following recipe — try it both ways and see which you prefer.

Scrambled Eggs

Tools: *Medium bowl, fork, 10-inch (preferably nonstick) skillet or omelet pan, metal spatula or wooden spoon*

Preparation time: *About 5 minutes*

Cooking time: *About 1 to 2 minutes*

Yield: *3 servings*

6 eggs

2 tablespoons light cream, low-fat milk, or water

2 tablespoons chopped chives (optional)

Salt and black pepper to taste

2 tablespoons butter

1 Break the eggs into a bowl. With a fork, beat the eggs until they are blended, but no more. Add the cream (or milk or water if you prefer), chopped chives (if desired), salt, and pepper and beat a few seconds to blend well.

2 Melt the butter in a 10-inch skillet over medium heat. (Do not let it burn.) Pour in the egg mixture. As the mixture begins to set, use a metal spatula or wooden spoon to pull the eggs gently across the bottom and sides of the pan, forming large, soft lumps. The eggs are cooked when the mixture is no longer runny.

You can dress up this basic scrambled eggs recipe by adding different seasonings to the liquid egg mixture, such as a dash of Tabasco sauce, a sprinkling of dry mustard or grated Parmesan cheese, 2 tablespoons of chopped fresh parsley or basil, or a teaspoon or so of freshly grated lemon peel.

Sauté pan

You also need at least one straight-sided, stainless steel sauté pan (see Figure 2-3) that's at least 10 or 12 inches in diameter, with a depth of 2 inches, for sautéing, braising, frying, and making quick sauces. These pans have a lid so that food can be covered and simmered in small amounts of liquid.

Figure 2-3:
You can use a nonstick sauté pan to sauté foods in just a little fat.

Nonstick coatings are the best aid to novice cooks since they started selling spaghetti sauce in jars. Nonstick pans have great appeal with today's emphasis on low-fat cooking. You can sauté potatoes, vegetables, fish, poultry, and meats in very little oil or butter. Nonstick pans do not brown foods as well as regular pans do, but they are easier to clean, and the convenience may be worth it.

In recent years, nonstick pans have improved tremendously, and the linings last longer than before (ten years or more) — as long as you don't use metal utensils with them. So many brands exist that keeping track of them all is difficult. Look for well-known manufacturers, such as All-Clad, Calphalon, Cuisinart, and WearEver.

Don't buy an inexpensive pan (whether nonstick or regular) that is thin and light — it will warp over time. Purchase pots and pans from a major manufacturer that stands behind its products and will quickly replace or repair damaged goods.

Rondeau (shallow, straight-sided pot)

A rondeau (pronounced *ron-DOE*) is great to have on hand when you entertain — and of course you will! A straight-sided pot with two handles and a lid, as shown in Figure 2-4, a 12-inch rondeau (the size we recommend) can hold enough food to serve eight people or more. If you just got a raise, splurge for heavy-gauge copper, which is expensive but beautiful to serve from. Stainless steel is good, too, but make sure that it has a copper or aluminum core for efficient heat conduction. Stainless steel alone is not an efficient heat conductor. (See the sidebar "Pros and cons of different materials," later in this chapter.)

Figure 2-4:
A rondeau
can go from
oven to
table.

A rondeau has many uses, among them braising, stewing, and browning large quantities of meat, poultry, or fish. Look for brands like All-Clad, Cuisinart, Sitram, Calphalon, Paderno, and Magnalite.

Saucepans

A saucepan can be stainless steel with a copper or aluminum core, heavy-gauge aluminum, or a combination of metals. It is an all-around pan used for cooking vegetables, soups, rice, and sauces for pasta and other dishes. (See Figure 2-5.) You will want to own a number of saucepans that range in size from small to large. A 1- to 1½-quart saucepan is perfect for melting small quantities of butter or chocolate, or for warming milk. A medium 2- to 3-quart saucepan is essential for making sauces. And saucepans that are 4 quarts or larger are suitable for making soups, steaming vegetables, or boiling a moderate amount of pasta or rice.

Figure 2-5:
You use a
saucepan to
boil foods
and make
sauces.

Sauteuse evasée (slope-sided saucepan)

This Gallic mouthful (also called a slope-sided saucepan) refers to a little pan that is the workhorse of the French kitchen. If you ever splurge on a piece of copper cookware, we recommend a *sauteuse evasée* (pronounced *saw-TOOZ eh-va-SAY*), which is 8 to 9 inches in diameter with a volume of about 3 quarts. (See Figure 2-6.) A *sauteuse evasée* may be referred to as simply a saucepan, which is its major role. Its sloped sides (*evasée* refers to the sloped sides) make for easy whisking.

Figure 2-6:
You use a *sauteuse evasée* mainly as a saucepan.

Copper (lined with stainless steel or tin) provides the best heat control of all metals. That control is the secret of well-textured sauces. Stainless steel with copper or aluminum sandwiched in the base works very well, too, and is less expensive than the all-copper variety.

Enameled cast-iron stew pot (or Dutch oven)

This attractive, all-around stew pot, also called a *Dutch oven,* is ideal for slow-cooking stews, soups, and all sorts of hearty winter meals. (See Figure 2-7.) Enamel does not brown food as well as cast-iron or stainless steel, however. You may want to brown or sear meat in a separate pan before adding it to the Dutch oven. A 4-quart version made by Le Creuset and a similar one from Copco are excellent.

Figure 2-7:
An enameled stew pot, or Dutch oven, is best for cooking stews and soups.

Stock pot

A stock pot is indispensable in any kitchen. It can serve many functions: soup making, braising, steaming, and poaching, to name a few. Look for a tall, narrow, 10- to 14-quart heavy-gauge pot with a tight-fitting lid that can hold a steamer basket (see Figure 2-8). Inexpensive circular steamers open and close like a fan to fit different sizes of pots and pans. Heavy aluminum is fine for a stock pot; stainless steel costs twice as much.

Figure 2-8:
In a stock pot, you make soups and much more. With a steamer basket, it doubles as a steamer.

stock pot

Pasta pot

A large, 8-quart stainless steel pot fitted with a lid is the perfect size for cooking ½ to 2 pounds of pasta (or you can use your stock pot instead).

Roasting pans

A well-equipped kitchen should have one oval roasting pan, about 12 inches long, and a large rectangular one, about 14 x 11 inches. An oval roasting pan is suitable for poultry and small roasts; a 14-inch rectangular one can handle two chickens or a large roast. The oval one should be enameled cast iron so that it can double as a gratin pan (see the following section); the rectangular pan can be heavy-gauge aluminum or stainless steel.

Gratin pan

Novice cooks tend to make many one-pot dishes. To give these entrees a delicious finishing touch, often by broiling to crisp the top, you should have a gratin dish, shown in Figure 2-9. Unlike Dutch ovens, gratin dishes are shallow, measure from 10 inches long and up, and do not have a lid. A 12-inch dish can feed six or more people. These pans are ideal for macaroni and cheese, turkey casserole, gratin of potatoes, and many other simple dishes. Some are attractive enough to go from oven to table.

Figure 2-9:
A gratin pan is handy for finishing one-pot dishes.

gratin pan

9-x-13-inch baking dish

Another classic you'll want to own is the versatile 9-x-13-inch baking dish. Whether made of glass or ceramic, it's great for making casseroles, roasting winter vegetables, or baking brownies and other bar cookies.

From Slicing to Dicing: Knives for All Occasions

Every department store carries kitchen knives these days, and some knives look quite impressive. But don't buy knives on appearance alone.

Hold a knife. If it's well constructed, it should feel substantial in your hand. The handle should be comfortable. The knife should be *balanced* — that is, the handle should not be significantly heavier than the blade or vice versa.

What you need

Knives are often sold in sets of six to eight, which can be a bargain. But think twice. Do you really need a boning knife or a filleting knife right now? Sometimes buying what you need as your skills progress makes more sense.

Home cooks really need only three essential knives: a 10- to 12-inch chef's knife, a 9- to 12-inch serrated (bread) knife, and a small paring knife. Investing in quality yields dividends for years.

Home cooks should buy high-carbon stainless steel knives with riveted wooden handles. These knives are durable and do not rust the way carbon steel knives do.

The best knives have a tapered blade that runs from the tip to the base of the handle — the technical term is *forged*. Among the most reputable brands are

- ✔ Henckels
- ✔ Wüsthof
- ✔ Sabatier
- ✔ Hoffritz
- ✔ International Cutlery
- ✔ Chef's Choice

A *chef's knife* (shown in Figure 2-10) is generally 10 to 12 inches long and can be used for all sorts of chopping, slicing, dicing, and mincing. This knife is really the workhorse of the kitchen, so investing in a great chef's knife always pays off.

Figure 2-10:
A chef's knife is handy for all sorts of chopping chores.

chef's knife

Here is a dish in which the chef's knife goes into action — chopping, slicing, and trimming.

This wonderful salad, typical of the Tuscan countryside in Italy, is ideal for entertaining. Serve it with grilled fish or chicken, or as a light lunch all on its own. If you have leftovers you can refrigerate it overnight; more than that and it gets soggy.

Tuscan Bread Salad

Tools: *Chef's knife, bread knife, cotton towel, two large bowls*

Preparation time: *15 minutes*

Cooking time: *None (30 minutes marination)*

Yield: *Serves 4 to 6*

1 country loaf of bread (or 1½ baguettes), sliced thinly and left out overnight

½ cup red wine vinegar

4 scallions, trimmed and chopped (including green part)

1 cucumber, peeled and sliced crosswise (⅛ inch thick)

1 red or yellow bell pepper, cored, seeded, and sliced into thin strips

3 tomatoes, halved, chopped

20 fresh basil leaves, sliced thinly

8–12 anchovy fillets, rinsed and chopped (optional)

6 ounces canned tuna (in oil), drained and flaked

6 tablespoons olive oil

1½ teaspoons salt

1½ teaspoons black pepper

1 teaspoon chopped fresh marjoram (or ½ teaspoon dried)

1 Tear the bread roughly and soak it in ¼ cup of the vinegar mixed with enough water to soak it through. After 2 minutes, place it in a towel and twist to squeeze out as much liquid as possible. Place the bread in a large bowl with the scallions, cucumber, bell pepper, tomatoes, basil, anchovies (if desired), and tuna.

2 In a separate bowl combine the olive oil, remaining vinegar, salt, and pepper. Stir to combine well. Add this dressing to the vegetable-bread mixture and toss well. Let sit for 30 minutes at room temperature. Taste for seasonings — it may need more salt and pepper. Sprinkle the marjoram over the top and serve.

Nothing evokes the fresh flavors of summer like fresh basil. But basil is very fragile. Shortly after you chop it, the pieces start to darken — the flavor is still there, but the appearance is off-putting. Always chop basil just before using it.

Have you ever tried to slice a baguette with a regular knife? It's not only frustrating, but also dangerous. So, to remedy that situation, we put a serrated knife in our list of essential knives.

A *serrated knife* (shown in Figure 2-11), generally with an 8- to 10-inch blade, is essential for cutting bread. Hard-crusted French or Italian bread dulls a chef's knife quickly. Look for a serrated knife that has wide teeth.

Figure 2-11:
A serrated knife is great for cutting crusty breads.

A *paring knife* (shown in Figure 2-12), with a blade from 2 to 4 inches long, is for delicate jobs like peeling apples and other fruits, trimming shallots and garlic, removing stems from strawberries, coring tomatoes, or making vegetable or fruit decorations.

Figure 2-12:
Use a paring knife for delicate cutting tasks.

A *mandoline* cuts vegetables in the shapes of French fries, crinkle cuts, thin disks, and more. The stainless steel and new composite fiberglass versions are expensive, but a much cheaper plastic version is also available. See Chapter 18 for an illustration of how to use it.

Using knives safely

Every year, hundreds of thousands of people wind up in hospital emergency rooms as a result of kitchen accidents involving knives. Many injuries have resulted from time-pressed, hungry people trying to pry apart frozen hamburgers or slice through hard bagels. Don't make their mistake! Slice away from your hand, keep your fingers clear of the blades, and don't ever use the palm of your hand as a cutting board.

Using a knife properly is just as important as choosing the right knife. In the following sections, we explain how the pros chop garlic and fresh herbs.

Chopping garlic

TOQUE TIP

Chef, author, and cooking teacher Jacques Pépin has a slightly unconventional method for chopping garlic that works exceptionally well for novices and professionals alike. Follow these steps:

1. **Peel off the outer skin of the garlic, smash the garlic slightly with the side of your knife, and remove the rest of the skin.**

2. **Hold the garlic clove on a cutting board with the knuckles of your index finger and middle finger leaning against the side of the blade.**

   Keep your fingertips folded over inward to prevent cuts. (This chopping technique works for most vegetables.)

3. **Start working the chef's knife up and down, slowly moving your knuckles toward the other end of the garlic as you chop. (This technique takes a little practice.)**

When Pépin slices the whole garlic, he runs the side of his knife over the slices to flatten them and presses them to adhere to the cutting board. Doing so makes the second round of chopping easier because the garlic is not moving around the board.

Chopping parsley and other fresh herbs

TOQUE TIP

The late Pierre Franey, chef and author, had this suggestion: "When you chop vegetables, you don't want to strain your wrists. With parsley, I chop it roughly and then go back over it with my chef's knife in a rocking motion, walking the blade all around as I do it." (See Figure 2-13.)

Chopping Parsley & Other Fresh Herbs

Figure 2-13: The correct way to chop parsley and other fresh herbs.

1. Rinse and dry well

2. chop roughly

   *NOTE: For herbs like rosemary and thyme, remove and chop leaves. Discard thick stem.

3. gather and chop some more

   Use rocking motion

   move knife around

Processors, Blenders, and Mixers

Food processor: A food processor, shown in Figure 2-14, is an extremely versatile tool. Robot-Coupe, Cuisinart, and KitchenAid make high-quality food processors that come with a full line of accessories for mixing, slicing, shredding, pureeing, kneading, and more. Food processors come in various sizes and are widely discounted.

Figure 2-14: Food processors can do a wide variety of tasks.

food processor

Blender: With good reason, a blender is up there with the coffee machine as one of the most popular appliances in the kitchen. A blender's ultrafast blades can puree fresh fruits such as strawberries into a smooth sauce, whip milkshakes, crush ice, and more. (Turn to Chapter 7 for specific blender sauce recipes.) Waring made the first blender, which is still considered a classic, but other companies produce reliable machines as well. Some blenders come with 12 or more speeds, which is like taking a Lear Jet to the grocery store. Stick with the simple ones instead.

Electric mixer: Electric mixers come in two types: handheld and standing. Either comes in handy for all kinds of batters, sauces, homemade mayonnaise (you won't believe how much better it is than the store-bought variety!), and various egg dishes. Whereas a handheld beater is terrific for lighter jobs like beating heavy cream and egg whites, a heavy-duty, freestanding mixer is designed to accommodate the more serious cook.

Most standing mixers come with a 5-quart stainless steel bowl and multiple removable attachments that paddle, knead dough, and whisk. A heavy-duty standing electric mixer also frees your hands, allowing you to accomplish other tasks as it churns away. Major brands of heavy-duty standing mixers include KitchenAid and Sunbeam.

Why a blender is one of the most useful kitchen machines

Although food processors are unsurpassed for chopping, slicing, and grating, blenders have an edge when it comes to liquefying and sauce-making. For example, the upcoming chapters show you how to make dishes like sautéed chicken breasts with a wonderful quick sauce of white wine, chicken stock, leeks, and herbs. The normal way to make this sauce is to cook down the leeks, stock, and other ingredients, maybe add a little butter for smoothness, and pass them through a strainer. With a blender, however, you just toss everything in the bowl and whizzzzzzz — instant sauce. The sauce is even more flavorful because the leeks and herbs dissolve into it. This technique does not work as well in a food processor, in which the two-level slicing blade cuts through liquids instead of blending them.

Bowls and Other Mixing Equipment

Stainless steel, glass, or ceramic mixing bowls: Mixing bowls are among the most frequently used items in every kitchen. Buy bowls with flat bottoms for good balance in these sizes: 8 quarts, 5 quarts, 3 quarts, and 1½ quarts. Buy them in sets that stack and store easily. You can use these bowls to mix salads and sauces, store leftovers, let bread dough rise, and send your kid down a snowy hill.

Whisks: Whisks should be made of stainless steel. You use a stiffer *sauce whisk,* about 8 to 10 inches long, to blend sauces, such as béchamel and some cream sauces. You use a larger, rounder one, sometimes called a *balloon whisk,* generally 12 to 14 inches long, for whipping eggs and heavy cream.

Spoons, spatulas, long-handled forks, and tongs: Look for a variety of spoons. A solid, one-piece stainless steel spoon, about 12 to 15 inches long, fills most needs. Buy wooden spoons of various sizes for scraping food bits off the bottom of a simmering casserole and countless other tasks. A slotted, stainless steel spoon removes food solids that are cooking in hot liquid, such as ravioli.

You can use a long-handled, stainless steel ladle with a 4- to 6-ounce bowl to dole out soups and pour pancake batter onto a griddle. Buy at least two rubber spatulas and a square-tipped hard plastic turner to flip burgers and other foods. You need metal tongs for turning over tender pieces of meat or fish. Inexpensive plastic spaghetti tongs are useful for serving cooked pasta.

Baking Equipment

Baking (or cookie) sheet: For baking cookies, biscuits, and breads, a heavy-duty steel or nonstick baking sheet with ½-inch flared edges (they prevent butter and juices from spilling onto your oven) is essential. Baking sheets come in different sizes. Buy two large ones that fit in your oven, leaving a 2-inch margin on all sides to allow an even flow of heat during baking.

Jelly roll pan: This 15-x-10-inch shallow rectangular baking pan holds cake batters and egg batters that are filled and rolled. If you ever saw a Yule Log and wondered how the filling ends up swirled into the center, this pan is the answer. Buy one made of heavy aluminum.

Round cake pans: Standard layer cake recipes call for two 9-x-2-inch pans. Choose anodized or nonstick aluminum.

Square cake pan: For making brownies or gingerbread, you need an 8- or 9-inch square, 2-quart capacity pan. Anodized aluminum and other nonstick materials make removing the brownies easier.

Muffin tins: For baking quick breads and muffins, you need a 12-cup tray of nonstick or heavy-gauge aluminum. And buy a box of paper muffin liners so you don't have to grease and flour each metal cup.

Pie pan: A glass or aluminum pan that is 9 inches in diameter suits most standard recipes.

Rolling pin: You don't need an arsenal of rolling pins like professional pastry chefs have. For home-baking, get a two-handled, hardwood rolling pin that is about 15 inches long.

Cooling racks: Cookies and cakes removed from the oven need to cool. Racks allow air to circulate around them and vent steam. They come in many shapes and sizes. Buy two 12- to 14-inch racks made of chromed steel.

Loaf pan: For baking breads, terrines, and meat loaf, you want a sturdy, 6-cup loaf pan. (See Figure 2-15.)

Figure 2-15:
You can bake all sorts of foods in a loaf pan.

loaf pan

Springform pan: With its hinged release, detachable bottom, a springform pan easily unmolds cheesecakes, delicate tarts, and cakes with crumb crusts. Get a 9- to 10-inch pan of heavy-gauge aluminum. (See Figure 2-16.)

Figure 2-16: Use a springform pan to make delicious desserts.

springform pan

Flour sifter: Not all baking recipes call for sifted flour, but when they do, you need a sifter to aerate the flour and eliminate lumps. A 3-cup stainless steel sifter with a rotating handle is a good choice.

If you don't have a sifter and need sifted flour for a recipe, you can use a strainer. (See Figure 2-17 for instructions.)

How to Sift Flour If You Don't Have a Sifter

Figure 2-17: In a pinch, you can sift flour by using a strainer.

1. Pour flour into a strainer

2. Use your hand to lightly tap the strainer

— OR — tap the strainer on the inside of the bowl

Pastry brush: To apply glazes and coatings to breads and cakes, use an all-purpose, 1½-inch pastry brush with natural bristles. Pastry brushes are also essential for basting food with pan drippings or sauces. Buy several brushes at a time because they wear out quickly. Clean the brushes with a mild dish soap, rinsing thoroughly.

Cake tester: A cake tester helps you determine whether your cake is finished. Pierce the cake with the needle-thin tester; if it comes out free of sticky batter, the cake is done. In a pinch, you can use a toothpick instead.

TIP

Half empty or half full: Measuring techniques

Measuring is important, especially for a beginning cook. Too much salt, and the stew is ruined. Too little baking powder, and the cake doesn't rise. Too much milk, and the pudding never sets.

But measuring does not replace tasting, and the more you cook, the less you need to measure. Experienced chefs are able to sense in their hands the feel of a tablespoon of salt or ½ teaspoon of lemon peel. But this comes with practice. Here are some basic measuring guidelines:

✔ **Measure dry and liquid ingredients in different cups.** The dry measure is a metal or plastic cup with a handle. To measure flour or rice, dip the measure into the canister or bag, scooping out more than you need. Then use the straight edge of a knife to level off the excess. Work over a piece of waxed paper or the bag or canister to catch any excess.

Measure liquids in a glass or plastic cup with a spout for pouring; do not fill the cup while holding it at eye level. Place the cup on the counter (so that you're sure the liquid is level) and lower yourself to read the mark.

✔ **Measure very precisely when baking cakes, breads, and desserts.** A baking recipe is a formula that requires an exact proportion of dry to wet ingredients.

✔ **Use a kitchen scale to measure dry ingredients accurately when a recipe calls for ounces or pounds.**

✔ **Use measuring spoons for small amounts of liquid and dry ingredients, such as a teaspoon of vanilla extract or ½ teaspoon of baking soda.** Don't use your table silverware — it's not equivalent to measuring spoons.

✔ **Do not measure over your working bowl, especially if it's filled with other ingredients.** You may accidentally add too much of an ingredient.

✔ **Pack solid fats and brown sugar into a cup.** For butter, use the measure marks on the wrapper to slice off a specific amount.

✔ **To easily remove sticky foods like honey, peanut butter, and molasses from a measuring cup, coat the cup first with a small amount of vegetable oil or spray.**

✔ **If the recipe calls for sifted flour, be sure to sift it.** Sifting incorporates air into the flour, and a cup of sifted flour is less — by 2 tablespoons or more — than a cup of unsifted flour. Using a dry measuring cup, scoop out the approximate amount of flour called for in the recipe and place it in the top of the sifter. Sift the flour into a large mixing bowl or over a piece of waxed paper. After sifting, so as not to lose the flour's new "lightness," gently spoon the flour into the appropriate measure cup, fill to overflowing, and then level it off with the straight edge of a knife.

Metal or plastic dry measuring cups: To follow precise recipes, you need a set of dry measuring cups — ¼ cup, ⅓ cup, ½ cup, and 1 cup. Metal is better than plastic, which isn't as durable.

Glass or plastic liquid measuring cup: Get one with a 2-cup capacity and a spout for pouring liquids. A 4-cup liquid measuring cup comes in handy, too.

Metal measuring spoons: Essential for many recipes, especially baking. Make sure that the set you purchase comes with ¼ teaspoon, ½ teaspoon, 1 teaspoon, and 1 tablespoon capacities.

Miscellaneous Tools

Kitchen timer: Don't stand in front of the oven staring at the clock like a monk at the shrine of Buddha. Set a timer and go watch *Jeopardy!* or read a book.

Salad dryer: An inexpensive plastic salad spinner, like the one shown in Figure 2-18, makes short work of drying lettuce. If lettuce is not completely dry, the dressing slides right off.

Figure 2-18:
Salad spinners are useful for drying greens so dressing adheres to them.

salad spinner

Colander: Buy one made of stainless steel or plastic for draining pasta and rinsing salad greens, vegetables, and berries.

Chinois: This cone-shaped sieve (so named because it is shaped like a Chinese hat) is well suited for straining sauces, stocks, and just about anything. (See Figure 2-19.) A *chinois* also looks funny when you put it on your head and chase the kids around the house with a rolling pin.

Figure 2-19:
Use a
chinois
to strain
liquids.

chinois

Cutting boards: Use cutting boards to save your counters from sharp knives and hot pots and pans. Plastic or composite boards are easier to clean than wooden ones and can be washed in the dishwasher. Chefs clean their wooden boards with a solution of water and bleach or rub them with lemon juice. Excessive soaking or placing wooden boards in the dishwasher causes them to splinter, warp, and crack.

Mcat thermometer: Unlike great chefs, most people can't tell that a roast has finished cooking by pressing its surface. You can use two types of meat thermometers to check: An instant-read thermometer, our favorite of the two kinds, has a thin rod that lets you pierce into the roast periodically to test for doneness. An ovenproof thermometer remains inside the meat or poultry from beginning to end of cooking. See Figure 2-20 for an illustration of both kinds of meat thermometers.

Figure 2-20:
Meat
thermo-
meters are
essential for
determining
whether a
roast is
done.

instant reading

meat thermometers

Bulb baster: Using this tool is the most convenient way to coat a roast or chicken with pan juices. A large spoon also works as a basting tool, but a bulb baster is quicker and safer for removing hot grease from the bottom of a roasting pan.

Following are ten more handy utensils to have around your kitchen:

- ✔ Vegetable peeler
- ✔ Lemon and cheese grater
- ✔ Citrus juicer
- ✔ Pepper mill
- ✔ Potato masher
- ✔ Shrimp deveiner
- ✔ Multipurpose kitchen shears
- ✔ Oven thermometer
- ✔ Pie server

Care and Feeding of Your Beautiful Utensils

So you have forgone a trip to Disney World and bought all these kitchen supplies. If you follow our advice and buy good stuff, your supplies should last a lifetime. Of course, you need to take care of your utensils. The following sections give you a few tips.

Pots and pans

If you have a high ceiling or spare wall space, hanging pots and pans on a rack is a great way to go. The cookware is safe and easily accessible. A low ceiling, however, risks concussion. For an inexpensive alternative, mount a pegboard on a wall and hang cookware from hooks.

To remove burned food from a pot, try boiling water in it until the food lifts off. Or sprinkle cleanser or a little dishwashing detergent onto the bottom, add water to cover, and let the pot soak for about an hour before scrubbing. If the burn is really severe, you'll have to repeat this process a couple of times. Or warm the burned pot in your oven; then remove and place it on a piece of newspaper. Wearing rubber gloves, spray all burned areas with oven cleaner and, after 15 minutes, wash in hot, soapy water. Don't try oven cleaner with nonstick pans, however — they require gentle cleaning. Wash them with hot, sudsy water and a sponge or soft plastic cleaning pad. Avoid harsh abrasives and steel wool pads that can damage the interior coating.

Not all pots and pans can be put in a dishwasher. Be especially careful with those made with copper, anodized aluminum, and nonstick coatings; harsh dishwasher detergents may cause them to discolor. Read the care and cleaning guide for specific instructions for handling your equipment.

Knives

Everyone has a kitchen drawer filled with an awesome stash of junk, from old calendars and chopsticks to unidentified keys and dried-up tubes of glue. People often consider these drawers to be convenient spots to store knives. *Don't do it!* Get a wooden knife block to protect your knives' edges. Or you can get one of those magnetic strips that you mount on the wall for hanging knives. The advantage of the magnetic strip is that you know exactly which knife you are choosing, whereas in a wood block you see only the handles. Just make sure that the knives are far from a child's reach.

Honing a knife with a steel

Grab the steel firmly and hold it slightly away from your body and at a slight angle as shown.

Then hold the knife firmly with the other hand and run the blade down the shaft at about a 30-degree angle. Start near the tip of the steel and, as you move down the steel, run the blade from near handle to tip.

Repeat on the other side of the blade. Keep alternating until you've honed each side of the blade (about ten times).

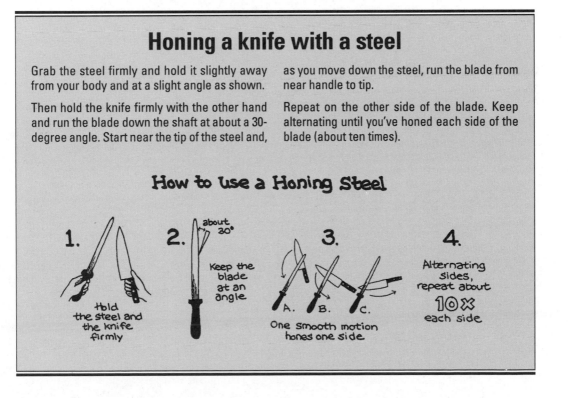

How to use a Honing Steel

1. Hold the steel and the knife firmly

2. about 30° Keep the blade at an angle

3. A. B. C. One smooth motion hones one side.

4. Alternating sides, repeat about 10x each side

Home cooks may want to have their knives (especially high-carbon stainless, the most common type) professionally sharpened only twice a year, because oversharpening wears down the blade. Your local butcher or gourmet retailer may sharpen them for free. Electric home sharpeners are okay, but they can't match a professional using a rotating stone.

To get the best from your knife, run the blade over a *steel* (a 12-inch-long steel shaft with a handle) every time you use it. Doing so realigns the molecules on the blade and restores the sharp edge. See the sidebar "Honing a knife with a steel" for illustrated instructions.

Part II
Know Your Techniques

The 5th Wave   By Rich Tennant

"Don't turn off the dryer, I'm tossing the salad."

In this part . . .

The focus of this book is cooking techniques — chopping, slicing, sautéing, braising, poaching, roasting, and a whole lot more. Granted, you have a lot to absorb, but you already exhibited superior intelligence by buying this book, so the rest should be a cakewalk.

The goal of this part — and indeed this book — is to give you the basic tools you need to cook from a recipe. We explain each technique from the ground up, giving you a variety of recipes to practice with. As you gain experience, you'll learn to improvise and maybe even invent some recipes yourself.

Chapter 3

Boiling, Poaching, and Steaming

In This Chapter

▶ Water follies: Simmering, boiling, and steaming defined

▶ Uncle Ben and friends: All about rice

▶ Surf's up: Poaching

"**I** can't even boil water" is the would-be cook's lament. Well, grab a pot so we can tell you about this bubbly experience — and faster than you can say "instant coffee."

In this chapter, we cover three vital cooking techniques: boiling, steaming, and poaching. We concentrate here on vegetables because there are no better ways to enjoy their fresh flavors and textures. We also tell you about the different types of rice, an incredibly versatile staple, and how to cook and season them. And who can forget potatoes? Finally, we talk about two important stocks, those flavor-packed liquids that fuel so many great dishes.

Into the Pool: The Techniques Defined

Relax; even Home Ec. dropouts can figure out these basic techniques. *Boiling* is bringing water to 212 degrees Fahrenheit for cooking. You don't need a thermometer. Let the water come to a full *rolling boil* (when the bubbles are rapidly breaking the surface). Covering the pot speeds the process by trapping surface heat. And no one knows why, but watching the pot indeed slows down the boiling process.

How would you like your meat boiled?

Boiling is an ancient method of cooking. Thank your lucky stars that you didn't live in medieval times, when they boiled just about everything. Meat was boiled to kill germs in food that sat out on a counter for days. Boiling also washed off salt, which was used heavily to preserve meat.

In *simmering,* tiny bubbles break the surface gently — like a soft summer shower on a still lake. (Sorry for going overboard with these similes.) Simmering occurs at a lower temperature — just below a boil — and is used for long, slow cooking and braising. (Chapter 5 talks more about braising.)

A soup or stock recipe often combines the techniques of boiling and simmering, instructing you to bring the liquid to a full boil and then to lower the heat and simmer, sometimes for a long time. Sauce recipes may ask you to *reduce* the stock or liquid. Reducing means boiling again to thicken and intensify the flavor of the cooking liquid by decreasing its volume. The result is often a delicious sauce.

Poaching and *simmering* are virtually identical; cookbook writers use the terms interchangeably just to confuse you. *Steaming* is the gentlest way to cook and is better than boiling or poaching for retaining a food's color, flavor, texture, shape, and nutrients. Steaming often involves placing food over simmering water on a perforated rack in a covered pot.

Making Rice

Before we get into recipes that demonstrate boiling, simmering, poaching, and steaming techniques, we'll say a few words about rice, an incredibly versatile food that is usually boiled and then simmered. Rice has an affinity with countless boiled and steamed foods, and you can season it to create exciting taste sensations.

The world is home to thousands of strains of rice. India alone has more than 1,100 types, which must make shopping a confusing endeavor. Fortunately, the rest of us can get away with remembering five types of rice:

- **Converted or parboiled rice:** Basic white rice used for home cooking in much of the Western world; medium to long grain

- **Long-grain rice:** Includes the Indian basmati

- **Short-grain rice:** The family of Italian Arborio; also used in sushi

> ✔ **"Wild rice":** Not really rice at all (We'll get to that.)
>
> ✔ **Brown rice:** Healthful, unrefined rice with a slightly nutty flavor

Each type has its textural and flavor differences, as the following sections explain.

Converted or parboiled rice

You've probably seen converted rice in the supermarket. The term *converted* is not apostolic but rather refers to a process by which whole grains of rice are soaked in water, steamed, and then dried. This precooking makes milling easier and also conserves nutrients that are otherwise lost. Steaming also removes some of the rice's sticky starch, leaving each grain smoother in texture. (If this sounds like Madison Avenue hype, just take a look at Uncle Ben on the rice box. His skin practically shines!)

Rice absorbs its cooking water while simmering, so getting your proportions right is important — too much water leaves the rice soupy, and too little water leaves it dry. To practice, try the following simple recipe for converted rice.

Converted Rice

Tools: *Medium (3-quart) saucepan fitted with a lid*

Preparation time: *About 5 minutes*

Cooking time: *About 25 minutes*

Yield: *3 to 4 servings*

2¼ cups water	1 tablespoon butter
1 cup converted rice	½ teaspoon salt, or to taste

1 Bring the water to a boil in a medium saucepan. Add the rice, butter, and salt. Stir and cover.

2 Reduce the heat to low and simmer for 20 minutes.

(continued)

3 Remove from the heat and let stand, covered, until all the water is absorbed, about 5 minutes. (If you have excess water, strain it off; if the rice is too dry, add a little boiling water and stir. Let sit for 3 to 5 minutes.) Fluff the rice with a fork; check the seasoning, adding more salt and pepper to taste, if desired; and serve.

This basic rice accompanies many dishes, including Pork Stir-Fry (see Chapter 17) and Salmon Steaks with Red Pepper Sauce (see Chapter 4).

 Basically, the more flavor in the cooking liquid, the better the rice tastes. The flavors permeate the grains, making them a superb complement to steamed vegetables or sautéed meats or poultry. You can use chicken or vegetable stock, seasoned herbs, a dash of saffron, lemon zest or juice, or any combination of herbs and spices you like to flavor the liquid. If adding fresh herbs, do so in the last 10 minutes of cooking.

Long-grain and short-grain rice

 Because rice goes with almost everything, making it well is a very important skill to master. Follow these tips for perfect long-grain rice:

- ✔ Always read package cooking directions.
- ✔ Always measure the amounts of rice and liquid.
- ✔ Time your cooking.
- ✔ Keep the lid on tightly to trap steam.
- ✔ At the end of cooking time, test for doneness. If necessary, cook for 2 to 4 minutes more.
- ✔ Fluff cooked rice with a fork to help separate the grains.

The term pilaf refers to a dish in which the grain (rice or other whole grains) is browned slightly in butter or oil, then cooked in a flavored liquid, like chicken or beef stock. After you get the technique down, you can add any flavors you like.

This rice pilaf recipe — seasoned with turmeric, cinnamon, garlic, and raisins — gives a rice casserole a Middle Eastern character.

Rice Pilaf with Raisins, Tomatoes, and Pine Nuts

Tools: *Chef's knife, one medium saucepan, one large heavy-bottom pot or saucepan, one small frying pan*

Preparation time: *10 minutes*

Cooking time: *About 35 minutes*

Yield: *4 servings*

2 cups chicken stock

1 tablespoon butter

1 tablespoon olive oil

½ cup chopped onion

1 large clove garlic, peeled and minced

1 cup long-grain white rice

1 teaspoon turmeric or quality curry powder

¼ cup golden raisins (optional)

1 lemon slice, seeds removed, about ¼-inch thick

¼ teaspoon salt

¼ cup pine nuts

1 large plum tomato, chopped

¼ cup chopped parsley

¼ teaspoon cinnamon

Black pepper to taste

1 In a medium saucepan, bring the chicken stock to a simmer. In another large, heavy-bottom pot or saucepan, melt the butter with the oil over medium heat. Add the onion and garlic and cook until the vegetables start to soften, about 3 minutes, stirring occasionally.

2 Add the rice and turmeric or curry powder to the pot with the onions; cook over medium heat, stirring often until the rice is lightly browned and completely coated in the melted butter and oil, about 2 to 3 minutes. Add the hot broth, raisins (if desired), lemon slice, and salt. Bring to a boil over high heat, stir with a fork, reduce heat to a low simmer and cook, covered, for about 15 to 20 minutes, or until the rice is cooked and the liquid evaporates.

3 Meanwhile, heat a small frying pan over medium-high heat; add the pine nuts and toast for 2 to 3 minutes, shaking the skillet and tossing the nuts with a fork to keep them from browning too quickly. When the nuts are toasted, remove them immediately from the pan.

4 When the rice is cooked, remove the lemon slice; stir in the pine nuts, tomatoes, parsley, and cinnamon. Adjust seasoning with additional salt and pepper to taste.

This slightly sweet, starchy side dish is delicious with Broiled Skirt Steak Cajun Style (see Chapter 16), Braised Chicken Legs in Red Wine (see Chapter 5), or Mustard-Brushed Barbecued Chicken (see Chapter 6).

Here are how different countries take basic boiled rice and make it special.

- ✔ **India:** Curry and hot spices, chicken, or vegetables
- ✔ **Spain:** Saffron, nuts, bell peppers, and other vegetables; also chicken, sausage, and seafood
- ✔ **Middle East:** Onions, raisins, cinnamon, allspice, turmeric, cardamom
- ✔ **Mexico:** Garlic, hot peppers, onions (sometimes dried beans)
- ✔ **Southern United States (Louisiana):** pork sausage, onions, garlic, cayenne; also with seafood
- ✔ **France:** Garlic, tomatoes, fresh herbs (thyme, tarragon, basil), and vegetables or seafood

The technique for cooking long-grain rice and short-grain rice is essentially the same, except when using Arborio rice (available in gourmet markets) to make *risotto,* the creamy, long-stirred specialty of northern Italy.

When making risotto, you want the rice to slowly absorb enough of the hot broth to form a creamy blend of tender yet still firm grains. Giving an exact amount of liquid for making risotto is difficult. The key is to keep stirring the rice over low heat, adding only enough liquid (a little at a time) so that the rice is surrounded by, but never swimming in, broth.

Make this basic recipe once or twice until you have the technique down. Then you can alter it by using the suggestions that follow the recipe or by improvising on your own.

Risotto

Tools: *Chef's knife, skillet or sauté pan, small saucepan with lid, wooden spoon*

Preparation time: *About 15 minutes*

Cooking time: *About 35 minutes*

Yield: *4 servings*

1 teaspoon olive oil	*About 5 cups chicken or vegetable stock*
3 strips lean bacon, cut into 1-inch pieces	*1½ cups Arborio rice*
½ cup chopped shallots or yellow onions	*Salt and black pepper to taste*

1 Place the olive oil and bacon in a large skillet or sauté pan and cook over medium heat, stirring occasionally until the bacon is brown, about 2 to 3 minutes. Add the chopped shallots (or onions) and lower the heat to medium-low. Cook the shallots until golden but not browned, stirring occasionally.

2 While the shallots are cooking, bring the stock to a boil in a small, covered saucepan. Reduce the heat to a simmer.

3 When the shallots are golden, add the rice to the skillet. Raise the heat to medium and cook 1 to 2 minutes, stirring constantly, until the rice is well coated with the oil.

4 Add ½ cup hot stock to the rice and stir it in with a wooden spoon. When most of the liquid is absorbed (and it will be absorbed quickly), add another ½ cup stock to the rice, stirring constantly. The rice should be surrounded by liquid but never swim in the stock. Be sure to loosen the rice from the bottom and sides of the pan to keep it from sticking.

5 Continue cooking, stirring and adding ½ cup stock after most of the broth is absorbed. (You may not need all of the broth.) The risotto should be creamy and tender but still firm to the bite after about 25 to 30 minutes. During the last 10 minutes, add only ¼ cup stock at a time so that most of the cooking liquid is absorbed when the rice is done.

6 Remove from the heat. Taste for seasoning and add salt and pepper, if desired. Serve immediately.

Risotto can be a course on its own or served as a side dish with entrees like Roast Loin of Pork (see Chapter 6) or Roasted Chicken (see Chapter 6).

Your risotto will be only as good as the chicken stock it absorbs. Make your own or buy the best commercial brand you can.

You can add an endless variety of ingredients to risotto. A few minutes before it's done, try stirring in l cup fresh or frozen peas or ½ cup chopped parsley. Or add chopped fresh kale, spinach leaves, sliced mushrooms, or broccoli rabe to the pan after browning the shallots.

Wild rice

Wild rice is a remote relative of white rice, actually a long-grain, aquatic grass. The wild version (it is now cultivated) grows almost exclusively in the Great Lakes region of the United States and has become quite expensive because of its scarcity. You can reduce the expense by combining it with brown rice. Wild rice is especially good with robust meat dishes, game, and smoked foods.

Mise en place

The French term *mise en place* (meeze-on-plahs) means to have on hand all the ingredients that you need to prepare a dish: For example, onions and herbs are chopped, garlic is minced, vegetables are rinsed, ingredients are measured, and so on. This preparation is very important, because it allows you to cook efficiently and without interruption. Practice *mise en place* and have all your prep work completed right up to the point of cooking.

Basic Wild Rice

Tools: *Colander, medium saucepan fitted with a lid*

Preparation time: *About 15 minutes*

Cooking time: *About 50 minutes*

Yield: *4 to 6 servings*

1 cup wild rice

2½ cups water

2 tablespoons butter

Salt and black pepper to taste

1 Wash the wild rice thoroughly before you cook it: Place the rice in a pot filled with cold water and let stand for a few minutes. Pour off the water and any debris that floats to the surface. Drain well in a colander.

2 Fill a medium saucepan with 2½ cups of water, cover, and bring to a boil over high heat. Add the rinsed rice, butter, and salt and pepper to taste. Stir once. Reduce the heat to low and simmer, covered, for 45 to 55 minutes or until the rice is tender.

3 Fluff the rice and add more salt and pepper, if desired, before serving.

If the rice is cooked but the cooking liquid is not completely absorbed, place it in a colander to drain off any excess liquid. If the liquid is completely absorbed before the rice is cooked, add a little more water or stock, about ¼ cup at a time, and continue to cook until the grains are tender.

Brown rice

If you associate brown rice with bare-wood, macramé-festooned health food cafes, think again. Brown rice can be cool; brown rice can be elegant.

The term *brown rice* refers to rice that has not been "polished"; that is, nothing but the tough, outer husk has been removed. With its bran layer intact, brown rice is superior in nutrition to polished rice and is also a little more expensive. Brown rice has a faintly nutty flavor and a shorter shelf life than white rice. You can store white rice almost indefinitely, but brown rice should be consumed within 6 months of purchase.

Flavored Brown Rice

Tools: *Chef's knife, wooden spoon, sauté pan or saucepan with a lid*

Preparation time: *About 15 minutes*

Cooking time: *About 45 minutes*

Yield: *4 servings*

2 tablespoons olive oil

½ cup finely chopped onion

2 teaspoons minced garlic, about 2 cloves (optional)

1 cup brown rice

2½ cups chicken stock, vegetable stock, or water

Salt and black pepper to taste

1 Heat the oil in a medium sauté pan or saucepan. Add the onion and garlic (if desired) and cook very slowly over low heat until the vegetables are just golden, stirring often. (Do not brown the garlic.) Add the brown rice and cook for another 1 to 2 minutes, stirring often.

2 Add the stock or water, raise the heat to high to bring to a boil, and cook, uncovered, for 2 minutes. Lower the heat, add salt and pepper to taste, cover, and simmer for about 45 minutes or until the liquid is absorbed and the rice is cooked but still firm to the bite.

3 Keeping the pan covered, set aside for 5 minutes to let the flavors meld. If desired, add more salt and pepper before serving.

Brown rice's nutty flavor complements hearty roasts as well as seasoned vegetables. Try it with Broiled Skirt Steak, Cajun Style (see Chapter 16), or Roasted Chicken (see Chapter 6).

Substitute 1 chopped leek (use the white section only) for the onion and add a bay leaf to the cooking liquid. Be sure to remove the bay leaf before serving. You also can stir ½ to 1 cup cooked, sliced carrots or other vegetables into the cooked rice.

Working with Other Whole Grains

Most grains, like rice, cook quickly in boiling water or flavored boiling liquid, like beef stock or chicken stock. They usually don't need to be soaked before cooking, but they should be rinsed to remove any surface grit. Here are some of the more common whole grains, other than rice:

- **Barley:** A great substitute for rice in soups and side dishes, barley is commonly sold as "pearl" barley, with its outer hull and bran removed. It cooks relatively quickly — about 25 minutes in boiling water or stock. Season with butter, salt, and pepper.

- **Bulgur:** Wheat grains that are steamed then hulled, dried, and cracked, bulgur cooks very quickly. In fact, in some recipes, like tabbouleh, you don't have to cook it at all (although you do soak it in water to soften it).

- **Quinoa:** A small grain that is power-packed with nutrients, quinoa (keen-wah) is available in most health food stores, Middle Eastern shops, and quality supermarkets. You must rinse quinoa a few times before cooking. Like rice, it takes about 2 parts liquid to 1 part quinoa, and cooks in about 15 minutes.

- **Buckwheat:** Although not really a grain, we treat buckwheat like one. Buckwheat is really a grass and a cousin of the rhubarb plant. It has an earthy, almost nut-like flavor and tastes more like brown rice than other grains — an acquired taste. Kasha, also called buckwheat groats, is simply buckwheat that has been roasted.

In the following recipe, the kasha is first sautéed pilaf-style and then combined with butternut squash, chicken broth, spinach, and ginger root for a hearty side dish that's teeming with nutrients and flavor.

Kasha with Butternut Squash and Spinach

Tools: *Large saucepan, chef's knife, colander, medium saucepan*

Preparation time: *10 to 15 minutes*

Cooking time: *About 25 minutes*

Yield: *4 to 6 servings*

2 tablespoons olive oil

1 tablespoon butter

1 medium onion, minced

1 large clove garlic, minced (optional)

1 cup kasha, rinsed and drained

1 tablespoon minced fresh ginger root

1 jalapeño pepper, seeded and minced

1 small butternut squash, about 1½ pounds, peeled and cut into 1-inch cubes

3 cups chicken stock or water, heated just to boiling

Salt and black pepper to taste

2 cups packed spinach leaves, stems removed, rinsed and coarsely chopped

1 In a large saucepan, heat the oil and butter over medium heat; add the onion and (if desired) the garlic, and cook until the onions are softened, about 2 to 3 minutes, stirring often.

2 Add the kasha to the pan and stir to coat the grains. Stir in the ginger and jalapeño pepper, followed by the squash, chicken stock or water, salt, and pepper. Cover and simmer for about 12 to 15 minutes, until squash and kasha are just tender.

3 When cooked, remove the pan from the heat and stir in the spinach. Cover and let stand for a few minutes. Adjust seasonings with salt and pepper before serving.

To give kasha a different flavor, add 1 red bell pepper (seeded and chopped) to the sautéed onion. Proceed with remaining recipe, but omit the spinach.

This simple dish, made with polenta (which is Italian for cornmeal), is a delightful change from pasta or rice; it's a quick and tasty light meal in itself when covered with a good tomato-meat sauce. This recipe works well with chicken stock or water — but stock adds more flavor. If you want a more garlicky finish, add a minced clove to the cooking liquid.

Polenta with Herbs

Tools: 2- or 3-quart heavy-bottom saucepan, wooden spoon, chef's knife

Preparation time: 5 minutes

Cooking time: 3 to 5 minutes for precooked or fine-grained polenta

Yield: 4 servings

(continued)

3¼ cups chicken stock or water

1 cup precooked polenta

⅓ cup freshly grated Parmesan cheese (optional)

1 tablespoon butter

1 tablespoon fresh, chopped tarragon, marjoram, or thyme, or 1 teaspoon dried

Salt and black pepper to taste

1 In a heavy, deep pot bring the stock or water to a boil.

2 Slowly stir in the polenta. Reduce the heat to low and continue stirring until the mixture thickens to a porridge consistency, about 3 to 5 minutes. Stir in the cheese, if desired, then the butter, tarragon (or marjoram or thyme), salt, and pepper. (If using salted chicken broth, little or no salt may be needed.)

This recipe is delicious as a side dish with chicken, pork, or veal stews; as a base for grilled vegetables; or smothered with any tomato-based meat sauce.

Add the polenta to the boiling cooking water *slowly,* and keep stirring to prevent it from getting lumpy. If lumps form, stir with a wire whisk to break them up. Also, polenta hardens very quickly after it is cooked and removed from the heat. Be sure to bring it to the table steaming and smothered with its sauce to prevent it from thickening into a glutinous mass. Prepare the sauce or stew-topping first and make the polenta at the last minute.

Most stores sell fine-ground cornmeal (commonly known as polenta in Italy), which cooks much faster than the coarsely ground meal. The latter has a nuttier texture and takes longer to cook. Try both to see which you prefer.

Substitute different herbs like thyme and marjoram, or add sautéed onion and garlic along with the butter and herbs. You can also blend in cooked carrots, celery, turnips, broccoli rabe, or even hot Italian sausages.

If you don't have time to make polenta you can buy it ready-made, wrapped in a fat-sausage-like tube of plastic; it is available in most supermarkets. Ready-made polenta is good sliced, brushed with a little butter or olive oil, and grilled on both sides until lightly browned. It can be used as a base for grilled chops, chicken or sausages, and vegetables.

In the following recipe, the basic polenta recipe is a base for a hearty sausage stew with tomatoes, red peppers, and onions. This recipe is a quick family dinner and a great change from traditional pasta dishes.

Sausage and Vegetable Stew on a Bed of Herbed Polenta

Tools: *Chef's knife, large Dutch oven, wooden spoon*

Preparation time: *10 to 15 minutes*

Cooking time: *25 to 30 minutes*

Yield: *4 servings*

1 pound mild Italian sausage, cut into 2-inch chunks

½ pound hot Italian sausage, cut into 2-inch chunks

1 tablespoon olive oil

1 large onion, chopped

1 large clove garlic, minced

2 medium zucchini, with skins, sliced into ½-inch rounds

1 large red bell pepper, cored and cut into 1-inch cubes

1 14½-ounce can diced tomatoes with liquid

⅓ cup red wine or water

¼ cup tomato paste

½ teaspoon sugar

1 bay leaf

Salt and black pepper to taste

Polenta with Herbs (see preceding recipe)

1 In a large, Dutch oven over medium-high heat brown the mild and hot sausage on all sides, turning frequently. This should take about 10 minutes. Remove the sausage to a plate.

2 Reduce the heat to medium. Add the olive oil, onion, and garlic and cook for 1 to 2 minutes, or until the onion is soft, stirring often. Add the zucchini, red pepper, and tomatoes, stirring to evenly mix.

3 Stir in the wine or water, tomato paste, sugar, and bay leaf. Return the sausage to the pan and bring to a boil. Reduce the heat to low and simmer, covered, about 10 minutes, or until the sausage is no longer pink in the center (cut into the center of the sausages with a sharp knife to determine doneness). Adjust seasonings with salt and pepper if needed.

4 As sausage and vegetables simmer, prepare Polenta with Herbs (see preceding recipe).

5 To serve, divide the polenta among four plates. Spoon the sausage-vegetable mixture over the polenta.

You can substitute any kind of sausage you like in this recipe, including low-fat turkey sausage.

After the polenta is cooked you can spread it over a greased baking pan, brush it with melted butter or olive oil (flavored, if you like), and place it under a broiler to brown. Then you can cut it into squares and serve like bread.

Boiling, Parboiling, and Blanching Vegetables

Sometimes a recipe calls for *parboiling* vegetables. Certain dense vegetables, such as carrots, potatoes, and turnips, are sometimes parboiled, or cooked briefly in boiling water, to soften them slightly before another method finishes cooking them. This technique guarantees that all the ingredients in the dish finish cooking at the same time. You might, for example, parboil green peppers before you stuff and bake them. Or you might parboil pieces of broccoli, carrots, and cauliflower before tossing them into a stir-fry of egg noodles and shrimp. (See Roasted Winter Vegetables in Chapter 6 for a recipe that uses this technique.)

Blanching is the technique of briefly plunging vegetables or fruits into boiling water for a few seconds and then into cold water to stop the cooking process. Cooks blanch tomatoes, nectarines, and peaches to remove their skins easily. (See Chapter 11 for instructions for removing the skins of tomatoes.) Some vegetables, like green beans, are blanched before they are frozen or canned to help retain their color and flavor.

Everyone's favorite boiling recipe

Although it sounds like a contradiction, "baking" potatoes (often referred to as Idaho potatoes) actually make fluffier, lighter mashed potatoes than "boiling" potatoes. Boiling potatoes get dense and gluey when they are mashed but are great for recipes in which they need to hold their shape — such as in potato salad.

When it comes to mashing potatoes, the slow way is the best. Mashed potatoes are much better when mashed by hand with a potato masher or fork or when pressed through a *ricer* (a round, metal device with small holes through which foods are pressed). Blenders and food processors whiz too fast and can leave you with excellent wallboard paste. Even when mashing by hand, don't overdo it. Mash just enough to get rid of the lumps.

Mashed Potatoes

Tools: _Chef's knife, medium saucepan fitted with a lid, potato masher or ricer, colander_

Preparation time: _About 15 minutes_

Cooking time: _About 20 minutes_

Yield: _4 servings_

4 large Idaho potatoes, about 2 pounds

½ teaspoon salt, or to taste

½ cup milk

3 tablespoons butter

Black pepper to taste

_1_ Peel the potatoes and cut them into quarters.

_2_ Place them in a medium saucepan with cold water to barely cover and ½ teaspoon salt, or to taste.

_3_ Cover and bring to a boil over high heat. Reduce heat to medium and cook, covered, for about 15 minutes or until you can easily pierce the potatoes with a fork.

_4_ Drain the potatoes in a colander and then return them to the saucepan. Shake the potatoes in the pan over low heat for 10 to 15 seconds to evaporate excess moisture, if necessary.

_5_ Remove the pan from the heat. Mash the potatoes a few times with a potato masher, ricer, or fork. (You can use a handheld mixer to mash them on low speed if you don't have a potato masher, but be careful not to overdo it!) Add the milk, butter, and salt and pepper to taste and mash again until smooth and creamy.

Mashed potato fiends think that they go with everything short of oatmeal. Try these potatoes with Broiled Skirt Steak, Cajun Style (see Chapter 16), Mustard-Brushed Barbecued Chicken Breasts (see Chapter 6), or Pork Loin Braised in Milk and Onions (see Chapter 16).

 For garlic mashed potatoes, wrap a whole, medium head of garlic (not just a clove — a whole head) in aluminum foil and roast it in a 350-degree oven for 1 hour. Remove the foil, allow the cloves to cool slightly, and then press the soft cloves to release the pulp. Mash the pulp into the potatoes with the butter and milk; then season with salt and pepper to taste. You can mash other cooked vegetables, such as broccoli, carrots, turnips, or sweet potatoes, and blend them into the potato mix.

You need to monitor dishes that are boiled, simmered, steamed, or poached to make sure that the water or other liquid doesn't steam away. (Otherwise, your pot will not be a pretty sight.) If necessary, add a little more liquid to prevent the food from burning.

Trying something new: Purees

Vegetable purees are simply cooked vegetables (usually boiled or steamed but sometimes roasted) that are mashed, blended, or processed to a thick consistency. Starchy root vegetables like potatoes, sweet potatoes, rutabagas, parsnips, and carrots generally make the best purees, but broccoli, cauliflower, and roasted red peppers are also wonderful, especially when mixed with a dense root vegetable. Try the following recipe for a winning combination.

Rutabaga and Potato Puree

Tools: *Chef's knife, citrus juicer, medium saucepan, small skillet, food processor*

Preparation time: *10 to 15 minutes*

Cooking time: *About 20 minutes*

Yield: *4 servings*

1 medium rutabaga, about 1 pound, peeled and cut into 1-inch cubes

1 large baking potato, peeled and cut into 1-inch cubes

2 tablespoons butter

¼ cup diced onion

Juice of ½ lemon

Salt and black pepper to taste

½ cup milk, light cream, or half-and-half

1 Place the rutabaga and potato cubes in a medium saucepan; cover with water and salt lightly. Bring to a boil, cover, and simmer for about 15 to 20 minutes, or until both vegetables are very tender (check with a fork).

2 Meanwhile, heat the butter in a small skillet over medium heat, add the onion and sauté until soft.

3 Drain the potato and rutabaga cubes well and transfer them to a food processor. Add the sautéed onion, lemon juice, salt, and pepper. Process until smooth while gradually adding the milk or cream.

This purée is perfect with any kind of grilled meat or poultry. You could try it with Glazed Leg of Lamb with Pan Gravy and Red Currant Glaze (see Chapter 6), Roast Loin of Pork (see Chapter 6), or Roasted Chicken (see Chapter 6).

In this recipe, the vegetables are mashed with a potato masher, not whirled in a food processor. The result is a totally different texture (a little chunky, not baby-food smooth) from the recipe above. Adding a little grated Parmesan really adds zip. This is a kid-friendly dish, and a wonderful way to surreptitiously get them to eat two vegetables in one sitting.

Broccoli and Potato Mash

Tools: *Vegetable peeler, chef's knife, potato masher, medium saucepan, small saucepan*

Preparation time: *About 5 minutes*

Cooking time: *15 to 20 minutes*

Yield: *4 servings*

2 large baking potatoes, peeled and thinly sliced

2 heaping cups broccoli florets

2 tablespoons butter

¼ cup chopped onion

¼ cup milk, light cream, or half-and-half

¼ cup grated Parmesan (optional)

Salt and black pepper to taste

1 Place the potato slices in a medium saucepan; add water to cover and salt lightly. Bring to a boil, and cook, covered, over medium heat for about 5 minutes. Add the broccoli florets and cook another 10 minutes or until both vegetables are very tender.

2 Meanwhile, heat the butter in a small saucepan, add the onion, and sauté over medium heat — 1 to 2 minutes, or until tender.

3 Drain the potatoes and broccoli and return them to the same saucepan. Add the sautéed onions, milk or cream, and grated cheese (if desired); mash with a potato masher until the mixture is nearly smooth. Adjust seasoning with salt and pepper to taste.

When making a puree like this, use only the florets of the broccoli and not the tough stems.

Here are a few other winning vegetable puree combinations: potatoes and carrots; parsnips and potatoes; sweet potatoes and apples; potatoes and roasted garlic; and potatoes and turnips.

You can add dried or fresh chopped herbs to taste, like tarragon, thyme, or sage.

What's more, you can turn these purees into instant soups by adding 2 to 3 cups of hot chicken or vegetable stock to about 1½ pounds of pureed vegetables until the mixture is thinned to a soup-like consistency.

Potato and Carrot Puree

Tools: *Chef's knife, vegetable peeler, large saucepan or pot, potato masher*

Preparation time: *5 minutes*

Cooking time: *25 to 30 minutes*

Yield: *4 servings*

3 carrots, cut into 1-inch pieces

1½ pounds baking potatoes, peeled and cut into 2-inch cubes

½ cup milk or cream

2 to 3 tablespoons butter

Salt and black pepper to taste

1 In a large covered saucepan, cook the carrots in lightly salted boiling water for 5 minutes; add the potatoes and enough water to just cover both; bring to a boil, reduce to a simmer, and cook, covered, for another 20 minutes or until both vegetables are tender. Drain well and return the vegetables to the pot.

2 Add the milk or cream and 2 to 3 tablespoons butter to the vegetables. Mash with a potato masher a few times until smooth. Adjust the seasoning with salt and pepper.

Simple tips for boiling and steaming a dozen fresh vegetables

Boiling other vegetables is as easy as boiling potatoes. Following are specific instructions for boiling and steaming common vegetables:

✔ **Artichokes:** Lay the artichokes on their side on a wooden cutting board. Using a sharp chef's knife, trim about ½ inch off the top. Use scissors to trim the prickly tips off each leaf. Pull off any very thick or tough leaves (but no more than 3 or 4) at the bottom of the artichoke. Place the artichokes in a deep pot with cold water to cover. (They should fit snugly to keep them from bobbing in the water.) Add salt and pepper and lemon juice to taste and bring to a boil. Boil gently for 30 to 40 minutes, depending on size. When the artichokes are done, you should be able to pierce the bottom with a fork or easily pull off a leaf. Use tongs to remove the artichokes and drain upside down on a plate or in a colander. Serve hot with a sauce of lemon juice and melted butter. Or marinate for several hours in a vinaigrette dressing (see Chapter 10) and serve at room temperature.

✔ **Asparagus:** Snap off the thick, woody stems at the natural breaking point. (If very coarse, use a vegetable peeler to remove some of the outer green layer at the thick end of each spear.) Rinse the stalks under cold water or soak them for about 5 minutes if they seem especially sandy. Place the spears in a wide, shallow pan in one layer, if possible (and never more than two). Add boiling water to cover and salt to taste. Cover and boil gently until crisp-tender, about 8 minutes for medium spears. Cooking time varies with the thickness of the stalks. Drain and serve immediately with butter, lemon juice, salt, and pepper, and, if desired, grated Parmesan cheese.

✔ **Brussels sprouts:** With a sharp paring knife, trim off the tough outer leaves. Using a paring knife, trim a very thin slice off the stem end. Then cut an X in the stem end to ensure even cooking of stem and leaves. Boil gently in about 1 inch of water for about 8 to 10 minutes or until crisp-tender. Test for doneness by tasting. Drain and serve with a simple lemon-butter sauce.

To steam brussels sprouts, place trimmed sprouts in a steaming basket over about 1 inch of boiling water. Cover the pot and steam for about 8 minutes, depending on size.

✔ **Cabbage:** Cut the head into quarters and cut out the hard core. Add the quarters to a large pot of lightly salted boiling water, cover, and boil gently for about 12 minutes. Cabbage should remain somewhat crisp.

To steam, place the quarters in a large deep skillet or saucepan with about ½ inch of water and cook, covered, over low heat until crisp-tender. Cabbage is also quite delicious when braised. (See Chapter 15 for a recipe for Braised Cabbage with Apple and Caraway.)

✔ **Carrots or parsnips:** Trim off the ends and peel with a vegetable peeler. Place them sliced into a pot with lightly salted water to just cover. Cover the pot and boil gently for about 12 to 15 minutes for sliced carrots, or about 20 minutes for whole ones. Or place in a steaming basket and steam in a covered pot over about 1 inch of boiling water. Sliced carrots or parsnips steam in 5 minutes; whole and large, 2- to 3-inch pieces need about 12 minutes. Serve with butter sauce flavored with lemon juice and grated lemon or orange zest or a sauce of melted butter and minced fresh dill.

✔ **Cauliflower:** To boil, cut a whole head into florets and boil gently in enough lightly salted water to cover the cauliflower for about 8 to 10 minutes or until crisp-tender. Adding the juice of half a lemon to the cooking water helps to retain cauliflower's whiteness.

To steam, place florets in a steaming basket over about 1 inch of boiling water. Cover pot and steam for about 5 minutes or until desired doneness. Toss in a sauce of melted butter, lemon juice, and chopped fresh parsley.

✔ **Corn:** Don't husk or remove the ears from the refrigerator until you're ready to boil them. (The sugar in corn rapidly turns to starch at room temperature. To retain sweetness, keep ears cold and cook the same day of purchase.) Heat a large pot filled with enough water just to cover the corn, add the husked corn, cover the pot, and boil for about 5 minutes. Remove with tongs and serve immediately with butter.

✔ **Green beans:** Trim by snapping off the stem ends. Add the beans to lightly salted boiling water to cover and cook for 8 to 10 minutes, or until crisp-tender. They should retain their bright green color.

To steam, place steaming basket over about 1 inch of boiling water. Add beans, cover the pot tightly, and check for doneness after 5 minutes. Serve hot beans with a simple butter sauce or toss in a vinaigrette dressing and chill before serving.

✔ **Pearl onions:** Peel and boil in a covered pot with lightly salted water to just cover for about 15 minutes or until tender but still firm. Don't overcook, or they will fall apart. Serve smothered in a sauce or gravy, or mixed with other vegetables.

✔ **Snow peas:** Rinse the peas, snap off the stem ends, and lift the string across the top to remove it. Place in boiling water to cover and cook for 2 minutes. Drain in a colander and run cold water over them to stop the cooking and retain their green color. (See the Roasted Pepper and Snow Pea Salad recipe in Chapter 10.)

✔ **Sweet potatoes:** Scrub the potatoes well, trim the tapered ends, and cut out any bruised spots. (Cut very large sweet potatoes in half crosswise or quarter them.) Place in a large pot, add cold water to cover the potatoes, cover the pot, and simmer for about 35 to 40 minutes for whole potatoes or 20 to 25 minutes for halved or quartered potatoes. Potatoes are done when you can pierce them easily with a fork. Don't overcook, or they will fall apart in the water. Drain and cool slightly before peeling. Mash or serve in large chunks with butter, salt, pepper, and ground ginger or nutmeg to taste, if desired.

✔ **Yellow squash and zucchini:** Scrub clean and trim the ends. Slice into ½-inch-thick rounds. Place in a steaming basket over about 1 inch of boiling water and steam in a covered pot for about 4 minutes or just until crisp-tender. These tender vegetables are also delicious sautéed.

How do you season to taste? Many recipes say to "taste for seasonings" or "add seasonings to taste," which is a critical part of a cook's discipline. No matter how well a recipe is written, it often needs a slight adjustment before serving — more salt, more pepper, and so on. To season "to taste" means just that. Adjust the seasoning by adding as much or as little as it needs, according to your taste. (Remember, while cooking, always taste, taste, taste!) But proceed gingerly at the beginning; seasonings can intensify while cooking. You can't remove seasonings after adding them.

Creating Two Great Stocks: Chicken and Vegetable

Scores of recipes call for either chicken stock or vegetable stock in lieu of water. By learning to make these building blocks of cuisine, which involve a simple simmering technique, you can vastly enhance many dishes.

Chicken Stock

Tools: *Stock pot or other large pot, slotted spoon, colander*

Preparation time: *About 15 minutes*

Cooking time: *About 2 hours*

Yield: *About 2 quarts*

3- to 4-pound, rinsed chicken

Water to cover

2 stalks celery, rinsed and halved crosswise

2 carrots, trimmed and halved crosswise

4 sprigs parsley

2 bay leaves

10 black peppercorns

1 Place everything in a large, deep pot and bring to a boil. Reduce heat; simmer and cook, uncovered, for 2 hours, skimming foam off the surface with a slotted spoon as necessary.

2 Strain the stock through a large colander set over a large pot or bowl to separate the broth from the chicken parts and vegetables. Let the strained stock cool slightly and then refrigerate. After the stock is completely chilled, scrape off any fat that has solidified on the surface. If desired, freeze the stock in small containers or in ice cube trays for later use.

When you are making stock, some scum or particles from the bones and vegetables may float to the surface. Remove them with a slotted spoon. An easy way to remove the fat from a meat stock is to let it cool and congeal. Then simply lift the fat off the surface and throw it away.

You can use the leftover cooked chicken to make chicken salad (see Chapter 10 for a mayonnaise dressing) or chicken pot pie (see Chapter 12).

If you don't have time to make a chicken stock, a flavorful vegetable stock is a wonderful substitute. It's traditionally used for poaching seafood. (A recipe for Poached Salmon comes later in this chapter.) You also can use vegetable stock as the base for all kinds of soups and sauces.

Vegetable Stock

Tools: *Cotton kitchen twine, cheesecloth, stock pot or other large pot, slotted spoon, colander, large bowl*

Preparation time: *About 25 minutes*

Cooking time: *About 1 hour*

Yield: *About 1½ quarts*

1 small bunch parsley, rinsed

10 black peppercorns

5 sprigs fresh thyme, or ½ teaspoon dried

1 bay leaf

Dash cayenne pepper

10 cups water

1 bottle dry white wine (see note)

5 carrots, peeled and cut into 2-inch pieces

5 stalks celery, rinsed and cut into 2-inch pieces

2 medium onions, each pierced with 1 whole clove

2 leeks, washed and coarsely chopped (including dark green parts)

1 Using cotton kitchen twine, tie the parsley, peppercorns, thyme, bay leaf, and cayenne in a double-thick, 8-inch-square of cheesecloth or a patch of white cotton of similar size. (You can even use part of an old white shirt.)

2 Combine with all remaining ingredients in a stock pot or other large pot and bring to a boil. Reduce heat to a simmer and cook, uncovered, for 1 hour, stirring occasionally and skimming foam off the surface with a slotted spoon as necessary.

3 Strain the stock through a colander or sieve placed over a large bowl or pot. Let cool. Discard the solids.

Note: Dry white wines are made from many grapes; you can use Chardonnay, Pinot Gris, Chenin Blanc, and Sauvignon Blanc, to name a few. There is no need to spend more than $8 to $10 on a bottle of wine for cooking. (See Ed McCarthy and Mary Ewing-Mulligan's Wine For Dummies, *2nd Edition, [published by IDG Books Worldwide] for more information about how wines complement food.)*

To make a fish stock for soups or for poaching seafood, simply add fresh fish bones and heads (gills removed) to the preceding vegetable stock at the outset. Ask your fishmonger for bones and heads — he or she is probably up to the ears in them and would be happy to get rid of some. Some soups use specialized stocks that also involve these techniques; you can find those stocks in Chapter 9.

Poaching Seafood in Stock

Poaching seafood is a fabulous way to preserve its flavor and texture. You just have to watch the clock to prevent overcooking and keep the poaching liquid to a gentle simmer. Vigorous boiling breaks up the fish's tender flesh.

Classic vegetable stock imparts a subtle, herby flavor to seafood. The carrots and onions give a touch of sweetness, and even the dash of cayenne plays an important role in the overall balance. Poaching works best with firm-fleshed fish: salmon, tuna, cod, halibut, and the like.

In the following recipe, simmer the salmon steaks in the vegetable stock for about 5 minutes. Remove the pot from the heat, and the steaks continue cooking gently off the heat for another 5 minutes. (See why a kitchen timer is so important?)

Poached Salmon Steaks with Vinaigrette Dressing

Tools: *Chef's knife, large skillet or small fish poacher, blender or food processor*

Preparation time: *About 25 minutes*

Cooking time: *About 10 minutes*

Yield: *4 servings*

1½ quarts vegetable stock (see previous recipe)

4 salmon steaks, 4 to 6 ounces each, with skin

Water (if necessary)

Vinaigrette Dressing (see Chapter 10 for a recipe)

1 Bring the vegetable stock to a boil over high heat in a large skillet or fish poacher. Submerge the salmon steaks in the vegetable stock. Add more water only if there is not enough stock to cover the steaks by about 1 inch.

2 Return to a boil; then lower the heat to a simmer and poach, uncovered, for about 5 minutes.

3 Turn off the heat and let the steaks stand in the poaching liquid about 3 to 5 minutes longer or until done. Be careful not to overcook. Cut into the center delicately to check for doneness. (See the sidebar "Is that fish done or just resting?" for details.) Remove the poached steaks to a platter.

4 Drizzle some Vinaigrette Dressing (see Chapter 10 for a recipe) over each salmon steak and serve immediately.

Serve this delicate, light dish with Braised Endive (see Chapter 5), Red and Green Pepper Rice (see Chapter 10), or Couscous with Yellow Squash (see Chapter 15).

Home cooks rarely think of poaching meat, but poaching is a wonderful way to infuse it with flavor and make it as tender as an Elvis ballad. The key is to start with a very flavorful stock. Homemade is best, but top-quality canned will do in a pinch.

TOQUE TIP

Is that fish done or just resting?

One traditional guideline for cooking fish is the so-called Canadian Fish Rule. Measure the whole fish steak or fillet at its thickest point and cook it (whether you are boiling, steaming, baking, broiling, or poaching) for precisely 10 minutes per inch. We've found that 8 to 9 minutes per inch is more like it; then check for doneness. If the thickest part of the fish is ¾ inch thick, for example, cook it for 6 to 7 minutes.

Whole fish is easiest to check. If the dorsal fin comes out easily, it is done; if not, it needs more cooking. Scallops turn opaque when done, and shrimp, which takes only a couple of minutes to cook, turns pink. Salmon and tuna are darkish pink at the center when medium. White fish should be glistening and wet looking *only* at the innermost core. Unless the recipe instructs you to do otherwise, remove all cooked fish from the heat or the poaching liquid immediately.

"One of the surest ways to tell if fish is cooked is to pierce its flesh using a very thin needle (like a cake tester) or a sharp knife. If it goes through, the fish is cooked," says Eric Ripert, executive chef of Le Bernardin in New York City.

Mussels, clams, and oysters give you a clear indication that they are cooked: Their shells open when they are done, no matter how you cook them.

Poached Filet of Beef with Vegetables and Horseradish Sauce

Tools: *Chef's knife, kitchen twine, large pot, mixing bowl, spatula or wooden spoon*

Preparation time: *About 20 minutes*

Cooking time: *About 10 minutes*

Yield: *4 servings*

1 pound center-cut filet of beef, divided into 4 equal pieces

2 leeks, white parts only (see Chapter 9 for more information on cleaning leeks)

5 cups homemade or canned beef or vegetable stock

1 large bouquet garni (a piece of cheesecloth holding 2 broken bay leaves, 3 sprigs parsley, and 3 sprigs fresh thyme — or 1 teaspoon dried each)

3 stalks celery, thinly sliced widthwise

3 medium carrots, trimmed, scraped, and thinly sliced widthwise

1 medium white onion, cut into thin strips

Salt and black pepper to taste

½ cup sour cream

2 teaspoons prepared horseradish, drained well, more to taste

1 teaspoon white wine vinegar

(continued)

1 Carefully tie the beef filets around the perimeter, and then crosswise. (Leave a long piece of string overhanging the pot to make it easier to remove the meat from the cooking liquid).

2 Slice the leeks down the center, starting at the root end and continuing ¾ of the way through the stalk. Open the leeks and rinse thoroughly to remove any sand. (See Chapter 9 for an illustration of this process.) Cut the leeks into 1½-inch pieces widthwise.

3 Pour the stock into a pot or deep saucepan large enough to hold the meat in one layer (you may need more stock, depending on the size of the pot). Bring to a simmer. Add the bouquet garni, leeks, celery, carrots, onion, salt, and pepper, and stir to distribute. Cover and simmer for 5 minutes.

4 Add the beef (with the strings overhanging the pot). Simmer for 5 minutes. Remove one of the filets and cut into the center. If it is still red, return to the pot; if it is pinkish, remove to a plate and cut off the strings.

5 Place the meat on warmed serving dishes (shallow bowls are best). Taste the broth for seasonings. With a slotted spoon, transfer some of the vegetables to the plate; then, with a large spoon or ladle, pour some of the broth over everything. Serve with horse-radish sauce on the side (see following recipe).

Horseradish Sauce

1 Put the sour cream in a mixing bowl.

2 Add the horseradish, vinegar, salt, and pepper. Stir well.

3 Taste. If desired, add more horseradish. Keep cool until serving.

As a starter for this meal you might serve Salmon Marinated in Ginger and Coriander (see Chapter 16) or Garlic and Goat Cheese Tartines (see Chapter 16).

Steamy Stuff

Steaming is the gentlest way to cook vegetables and seafood. It is also one of the most healthful because nutrients are not lost in the cooking liquids. This method is a particularly good way to cook delicate seafood, especially shellfish.

You can steam in two ways: in a perforated steamer set over simmering water (and covered) or in a deep, covered pot or saucepan holding about 1 to 2 inches of water. The latter method works especially well for large vegetables like broccoli and asparagus.

If you steam foods often, you may want to invest in some sort of steamer. The conventional steamer model is a pair of pots, the top one having a perforated bottom and a lid. (See Chapter 2 for more information about steamers.)

Simple steamed red potatoes are a quick and easy side dish for so many meals, from the lightest grilled fish to the thickest steak.

Steamed Red Potatoes with Dill

Tools: Large pot, steamer attachment

Preparation time: 2 minutes

Cooking time: About 20 minutes

Yield: 6 servings

8 to 12 small, red-skinned potatoes

2 to 3 tablespoons butter or to taste

1 to 2 tablespoons minced fresh dill or to taste

Salt and black pepper to taste

1 Place the potatoes in a steamer attachment over a pot filled with about 2 inches of salted water.

2 Bring the water to a boil. Reduce the heat, cover, and simmer 20 minutes or until the potatoes are tender. Drain, halve, and serve with a little butter and some fresh minced dill, seasoning with salt and pepper to taste.

With today's year-round food supply, you never know what produce will be at your supermarket. Don't just grab any bag of potatoes; you may get home to find them spongy and wet. All potatoes, including red, should be free of soft spots and sprouts.

Try the following recipe for steamed broccoli. You also can substitute vegetables like cauliflower, kale, and asparagus. Make sure that you trim and cut the vegetables into equal-sized pieces so that they cook evenly.

Fresh vegetables have more flavor and retain their nutrients better if you cook them only until *crisp-tender,* or firm to the bite. (The B vitamins and vitamin C are water soluble and leach into the cooking water as the vegetables cook.) Save the vitamin-packed cooking liquid to fortify soups and stews.

Steamed Broccoli

Tools: *Paring knife, deep 3- or 4-quart saucepan fitted with a lid, tongs, small saucepan*

Preparation time: *About 15 minutes*

Cooking time: *About 10 minutes*

Yield: *4 servings*

1 head broccoli	*3 tablespoons butter*
Salt and black pepper to taste	*Juice of ½ lemon*

1 Wash the broccoli thoroughly. Trim off only the thickest part of the stems and the large leaves. Divide the larger florets by slicing through the base of the flower and straight down through the length of the stem. All pieces should be roughly the same size.

2 Place the broccoli in a deep 3- or 4-quart saucepan holding about 2 inches of water. (The stalks should stand on the bottom with the florets facing up.) Add salt and pepper to taste and cover the pan.

3 Bring to a boil over high heat, then reduce the heat to low and simmer, covered, for about 8 minutes or until the stalks are tender but not soft. When done, the stalks should be firm but easy to pierce with a sharp knife.

4 While the broccoli steams, melt the butter in a small saucepan and add the lemon juice. Stir to blend.

5 Using tongs, carefully remove the broccoli to a serving dish. Pour the lemon-butter sauce over the broccoli and serve.

Fresh broccoli adds color and flavor to innumerable meals, including Roasted Fillet of Beef (see Chapter 6) and Glazed Leg of Lamb with Pan Gravy and Red Currant Glaze (see Chapter 6).

Delicate spring asparagus needs little more than butter, salt, and pepper to be delicious. The addition of fresh dill, however, gives it a new twist.

Steamed Asparagus with Dill

Tools: *Vegetable peeler, steamer or pan, chef's knife*

Preparation time: *10 minutes*

Cooking time: *About 5 minutes*

Yield: *4 servings*

1½ pounds asparagus spears	*2 tablespoons melted butter*
Salt to taste	*1 tablespoon finely chopped dill or parsley*

1 Snap off the hard bottom stems of the asparagus. If the spears are thick and the ends tough, use a vegetable peeler to remove 1 to 2 inches of the outer green layer at the thick end of each spear.

2 Heat about 2 inches of lightly salted water in the bottom of a vegetable steamer or pan; when it comes to a boil, place the asparagus in the top of the steamer, cover, and steam 3 to 5 minutes, depending on the thickness of the asparagus.

3 Transfer the asparagus to a warm serving dish and season with salt, butter, and dill or parsley.

Steaming and boiling are the most common ways to cook lobster; we have found that the former yields a slightly better texture and flavor. Strictly speaking, steaming calls for a trivet or basket to keep food off the bottom of the pot; because lobsters do not lie flat, that is not necessary. Check out Table 3-1 for guidelines on cooking lobster either way.

Table 3-1	Lobster Boiling and Steaming Times	
Lobster Weight	**Boiling Time**	**Steaming Time**
1 pound	8 minutes	10 minutes
2 pounds	15 minutes	18 minutes

It's difficult to foul up a fresh lobster — the worst thing you can do is overcook it. If you are lucky enough to be near the ocean, steam the lobster in sea water. You can add some seaweed to the cooking liquid for extra flavor. Serve this recipe with basic orange-lemon butter. You can use the recipe for orange-lemon butter with many kinds of steamed or roasted seafood, especially tuna, salmon, and bluefish. The dash of orange contributes a touch of sweetness that goes especially well with the sweet lobster meat.

Steamed Lobsters with Orange-Lemon Butter

Tools: *Large pot, long chef's knife, mallet, grater, small pot, wooden spoon*

Preparation time: *None for the lobsters, 5 minutes for the orange-lemon butter*

Cooking time: *About 15 to 18 minutes for a 1½- to 2-pound lobster, about 2 minutes for the orange-lemon butter*

Yield: *4 servings*

4 live lobsters, about 1½ to 2 pounds each

Salt to taste

½ cup (1 stick) butter, room temperature

1 tablespoon freshly grated lemon zest

¼ teaspoon freshly grated orange zest

1 Add 3 inches of water to a large, heavy pot. Salt the water generously and bring to a boil.

2 Add the lobsters and cover with a heavy lid. Let steam 14 to 16 minutes, depending on the lobsters' weight. (Unlike fish, lobsters give no visual clue regarding when they are done. If you crack one claw and the meat is not cooked, cook a little longer.)

3 Remove the lobsters with tongs. See Figure 3-1 for how to eat a lobster. Serve with Orange-Lemon Butter.

Orange-Lemon Butter

In a small pot, melt the butter. Remove from heat, add the zest, and stir to combine.

Flavored butters come in all colors and aromas. Turn to Chapter 7 for more flavored-butter recipes.

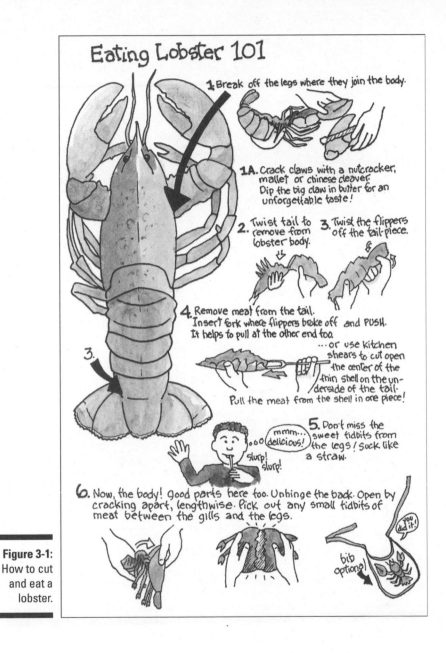

Figure 3-1:
How to cut
and eat a
lobster.

Chapter 4

Sautéing

The common technique of sautéing, or *pan-frying,* as many hip restaurants call it today, is generally associated with French cuisine. But in fact, many other nationalities sauté routinely to sear steaks, cook fillets of fish, glaze vegetables, and quick-cook shellfish.

Sautéing is nothing more than cooking food in a hot pan, usually with a little fat (butter or oil, for example) to prevent sticking. Sautéing imparts a crispy texture to foods and brings out all sorts of flavors from herbs and spices.

The French word *sauté* translates literally as *to jump.* Chefs shake the sauté pan back and forth over the heat, tossing the food without using utensils, to keep the food from burning and to expose all sides to the intense heat. Practice this technique in an empty cold skillet by using small candies, such as M&M's.

Because sautéing is done at high or medium-high heat, you have to be careful not to leave food in the pan too long. For example, if you drop a steak onto a roaring-hot pan (maybe with a little oil to prevent sticking), it develops a dark crust in a few minutes. This effect is desirable because you want to trap the juices inside the steak. If you do not flip the steak quickly to sear the other side, however, it may blacken and burn.

After your steak is browned on both sides, you should turn down the heat to medium to finish cooking. Doing so gives you the best of both worlds — a crispy outside and juicy inside.

Seafood benefits from sautéing in the same way; sautéing gives it texture and flavor. Likewise, sautéed vegetables become glazed with butter and absorb seasonings — that is, the seasonings are cooked into the vegetable, not added at the table.

Oil or Butter?

The type of fat in which you sauté foods makes a big difference. Butter is flavorful but can burn at too high a heat. Oils don't burn as easily, but they don't add much flavor unless they're seasoned.

We asked our friend André Soltner, former owner and chef of the celebrated Lutèce in Manhattan, about sautéing. He told us, "You have to understand the heat. If the sauté pan is not hot enough, the pores of your meat will not close and the juices will run out.

"The next most important factor is the type of fat you use. Oil is best for meat; it can get very hot without burning. Butter is fine for vegetables and pasta. I also like rapeseed oil (also called canola oil) because of its high smoke point," Soltner said.

Oil should be hot but not smoking in the pan before you add food. Butter should foam at its edges but not brown. Some chefs insist on using only *clarified* butter when sautéing.

To clarify, you melt butter in a saucepan to separate its milk solids, which sink to the bottom of the pan. Transfer the butter to a small bowl and let it sit for a minute to let the solids (foam) rise to the surface. Use a spoon to skim off the foam and discard it. Without milk solids, clarified butter has a higher smoke point and is less likely to burn. To avoid clarifying butter but still impart some of butter's delicious flavor, you can use a combination of equal parts butter and oil.

Deglazing

A very hot sauté pan begins to cook meat, poultry, or fish right away, browning the juices that flow from it and leaving bits of food sticking to the bottom of the pan. These browned bits are loaded with flavor. If *deglazed* (moistened and scraped up) in the pan, they become a delicious sauce.

To deglaze, remove the meat, poultry, or fish from the pan onto a serving platter. Immediately add liquid — you can use water, wine, stock, or a combination. The liquid should be twice the amount of sauce you want to make.

Raise the heat to high, bringing the liquid to a boil while you stir and scrape the browned bits off the bottom of the pan until they dissolve into the sauce. Boil until the sauce is reduced by half the volume. Season to taste and maybe stir in a teaspoon or more of butter for flavor and to add a smooth texture. Then spoon it over the cooked meat, poultry, or fish and serve. (See Figure 4-1.)

Deglazing a Pan

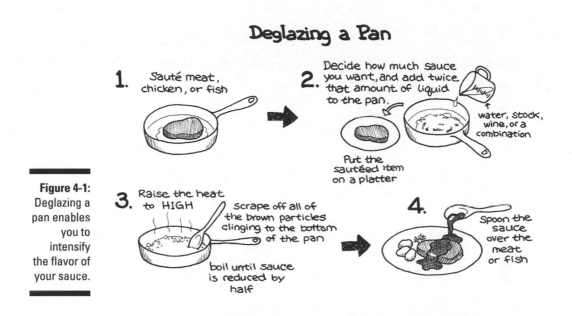

Figure 4-1: Deglazing a pan enables you to intensify the flavor of your sauce.

As a rule, the wine you use for deglazing depends on what you're sautéing: Use white wine for poultry and seafood, and red wine for meat.

Versatile Sautéing

Notice how the following recipes use the same basic sautéing technique and change only the types of fat and seasonings.

Vegetables

Vegetables are excellent when boiled or steamed until about 90 percent done and then transferred to a skillet to be finished in butter and maybe fresh herbs. Many classic recipes for potatoes call for sautéing; thinly sliced raw potatoes are delicious when cooked this way. In the following recipe, you cut the potatoes into fine cubes and toss them in a hot pan until crispy.

These potatoes, an excellent accompaniment to steak or veal chops, are cubed and sautéed in oil and butter until well browned. By using a combination of butter and oil, you give them a rich flavor and eliminate the risk of burning.

Sautéed Cubed Potatoes

Tools: *Vegetable peeler, chef's knife, colander, large nonstick skillet, slotted spoon*

Preparation time: *About 15 minutes*

Cooking time: *About 15 minutes*

Yield: *3 to 4 servings*

2 large baking potatoes, about 1½ pounds	*2 tablespoons butter*
⅓ cup vegetable or corn oil	*Salt and black pepper to taste*

1 Peel the potatoes and cut each into cubes of about ¼ inch.

2 When ready to cook, place the cubes in a colander in the sink. Run very hot water over the potatoes for about 10 seconds. (The hot water rinses off the starch so that the potatoes don't stick together in the pan and removes any discoloration from peeling and cutting the potatoes.) Drain well and dry on paper towels.

3 Heat the oil in a large nonstick skillet over high heat until it is hot. Add the potatoes and cook, stirring the potatoes often (to brown them evenly) for about 5 to 6 minutes. With a slotted spoon, remove the potatoes from the pan to a platter. Pour all the fat out of the pan and wipe out the skillet with paper towels.

4 Melt the butter in the skillet over medium-high heat. Do not let it burn. Add the potatoes and salt and pepper. Cook, stirring occasionally, for 4 to 5 minutes or until the cubes are browned and crisp. Serve immediately, removing the potatoes with a slotted spoon.

These potatoes are a delicious side dish to omelets (see Chapter 8), Roasted Fillet of Beef (see Chapter 6), or Grilled Brochettes of Pork with Rosemary (see Chapter 6).

Be very careful when you put rinsed vegetables (or other foods) into a pan of hot fat. The water that clings to the vegetables makes the fat splatter, which can cause serious burns.

Following is a quick and healthy side dish that is a fine match with the Salmon Steaks with Sweet Red Pepper Sauce recipe later in this chapter.

Sautéed Spinach Leaves

Tools: *Large sauté pan or skillet fitted with a lid*

Preparation time: *About 15 minutes*

Cooking time: *About 4 minutes*

Yield: *4 to 6 servings*

1½ pounds fresh spinach	*¼ teaspoon ground nutmeg*
1 tablespoon olive oil	*Salt and black pepper to taste*
1 tablespoon butter	

1 Cut away and discard any tough spinach stems and blemished leaves. Wash spinach thoroughly in cold water and drain well. (See Chapter 10 for complete instructions for rinsing and trimming greens.)

2 Heat the oil and butter in a large sauté pan or skillet over medium heat. Add the spinach, nutmeg, salt, and pepper.

3 Stir the spinach leaves to coat with the oil. (The spinach wilts so fast that you may think you barely have enough for one portion — don't worry, you do.) Cover and cook over medium-high heat for about 2 to 3 minutes or until the spinach leaves wilt thoroughly. Remove from heat and serve.

Sautéed spinach also complements Grilled Swordfish Steaks with Lemon and Thyme (see Chapter 6) or Mustard-Brushed Barbecued Chicken Breasts (see Chapter 6).

Firm, rich fish

Rich fish, with a high fat content, such as salmon, tuna, and bluefish, are exceptionally good when sautéed. And you can enhance them with countless sauces that you can make in 15 minutes or less. Because these fish have relatively high fat contents, they also stand up to spicy sauces.

However, a spicy sauce paired with a delicate fish, like sole or snapper, can be a culinary train wreck. In general, firm-fleshed fish (or rich fish) stand up to spiciness.

In the following easy recipe, which is faintly sweet from sautéed red bell peppers and shallots, note that you first sear the salmon to seal in moisture and then remove it from the pan. You make the quick sauce in the same pan, and then you return the fish to the sauce for the rest of the cooking. This technique helps to keep the salmon moist and infuses it with some of the sauce flavors. Note that this recipe calls for ½ cup of heavy cream (or half-and-half) at the end to bind the sauce, which works out to only 2 tablespoons of cream per person.

Binding a sauce means simply pulling together sauce ingredients in the pan and creating a smoother and thicker texture by stirring in butter, cream, or starch, like cornstarch or flour. Binding is done at the very end of the sauce-making process, just before serving.

The following salmon dish goes well with sautéed spinach accented with nutmeg.

Salmon Steaks with Sweet Red Pepper Sauce

Tools: *Paring knife, chef's knife, large nonstick skillet or sauté pan*

Preparation time: *About 15 minutes*

Cooking time: *About 15 minutes*

Yield: *4 servings*

2 medium red bell peppers

4 salmon steaks, each about 6 to 7 ounces and ¾ inch thick

Salt and black pepper to taste

2 tablespoons butter

¼ cup finely chopped shallots or onion

¼ teaspoon cayenne pepper

¼ cup dry white wine

½ cup heavy cream or half-and-half

2 tablespoons finely chopped fresh dill, plus dill sprigs for garnishing

1 Core and remove the seeds from the red peppers and then cut them into ¼-inch cubes. (Refer to Figure 4-2.)

2 Season both sides of the salmon steaks with salt and pepper. Melt the butter over medium-high heat in a large nonstick skillet or sauté pan large enough to hold the steaks in one layer.

3 Add the salmon to the pan and cook until lightly browned on both sides, about 3 to 4 minutes per side for medium doneness. The cooking time varies with the thickness of the fish and the doneness desired.

4 Transfer the steaks to a warm platter and cover with foil. Leave the cooking butter in the skillet and scrape the bottom of the pan with a wooden spoon to loosen the browned bits clinging to the pan. Add the shallots, cayenne pepper, and red peppers. Cook over medium-high heat, stirring occasionally, for about 4 to 5 minutes or until the vegetables are softened.

5 Add the wine, turn up the heat to high, and cook until about half the liquid in the pan evaporates. (This step intensifies the flavor of the sauce.) Lower the heat to medium-high, add the cream, and cook, stirring often, until the liquid reduces again by about half.

6 Add the salmon steaks, chopped dill, and any juices that have accumulated around the steaks and bring to a simmer. Cook for about 1 minute more or until warmed through. Do not overcook. Check the seasoning and add salt and pepper if desired. Using a flat metal spatula, remove each salmon steak to an individual plate; spoon a little of the sauce over each serving and serve immediately with dill sprigs or a decorative garnish.

How to Core and Seed a Pepper

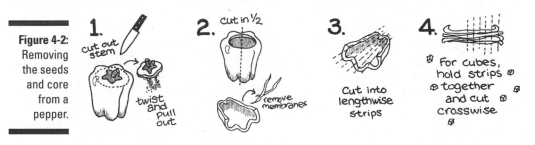

Figure 4-2: Removing the seeds and core from a pepper.

Chicken

Sautéing is probably the best method to impart flavor to chicken. The following simple recipe combines chicken with the sweet flavors of onions and tomatoes. This recipe is an easy one to modify.

Sautéed Chicken Breasts with Tomatoes and Thyme

Tools: *Chef's knife, large sauté pan or skillet, meat mallet or heavy pan, waxed paper, aluminum foil*

Preparation time: *About 20 minutes*

Cooking time: *About 10 minutes*

Yield: *4 servings*

4 boneless, skinless chicken breast halves

Salt and freshly ground pepper to taste

2 tablespoons olive oil

1 medium onion, chopped

1 large clove garlic, chopped

2 medium tomatoes, peeled, seeded, and chopped (see Chapter 11 for instructions)

1 teaspoon chopped fresh thyme, or ¼ teaspoon dried

2 tablespoons chopped fresh basil (optional)

⅓ cup white wine or chicken stock

1 Place the chicken breasts on a cutting board, season generously on both sides with salt and pepper, cover with waxed paper, and pound them lightly so that they are of equal thickness. (Use the bottom of a heavy pan or a meat mallet.)

2 Heat the olive oil in a large sauté pan or skillet over medium heat. Add the chicken and sauté for about 4 to 5 minutes per side or until done. (To test for doneness, make a small incision in the center of each piece. The meat should be white, with no trace of pink.) Remove the pieces to a platter and cover with aluminum foil to keep warm.

3 Add the onion to the pan over medium heat. Stir for 1 minute, scraping the bottom of the pan. Add the garlic, stirring occasionally for another minute. Add the tomatoes, thyme, basil (if desired), and salt and pepper to taste. Stir for 1 minute. Add the white wine or stock, increase the heat to high, and cook, stirring ocassionally, for about 2 to 3 minutes or until most of the liquid evaporates. (The mixture should be moist but not soupy.)

4 Place the chicken on 4 plates. Spoon equal portions of sauce over each piece.

You can serve the chicken with side dishes of Mashed Potatoes (see Chapter 3) or Ginger Rice with Fresh Coriander (see Chapter 16).

You can modify this recipe in many ways. For example, use turkey breasts or slices of veal instead of chicken; add 1 cup fresh, frozen, or canned corn kernels with the chopped tomatoes; add 2 tablespoons heavy cream with the stock or wine; substitute tarragon, marjoram, or other herb of choice for the thyme; or grate some Parmesan cheese over the top of each serving.

Steak

One of the most popular beef dishes in restaurants is what the French call *steak au poivre,* in which beef is coated liberally with cracked black pepper before it is cooked in a hot pan. The sauce is usually made with beef stock, shallots, red wine, and maybe a little brandy. The combination is compelling if the cook skillfully balances the pepper with sweet elements.

Sautéed Peppered Sirloin of Beef

Tools: *Chef's knife, large cast-iron skillet or other heavy-bottomed skillet, mortar and pestle or heavy pan*

Preparation time: *About 20 minutes*

Cooking time: *About 15 minutes*

Yield: *4 servings*

3 to 4 tablespoons black peppercorns, or to taste

2 boneless sirloin steaks, trimmed, each about 1 pound and 1¼ inches thick

2 tablespoons vegetable oil

3 tablespoons minced shallot

2 tablespoons minced onion (see following sidebar for instructions)

2 tablespoons butter

¾ cup dry red wine

2 tablespoons brandy

¼ cup homemade or canned beef or chicken stock

1 teaspoon tomato paste

Salt to taste

1 Crush the peppercorns finely by using a mortar and pestle or on a hard surface (such as a wooden cutting board) with the bottom of a heavy pan, as shown in Figure 4-3. Doing so shortly before cooking gets the most potency from the pepper.

2 Press the steaks into the peppercorns, covering both sides evenly. (Three to four tablespoons of peppercorns makes for a wonderfully hot and spicy sauce, but if you prefer a milder sauce, use only 2 to 3 tablespoons.)

3 Heat the oil in a large cast-iron skillet over high heat. When the pan is very hot, lay the steaks in and cook for about 2 to 3 minutes per side to sear. Lower the heat to medium and cook another 6 to 7 minutes, flipping periodically to finish. Cooking times vary with the thickness of the meat, so make a small incision in the meat and check for the desired degree of doneness. Medium doneness has a slightly pink center with soft-brown edges. (For medium-well or rare doneness, cook a minute or two more or less per side.)

(continued)

4 Remove the steaks from the pan and set aside on a plate. Cover the plate with foil to keep the steaks warm. Let the cooking pan cool slightly and remove any little burned particles, but do not rinse under water!

5 Return the pan to medium heat and add the shallot, onion, and 1 tablespoon of the butter. Cook for about 1 minute, stirring. Add the red wine and brandy. Raise the heat to high and boil the sauce to evaporate, or reduce, to about half its original volume, stirring often. Add the stock and tomato paste. Reduce the sauce again until it is about ½ cup total, stirring. Lower the heat to medium.

6 Add the remaining 1 tablespoon butter and stir well until it melts to finish, or pull together, the sauce. Spoon the sauce over the steaks. Check for seasoning, adding salt if necessary, and serve immediately.

We recommend serving this with a side of Mashed Potatoes (see Chapter 3) and Sautéed Spinach Leaves (in this chapter).

If you'd like to flambé the steaks, bring the steaks and the pan to the table. Pour 2 tablespoons of brandy over the steaks and ignite them with a match. Even if you don't taste the difference, your guests will be impressed. After the flame dies out, distribute the sauce over the steaks. You may want to practice this once before attempting it in front of a hungry audience.

To prevent peppercorns from flying all over the place when you crush them, wrap them first in aluminum foil.

How to Crush Peppercorns

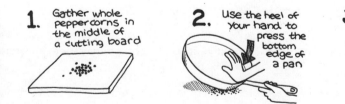

Figure 4-3: Crushing peppercorns with a heavy pan.

1. Gather whole peppercorns in the middle of a cutting board

2. Use the heel of your hand to press the bottom edge of a pan

3. Repeat steps 1 & 2 until peppercorns are crushed to desired size.

The doneness of steaks is defined by the meat's interior color. Rare meat is bright red and juicy. Medium meat has a light pink center with light brown edges. Well-done, which we don't recommend, is brown-gray and dry throughout.

ESSENTIAL SKILL

Mincing onions and garlic

A sliced onion releases intense flavor and juice, which is why so many recipes call for chopped, minced, or diced onion. To avoid tears, the best strategy is a sharp knife that reduces cutting time. Follow these steps (also illustrated below) to mince an onion:

1. Cut the onion in half lengthwise through the bulbous center. Peel back the papery skin and chop off the top, but leave the root end intact. (As you slice through the onion, the intact root end helps you to keep the slices from slipping out from under the knife.) Place each half cut side down.

2. With your knife tip just in front of the root end, slice the onion lengthwise in parallel cuts, leaving ⅛ to ¼ inch between the slices.

3. Now make several horizontal cuts of desired thickness, parallel to the board.

4. Cut through the onion at right angles to the board, making pieces as thick as desired. Finally, cut through the root end.

Just as with onions, slicing, chopping, and mincing garlic releases its pungent juices. The more you chop it, the stronger its flavor becomes. Raw, mashed garlic carries the biggest punch, while whole roasted garlic cloves release a nutty, slightly sweet flavor (see the "Using the knives properly" section in Chapter 2).

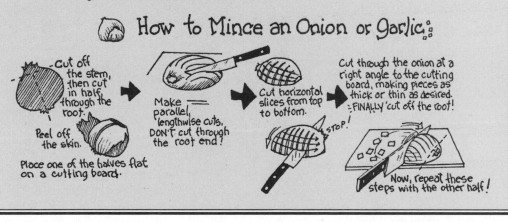

How to Mince an Onion or Garlic:

Cut off the stem, then cut in half through the root.

Peel off the skin.

Place one of the halves flat on a cutting board.

Make parallel, lengthwise cuts, DON'T cut through the root end!

Cut horizontal slices from top to bottom.

STOP!

Cut through the onion at a right angle to the cutting board, making pieces as thick or thin as desired. FINALLY 'cut off the root!

Now, repeat these steps with the other half!

Chapter 5

Mom Food: Braising and Stewing

. . . .

In This Chapter

▶ Braising and stewing: Twin tenderizers

▶ Sniffing your way through the herb garden

▶ Bang for the buck: Homey recipes for braising and stewing

. . . .

> **Recipes in This Chapter**
>
> ▶ Old-Fashioned Beef Stew
>
> ▶ Pot Roast with Vegetables
>
> ▶ Braised Chicken Legs in Red Wine
>
> ▶ Braised Lamb with White Beans
>
> ▶ Mediterranean Seafood Stew
>
> 🦐 🧅 🍅 🧄 🌿

*I*f you're like most people, you have precious little time, especially during the week, to stand over a pot. This chapter is for you. Braising and stewing are slow cooking methods that allow you to put all the ingredients in a pot, turn the heat to low, and do something else for an hour or two — maybe dust the TV or return the neighbor's newspaper that your dog retrieves every day.

Because braising and stewing dishes take so much time, they are best cooked the day before and reheated — the flavors are actually more pronounced that way. They are also great for parties because they are easily made in large batches and are inexpensive (usually using less expensive cuts of meat).

Most meat dishes in this chapter use the less expensive front cuts of beef: the chuck, brisket, shank, and plate. (See Chapter 14 for an illustration of the various cuts of beef.) These more muscular cuts do not make much of a steak, but when you braise them for hours, their fibers break down and they become succulent. In some ways, these cuts are more flavorful than expensive tenderloin.

Braising versus Stewing

Both braising and stewing involve long, slow cooking in liquid. The major difference is that braised foods lie in a few inches of liquid, not quite submerged, so that they stew and steam at the same time.

Stewing involves submerging ingredients in a liquid and simmering the mixture for a long time. Larger cuts of meat — and the very toughest — tend to be braised, whereas cut-up meat is stewed.

Exotic Flavors to Fill Your Pantry: Herb and Spice Charts

Herbs and spices energize virtually every type of cooking. Change the herb or spice, and the dish takes on entirely different tastes and aromas. Herbs and spices are particularly important in braising and stewing, where a last-minute addition of the right herb and spice combination can make a dish soar.

Purchasing and storing herbs and spices

Purchase dried herbs and spices in small quantities, keep them in tightly sealed containers away from heat and light, and try to use them within 10 to 12 months. The flavor of dried herbs fades over time.

You also can cultivate fresh herbs in a container box for your window or patio. Rinse fresh herbs thoroughly, wrap them in damp paper towels, and store them for up to a week in the refrigerator.

Cooking with herbs and spices

Elizabeth Terry is one of the South's most acclaimed chefs, owing to the pure and unfussy regional fare she turns out at Elizabeth on 37th in Savannah, Georgia. Fans of family-style Southern food come from hundreds of miles away to experience this unpretentious and unforgettable place.

Terry says, "Use fresh herbs rather than dried whenever possible. The full flavor of the fresh herb or spice is best released if you add it to the dish just before serving."

Where does a fricassee fit in?

A *fricassee* is a variation on stew. A traditional fricassee is made with poultry, usually chicken. Moreover, the poultry in a fricassee is not seared and browned first, as in a stew. The lack of browning makes the sauce paler than that of a stew.

Following are some of Chef Terry's favorite ways to add fresh herbs and spices to food:

- ✔ **Basil and mint combined:** Delicious with tomato sauces and salads, potato salads, and marinated vegetable salads.

- ✔ **Rosemary and thyme:** Go well with oven-roasted potatoes and roasted chicken. Rub the rosemary into the poultry before roasting it and then sprinkle it with the fresh thyme when it comes out of the oven. One herb is roasted, the other is fresh, and the flavors are perfect together.

- ✔ **Curry powder and sautéed onions:** Add curry powder to sautéed onions for a wonderful cold vegetable garnish.

- ✔ **Cumin:** Use in soups and sauces. Especially good sautéed with red cabbage, apple, and a little cream.

- ✔ **Fresh ginger, red bell peppers, and onions:** Make a sauce for fish, shrimp, and grilled vegetables by pureeing fresh ginger, red bell peppers, and onions in a blender.

- ✔ **Cinnamon, allspice, finely chopped red bell pepper, crushed garlic, and oil:** Make a paste for coating and marinating shrimp before cooking it on the grill.

- ✔ **Whole mustard seeds:** Rub whole mustard seeds on the outside of salmon and sear in a pan of hot oil until the seeds form a crunchy crust and the fish is cooked.

Table 5-1 can help you decide which herbs go best with which kinds of dishes. (Also see Figure 5-1.) After you become familiar with the properties of these flavor enhancers, you can toss the chart and navigate on your own.

Table 5-1	A Few Fresh Herbs You Should Know
Herb	*Description*
Basil	Pungent, sweet flavor. Most fresh varieties are dark green, except for the purple-leafed opal basil. Available as fresh sprigs or crumbled dry. Essential to Mediterranean cooking, especially Italian and French cuisine. Excellent with tomatoes, eggs, pasta, poultry, fish, and green salads, and in vinaigrettes.
Bay leaf	Strong, herbaceous taste. Sold as a whole, dried leaf. Excellent in long-cooking dishes like soups, stews, poaching liquid, marinades, pot roasts, rice casseroles, stuffings, and barbecue sauces. Remove the leaf before serving the dish.

(continued)

Table 5-1 *(continued)*

Herb	Description
Chervil	Quite aromatic, with delicate licorice-like flavor. Available as fresh sprigs (mostly in summer) or crumbled dry. Use with fish and shellfish, eggs, chicken, tomatoes, asparagus, summer squash, eggplant, herb butters, sauces, green salads, and soups.
Chives	Delicate mild-onion flavor. Sold in thin, fresh stalks, chopped, or dried. Wonderful in cream sauces or soups, with chicken, eggs, shellfish, or marinated salads, or as a plate garnish.
Cilantro or Chinese parsley	Extremely pungent and aromatic. Sold in fresh, curly-leafed bunches. Found in Mexican and Asian dishes and works well with rice, fish, pork, ham, salsa, avocado, and tomato.
Dill	Delicate caraway flavor. Sold in feathery, fresh bunches or as dried seeds. Use seeds in pickling recipes; use fresh leaves with fish and shellfish, omelets, chicken, turkey, dressings and vinaigrettes, cold salads and marinades, fish mousses, and pâtés.
Marjoram	A little like oregano in taste, but much milder and sweeter. Sold fresh or crumbled dry. Extremely versatile herb. Add to almost any vegetable dish, especially good with sweet potatoes, squash, tomatoes, corn, stuffings, stews, omelets, soups, herb butters, rice, pork, lamb, beef, poultry, or any fish.
Mint	Fresh scent and a sweet, pungent flavor. Most common varieties are standard peppermint and spearmint. Sold in fresh bunches or crumbled dry. Terrific in cold grain and rice salads, with fresh fruit, in cold fruit soups and sauces, and with marinated vegetable salads of cucumber or tomato; also good with grilled chicken, pork, lamb, and shellfish and in cold drinks like iced tea.
Oregano	Intense flavor. Sold fresh or crumbled dry. An essential ingredient in Italian and Greek cooking. A little goes far with poultry, tomato sauces, egg dishes, vegetable stews, and stir-fries.
Parsley	Fresh-flavored and slightly tart. Available year-round in fresh bunches or crumbled dry. Two common fresh varieties are the stronger-flavored Italian flat leaf and the curly leaf. An all-purpose herb; use in savory soups or stocks in bouquet garni, stews, dressings, stuffings, and frittatas, with fish, poultry, beef, pork, lamb, veal, game, and all vegetables. Also a pretty plate garnish.

Herb	Description
Rosemary	Quite aromatic, needle-shaped leaves smell a little like lemon and pine. Sold as fresh sprigs or dried. Use sparingly with vegetables and in stuffings, rice dishes, and stews. Excellent with game, meats (especially grilled), chicken, halibut, salmon, tuna; in herb breads; or to flavor oils and marinades. The stem of the rosemary herb is rather tough and woody. Pull the needles or leaves off the stem, and mince them finely before using. Discard the tough stem.
Sage	Green-gray or purple oval leaves with a slightly bitter mint taste. Available in fresh sprigs, crumbled dry, and ground. Use sparingly. Excellent in poultry stuffings, pâtés, fish and chicken stews, chicken salads, meat loaves, and herb butters, with halibut and salmon, and for seasoning meat and poultry roasts.
Savory	Full-bodied herb that some people say tastes like a cross between mint and thyme. Fresh sprigs available in two varieties: winter savory and milder summer savory. Crumbled dry available year-round. Excellent with fresh or dried bean salads, most fish and shellfish dishes, omelets, soufflés, rice dishes, stuffings, meat and poultry, tomatoes, potatoes, artichokes, and onions.
Tarragon	Aromatic herb with assertive, licorice-like flavor. Sold as fresh whole sprigs, crumbled dry, and whole dried leaves. Fresh tarragon, widely available in the summer months, has the most subtle flavor. Use with chicken, pork, lamb, veal, fish, shellfish, omelets and other egg dishes, dips and dressings, mayonnaise, vegetable casseroles and salads, herb butters, and as flavoring for white vinegar and hot or cold potato dishes.
Thyme	Tiny leaves with minty aroma and tea-like taste. Sold as fresh sprigs and crumbled dry. Fresh varieties include lemon, orange, and French (the common variety). Add to vegetables, meat, poultry, fish, egg dishes, soups, stews, cream sauces, meat loaf, pâtés, chowders, stuffings, and bouquet garni.

Spices, which are almost always sold dried, have been a vital element in international cooking since Byzantine times. Most spices come from the East, where they were introduced to Europe during the Crusades.

Dried spices are generally more concentrated than dried herbs, so use them carefully. If a recipe calls for 1 tablespoon of fresh oregano, you need only use ½ teaspoon dry oregano. After you become familiar with the qualities of different spices, your cooking repertoire expands exponentially.

Figure 5-1:
Types of
herbs.

The flavor of freshly ground spices is much more potent than those sold already ground. Whenever possible, buy whole spices, like nutmeg and peppercorns, and grate or grind them yourself before using them. You can purchase a small spice grater for just this purpose.

Whole spices also can be wrapped and tied in a piece of cheesecloth, added to soups and stews, and then removed before serving. Cloves are often stuck into an onion and then added to a stew.

Store spices in a cool, dry place and try to use them within 6 to 10 months. Table 5-2 lists the more common spices.

Table 5-2	A Few Spices You Should Know
Spice	*Description*
Allspice	Spice berries of the evergreen pimiento tree with tastes of cinnamon, nutmeg, and cloves — hence the name. Sold as whole, dried berries or ground. Excellent in both sweet and savory dishes — pâtés, stews, chilies, poached fish, meat loaf and meatballs, pumpkin and fruit pie fillings, barbecue sauce, stuffed cabbage, winter squash, chutneys and preserves, and gingerbread.
Caraway	Has a nutty, faint anise flavor and is commonly used in German cooking. Sold as dried seeds. Found in rye bread and also in cakes, stews, and some European cheeses.
Cardamom	Pungent, spicy-sweet flavor. Sold as whole dried seeds and ground. Excellent in baked goods, fruit salads, pumpkin pie, and Indian curries, one of the main ingredients in barain masala, an essential spice mixture in Indian cooking.
Cayenne or red pepper	A hot, powdered mixture of several chili peppers. Sold ground. Use sparingly. Especially good in dishes with egg, cheese, rice, fish, chicken, or ground beef.
Chili powder	A hot and spicy mixture of dried chilies, cumin, oregano, garlic, coriander, and cloves. Sold ground. A multipurpose hot seasoning; use sparingly in stews, soups, chili, egg dishes, dressings, guacamole and bean dips, barbecue sauces, and rice and bean casseroles.
Cinnamon	Sweet and aromatic spice from the bark of a tropical tree. Sold whole, in dry sticks or ground. Primarily a baking spice in cakes, cookies, and pies, but also adds a savory touch to stews, curries, baked sweet potatoes, and yellow squash.
Clove	Sharp and deeply fragrant. Sold as whole dried buds or ground. Use much like cinnamon, but more judiciously. Excellent in stocks, vegetable soups, and glazes.
Coriander	Similar in flavor to caraway. Sold as whole dried seeds and ground. Seeds used for pickling; powder used for curries, lamb, pork, sausage, and baked goods.

(continued)

Table 5-2 *(continued)*

Spice	*Description*
Cumin	Slightly acidic aroma; nutty-flavored seed. Sold as whole dried seeds and ground. Essential to Middle Eastern and Asian cooking. Use in curries, chili, and bean dips and with fish, lamb, poultry, and beef.
Curry powder	A spice blend that can include more than a dozen different herbs and spices, often with cinnamon, cloves, cardamom, chilies, fenugreek seeds, mustard seeds, turmeric (which gives curry its distinctive golden color), and red and black pepper. Commercial blends tend to lose their flavor fast and should be used within 2 months of purchase. Use to season lamb, pork, chicken, rice, stuffings, and sautéed vegetables like onions, cabbage, and baked squash.
Ginger	Sharp and faintly sweet flavor; intensely aromatic. Sold dried ground, crystallized, preserved, and fresh. Use ground sparingly in curries, spice cakes, and marinades and with pork, chicken, and seafood. Use crystallized (candied) in fruit syrups and glazes and with pies and cakes. Grate fresh ginger into stir-fries of pork, chicken, beef, and fresh vegetables.
Nutmeg	Pleasing aroma; slightly sweet and nutty taste. Sold as whole seeds and ground. Delicious in white sauces, sweet sauces, and glazes, pureed vegetables and soups, eggnog, fruit pies, spice cakes, and pumpkin pie. Best freshly grated. Use very sparingly.
Paprika	Beautiful red powder; varieties range from sweet to hot. Sold ground (the Hungarian variety is considered best). Accents dips, creamy salads, dressings, stews (like goulash), sautéed meats, chicken, and fish. Imparts rusty red color to creamed dishes and sauces.
Peppercorns	Black peppercorns are intense, hot, and aromatic. Sold cracked, finely ground, or as whole peppercorns in black and white, with black being the strongest. (All are berries from the same vine, picked at various stages of maturity.) Black pepper is perhaps the world's most popular spice, used to accent nearly every savory dish. Use freshly ground peppercorns for best effect — ground pepper quickly loses its intensity. Use white pepper to enrich cream sauces and white dishes if you don't want the pepper specks to show.

Spice	Description
Saffron	The world's most expensive spice. Made from dried stigmas hand-picked from a special variety of purple crocus flowers. Available as powder or whole red threads (which are of better quality). A little goes a long way. Essential to classic dishes like bouillabaisse and paella, but also delicious in rice casseroles, creamed dishes, risotto, and with seafood. Imparts a pale yellow color to cream sauces and rice dishes.
Turmeric	Yellow-orange powder that is intensely aromatic and has a bitter, pungent flavor; gives American-style mustard its color. Sold as a powder. Essential ingredient in curries; use in rice and chili and with lamb and winter squash.

Brawny Beef Stew

Dollar for dollar, beef stew goes a long way. Lean, boneless chuck is one of the least expensive cuts of beef, and the root vegetables (carrots and turnips) that surround it are as economical as they are healthful. Other good cuts to ask for are neck, brisket, and shank.

The following recipe serves 8 to 10 and is a perfect make-ahead meal for a small party. To reduce the yield to serve 4 or 5, use half the ingredients. But remember, stews are always better the next day, after the seasonings have a chance to permeate the meat. If you make too much, you'll have delicious leftovers.

ESSENTIAL SKILL

Learning your herbs and spices

Because the rainbow of herbs and spices available to home cooks is so exciting, it can be easy to overdo it. The best way to get to know herbs and spices is to cook dishes that contain only one herb or spice — learn how it interacts with different foods, watch how it intensifies with cooking, and find out whether you really like it.

For example, with rosemary, you can make a quick sauce for sautéed or grilled chicken breast by combining 3 parts chicken stock to 1 part white wine in a saucepan. Then add a teaspoon of minced fresh rosemary (or ½ teaspoon dry), some very thin slices of garlic, and salt and black pepper to taste. Cook down the liquid until it is reduced by three-quarters. Then strain the sauce and serve it over the chicken.

This dish gives you a pure rosemary flavor. If you like it, you can refine it by adding more or less rosemary or even by adding a complementary herb, such as thyme, tarragon, or chives.

TIP

You also can store meat stews in the freezer in tightly covered containers for up to six months.

Old-Fashioned Beef Stew

Tools: *Chef's knife, stew pot (cast iron is best), large spoon, long tongs*

Preparation time: *About 25 minutes*

Cooking time: *About 1 hour and 40 minutes*

Yield: *8 to 10 servings*

¼ cup olive or vegetable oil

4 pounds lean, boneless chuck, cut into 2-inch cubes

2 large onions, coarsely chopped

6 large cloves garlic, chopped

6 tablespoons flour

Salt and black pepper to taste

3 cups dry red wine

3 cups homemade or canned beef or chicken stock

2 tablespoons tomato paste

4 whole cloves

2 bay leaves

4 sprigs parsley, tied together (see following note)

4 sprigs fresh thyme, or 1 teaspoon dried

1 tablespoon minced fresh rosemary, leaves only, or 1 teaspoon dried and crumbled

1 pound small turnips, trimmed and cut into 2-inch pieces

6 large carrots, trimmed and cut into 1-inch lengths

1 Heat the oil in a large stew pot over medium-high heat. Then add the beef cubes (see following What If icon). Cook, stirring and turning the meat as necessary, for 5 to 10 minutes or until evenly browned. **Warning:** Meat or poultry browned in hot oil or fat of any kind splatters hot grease. Use long tongs to turn the meat carefully. If the oil becomes too hot, lower the heat to medium for the remainder of the browning.

2 Add the onion and garlic and cook over medium heat, stirring occasionally for about 8 minutes. Sprinkle the flour, salt, and pepper and stir to coat the meat evenly.

3 Add the wine, stock, and tomato paste and stir over high heat until the cooking liquid thickens as it comes to a boil. Add the cloves, bay leaves, parsley, thyme, rosemary, and turnips. Cover and reduce the heat to low. Simmer for 1 hour, occasionally stirring and scraping the bottom of the pot. Add the carrots and cook until meat and carrots are tender, about 20 minutes more. Remove the herb sprigs and bay leaves before serving.

Note: *If using fresh herb sprigs, tie them together with a little kitchen twine. Doing so makes removing the herb sprigs easier, and you get the benefit of parsley flavor without stringy stems.*

You can serve this stew with country bread and Tomato, Red Onion, and Basil Salad (see Chapter 10).

Before adding a dried herb, like rosemary, to a stewing pot, crush the brittle leaves in a mortar and pestle or with your fingers into smaller, more palatable pieces. Doing so also releases more of the herb's flavor.

If you don't have a stew pot big enough to brown the meat in one layer, cook the meat, in batches, a little at a time, moving the pieces to a platter as they brown. Return the pieces to the pot after they are all browned.

Hanging Out at Home? Try Pot Roast

Pot roast is a good dish to make when you intend to be around the house all afternoon. The braising technique is the same as in the preceding recipe. First you brown the piece of meat well on all sides; then you braise it in its juices and the cooking liquids for about the duration of one football game, or almost 3 hours.

The best cut of beef for a pot roast is the *first-cut* brisket. Sometimes referred to as the *flat cut,* the first-cut brisket has just the right amount of fat so it is not too dry after it's cooked. Ask your butcher for the first cut.

Pot roast is also relatively inexpensive. We made this dish for less than $20, with an individual serving costing about $2.50. This rich and satisfying dish is excellent served hot or cold with Dijon-style mustard or a horseradish sauce (see Chapter 3 for a recipe).

Pot Roast with Vegetables

Tools: *Large Dutch oven, chef's knife*

Preparation time: *About 20 minutes*

Cooking time: *About 3 hours*

Yield: *6 to 8 servings*

(continued)

2 tablespoons vegetable oil

4 pounds first-cut beef brisket

2 large onions, chopped

3 large cloves garlic, chopped

½ cup dry white wine

½ cup water, more if needed

1 bay leaf

¼ teaspoon dried thyme

Salt and black pepper to taste

4 large Idaho potatoes, peeled and cut into bite-size chunks

3 large carrots, peeled and sliced crosswise into 2-inch pieces

3 tablespoons chopped fresh parsley

1 Heat the oil in a large (preferably cast iron) Dutch oven over high heat; add the brisket and brown on both sides, about 7 to 8 minutes. Allow the meat to sear to a golden brown without burning. Remove the brisket from the pot and set aside on a large plate.

2 Reduce the heat to medium; add the onions and garlic, and sauté until the onions are lightly browned, stirring frequently. (Do not let the garlic brown.)

3 Return the brisket to the pot. Add the wine, water, bay leaf, thyme, salt, and pepper. Cover, bring to a boil, adjust heat as necessary, and simmer for 2 ¾ to 3 hours, turning the meat several times and adding ½ to 1 cup water as necessary if the liquid evaporates.

4 About 10 minutes before the end of the cooking time, add the potatoes and carrots to the saucepan.

5 When the meat is so tender that you can pierce it easily with a fork, carefully remove it to a carving board with a long-handled fork; cover with foil and let it rest for 10 to 15 minutes. Continue cooking the potatoes and carrots in the covered pot, for about 10 to 15 minutes more, or until tender.

6 To assemble the meat and vegetable platter, slice the brisket across the grain, as shown in Figure 5-2. (If you cut *with* the grain — see the following tip — you'll shred the meat.) Arrange the slices on a serving platter.

7 Remove the cooked potatoes and carrots from the gravy and spoon them around the meat. Skim off the fat from the surface of the remaining juices, heat the juices through, and spoon over the meat and vegetables. Sprinkle with the chopped parsley. Serve the extra gravy in a sauceboat.

Pot roast is delicious served with a mixed green salad and country bread.

Leftover terminology

The term *leftover* is unfortunate in some cases. Its unsavory connotation — something you "left," like your briefcase — hardly does justice to foods that can be just as good, or better, the next day, such as stews, soups, and certain one-pot dishes.

We invite you to join our campaign to find a new term for *leftovers*. Possibilities include

- ✔ Previously prepared
- ✔ Tested
- ✔ Enjoyed again
- ✔ Golden oldie
- ✔ Broken in

TIP

Most meat has a *grain,* or visible layers of muscle tissue that hold it together. As Figure 5-2 shows, you should cut *across* the grain.

Cutting Pot Roast Across the Grain

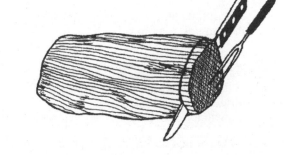

Figure 5-2:
Cut across the grain to avoid shredding the meat.

Downright Regal Chicken Legs

A dinner of chicken legs may not sound like reason to get excited, but slow braising can turn them into something special. This technique makes the legs tender and succulent (it also works with tough duck legs), and the red wine sauce is packed with flavor. Chicken legs, with the thighs, are the most flavorful part of the bird, much better than breast meat. When braised, the legs loosen up and absorb some of the red wine sauce.

We were amazed to discover upon preparing this dish that the cost of all the ingredients came to about $4. Serve this dish with rice, egg noodles, or instant couscous (see Chapter 15).

Braised Chicken Legs in Red Wine

Tools: *Large sauté pan with lid, chef's knife, vegetable peeler*

Preparation time: *About 25 minutes*

Cooking time: *About 45 minutes*

Yield: *4 servings*

4 chicken legs with thighs attached, about 2½ to 3 pounds total

Salt and black pepper to taste

About ¼ cup flour

2 tablespoons vegetable oil

8 small white pearl onions, peeled

½ pound small white mushrooms, cleaned, trimmed

2 cloves garlic, chopped

4 sprigs fresh thyme, or 1 teaspoon dried

1 bay leaf

1½ cups dry red wine

8 baby carrots, trimmed

2 whole cloves

4 parsley sprigs plus 2 tablespoons finely chopped parsley (for garnish)

1 Rinse the chicken legs under cold running water and pat dry. Trim the legs of all excess flaps of skin and fat. Sprinkle with salt and pepper on both sides. Coat the legs lightly with flour (see the following Tip icon).

2 Heat the oil in a heavy sauté pan that is large enough to hold the chicken legs in one layer. Place the legs in the pan and cook over medium-high heat until they are nicely browned on one side, about 5 minutes. Turn the chicken legs over and continue cooking about 5 minutes more or until browned. Remove the legs to a large platter.

3 Add the onions to the pan and cook about 4 to 5 minutes, turning occasionally. Add the mushrooms and cook about 3 minutes more or until nicely browned, turning occasionally.

4 Remove the onions and mushrooms from the pan to the large platter and carefully pour off all the fat — but not down the sink! (You can pour fat into an old coffee can. After the fat cools and hardens, throw the can away.)

5 Return the chicken and vegetables to the pan over medium heat. Add the garlic, thyme, and bay leaf and cook for 1 minute, stirring often. Do not brown the garlic. Add the wine, carrots, cloves, and parsley sprigs; then raise the heat and bring to a boil.

6 Cover tightly, adjust the heat as necessary, and simmer for 25 to 30 minutes or until the chicken and vegetables are tender.

7 Transfer the chicken, onions, mushrooms, and carrots to a serving dish. Discard the thyme and parsley sprigs, the bay leaf, and whole cloves. Turn up the heat to high and reduce the sauce, if necessary, for 2 to 3 minutes or until slightly thickened. Season to taste with salt and pepper. Pour the sauce over the chicken and sprinkle with the chopped parsley.

To seal in the moisture of meat, fish, or poultry before sautéing, you *dredge,* or coat, with flour and shake off the excess. Simply drag or roll the food in flour to coat all sides, then pat or shake the pieces gently to remove excess before cooking.

To give the chicken sauce a rich, smooth texture, stir in 2 to 3 tablespoons light cream, after reducing the sauce, and heat through. To reduce the number of calories in this dish, remove all skin from the chicken legs before serving.

The Best Lamb You've Ever Had

Lamb and white beans are a classic combination in many of the world's cuisines. This wonderful, rustic dish uses a shoulder of lamb, which is lean and sinewy but exceptionally tasty — and ideal for long, slow cooking.

Cooking with wine

An adage goes, "If you wouldn't drink it, don't cook with it." That is really the only rule you need to remember when cooking with wine. If you see a bottle in the store labeled *cooking wine,* keep walking.

Fortified wines, such as Madeira, Port, sherry, and marsala, can add a lovely touch to stews and braised dishes. All have their places in certain recipes.

Note: In an episode of *The Honeymooners,* Alice Kramden says that her husband, Ralph, has so little tolerance for alcohol that he gets tipsy eating rum cake. Although some residual alcohol may be found in rum cake, none survives in a long-cooked stew. What you get are flavors from the wine or spirit and maybe some added body. If you want to have a wild and crazy night, you'll have to drink lots of wine along with the stew. (See *Wine For Dummies,* 2nd Edition, by Ed McCarthy and Mary Ewing-Mulligan [published by IDG Books] for more information about which wines go with which foods.)

Braised Lamb with White Beans

Tools: *Large saucepan, wooden spoon, chef's knife, nonstick pan, heavy pot or Dutch oven*

Preparation time: *About 20 minutes, plus soaking time for beans*

Cooking time: *About 2 hours*

Yield: *8 servings*

1 pound dried white beans (such as Navy or Great Northern)

8 cups water

4 large carrots, trimmed and cut widthwise into ¼-inch pieces

1 medium onion stuck with 2 whole cloves (see following note)

4 sprigs fresh thyme, or l teaspoon dried

2 bay leaves

Salt and black pepper to taste

3 pounds lean lamb shoulder, cut into 2-inch cubes

1 large onion, chopped

3 cloves garlic, chopped

28-ounce can crushed tomatoes

1 cup dry white wine

4 sprigs fresh thyme, or 1 teaspoon dried

1 Soak the beans in a large bowl of cool water, for 8 to 10 hours. (To shorten the soaking process, boil the beans for 3 minutes, then let soak, covered, for 1 to 2 hours.)

2 Drain the beans, transfer them to a large saucepan, and add 7 cups of the water, carrots, onion with cloves, thyme, 1 of the bay leaves, salt, and pepper. Bring to a boil, reduce heat, and simmer for 45 minutes or until the beans are tender, skimming the surface frequently to remove any foam. As the beans cook, you can prepare the lamb.

3 Over medium high setting, heat a heavy pot or Dutch oven. Add the meat and cook, stirring, about 10 to 15 minutes or until well browned on all sides.

4 Reduce the heat to medium and add the chopped onion and garlic. Cook and stir often over medium heat for 3 minutes. Add the tomatoes, the wine, the remaining 1 cup of the water, thyme, the remaining 1 bay leaf, salt, and pepper. Stir well, cover, and simmer for about 1½ hours, or until the lamb is tender.

5 After the lamb is cooked, drain the cooked beans, reserving 1 cup of the cooking liquid. Remove the thyme sprigs, bay leaf, and onion with cloves from the pot of cooked beans. Remove the cloves from the onion. Cut the onion into small cubes and add the onion, beans, and carrots to the lamb casserole. Stir well. Simmer for 5 minutes, stirring occasionally. If the dish seems too thick, add some of the reserved bean liquid. Remove thyme sprigs and bay leaf before serving.

Note: Clove adds a lovely perfume to dishes like this one. However, you must remove the clove before serving — chomping on it is like biting a nail.

This one-dish meal needs no side dish — just good bread.

A Fish in Every Pot

This fish stew combines different compatible flavors in one pot. Like other stews, you can prepare it several hours ahead of serving time. Simply complete the recipe up to step 3. Five minutes before you want to serve the stew, add the fish and finish cooking.

Note that you add cilantro to this dish at the very last minute — that is because fresh herbs are at their most fragrant that way. Cooking delicate chervil, cilantro, or parsley mutes its flavors. Moreover, herbs are more colorful when added at the last minute.

Mediterranean Seafood Stew

Tools: *Large, deep sauté pan or skillet, chef's knife, shrimp deveiner (optional)*

Preparation time: *About 30 minutes*

Cooking time: *About 25 minutes*

Yield: *4 servings*

3 tablespoons olive oil

2 large leeks, white and light green parts only, washed and cut into ½-inch pieces (see Chapter 9)

2 large cloves garlic, chopped

1 red bell pepper, cored, seeded, and diced

¾ teaspoon ground cumin

¼ to ½ teaspoon red pepper flakes, or to taste

3 ripe plum tomatoes, cored and diced

1 cup dry white wine

1 cup water

Salt and black pepper to taste

1 pound medium shrimp, shelled and deveined

¾ pound sea scallops, cut in half

¼ cup coarsely chopped cilantro or parsley

(continued)

1 Heat the oil in a large, deep sauté pan or skillet over medium heat. Add the leeks and cook, stirring occasionally, about 4 minutes or until they wilt. Add the garlic and cook, stirring often, for another 1 to 2 minutes or until just golden. (Don't let the garlic brown.)

2 Add the red bell pepper, cumin, and red pepper flakes and cook over low heat about 8 minutes, or until the peppers are tender, stirring occasionally.

3 Add the tomatoes, wine, water, salt, and pepper to taste. Cover and raise the heat to bring the mixture to a boil. Reduce the heat to medium and cook, partially covered, for 6 to 8 minutes.

4 Add the shrimp and scallops and cook, partially covered, about 5 minutes more, or just until the shrimp is evenly pink and the scallops are opaque. Remove from heat, stir in the cilantro or parsley, and serve.

Serve this dish with noodles or rice. A salad and good bread are also great accompaniments to this dish.

You can make fish stew with species such as cod, halibut, porgy, squid, tilefish, and weakfish, some of which are quite inexpensive. Think of the texture and flavor of different fish. In stew, you want a relatively firm-fleshed fish that does not fall apart. Sole, for example, would be too delicate. Dark-fleshed fish, like mackerel, would overpower the stew.

Solving cooking woes

What do you do if a stew or a braised dish is . . .

✔ **Flat-tasting?** Add salt and pepper. Or try a little sherry or Madeira.

✔ **Tough?** Cook it longer. Additional cooking breaks down the sinew in muscular cuts of meat. You may want to remove the vegetables in the dish with a slotted spoon to prevent them from overcooking.

✔ **Burned on the bottom?** Carefully scoop out the unburned portion of the stew into a separate pot. Add water or stock to stretch it if necessary, and add sherry and a chopped onion. (The sweetness in an onion can mask many mistakes.)

✔ **Too thin?** Blend 1 tablespoon flour with 1 tablespoon water. Mix this mixture with 1 cup stew liquid and return to the pot with the rest of the stew. Stir well. Heat slowly until thickened.

Chapter 6

Grate Possibilities: Roasting and Grilling

*H*ere's where we get to the meat of the matter, so to speak. In theory, if you had only an oven with a broiler, you could survive quite well — you might get a hankering for pasta once in a while, but it would pass. Similarly, if you lived in a sunny spot with little rain, you could probably make do with just a barbecue grill. In this chapter, we take a look at both.

Roasting

The strict definition of *roasting* is cooking uncovered in an oven in which heat emanates from the walls.

When it comes to ease and simplicity, roasting is a valuable technique. You simply buy a big hunk of meat or a variety of vegetables, crank up the oven, and toss it in (well, almost). Whole fish are sublime when seasoned well and roasted. And root vegetables — carrots, onions, and beets, for example — become particularly sweet and succulent when you roast them.

The art of roasting is 90 percent timing and 10 percent patience. And if you use a meat thermometer when roasting meats, fouling up is almost impossible. After you understand timing, you can focus on the finer points of roasting.

Seasoning a roast

Have you ever eaten a superb, charbroiled steak that lingers on the palate like an aged wine? Part of its appeal comes from being salted generously before cooking. Salt is a flavor enhancer that brings out the best in many foods. For that reason, salting meat, fish, poultry, and vegetables before roasting is important. However, because some people are advised to limit salt in their diets, you should ask guests ahead of time.

To sear or not to sear?

Searing refers to the technique of putting meat in a very hot pan before roasting, in order to seal the surface and add flavor by browning (doing this also keeps the juices inside). You often sear steaks by placing them in a very hot pan and then turning them all around until a crust forms on the surface.

"Searing a roast helps to caramelize the juices and sugars on the roast's surface and give it a nice, flavorful crust," says Waldy Malouf, chef of the Rainbow Room in New York City. "Be sure to reduce the oven temperature to an even 350 or 325 degrees after the surface of your roast is seared so that it doesn't shrink or dry out."

Basting

Many recipes call for *basting* the roast, which means brushing or pouring pan juices over it during cooking. To baste, use a large spoon, bulb baster, or basting brush to coat the roast's surface with the pan juices or oil. Basting keeps the meat or vegetables moist, prevents shrinkage, and gives the crust or skin an even brown color.

Chill out: Resting

If you're like us, by the time a roast emerges from the oven you are so hungry that you could tear at it like a dog. Instead, go have some Cheez Whiz and crackers and let the roast sit out, covered with aluminum foil, for 15 to 20 minutes (if the cut of meat is large). Even a roast chicken or duck should sit for 10 minutes out of the oven before you carve it. Sitting lets the meat *rest:* that is, loosen up a bit, allowing the internal juices to distribute more evenly.

Chef Malouf has a different technique. He says, "I like to slightly undercook the roast and then turn my home oven off and let it rest undisturbed (in the oven) about 20 minutes before carving. The roast will continue to cook, with its internal temperature increasing about 10 degrees during this time."

Roasting times and temperatures

Tables 6-1 through 6-4 give approximate cooking times and temperatures for various roasts and weights. Remember to remove a roast when its internal temperature is 5 to 10 degrees *less* than final internal temperature, and then let it rest for about 15 minutes. During the resting time, the roast cooks 5 to 10 degrees more. None of this is exact science, though; you have to use a meat thermometer to get the results you like. See Figure 6-1 for illustrated instructions for using a meat thermometer.

When inserting a meat thermometer into a roast, do not let the metal touch the bone — the bone is hotter than the meat and registers a falsely higher temperature.

Figure 6-1:
How to insert a meat thermo-meter in var-ious roasts.

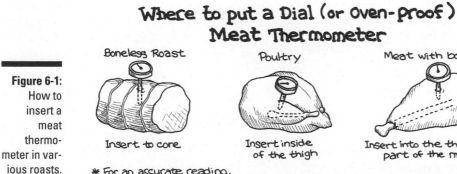

Where to put a Dial (or Oven-proof) Meat Thermometer

Boneless Roast — Insert to core

Poultry — Insert inside of the thigh

Meat with bone — Insert into the thickest part of the meat

* For an accurate reading, do NOT touch the bone, fat, or bottom of the pan with the thermometer

Table 6-1		Beef Roasting Chart		
Beef Roast	*Preheated Oven Temperature (°F)*	*Weight*	*Approximate Total Cooking Time*	*Remove from Oven at This Meat Temperature*
Boneless rib-eye roast (small end)	350°	3 to 4 pounds	Medium rare: 1½ to 1¾ hours	135°
			Medium: 1¾ to 2 hours	150°
		4 to 6 pounds	Medium rare: 1¾ to 2 hours	135°
			Medium: 2 to 2½ hours	150°
		6 to 8 pounds	Medium rare: 2 to 2¼ hours	135°
			Medium: 2½ to 2¾ hours	150°
Bone-in rib roast (chine bone removed)	350°	4 to 6 pounds (2 ribs)	Medium rare: 1¾ to 2¼ hours	135°
			Medium: 2¼ to 2½ hours	150°
		6 to 8 pounds (2 to 4 ribs)	Medium rare: 2¼ to 2½ hours	135°
			Medium: 2¾ to 3 hours	150°
		8 to 10 pounds (4 to 5 ribs)	Medium rare: 2½ to 3 hours	135°
			Medium: 3 to 3½ hours	150°
Round tip roast (sirloin tip)	325°	3 to 4 pounds	Medium rare: 1¾ to 2 hours	140°
			Medium: 2¼ to 2½ hours	155°

Beef Roast	Preheated Oven Temperature (°F)	Weight	Approximate Total Cooking Time	Remove from Oven at This Meat Temperature
Round tip roast (sirloin tip)	325°	4 to 6 pounds	Medium rare: 2 to 2½ hours	140°
			Medium: 2½ to 3 hours	155°
		6 to 8 pounds	Medium rare: 2½ to 3 hours	140°
			Medium: 3 to 3½ hours	155°
Tenderloin roast	425°	2 to 3 pounds	Medium rare: 35 to 40 minutes	135°
			Medium: 45 to 50 minutes	150°
		4 to 5 pounds	Medium rare: 50 to 60 minutes	135°
			Medium: 60 to 70 minutes	150°

Medium rare doneness: 140° to 145° final meat temperature after 10 to 15 minutes standing time
Medium doneness: 155° to 160° final meat temperature after 10 to 15 minutes standing time
Allow ¼ to ⅓ pound of uncooked boneless beef per serving and ½ to 1 pound of bone-in meat per serving, depending on the cut.
Source: National Cattlemen's Beef Association

Table 6-2	Poultry Roasting Chart		
Bird	Weight	Preheated Oven Temperature	Cooking Time
Chicken, broiler/fryer (unstuffed)	3 to 4 pounds	350°	1¼ to 1½ hours
Chicken, roaster (unstuffed)	5 to 7 pounds	350°	2 to 2¼ hours
Whole turkey (thawed and unstuffed)	8 to 12 pounds	325°	2¾ to 3 hours

(continued)

Table 6-2 (*continued*)

Bird	Weight	Preheated Oven Temperature	Cooking Time
Whole turkey (thawed and unstuffed)	12 to 14 pounds	325°	3 to 3¾ hours
	14 to 18 pounds	325°	3¾ to 4¼ hours
	18 to 20 pounds	325°	4¼ to 4½ hours
Duck (whole, unstuffed)	4 to 5½ pounds	325°	2½ to 3 hours

Depending on the size of the bird, allow 15 to 20 minutes additional cooking time if stuffed. Internal temperature for stuffing should be 165°. Internal temperature for meat should be minimum 180° in the thigh. Allow about ¾ to 1 pound of uncooked chicken or turkey on the bone per serving.
Source: National Chicken Council

The associations and companies that produce and market poultry use these roasting tables only as a rough guideline. For actual cooking times, they recommend always using a meat thermometer when cooking poultry of any kind.

Table 6-3   Pork Roasting Chart

Cut	Thickness/Weight	Final Internal Temperature	Cooking Time
Loin roast (bone-in)	3 to 5 pounds	155° to 160°	20 minutes per pound
Boneless pork roast	2 to 4 pounds	155° to 160°	20 minutes per pound
Tenderloin (roast at 425° to 450°)	½ to 1½ pounds	155° to 160°	20 to 30 minutes
Crown roast	6 to 10 pounds	155° to 160°	20 minutes per pound
Boneless loin chops	1 inch thick	155° to 160°	12 to 16 minutes
Ribs		Tender	1½ to 2 hours

Roast in a shallow pan, uncovered, at 350°.
Allow about ¼ to ⅓ pound of uncooked boneless meat per serving and about ½ to 1 pound of bone-in meat per serving, depending on the cut.
Source: National Pork Producers Council

Table 6-4		Lamb Roasting Chart	
Roast	*Weight*	*Final Internal Temperature*	*Approximate Cooking Time Per Pound*
Leg (bone-in)	5 to 7 pounds	Medium rare: 145° to 150°	15 minutes
		Medium: 155° to 160°	20 minutes
Boneless (rolled and tied)	4 to 7 pounds	Medium rare: 145° to 150°	20 minutes
		Medium: 155° to 160°	25 minutes
Sirloin roast (boneless)	about 2 pounds	Medium rare: 145° to 150°	25 minutes
		Medium: 155° to 160°	30 minutes
Top round roast	about 2 pounds	Medium rare: 145° to 150°	45 minutes
		Medium: 155° to 160°	55 minutes

Preheat oven to 325° and remove from oven about 10° below desired temperature.
Allow ¼ to ⅓ pound of boneless lamb per serving and ⅓ to ½ pound of bone-in lamb per serving.
Source: American Lamb Council

Every oven is different, no matter how much you spend for it. Some ovens are off by as much as 50 degrees, which can be like trying to make gourmet coffee with hot tap water. Baking can be a disaster without precision. Investing in an oven thermometer is worthwhile.

Don't keep opening the oven door to see whether the roast is done. Your kitchen will get hot, and the meat or vegetables will take longer to cook.

Roasting poultry

Roasting a chicken may seem challenging, but don't be intimidated. Although it's not just a matter of tossing it in the oven and mixing a gin and tonic, attention to a few details will yield a memorable result.

Eat your chicken liver

A cardinal rule of many chefs (who hate to throw out food of any kind) is to never discard the giblets. You can add giblets to homemade soup or to canned stock to enrich its flavor.

The most common mistake home cooks make when roasting chicken is using an insufficiently hot oven. The following recipe calls for a 425-degree oven, which yields a brittle, golden-brown skin.

Again, use a meat thermometer! (When you feel feverish, which would you prefer: a doctor who places a hand on your forehead or one who uses a thermometer?) Whatever the type of thermometer you use, instant-read or ovenproof (see Chapter 2 for information about the different types), insert it deep into the flesh between the bird's thigh and breast. If you don't have a thermometer, insert a knife into the thick part of the thigh; if the juices run clear, the bird is thoroughly cooked. If they run pink, let the meat cook for another 15 minutes or so before testing for doneness again. Then go buy a thermometer so that you have one next time!

Before you roast a chicken, remove the packaged giblets (the neck, heart, gizzard, and liver) inside the cavity and save them. Rinse the bird thoroughly, inside and out, under cold running water. Then pat the skin dry with paper towels and season. The following recipe uses the giblets to make a delicious pan gravy.

If you want your chicken to hold its shape perfectly while roasting, you can truss it. You can do without this step if you're in a hurry, but we'll explain the technique anyway. See Figures 6-2 and 6-3 for illustrated instructions.

Trussing a Chicken

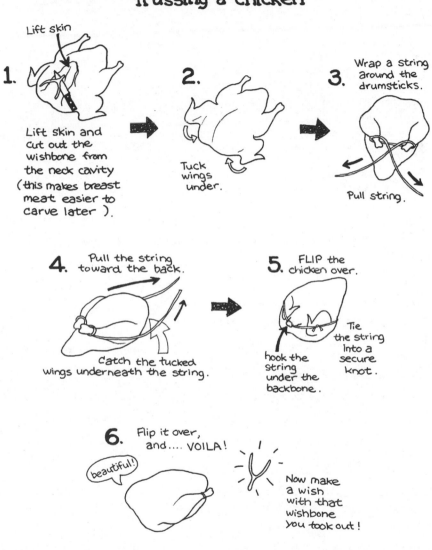

1. Lift skin

Lift skin and cut out the wishbone from the neck cavity (this makes breast meat easier to carve later).

2. Tuck wings under.

3. Wrap a string around the drumsticks.

Pull string.

4. Pull the string toward the back.

Catch the tucked wings underneath the string.

5. FLIP the chicken over.

hook the string under the backbone.

Tie the string into a secure knot.

6. Flip it over, and.... VOILA!

beautiful!

Now make a wish with that wishbone you took out!

Figure 6-2:
Trussing helps chicken keep its shape.

Even Quicker ... Truss Me!

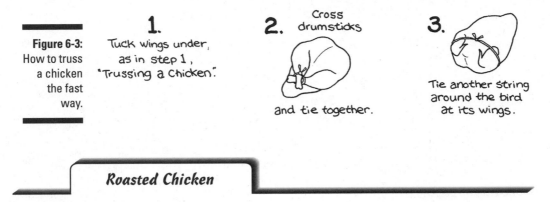

Figure 6-3:
How to truss a chicken the fast way.

1.
Tuck wings under, as in step 1, "Trussing a Chicken."

2. Cross drumsticks

and tie together.

3.
Tie another string around the bird at its wings.

Roasted Chicken

Tools: *Chef's knife, large metal roasting pan, roasting rack, meat thermometer, kitchen string (if trussing)*

Preparation time: *About 15 minutes (or 20 if trussing)*

Roasting time: *About 1 hour and 15 minutes, plus 15 minutes resting time*

Yield: *4 servings*

1 chicken, 4 to 4½ pounds, with giblets

Salt and black pepper to taste

1 lemon, pricked several times with a fork

2 sprigs fresh thyme, or ½ teaspoon dried

1 clove garlic, peeled whole

2 tablespoons olive oil

1 medium onion, quartered

½ cup homemade or canned chicken stock

½ cup water, or more as necessary

2 tablespoons butter

Parsley, rosemary, tarragon, or other fresh herbs to taste (optional)

1 Preheat the oven to 425 degrees. Remove the giblets from the chicken's cavity; rinse and reserve. Rinse the chicken under cold running water, inside and out, and pat dry with paper towels.

2 Sprinkle the chicken inside and out with salt and pepper. Insert the lemon, thyme, and garlic into the cavity of the chicken. Rub the outside of the chicken all over with olive oil.

3 Truss the chicken with string, if desired. (See Figures 6-2 and 6-3 for instructions.)

4 Place the chicken, breast side up, on a rack in a shallow metal roasting pan. Scatter the giblets and onions on the bottom of the pan.

5 Place the chicken in the oven and roast for 45 minutes.

6 Carefully remove the roasting pan from the oven and close the oven door. Using a large spoon, skim any fat from the roasting pan juices. Add the chicken stock, water, and butter to the pan. Roast for another 20 to 30 minutes.

When cooked, the chicken should be golden brown all over, and no red juice should flow when you pierce the joint between the thigh and leg with a knife. A meat thermometer in the thigh should read 180 degrees (refer to Figure 6-1) before you remove the bird from the oven. Lift up the chicken to let the cavity juices (which should be clear, not pink) flow into the pan. Transfer to a carving board or serving platter, cover with aluminum foil, and let rest for 10 to 15 minutes.

7 Meanwhile, place the roasting pan on top of the stove. Using a slotted spoon, remove and discard any pieces of giblets or onion. Add water or stock if necessary to make about 1 cup liquid. (You can pour the juices into a glass measuring cup to gauge how much liquid is in the pan.) Bring to a boil and reduce for 1 to 2 minutes (letting the sauce evaporate and condense as it cooks over high heat), stirring and scraping the bottom of the pan. If desired, add fresh parsley, rosemary, tarragon, or other fresh herbs to taste. Turn off the heat when the sauce is reduced to about ¾ cup. Strain the sauce into a gravy boat or a small bowl just before serving.

8 Untruss the chicken (if necessary), cutting the string with a sharp knife or kitchen shears. Remove and discard the lemon and thyme sprigs.

9 Carve the chicken into serving pieces, as shown in Figure 6-4, and serve with the hot pan juices.

Serve this dish with any of the following side dishes: White Beans with Tomato and Thyme, Carrots with Cumin Butter, Couscous with Yellow Squash, Homestyle Kale (all in Chapter 15), or Sautéed Cubed Potatoes (see Chapter 4).

Roasted chicken, either hot or cold, goes well with a mildly spicy mustard mayonnaise. Blend Dijon mustard to taste into ½ cup of mayonnaise. Season with salt and pepper, and freshly chopped herbs like tarragon, basil, chervil, parsley, or oregano. This is also good with cold pork, poultry, fish, and grilled meats.

Roasting your veggies

All kinds of vegetables, either alone or in combination with others, can be roasted using the simple technique here — in fact, this is so convenient for home cooks that we decided to give you two recipes, one for summer vegetables and one for winter root vegetables.

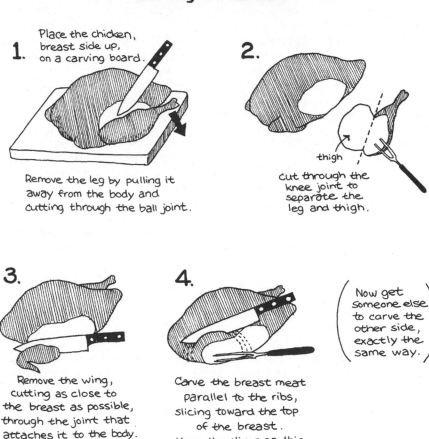

Carving a Chicken

1. Place the chicken, breast side up, on a carving board.

Remove the leg by pulling it away from the body and cutting through the ball joint.

2. thigh

Cut through the knee joint to separate the leg and thigh.

3. Remove the wing, cutting as close to the breast as possible, through the joint that attaches it to the body. (cut off the wing tips, if desired.)

4. Carve the breast meat parallel to the ribs, slicing toward the top of the breast. Keep the slices as thin as possible.

(Now get someone else to carve the other side, exactly the same way.)

Figure 6-4:
How to carve a chicken.

In the next recipe all you do is take a large roasting pan and scatter the chopped vegetables in it. Drizzle them with olive oil, toss to coat well, and season generously with salt and pepper. Then you can add any fresh or dried herbs of your choice: tarragon, rosemary, basil, marjoram, and so on. Roast the vegetables in a 400- to 425-degree oven until they are tender, turning them over in the oil every so often.

If you combine different vegetables on the same roasting pan, be sure to choose those that will cook in about the same amount of time — for example, tomatoes cook much faster than carrots. Another way to achieve even cooking is to cut the hardest vegetables (carrots, parsnips, potatoes, and so on) into smaller pieces than the soft vegetables (celery, bell peppers, eggplant, and so on).

Crispy Roasted Root Vegetables

Tools: *Vegetable peeler, chef's knife, large mixing bowl, baking dish*

Preparation time: *About 10 minutes*

Cooking time: *About 25 minutes*

Yield: *4 servings*

4 medium carrots, washed (skins on), halved, and chopped crosswise into about 4 pieces

2 red or yellow bell peppers, cored, seeded, and sliced into ½-inch strips

3 medium red potatoes, quartered

3 small turnips, peeled and quartered

2 medium onions, quartered

2 small bulbs fennel, trimmed and quartered

1 tablespoon minced fresh rosemary, or ½ tablespoon dried

¼ cup olive oil

Salt and black pepper to taste

1 Preheat the oven to 400 degrees.

2 Place the vegetables and rosemary in a large mixing bowl. Pour the olive oil over them. Season generously with salt and pepper. Toss well to blend. Transfer to a roasting pan that can hold them in one layer. Place the pan in the oven and roast for 25 to 30 minutes, turning the vegetables several times. (If after 25 minutes the vegetables are tender but not browned, place them under the broiler for a minute or two — but don't let them burn).

These vegetables go well with all sorts of roasted meats, like Roasted Fillet of Beef and Roasted Chicken, both in this chapter.

Summer vegetables release quite a bit of water when roasted. To get them brown and crisp, be sure to place them on the lowest oven rack, close to the heating element. You may also sprinkle a little brown sugar over the vegetables; this brings out their natural sweetness and counterbalances the tastes of fresh ginger, garlic, and hot pepper.

If you have any leftovers, serve them as a side dish the next day with sandwiches, or roll them in soft flour tortillas, maybe with some lettuce and hot sauce; they also are great over pasta with a little grated Parmesan cheese.

Roasted Summer Vegetables

Tools: *Vegetable peeler, chef's knife, spatula or wooden spoon*

Preparation time: *About 15 minutes*

Cooking time: *About 25 minutes*

Yield: *4 servings*

3 medium carrots, peeled and cut into ¼-inch slices

2 to 3 tablespoons olive oil

1 red or yellow bell pepper, cored, seeded, and cut into ½-inch cubes

1 small zucchini, halved lengthwise and cut into ½-inch-thick slices

1 small yellow squash, halved lengthwise and cut into ½-inch-thick semi-round slices

½ pound asparagus, trimmed of thick stems, cut diagonally into 1-inch pieces

1 small red onion, chopped into ⅛-inch cubes

1 large clove garlic, chopped

½ to 1 jalapeño pepper or small red chili pepper (according to taste), seeded and minced

1 tablespoon chopped fresh basil, marjoram, or thyme (or 1 teaspoon dried)

2 teaspoons peeled and minced fresh ginger

1 teaspoon brown sugar (optional)

Salt and black pepper to taste

1 Preheat the oven to 425 degrees.

2 Scatter the carrots over a large roasting pan. Drizzle them with 1 tablespoon of the olive oil; toss to coat. Place the pan on the oven rack closest to the heating element, and roast for 10 minutes.

3 Take the pan from the oven and add the bell pepper, zucchini, squash, asparagus, onion, garlic, and jalapeño. Sprinkle with the herbs, ginger, brown sugar (if desired), salt, and pepper; drizzle the remaining 1 to 2 tablespoons of olive oil over the vegetables, using only enough to lightly coat them. Toss well, spreading the vegetables out in a single layer.

4 Return the roasting pan to the oven and roast about 20 to 25 minutes, or until tender, turning once with a spatula or wooden spoon after 15 minutes so the vegetables brown evenly. If after 25 minutes the vegetables are tender but not browned, place them under the broiler for a minute or two — but watch carefully that they don't burn.

Serve these vegetables, hot or cold, with Grilled Swordfish Steaks with Lemon and Thyme or The Perfect Hamburger, both in this chapter.

The big guns: Beef, pork, and lamb

Americans have two immutable love affairs: automobiles and meat. And little the government says about them seems to change that.

In the past decade, the American pork industry has made great strides in breeding leaner animals without sacrificing tenderness. What's more, pork remains a relative bargain. You can assemble this uncomplicated dish in about half an hour and then pop it in the oven.

Roast Loin of Pork

Tools: *Chef's knife, vegetable peeler, large roasting pan, meat thermometer*

Preparation time: *About 25 minutes*

Roasting time: *About 1 hour and 5 minutes, plus 15 minutes resting time*

Yield: *6 servings*

Center-cut boneless loin of pork, about 3 pounds

4 tablespoons olive oil

2 tablespoons chopped fresh thyme, or 1 teaspoon dried

Salt and black pepper to taste

6 medium red potatoes, peeled and halved lengthwise

3 medium onions, peeled and quartered

4 carrots, peeled and cut into 2-inch pieces

1 bay leaf

2 large cloves garlic, finely chopped

½ cup water

¼ cup chopped fresh parsley

2 cups applesauce (optional)

1 Preheat the oven to 400 degrees.

2 Place the pork in a large roasting pan (without a rack) and brush or rub the meat all over with 3 tablespoons of the oil. Season with the thyme, salt, and pepper. Roast, fat side up, for 15 minutes.

3 Remove the pan from the oven and scatter the potatoes, onions, carrots, and bay leaf around the roast. Drizzle the remaining 1 tablespoon of oil over the vegetables, and, using a large spoon, turn the vegetables in the cooking juices. Sprinkle the garlic over the vegetables, and season the vegetables with salt and pepper. Add the water to the pan.

4 Reduce the oven temperature to 350 degrees and roast for 45 to 50 minutes or until a meat thermometer registers 155 degrees in the thickest part of the roast.

(continued)

5 Remove the pan from the oven, and transfer the roast to a cutting board. Cover with aluminum foil and let rest for 15 minutes before carving. Reduce the oven temperature to 300 degrees and place the pan with the vegetables in the oven to keep warm.

6 To serve, transfer the carved meat and vegetables to a large platter. (Pour any juices that have collected around the meat into the roasting pan.) Remove the bay leaf from the pan, and place the pan over two burners on high. Bring the juices to a boil, stirring and scraping the bottom and sides of the pan with a wooden spoon. Cook about 1 to 2 minutes or until the sauce is reduced and slightly thickened. Pour the juices over everything, sprinkle with the chopped parsley, and, if desired, serve with applesauce.

This hearty dish is delicious with winter vegetables like Homestyle Kale (see Chapter 15) or Sautéed Spinach Leaves (see Chapter 4), or a simple salad of mixed greens (see Chapter 10).

Roasted pork tenderloin is great with a fillip of sweetness, in this case apples. Another way to sweeten it is by applying a simple glaze toward the end of cooking: apricot jam, ginger marmalade, or even brown sugar melted with orange juice.

Use an ovenproof casserole that can go from stovetop to oven.

Pork Tenderloin with Potatoes and Apples

Tools: *Vegetable peeler, pot, large pan, chef's knife, meat thermometer*

Preparation time: *20 minutes*

Cooking time: *About 40 minutes*

Yield: *4 to 6 servings*

8 small red potatoes, about 1 pound

2 or 3 boneless pork tenderloins, 1½ to 2 pounds total

Salt and black pepper to taste

4 tablespoons olive oil

2 teaspoons minced fresh rosemary, or 1 teaspoon dried

2 medium onions, cut into 4 equal pieces

2 Golden Delicious (or Granny Smith) apples

½ cup homemade or canned chicken stock

2 tablespoons finely chopped parsley

1 Preheat the oven to 450 degrees.

2 Peel the potatoes and put them in a pot with cold salted water to cover. Bring to a boil and cook until just tender, about 10 minutes. Remove the potatoes from the water and set aside.

3 Sprinkle the tenderloins generously with salt and pepper. Put 3 tablespoons of the olive oil in a metal roasting pan large enough to hold the tenderloins in one layer. Sprinkle with rosemary and turn the pork in the mixture to coat it all over. (You can let it marinate for several hours, refrigerated, until needed. Bring to room temperature before cooking.)

4 Place the roasting pan on top of the stove until very hot. Brown the pork over high heat, turning to sear it all over. Remove from heat. Arrange the onions, cut side down, around the pork, and the potatoes. (If you don't have a pan that is large enough, place the vegetables in a separate roasting pan.) Season the onions with the remaining olive oil, salt, and pepper. Place everything in the oven and roast for about 20 minutes, turning once. Check the meat by slicing into the middle — it should be pinkish in the center, or 155 degrees on a meat thermometer. Meanwhile, core and peel the apples; cut each into 8 wedges. When the roast has cooked for 15 minutes add the apples.

5 Remove the meat to a cutting board and cover with foil. Remove the vegetables and apples to a large serving platter and cover with foil as well. Add the broth to the meat pan. Stir, scraping up any particles on the bottom of the pan, and bring to a boil; reduce for about 3 minutes, stirring. Remove the pan from the heat. Cut the pork crosswise on a bias into thin slices. Transfer the slices to the platter with the apples and vegetables; spoon the pan sauce over the meat. Serve sprinkled with chopped parsley.

This dish is great with Garlic-Grilled Mushrooms (in this chapter), White Beans with Tomato and Thyme (see Chapter 15), or Baby Carrots in Cumin Butter (see Chapter 15).

 If you have leftover roasted vegetables, use them the next day in a salad, rolled in a tortilla with hot sauce, or in an omelet. If you want to make them crisp again, before serving, place them in a 400-degree oven for about 5 minutes.

 If you are roasting a side of beef or a chicken, scatter a variety of root vegetables (such as cut up carrots, onions, and peeled potatoes) in the roasting pan. Turn them every so often in the pan drippings so they cook evenly. This makes for a great presentation at the table — that is, if you don't eat them all in the kitchen.

Pork paranoia

Cooks used to believe that if you ate pork cooked under 185 degrees, you could contract *trichinosis*. The average person didn't know what that was — or how many days of school kids could miss because of it — but it sure sounded unpleasant. Thus, for years, everyone ate overcooked pork. About a decade ago, scientists discovered that harmful trichinae are killed at 135 degrees. Cooking pork to 155 degrees is considered plenty safe and yields a much juicier result than the 185 degrees of the past.

Concerning pork or other meats, good butchers are also knowledgeable cooks. They can offer recipes, tips, and information on preparing your roast so that it is "oven-ready." An oven-ready roast is trimmed of excess fat and sometimes tied with butcher's string to make it as uniform as possible for even cooking. For example, a leg of lamb should have its fat and shank bone removed. The skin and rind of a smoked ham are trimmed away, leaving just a thin layer of fat that you can score to make a diamond pattern on the meat's surface for a pretty effect.

Following is a basic recipe for leg of lamb. Feel free to add vegetables such as carrots, onions, and potatoes to the pan during the last hour of cooking.

Glazed Leg of Lamb with Pan Gravy and Red Currant Glaze

Tools: *Paring knife, roasting pan, roasting rack, basting brush, meat thermometer, small saucepan*

Preparation time: *About 15 minutes for the lamb, about 5 minutes for the glaze*

Roasting time: *About 1 hour and 40 minutes, plus 20 minutes resting time*

Yield: *8 to 10 servings*

One 6- to 7-pound leg of lamb, well trimmed and ready for roasting

3 cloves garlic, thinly sliced

1 tablespoon vegetable oil

½ teaspoon ground ginger

Salt and black pepper to taste

¼ cup red currant jelly

Juice and grated peel of ½ lemon

1½ teaspoons Dijon-style mustard

1 Preheat the oven to 425 degrees.

2 With a paring knife, make small incisions along the leg and then insert the garlic slivers into the incisions.

3 Rub the lamb with the olive oil and place it on a rack in a shallow roasting pan, fat side up. Sprinkle the meat with the ginger, salt, and pepper.

4 Roast the lamb for 20 minutes; reduce heat to 350 degrees and roast for an additional 1 hour and 20 minutes or until a meat thermometer registers 145 degrees in the thickest part of the leg for medium rare or 155 degrees for medium. (See the What If icon following this recipe for more information.) As the lamb roasts, make the Red Currant Glaze.

5 During the last 30 minutes of roasting, brush the top and sides of the lamb every 10 minutes with Red Currant Glaze and pan juices. (Start brushing when meat thermometer in lamb registers about 115 degrees.)

6 Remove from the oven, cover with foil, and let rest for 20 minutes. Carve (see Figure 6-5) and serve with some natural pan juices spooned over the top of the slices.

Red Currant Glaze

Combine all ingredients in a small saucepan and heat until jelly is melted (about 1 minute). Use as a basting sauce for a leg of lamb, brushing every 10 minutes during the last 30 minutes of roasting.

Serve with Crispy Roasted Root Vegetables (earlier in this chapter) and a tossed green salad (see Chapter 10). Or try serving it with a rich dish like Creamed Spinach (see Chapter 7).

If you enjoy your lamb cooked medium to well, just roast it a little longer until the internal temperature reaches 155 or 160 degrees or more. But you may not need to. A roasted leg of lamb offers meat of varying degrees of doneness. The meat at the thin, shank end, very close to the bone, is browned and well done, and the meat at the thicker end ideally is quite pink and medium rare. Use the drier meats for hash or to train your dog to separate the sports section of the newspaper and bring it to you.

Carving a Leg of Lamb

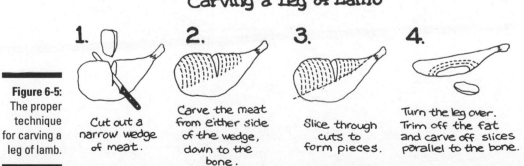

Figure 6-5: The proper technique for carving a leg of lamb.

1. Cut out a narrow wedge of meat.

2. Carve the meat from either side of the wedge, down to the bone.

3. Slice through cuts to form pieces.

4. Turn the leg over. Trim off the fat and carve off slices parallel to the bone.

If you're lucky, a whole leg of lamb will leave you with delicious leftovers. You can make cold lamb sandwiches, Shepherd's Pie (see Chapter 12), or Lamb Barley Soup (see Chapter 9). Or turn to Chapter 17 for a delicious Lamb Curry recipe using leftover cooked lamb.

The following savory dish, although on the pricey side, is fast, simple and always delicious — a real last-minute party saver. Serve it with simple dishes like garlic-flavored mashed potatoes and fresh-steamed asparagus (see Chapter 3).

Roasted Fillet of Beef

Tools: *Roasting rack, roasting pan, meat thermometer*

Preparation time: *About 10 minutes*

Roasting time: *About 45 minutes, plus 10 minutes resting time*

Yield: *6 to 8 servings*

1 beef tenderloin roast, oven-ready from the butcher, about 4 pounds

Salt and black pepper to taste

2 tablespoons vegetable oil

Herb butter (optional)

1 Preheat the oven to 425 degrees.

2 Sprinkle the fillet of beef with salt and pepper to taste.

3 Place the meat on a rack in a heavy roasting pan and brush or rub it with the oil. Roast for about 45 minutes for medium rare or until desired doneness. A meat thermometer should read 135 to 140 degrees for medium rare and 150 to 155 degrees for medium. Halfway through the roasting time, invert the meat and baste once with the pan juices.

4 Transfer to a carving board, cover with aluminum foil, and let stand for 10 minutes before carving.

5 Carve the fillet into approximately ½-inch-thick slices and serve immediately, perhaps topped with a pat of herb butter. (See Chapter 7.)

You can serve tenderloin with almost anything, from a simple avocado and tomato salad to Couscous with Yellow Squash (see Chapter 15).

WHAT IF?

You overcooked the roast beef

Unfortunately, ovens do not have reverse gears. But you can salvage overcooked roast beef in many tasty ways. You can always make roast beef hash or beef pot pie. Various soups. Beef Stroganoff. Any recipe that calls for liquid or a cream-based sauce is good, too.

For centuries, prime rib of beef has been an icon of prosperity and refined taste. Regal, thick-ribbed, and rosy, this cut of beef is one of the most elegant to prepare. A 6-pound, 3-rib roast will be medium rare in the center and medium well on the outside — and someone always grabs for those pieces. A skilled and organized cook can easily handle making all the wonderful elements of this recipe. However, if this is your first rib-roasting experience, you may want to skip the pudding with its many last-minute steps. The roast is also exquisite served simply with pan gravy.

Standing Rib Roast of Beef with Pan Gravy and Yorkshire Pudding

Tools: Chef's knife, shallow roasting pan, meat thermometer, large measuring cup, mixing bowl, wire whisk, 9-inch baking pan

Preparation time: 20 minutes

Cooking time: About 3 hours and 25 minutes

Yield: 6 servings

1 beef rib roast, 5 to 6 pounds (3 ribs), trimmed of excess fat (see Toque Tip following this recipe)

3 large cloves garlic, peeled and minced

Salt and black pepper to taste

Roast beef pan drippings

½ cup red wine

1¼ cups homemade or canned beef stock

2 tablespoons plus 1 cup flour

1 tablespoon chopped fresh parsley or thyme

2 eggs

1 cup milk

½ teaspoon salt

1 Preheat the oven to 350 degrees. Place the roast, fat-side up, in a large, shallow roasting pan. (Do not place the meat on a rack or add any liquid to the pan.) Smear minced garlic onto the top and sides of the meat, and sprinkle generously with salt and pepper.

(continued)

2 Place the roast in the oven and cook for about 20 minutes per pound, or until an instant-read meat thermometer inserted into the center reaches 130 to 135 degrees (medium rare) or 140 to 145 degrees for medium. The temperature will rise another 5 to 10 degrees as the roast rests.

3 Remove the meat from the oven, set it on a large cutting board, leaving the drippings in the pan, and cover the meat loosely with aluminum foil. Let rest 20 minutes before carving. Prepare the gravy while letting the meat rest.

Pan Gravy

1 Pour the pan drippings into a large measuring cup. Skim 4 to 5 tablespoons fat from the drippings into a small bowl; skim and discard the remaining fat from the drippings.

2 Add the wine and ½ cup of the broth to the roasting pan; place the pan over medium heat (over both burners, if you can), and stir the mixture, scraping the bottom of the pan to loosen any browned bits. Pour the mixture into the measuring cup; add ¾ cup stock and set aside.

3 Add 2 tablespoons of the reserved fat to the roasting pan (if making the Yorkshire Pudding, reserve the remaining 2 to 3 tablespoons fat). Sprinkle in 2 tablespoons of flour, stirring until well blended. Cook over medium heat, stirring constantly until the flour turns golden. Slowly stir in the wine-broth mixture; cook over medium-high heat, stirring, until the gravy boils and thickens slightly. If the gravy is too thick, stir in a little more wine, water, or broth. Taste for seasoning.

4 Carve the roast (see Figure 6-6 for illustrated instructions). Ladle over slices of the carved roast, on warm serving plates, and garnish with chopped fresh parsley or thyme.

Yorkshire Pudding

This famous English roast beef side dish, which uses some of the roast's delicious pan drippings, is not actually a pudding at all, but rather a large popover. This is one of those dishes that requires a few last-minute preparation steps to get it just right. If you want to try it, the ideal time to bake the pudding is when the roast is resting for 15 minutes or so, and right before you've made the gravy. The batter can be made and chilled 4 to 5 hours ahead of roasting time — but let it rest about 20 minutes at room temperature before baking. An ideal pudding is crusty on its edges, puffed and somewhat soft and custardy in its center. Don't be tempted to open the oven door and peek at the pudding's progress, because doing so could cause it to deflate.

1 In a medium mixing bowl, whisk the eggs until they are light and foamy; add the milk and whisk well to combine. Add 1 cup of flour and the salt and pepper and whisk just to combine. The batter should be a little lumpy. (This batter may be made up to 4 to 5 hours in advance and refrigerated. Before using, let it rest for about 20 minutes to bring it to room temperature.)

2 About 10 minutes before the roast is done, preheat a 9-inch-square baking pan by placing it on a rack in the oven, above or below the roast; immediately after removing the roast, increase the oven heat to 450 degrees.

3 Place 2 to 3 tablespoons of the reserved warm roast beef drippings in the preheated pan; slowly pour the batter over the drippings. Bake on the center rack of the oven for 15 minutes. Reduce the temperature to 350 degrees and continue baking until the pudding has risen and is golden brown around the edges — about 10 minutes more. (The pudding will rise up the sides of the pan and puff up in the center). To serve, cut into squares and serve immediately with the meat and gravy. Don't worry, the pudding will deflate like a grounded hot air balloon — but it will still taste great.

 To serve roasted potatoes with the beef, peel and quarter 2½ pounds of baking potatoes. The chunks should be about 2 inches wide and fairly uniform to ensure even roasting. Remove the roast from the oven after 1 hour and 10 minutes; scatter the potatoes around the roast in the bottom of the pan; turn them over in the fat to coat all sides. Return to the oven and roast a total of 50 minutes, turning once after 25 minutes (depending on the size of the roast it may need to continue cooking). Transfer the potatoes to an ovenproof serving dish, covered with aluminum foil; keep warm in the oven until ready to serve.

 The most flavorful and tender rib roasts come from the small end, which some butchers identify as the 12th through 9th ribs, or "first cut." Ask your butcher for this. Have it trimmed and cut to order, which means the butcher removes the short ribs (if not already removed) and the shinbone. (Short ribs are delicious braised or roasted separately in a seasoned tomato sauce.) The chine bone is removed to make carving the roast easier. The butcher can also partly separate the ribs to ease carving — once loosened they should be tied back together with twine for roasting.

 Nothing is more embarrassing than running out of food at a dinner party — well, having the dog drag it onto the floor comes close. Always calculate before you start cooking. For example, the serving guideline for a rib roast is one rib for every 2 people; to feed 6 you'll need three ribs, weighing about 6 pounds total.

To avoid overcooking, take the roast out of the oven when it reaches about 5 to 10 degrees below the desired temperature. The internal temperature rises most rapidly at the end of roasting. Check the temperature frequently during the last 30 minutes to avoid overcooking.

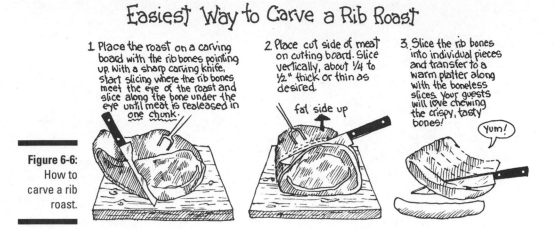

Figure 6-6:
How to
carve a rib
roast.

If you overestimated the cooking time and the roast is cooking so fast that it will be done before your dinner guests arrive, reduce the oven temperature to 325 degrees to slow down and extend the cooking time a bit. A large, uncarved roast, loosely covered with foil, will hold onto its internal heat for up to 45 minutes after it's removed from the oven.

Don't make the critical mistake of thinking that a large, 10-pound roast needs twice as much time to cook as a roast half its size. Larger roasts cook in fewer minutes per pound than smaller roasts. For example, a 5-pound rib roast may need 20 minutes per pound to reach medium rare, while a 10-pound roast will require only about 15 minutes per pound to attain that same degree of doneness. Our best advice is to rely on your meat thermometer to test accurately for doneness, and to use the minutes per pound rule only as a guideline.

If you slightly overcook the prime rib, or have pieces of well-done meat leftover, use it to make a terrific hash. Here is a quick recipe: Place about 1½ pounds of chopped (bite-sized) cold roast beef in a large mixing bowl. Peel two medium baking potatoes, cut them into ¼-inch cubes, and set aside. Add to the bowl one minced onion; 1 cored, seeded, and diced green bell pepper; ½ cup homemade or canned beef stock; ¼ cup tomato paste; and lots of salt and black pepper. Mix well; if it appears a little dry, add some more beef stock. Pour about a tablespoon of olive oil in a skillet (preferably nonstick), over medium heat. Sauté the potatoes, stirring with a wooden spoon, for 3 to 5 minutes, or until barely cooked through. Add the rest of the hash ingredients to the potatoes and stir to combine. Cook until the hash is thoroughly hot and the green peppers are soft. Continue cooking until crispy on the bottom. Serve the hash on a warm platter.

A Sunday dinner winner

A *round tip roast,* also referred to as a *sirloin tip roast,* is leaner and less tender than a roasted prime rib. However, it is very economical, and, if cooked properly, makes a great family dinner.

To serve 6 people, purchase a 3- to 4-pound sirloin tip roast. Rub it with fresh chopped garlic, a little olive oil, salt, pepper, and your favorite herbs. Place it on a rack in a shallow roasting pan in a preheated 325-degree oven. Cook until a meat thermometer inserted into the center of the roast registers 140 degrees for medium-rare; 150 degrees for medium. Remember that a resting roast continues cooking, adding about 5 degrees on a meat thermometer. A 3- to 4-pound roast will cook to medium-rare in between 1¾ and 2 hours and to medium in between 2¼ and 2½ hours.

Remove the roast from the oven and let stand, loosely covered with foil, for 15 minutes before carving.

Ham it up

Hams have more identities than an international spy. Sorting it all out is not terribly complicated, however. Remember that all hams are cured (which means seasoned and aged), and some are also smoked. The two most common methods of preparing a ham are *dry curing* and *wet curing.* In the dry method, a ham is rubbed with salt and seasonings and hung in a cool, dry place to age, anywhere from a few weeks to a year or more. Wet cured hams are soaked in brine, or injected with brine, to give them more flavor.

Here is a primer on some other terms for hams.

- **Country ham:** This is a dry cured ham that is smoked, salted, and then aged for at least 6 months.

- **Sugar-cured ham:** This is a ham that is rubbed with salt and brown sugar or molasses before aging.

- **Canned ham:** Cured but not always smoked, these cooked hams are ready to eat. A little cooking, though, improves the flavor.

- **Fully cooked hams:** These are the same as "ready-to-eat" hams. You can eat them without cooking.

- **Aged ham:** These are heavily cured and smoked hams that have been dry-aged at least one year.

- **Half ham:** These come from the shank bone, butt, or ham end. The shank portion is best and easiest to deal with.

- **Bayonne ham:** A dry-cured ham from the Basque country of France, specifically the city of Bayonne.

- ✔ **Prosciutto:** Strictly speaking, this is ham from Parma, Italy. It is seasoned, salt cured, air dried and pressed to make the meat very firm. It is usually eaten in very thin slices over bread.

- ✔ **Westphalian ham:** A rosy, sweetish, German ham made from hogs that are fed sugar beet mash. It is usually eaten like prosciutto.

- ✔ **Smithfield ham:** The pride of Smithfield, Virginia, this salty, wonderfully flavorful ham is seasoned, smoked, and hung for at least a year.

- ✔ **Virginia ham:** Another salty, dry-cured ham; it is made from hogs that eat peanuts, acorns, and other high-protein foods.

The term "scoring" has nothing to do with a long pass into the end zone; rather, it means making small incisions all around a piece of meat or fish (see Figure 6-7 for an illustration). The purpose is to let marinades, basting sauces, or glazes penetrate food. It is best done with a sharp paring knife or chef's knife.

Figure 6-7:
How to
score a
ham.

Sweet little piggies

Baked hams — more accurately called "roasted hams" — are often brushed with a sweet marmalade or other glaze that counterbalances the saltiness of the meat. The thick skin, or rind, is first cut away to expose a thin layer of fat. This fat can be trimmed then scored and studded with whole cloves for a pretty effect. The glaze is applied during the last 30 minutes of baking, or when the ham has reached an internal temperature of 120 degrees; if applied sooner, the glaze could burn. Glazes can be mixtures of all sorts of flavors: jams, brown sugar, molasses, corn syrup, mustard, cinnamon, cloves, ginger, whiskey, rum, orange juice, port, or white wine. Some producers douse the ham with Coca-Cola to produce a syrupy coating — no kidding.

In the next recipe in this chapter, the ham is brushed with an apricot-and-mustard glaze and then served with a pan sauce made from the luscious drippings.

TIP

Skimming the fat from gravies and sauces is very important, from both a flavor and health standpoint. There are many ways to skim. You can pour the juices into a wide glass and refrigerate — fat solidifies on the surface so it is easy to remove. When you don't have time do that, you can pour the liquid into a wide container and skim the fat layer with a spoon. The easiest way is to use a *skimmer* (see Figure 6-8), which resembles a measuring cup with a spout coming out of the bottom. Because fat floats to the surface, the clear liquid comes out first.

fat skimmer

2 cups

FAT

Figure 6-8:
A fat
skimmer.

Smoked Ham with Apricot Glaze

Tools: *Roasting pan, chef's knife, meat thermometer, brush for applying glaze, gravy skimmer (optional), fine strainer, wooden spatula*

Preparation time: *20 minutes*

Cooking time: *About 2 hours and 15 minutes*

Yield: *12 to 14 servings*

½ of a smoked cooked ham, bone-in (7 to 9 pounds)

About 30 whole cloves (optional)

About 1 cup water

½ cup apricot preserves or orange marmalade

2 tablespoons Dijon-style mustard

1 tablespoon dark rum (optional)

Black pepper to taste

1 cup homemade or canned chicken stock

1 Preheat the oven to 325 degrees. Remove the rind from the ham with a sharp knife, and discard. It should have a thin layer of fat underneath.

2 Using a sharp knife, score the meat by making small cuts in the fat all over the ham — this helps the glaze penetrate the meat. (If you want to add a decorative effect, insert a clove into the center of each diamond cut.) Place the ham in a heavy roasting pan; add ½ cup of water to the pan and bake until a meat thermometer inserted into the center registers 120 degrees — about 1½ to 2 hours. (Add an additional ½ cup of water to the roasting pan if it gets dry.)

3 Meanwhile, prepare the glaze. In a small pan, heat the apricot preserves over low heat; mash any large pieces of fruit with a fork. Stir in the mustard and, if desired, 1 tablespoon rum. Season with pepper. Boil, stirring occasionally, until the mixture thickens enough to coat a spoon, about 3 minutes.

4 When the ham reaches an internal temperature of 120 degrees, increase the oven temperature to 400 degrees. Pull out the ham and brush or spoon the glaze all over. Return the ham to the oven and bake for another 20 to 25 minutes, or until a thermometer inserted in the center registers 140 degrees (be careful not to burn the glaze). Place the ham on a large carving board; cover with foil and let rest 15 minutes.

5 While the ham rests, prepare the pan sauce. Pour the juices from the roasting pan into a small shallow bowl. Tilt the bowl and skim the fat that accumulates on the surface with a spoon (or use a skimmer, as shown in Figure 6-8). Return the skimmed juices to the pan and place it over a burner on high heat; add the chicken stock. Cook, stirring and scraping up browned bits on the bottom of the pan (a wooden spoon or spatula will not scratch your pan), until the liquid is reduced and slightly thickened. Pass the sauce through a fine strainer before serving with the ham.

6 Thinly slice the ham (see Figure 6-9); serve with pan juices and, if desired, a good mustard.

Ham always goes well with dishes like Braised Cabbage with Apple and Caraway (see Chapter 16), Homestyle Kale (see Chapter 15), and Basic Wild Rice (see Chapter 3).

 You can flavor a ham's pan sauce in many ways. Try adding 2 to 3 tablespoons of dark raisins, 2 tablespoons of dark rum, or some dry white wine or apple cider. Grated orange zest and freshly squeezed orange juice also give the sauce a clean, citric edge.

 To carve a ham, follow the steps in Figure 6-9.

How to Carve a Ham

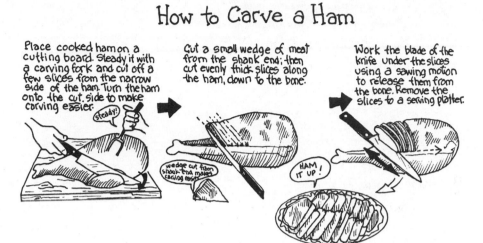

Place cooked ham on a cutting board. Steady it with a carving fork and cut off a few slices from the narrow side of the ham. Turn the ham onto the cut side to make carving easier.

Cut a small wedge of meat from the shank end; then cut evenly thick slices along the ham, down to the bone.

Work the blade of the knife under the slices using a sawing motion to release them from the bone. Remove the slices to a serving platter.

Figure 6-9:
How to carve a ham.

The best way to tenderize spareribs is to cook them slowly in a covered gas or charcoal grill over hickory chunks. The ribs should be cooked indirectly, which means that they should be placed just to the side of the fire and not directly above it (see *Grilling For Dummies* by Marie Rama and John Mariani, published by IDG Books Worldwide, Inc.), for a complete explanation).

Whether done over a grill or in an oven, ribs need long, slow cooking. Some recipes call for parboiling ribs before roasting or grilling, but we have found that a lot of the flavor winds up in the cooking water when you do it this way. The best alternative we've found is roasting spareribs in a 300-degree oven for 2 hours, which leaves them succulent and flavorful.

Ribs are delicious when rubbed with spices before cooking. The recipe here calls for brown sugar, salt, and pepper. A sweet element always give the ribs a seductive flavor; the other ingredients can vary according to your taste. If you like them spicy, add some cayenne pepper to the mix. Other seasonings you could experiment with include sweet paprika, onion powder, garlic powder, ground cumin, ground coriander, cinnamon, dried thyme, and dried basil.

This dish is great for casual entertaining. Just be sure to have lots of moist towels around.

Roasted Pork Ribs with Country Barbecue Sauce

Tools: *Chef's knife, roasting pan, basting brush*

Preparation time: *10 minutes, plus 30 minutes refrigeration*

Cooking time: *About 2 hours and 30 minutes*

Yield: *4 servings*

1 tablespoon brown sugar, packed	*⅔ cup ketchup*
1½ teaspoons salt, or to taste	*½ cup dark brown sugar, packed*
1 teaspoon black pepper, or to taste	*6 tablespoons cider vinegar*
3 to 4 pounds pork spareribs	*1 tablespoon Worcestershire sauce*
2 tablespoons vegetable oil	*1 tablespoon molasses*
1 small onion, minced	*l teaspoon ground cumin*
2 cloves garlic, minced	*Salt and black pepper to taste*
¾ cup water	

1 Preheat oven to 300 degrees. Combine the brown sugar, 1½ teaspoons salt, and 1 teaspoon pepper in a small bowl. Stir well. Trim excess fat from the ribs. Place them on a cutting board. Cut the slabs into pieces of one to two ribs each.

2 Arrange the spareribs in one layer on a roasting pan. Sprinkle the ribs with the spice rub, pressing the seasonings firmly onto the meat all around. Cover loosely and refrigerate about 30 minutes.

3 Roast in oven for 1½ hours, turning them over after 45 minutes. (While the ribs cook, make the barbecue sauce.)

4 Increase oven temperature to 350 degrees. Remove the roasting pan from the oven; carefully pour off all the fat (or transfer ribs to a clean roasting pan). Brush the ribs generously on all sides with the barbecue sauce and roast another 25 to 30 minutes, or until the meat is so tender it easily "wiggles" or pulls away from the bone. Serve the ribs with extra sauce on the side.

Country Barbecue Sauce

This sauce also works exceptionally well with barbecued chicken and beef.

1 Heat the oil in a saucepan over medium heat. Add the onion and cook, stirring often, until it starts to wilt; add the garlic and continue cooking and stirring for about 1 minute longer.

2 Add the water, ketchup, brown sugar, cider vinegar, Worcestershire sauce, molasses, cumin, salt, and pepper, and stir well. Increase the heat to high and bring to a boil. Reduce the heat and simmer 25 to 30 minutes or until thickened, stirring occasionally. (The sauce may be prepared a day or two in advance, refrigerated, and reheated before using.)

These succulent ribs are great with Roasted Winter Vegetables (see the recipe earlier in this chapter), White Beans with Tomato and Thyme (see Chapter 15), or with any of the side dishes in Chapter 18.

 As pork ribs cook they leave a good amount of fat in the roasting pan. This fat should be carefully poured off and discarded before the ribs are brushed with barbecue sauce. Never pour hot fat down the sink drain or into a garbage disposal where it could clog the lines. Pour it into an empty soup or coffee can, let it cool and harden, and then throw it out.

Coals and Coils: Grilling and Broiling

An interesting thing about cooking is that a single food can be exposed to various cooking techniques and take on different characteristics. This difference is most dramatically seen in charcoal grilling and oven broiling, which impart very different flavors to foods than roasting does.

Here are a few axioms of outdoor grilling:

- ✔ The fire is always at its peak 15 minutes after you finish cooking the food.

- ✔ If you overhear the cook say, "No problem, I'll just dust it off," it's time to visit the salad bowl.

- ✔ The chances of getting good food at a home barbecue are in inverse proportion to the silliness of the chef's apron. If the apron is plain and solid in color, you have reason for hope; if it says, "Who Needs Mom?" or "Dog Catcher," hit the onion dip fast.

- ✔ Barbecues benefit from the "Hot dogs taste better at the ballpark" syndrome. That is, ambience makes everything taste better.

Wolfgang Puck, owner and chef of Spago in Los Angeles, and a preeminent authority on the subject of grilling, says, "Just about anything can be grilled, and it's probably a more healthy way to cook because the food isn't swimming in oil. But it doesn't have to be steak or hamburgers. It can be a simple grilled olive bread, drizzled with oil, or grilled vegetables — even pieces of cornbread can be toasted on the grill. Americans think of grilling as BBQ or spicy, southwestern foods — but you can grill even the most refined piece of fish for wonderful flavor."

The terms *barbecuing* and *grilling* are often incorrectly interchanged. Grilling, like broiling, is a quick technique that cooks relatively small, tender pieces of food (such as chicken breasts, pork kebobs, or skewered shrimp) directly over the heat source. Barbecuing is more like oven roasting and almost the opposite of grilling. With barbecuing, larger cuts of meat (such as spare ribs, pork butts, or whole turkeys) are slowly roasted over an indirect fire, in a covered grill, sometimes for hours, until the food is very tender and succulent. To make an indirect fire, the coals are moved to one side of the grill in the fire box. (On a gas grill, only one side of the grill is heated.) The food is cooked opposite the fire and covered, to trap the heat and smoke. This chapter focuses on grilling only. For barbecuing information, tips, and recipes, check out *Grilling For Dummies,* by Marie Rama and John Mariani (published by IDG Books).

If you can grill, you can broil

Loosely speaking, the terms *grilling* and *broiling* are interchangeable. In grilling, which is done on a barbecue grill, the heat source is below; in oven broiling, it's above. Because both methods involve intense heat, they are best reserved for relatively thin pieces of meat, poultry, or vegetables — thick cuts of meat can burn on the outside before cooking sufficiently in the middle. The advantage of grilling or broiling is that the surface of the food being cooked, especially meat, turns dark brown and develops a characteristic "charcoal" flavor.

You do most broiling about 4 to 6 inches from the heat source. It is always best to put the food, whatever it is, on a broiler pan, which has a grated top that allows juices to fall into a pan below. And watch out for flare-ups, either in the oven or on the grill. Flare-ups not only pose a fire danger, but they also can burn meat and give it an acrid flavor. Use the grill's cover to extinguish flames, and keep a box of baking soda or salt handy in the kitchen for broiler flare-ups.

The barbecue recipes in this chapter work for broiling as well. Because you cannot see food that is broiling as readily as food on a grill, check it more often until you get used to the timing. Just watch and vary your cooking times because broiler heat is slightly more intense and the food generally cooks more quickly.

Gas versus charcoal

About 80 percent of all American households do some kind of grilling at home or on vacation, whether it is with a $12 hibachi or a $500 "grilling unit" that is roughly the size of a Fiat and sports everything from gas burners (for sauce-making and so on) and cutting boards to rotisseries and satellite TV (just kidding). The following sections explore the specifics of gas and charcoal grills.

Charcoal grills

The key to successful charcoal grilling is the same as for stovetop cooking: an even source of heat. Probably the most common failing of amateur cooks is trying to work with a charcoal fire that is too hot. If you're using charcoal, the coals should spread in a solid layer about 4 to 6 inches below the food grate. Wait until they are about 75 percent white to start grilling; don't overload your grill with charcoal — too hot a fire will char food before it is fully cooked.

Allow 30 to 35 minutes for the coals to burn to medium. To gauge the temperature of the coals, place the palm of your hand just about the grill's grid. If you can hold your hand in that position for 2 seconds, the coals are hot; a 3-second hold tells you the coals are medium-hot; 4 seconds is medium; and 5 indicates low heat.

If you are cooking a large quantity of food and the fire begins to fade before you finish, add a small amount of fresh charcoal from time to time to keep the fire alive. And store your charcoal in a dry place to help it light faster and burn more quickly.

As a general rule, 30 charcoal briquettes will cook about 1 pound of meat. If you're cooking 2 pounds of meat, you need around 45 briquettes.

Using a grill's lid

Many barbecue grills come with lids, which, when secured, create an oven that can exceed 450 degrees. Certain foods that take a relatively long time to cook — chicken legs, thick slices of steak, and so on — grill faster and better with the lid on. Essentially, you are grilling and roasting at the same time. A lid traps much of the heat, directing it into the food rather than allowing it to blow away. The lid also creates a smoky effect that envelopes the food with delicious aroma and flavor. But be sure to lift the lid frequently to check on (and avoid burning) your food.

Never light cooking fires with kerosene, gasoline, or other chemicals unless you have a terrific home insurance plan. Dry newspaper and a little patience work wonders. A good alternative is the *plug* — an electric rod that you place in the center of a charcoal pile until it ignites. Using lighter fluid remains the most popular way of starting a fire.

Gas grills

The gas-powered grills that have become increasingly popular in recent years have an advantage over charcoal in that they maintain high heat without fading. Some gas grills use lava rocks to simulate charcoal, which works exceedingly well. The cooking technique is the same as for charcoal grills.

If you add wood chips to a barbecue, soak them first in water for about 15 minutes. Doing so makes them smolder and smoke rather than burn up in a flash.

Grilling tips

Before you get started with grilling, keep in mind the following tips:

✔ Clean the grill grate well with a wire brush between uses. Before igniting the fire, brush some vegetable oil over the grates to prevent food, particularly fish, from sticking.

✔ Trim meat of excess fat to avoid grease flare-ups that blacken the meat and give it a burned flavor.

✔ Cooking times in outdoor grill recipes are approximate; don't throw the meat on and jump in the pool for 15 minutes. Many variables affect cooking time: wind, intensity of coals, thickness of meat, and your fondness for dancing every time a Supremes song comes on.

✔ Do not apply sweet barbecue sauces to meat until the last 10 minutes or else the sugar in them may burn.

✔ Grilling demands you to be organized. Set up a small table right next to the grill with all of your ingredients, utensils, serving platters, and so on.

✔ Marinate, marinate, marinate — to add moisture and flavor to almost all foods.

✔ Be sure to shut off the valve that leads gas into your grill after you turn off the burners. On a charcoal grill, close all the vents after grilling and close the lid to extinguish the hot coals.

Marinating myths and facts

A common misperception is that marinades tenderize meat. They don't. A marinade barely penetrates the outer ⅛ inch of meat, poultry, or game. What a marinade *can* do is add flavor to the surface, which is, of course, the first thing you taste.

We could write a whole book about marinades. Suffice it to say that most marinades involve an acidic ingredient (vinegar, lemon, or some kinds of wine), oil, herbs, and perhaps a base flavor ingredient (beef or chicken stock, for example). You want to end up with a marinade that is well balanced and flavorful. The only way to know what you have made is to taste it.

Consider this example: You have a chuck shoulder steak. Ask yourself whether you want to add a hot, medium, or sweet flavor. Much of this depends on the main ingredient. You may not want a sweet flavor on fish, for example. With pork, though, you might.

Say for now that you want a hot marinade for the steak. You want to give the steak some zip. Start with red chili flakes (carefully!). Then what? You need a liquid that goes with beef as well as chilies. You can use beef stock (home-made or canned beef broth) or red wine. Try red wine. So here you have the foundation of your hot marinade. Now you can jazz it up. What goes well with hot things? Minced garlic and black peppercorns maybe. Chopped cilantro adds flavor, too. (As you begin to cook, you will discover more about ingredients in the supermarket and how to blend them.) Depending on your taste, you may want to add a little dried cumin or coriander seed. Then, at the end, add 2 to 3 tablespoons of good olive oil, salt, and black pepper.

So there you have your basic hot marinade for steak, which you can vary as you go along to make it hotter, milder, or whatever.

What's your beef?

If you want a great hamburger — juicy and meaty, moist and not fatty — you have to start with the right meat. Many people think that if they buy the "best" meat, like ground sirloin or ground round, they will have a superior burger. The flavor may be good, but those cuts are so lean that they tend to be dry.

The best all-around meat for hamburgers is ground chuck, which has about 15 to 20 percent fat, just enough to keep it moist. Supermarkets usually list the percentage of fat on the label. Also look for coarsely ground meat, which yields a looser patty.

Be sure to marinate meats, fish, poultry, and vegetables in the refrigerator. Bacteria forms on the surface of room-temperature food very quickly. And don't reuse marinade from pieces of raw chicken or fish unless you bring it to a boil first.

Grill time

Following are some recipes to get you started grilling. Novice cooks should follow the recipes exactly before modifying them to fit personal tastes.

The burger basics

We start with the most basic of American foods: the burger. The classic all-American hamburger — said to be invented at Louis' Lunch in New Haven, Connecticut — is usually made with ground chuck or sirloin. You can get more extravagant if you like, but more expensive cuts of beef have less *marbling* (visible veins of fat that run throughout a piece of raw sliced or chopped meat). You need marbling to keep the burger moist. Generally, more marbling means higher fat content, richer flavor and texture.

Hamburgers for the grill should be plump and well seasoned. The flavors you can add are limitless. If you like it hot, add Tabasco sauce or one of the scores of hot sauces on the market. Soy sauce makes hamburgers salty-sweet. And you don't even have to stick to beef; lamb and turkey burgers, or blends of all three, are super, too.

We all know how much fun it is getting our hands (washed please!) into a mound of rosy ground meat and playing sculptor. But if you get too aggressive when forming your hamburger patties and mold them too firmly, they will tighten up on the grill. And nobody wants a tight hamburger!

The Perfect Hamburger

Tools: *Mixing bowl, spatula*

Preparation time: *About 12 minutes*

Cooking time: *12 to 15 minutes*

Yield: *4 servings*

1½ pounds ground chuck

¼ teaspoon salt or to taste

¼ teaspoon black pepper, or to taste

4 hamburger buns

1 Oil the grill and prepare a medium fire in a charcoal or gas grill, or heat an oven broiler.

2 While the grill is heating, combine in a bowl the ground chuck, the salt, and the pepper. Mix lightly but thoroughly, using your hands. Shape the mixture into four patties, each about ¾-inch thick.

3 Place the patties on the oiled grill grid. Grill directly over the heat for 5 to 7 minutes per side for medium, less for rare or medium rare. (The United States Department of Agriculture suggests an internal temperature of 160 degrees for safety; the inside of the burger should not show any pink.) Make a small incision in each patty to determine doneness — they should be just cooked through and still juicy in the center.

4 Just before the burgers are cooked, toast the buns on the edges of the grill. Serve.

Nothing goes better with a great burger than French Potato Salad (see Chapter 10).

To avoid flare-ups from oil dripping on the coals, the grill grid should be oiled *before* you start the fire.

Many ingredients can be blended in with the ground beef: minced onions, minced garlic, minced basil, and chopped thyme or rosemary; soy sauce, seasoned breadcrumbs, and a beaten egg; minced bell peppers; and much more.

Quick and tasty burger toppings include thinly sliced red or yellow onions, tomato slices marinated in a basil vinaigrette dressing, flavored mustards, mango or tomato chutney, tomato-based salsa, grilled peppers, and garlic-grilled mushrooms. (You can find recipes for the last dish later in this chapter.)

Lamb burgers are a moist and tasty change from ground beef burgers.

Lamb Burgers

Tools: *Chef's knife, mixing bowl, spatula*

Preparation time: *About 5 minutes*

Cooking time: *About 12 minutes*

Yield: *4 servings*

(continued)

1¼ to 1½ pounds ground lamb

3 tablespoons minced red or yellow onion

2 tablespoons dark raisins, minced (optional)

2 tablespoons chopped fresh parsley or cilantro

2 cloves garlic, minced

¾ teaspoon ground cumin

¼ teaspoon ground cinnamon

¼ teaspoon salt, or to taste

Black pepper to taste

4 warmed buns or pitas

Fruit chutney (optional)

Chopped tomatoes and cucumbers (optional)

1 Oil the grill and prepare a medium-hot fire in a charcoal or gas grill, or heat an oven broiler (put the rack about 4 to 6 inches from the heating element).

2 In a large mixing bowl, combine the ground lamb, onion, raisins (if desired), parsley or cilantro, garlic, cumin, cinnamon, salt, and pepper. Mix well. Shape the meat into 4 patties, each 1-inch thick.

3 Place the patties on the grill grid, or in a small roasting pan set under the broiler. Cook 5 to 7 minutes per side on a grill, or 4 to 5 minutes per side under the broiler for burgers that are cooked to medium. Cut into the center of each patty to check meat color. (The United States Department of Agriculture recommends cooking all ground meat to medium, or until the center is no longer pink.) Serve on warm buns with tomato, mango, or other fruit chutney; or stuff into pita pockets with chopped tomatoes and cucumbers.

The assertive flavor of lamb marries well with side dishes like French Potato Salad (see Chapter 10), or Watercress, Endive, and Orange Salad (see Chapter 10). You could also serve this recipe with the Mediterranean Rice Casserole (see Chapter 3).

Grilling vegetables

When it comes to vegetables, even those that you're not wild about can taste terrific when grilled. Charcoal imparts an alluring texture and a smoky essence that is irresistible. Moreover, preparation is easy and quick. Here are some examples:

✔ **Eggplant and zucchini:** Cut them lengthwise into 1-inch-thick slices before grilling. Brush with oil, season to taste, and grill for 15 to 20 minutes or until charred and tender, turning occasionally. For additional flavor, marinate first in a 3-to-1 oil/vinegar mixture with salt and pepper and maybe Dijon-style mustard for about 15 minutes before grilling.

✔ **Corn:** Pull back the husks to remove the silk, but leave the husks attached to the base of the ear. Wrap the husks back around the corn and tie at the top with string or a strip of husk. Grill 20 minutes or until tender, turning frequently. Serve with melted butter flavored with herbs and fresh lemon juice.

✔ **Potatoes, carrots, onion, and turnips:** Peel and slice into uniform pieces and precook in boiling water until almost tender. Rinse in cold water to stop the cooking and drain well. Wrap in aluminum foil with seasonings such as olive oil, lemon juice, fresh herbs, and salt and pepper to taste, and grill for 10 to 15 minutes or until tender. (You can also thread them onto skewers before grilling.)

✔ **Tomatoes:** Slice firm, ripe tomatoes into 1-inch-thick slices. Brush with olive oil; sprinkle with dried basil or parsley and salt and pepper. Grill until heated through, about 5 minutes total, turning once.

Porous vegetables, such as mushrooms and sliced eggplant, need not be marinated. You simply brush them with a flavorful liquid, as in the following recipe.

Garlic-Grilled Portobello Mushrooms

Tools: *Chef's knife, small bowl, basting brush*

Preparation time: *About 10 minutes, plus time to preheat grill*

Cooking time: *About 6 minutes*

Yield: *4 servings*

1 pound portobello mushrooms

⅓ cup extra-virgin olive oil

3 tablespoons lemon juice

2 large cloves (about 2 teaspoons) minced garlic

Salt and black pepper to taste

2 tablespoons minced fresh parsley (optional)

1 Oil the grill grid and prepare a medium-hot fire in a charcoal or gas grill.

2 Clean the mushrooms with a damp paper towel. Remove the stems, as shown in Figure 6-10. (You can save them to put in soups or stocks.)

3 In a small bowl, combine the oil, lemon juice, and garlic. Brush the caps with the flavored oil and season with salt and pepper.

(continued)

4 Place the caps on the grill, top side down, and grill for about 3 minutes. (Do not let them burn.) Turn the caps over and grill for another 3 to 4 minutes or until you can easily pierce the caps with a knife and the mushrooms are nicely browned.

5 Remove the mushrooms to a platter, garnish with parsley, and serve.

Steak — such as the Broiled Skirt Steak, Cajun Style (see Chapter 16) — is the natural accompaniment to these savory mushrooms.

How to Trim and Slice Mushrooms

Figure 6-10:
Trim the stems off the mushrooms before grilling the caps.

Cleaning mushrooms thoroughly is important. The wild varieties especially can be full of sand and dirt. But if you soak or rinse mushrooms too long, they can become water-drenched and mushy. Rinsing and using a damp paper towel to gently brush off any dirt is best. If the mushrooms are very dirty, rinse more thoroughly with cold water and drain in a colander, wiping away excess moisture with a cloth or paper towel.

Getting fancy: Pork, mushrooms, and swordfish

In this savory recipe for brochettes of pork, you cube the meat and marinate it in olive oil, red wine vinegar, garlic, rosemary (preferably fresh), cumin, salt, and hot pepper. Cumin is a lovely match for pork (and lamb, too). Rosemary gives it a sunny Provençale flavor.

Grilled Brochettes of Pork with Rosemary

Tools: *Chef's knife, mixing bowl, wooden or metal skewers*

Preparation time: *About 25 minutes, plus time to preheat grill*

Marinating time: *About 30 minutes*

Cooking time: *About 15 minutes*

Yield: *4 servings*

1½ pounds lean boneless pork loin, cut into 1-inch cubes

3 tablespoons olive oil

2 tablespoons chopped fresh rosemary, or 2 teaspoons dried

1 tablespoon red wine vinegar

1 large clove (about 1 teaspoon) finely chopped garlic

1 teaspoon ground cumin

¼ teaspoon red pepper flakes

Salt and black pepper to taste

1 Place the pork in a mixing bowl. Add the remaining ingredients and mix well. Cover with plastic wrap and allow to marinate in the refrigerator for about 30 minutes.

2 Oil the grill grid and prepare a medium fire in a charcoal or gas grill. If you use wooden skewers, soak them for 30 minutes in cold water and cover the tips with foil to prevent burning. (**Note:** Don't pack the meat too tightly on the skewers, but allow a little space between each piece to allow the heat to circulate and ensure even cooking.)

3 Arrange the pork cubes on four skewers.

4 Place the meat on the grate and grill for about 10 to 15 minutes or until just pink in the center, turning the skewers every 4 to 5 minutes. Serve immediately.

Add color to these brochettes by serving them with Couscous with Yellow Squash (see Chapter 15).

Fish and shellfish lend themselves particularly well to grilling, too. Use firm-fleshed fish that holds together on the grill, such as salmon, halibut, tuna, swordfish, mako shark, or monkfish. Delicate fish such as sole tends to flake and fall apart. Species with relatively oily flesh, such as bluefish and mackerel, also grill well.

Notice that in this next recipe the marinade for the swordfish is retained and used to make a quick pan sauce. As long as the sauce comes to a boil there is no health problem. By tossing the fish in the hot marinade you infuse it with all of the wonderful herb flavors.

Grilled Swordfish Steaks with Lemon and Thyme

Tools: *Large metal roasting or broiling pan, brush for basting*

Preparation time: *About 10 minutes, plus time to preheat grill*

Marinating time: *About 30 minutes*

Grilling time: *About 10 minutes*

Yield: *4 servings*

4 swordfish steaks, each about 1 inch thick, about 1½ pounds total	*Juice of one large lemon*
Salt and black pepper to taste	*2 sprigs fresh thyme, chopped, or ½ teaspoon dried*
2 to 3 tablespoons corn or vegetable oil	*2 tablespoons butter at room temperature*

1 Thirty minutes before cooking, sprinkle the swordfish steaks on all sides with salt and pepper. Mix together the oil, lemon juice, and thyme in a large metal roasting or broiling pan. Add the fish steaks, turning them in the marinade to coat evenly. Cover with plastic wrap and refrigerate for no more than 30 minutes.

2 Brush the grill grid with oil and prepare a medium-hot fire in a charcoal or gas grill.

3 Remove the swordfish from the pan, reserving the marinade. Grill the swordfish steaks for about 4 to 5 minutes per side or until cooked through, depending on their thickness and the grill's temperature. (The fish is cooked when the center is opaque and no longer transparent.) Then return the fish to the metal pan with the marinade. Add the butter and place the dish on the grill to simmer the marinade and melt the butter, about 2 to 3 minutes. Coat the fish with sauce and serve.

You can enliven swordfish like this with Lentils with Balsamic Vinegar (see Chapter 15) or Orzo Medley (see Chapter 10). Gazpacho beforehand is great, too (see Chapter 9).

Scallops require minimal cooking time, and are even eaten raw in the form of a well-seasoned *ceviche* (a cold seafood salad in which the seafood is thinly sliced) with lime juice (the acid "cooks" the scallops somewhat). Be sure not to overcook them because they quickly become rubbery.

We use the term "Portuguese" loosely in the next recipe, but we don't think we'll get in trouble for it because this book is not yet published in that language — or is it? Indeed, this recipe includes some ingredients commonly found in Portuguese cooking, specifically red and green bell peppers, capers, garlic, parsley, and wine.

Broiled Scallops Portuguese Style

Tools: *Chef's knife, large pan, roasting sheet, large skillet*

Preparation time: *10 minutes*

Cooking time: *About 3 minutes*

Yield: *4 servings*

1½ pounds sea scallops, halved widthwise

Salt and black pepper to taste

2 tablespoons olive oil

2 tablespoons butter

1 medium green bell pepper, cored, seeded, and finely chopped

1 medium red bell pepper, cored, seeded and finely chopped

1 clove garlic, minced

¼ cup drained capers

3 tablespoons chopped parsley

½ cup fine fresh bread crumbs

¼ cup dry white wine

1 Preheat the broiler.

2 Sprinkle the scallops with salt and pepper.

3 Heat the oil in a large, heavy pan and add the scallops. Cook over very high heat, stirring often, about 2 minutes. Transfer the scallops to a baking dish that will hold them in one layer. Set aside briefly.

4 Add the butter to a large skillet over medium heat. When the butter is hot and melted, add the peppers and garlic. Cook, stirring, until wilted, about 1 to 2 minutes.

5 Add the capers. Stir. Add the parsley, bread crumbs, and wine. Heat thoroughly. Spoon the mixture over the scallops. Place the scallops about 6 inches from the broiler and broil until the bread crumb mixture is just crisp — less than 1 minute. Serve on warm plates.

Try this dish with a light accompaniment like Sautéed Spinach Leaves (see Chapter 4), or Braised Endive (see Chapter 5).

Grilled Tuna with Niçoise Dressing

Tools: *Chef's knife, spatula, medium mixing bowl, roasting pan*

Preparation time: *15 minutes*

Cooking time: *6 to 7 minutes*

Yield: *4 servings*

1 green onion, trimmed and minced

1 tablespoon finely chopped black olives

1 tablespoon finely chopped capers

2 tablespoons balsamic vinegar

1 teaspoon finely chopped anchovy fillets or anchovy paste (optional)

2 tablespoons chopped parsley

½ cup plus 3 tablespoons olive oil

4 tuna steaks, about 1-inch thick, 1½ pounds total

1 teaspoon minced fresh thyme leaves, plus 1 bunch fresh thyme, brushed with oil

Salt and black pepper to taste

Niçoise Dressing

Combine in a bowl the green onion, olives, and capers. Stir in the vinegar and pepper. Beat in the anchovy (if desired) and parsley, then ½ cup of the oil. Set aside.

Grilled Tuna

1 Put the tuna on a roasting pan and add the remaining 3 tablespoons of oil, 1 teaspoon minced thyme, salt, and pepper. Turn the steaks to coat well. Let sit, refrigerated, 10 to 25 minutes.

2 Brush the grill grid with oil and heat a gas or charcoal grill to medium-high (see the "Charcoal grills" section earlier in this chapter for a definition). When the fire is ready, lay 4 clusters of fresh thyme on the grate. Place a piece of tuna over each cluster of thyme. Cook for about 3 minutes. Using a spatula, turn the fillets (the thyme sprigs may come up with them, but this isn't a problem) and grill for 3 minutes on the other side. Remove one of the steaks and test for doneness by making a small incision in the center — some people like grilled tuna very rare, others medium, so don't overcook it.

3 When the steaks have cooked, transfer them to warm serving dishes. Spoon half of the sauce over the steaks. Serve the remaining sauce on the side.

This entrée salad would go nicely with a soup, warm or cold; try Carrot Soup with Dill (see Chapter 9) or Fresh Tomato Gazpacho (see Chapter 9).

Chapter 7

Sauces

> *A great meal without a sauce is like a beautiful woman without clothes. It can provoke and satisfy the appetite, but it lacks the coating of civilization that would arouse our fullest interest.*
>
> — Raymond Sokolov, from *The Saucier's Apprentice*

*P*robably no aspect of cooking sends a kitchen novice running for a restaurant like sauce-making. All this reducing and blending and seasoning and adjusting seems about as arcane as DNA testing.

In fact, sauce-making is within the reach of the absolute cooking rookie. Some sauces require nothing more than cooking several ingredients in a pan and tossing them in the blender. We tell you how to do that in this chapter. From there, you can progress to some of the more important basic sauces in American and European cooking, with all kinds of variations.

Don't think of today's sauces only as those old triple-bypass, cream-and-butter concoctions. Most sauces in restaurants today are Mediterranean or Californian in style, made with olive oil, aromatic herbs, vegetables, and maybe wine. The gelatin-like *demi-glace,* essentially a heavy, concentrated stock, also adds wonderful flavor to many low-fat sauces today.

Not only are these sauces easier to make than the classic sauces (although we explain the classics because they can be superb in moderation), but they also keep you light on your feet.

Who came up with this saucy idea anyway?

Throughout the Middle Ages and the Renaissance, *gravies,* or thickened pan juices, were served with meat, game, and fowl; they were not sophisticated sauces as we know them today. But what would you expect from people who ate with their hands and tossed bones under the table? It wasn't until the eighteenth century that modern sauces entered the cooking vocabulary. By 1800, a celebrated French chef known as Carême had compiled more than a dozen classical recipes for sauces, each of which could be modified in different ways. These recipes include some of the most famous of French sauces today: *ravigote* (highly seasoned white sauce), *Champagne* (white sauce made with Champagne), *bourguignonne* (red wine with mushrooms and onions), *poivrade* (red wine sauce with black pepper), tomato (red sauce), *raifort* (horseradish and cream), mayonnaise (egg yolk and oil emulsion), and *Provençale* (usually tomatoes along with other ingredients and fresh herbs).

Today, the French cooking repertoire includes several hundred sauces. (Annoyingly, most of these sauce recipes are written in French.) Add to those the sauces of Spain, Italy, and America, and the list is mind-boggling. But don't fret. Most cooks use no more than a dozen sauces and their variations — and those are within the grasp of anyone who can boil a hot dog and carry on a conversation at the same time.

What Is a Sauce?

Think of a sauce as a primary liquid (chicken stock, beef stock, fish stock, vegetable stock, or wine, for example) flavored with ingredients (sautéed shallots, garlic, tomatoes, and so on) and seasoned with salt and pepper and herbs of choice.

Before it's served, a sauce is often *reduced.* Reduced simply means that the sauce is cooked and evaporated over high heat so that it thickens and intensifies in flavor. Sometimes you strain a sauce through a sieve to eliminate all the solids. Other times you puree everything in a blender.

The Family Tree of Sauces

The best way to understand sauces is to become familiar with their foundations:

- *White sauces* usually contain milk or cream.
- *White butter sauces* are based on a reduction of butter, vinegar, and shallots.
- *Brown sauces* are based on dark stocks like lamb or veal.

> ✔ *Vinaigrettes* are made up of oil, vinegar, and seasonings.
>
> ✔ *Hollandaise* is based on cooked egg yolks and butter.
>
> ✔ *Mayonnaise* is based on uncooked or slightly cooked egg yolks and oil.

For the purposes of this book, subcategories might include compound butters, which we discuss later in this chapter, and tomato sauces.

Classic White Sauce: Béchamel

For centuries, béchamel has been the mortar that supports the house of French cuisine. With its buttery, faintly nutty flavor, béchamel is also the base of hot soufflés and such homey dishes as macaroni and cheese and pot pies. You can modify béchamel in many ways to suit the dish it garnishes. For example, if you are cooking fish, you can add fish stock to the sauce. If you are cooking poultry, you can add chicken stock. Like most white sauces, béchamel is based on a *roux,* which is nothing more than butter melted in a pan and then sprinkled with flour (equal quantities of each) and stirred into a paste over low heat. Note how, in the following recipe, béchamel begins with a roux.

Béchamel and its variations go with all kinds of foods, including poached and grilled fish, chicken, veal, and vegetables like pearl onions, brussels sprouts, broccoli, and cauliflower. (See Chapter 3 for information about steaming and boiling these vegetables before coating with béchamel.) The thickness of béchamel varies from dish to dish.

Béchamel

Tools: *Small saucepan, medium saucepan, wire whisk*

Preparation time: *About 5 minutes*

Cooking time: *About 8 minutes*

Yield: *About 1 cup*

1¼ cups milk	¼ teaspoon ground nutmeg, or to taste
2 tablespoons butter	Salt and black pepper to taste
2 tablespoons flour	

1 Heat the milk over medium heat in a small saucepan until almost boiling. (If the milk is hot when you add it to the butter and flour, there's less chance that the béchamel will be lumpy.)

(continued)

2 Meanwhile, in a medium saucepan, melt the butter over medium heat (don't let it darken or burn). Add the flour and whisk constantly for 2 minutes. (You are cooking the loose paste, or roux, made from the butter and flour.) The roux should reach a thick paste consistency.

3 Gradually add the hot milk while continuing to whisk the mixture vigorously. When the sauce is blended smooth, reduce heat and simmer for 3 to 4 minutes, whisking frequently. The béchamel should have the consistency of a very thick sauce. Remove from heat, add the nutmeg and salt and pepper, and whisk well.

If the butter burns or even gets brown, you should probably start over, or your white sauce will have a brown tint.

Whipping up some creamed spinach (or creamed vegetables in general) is a good way to try out your béchamel-making skills.

If creamed spinach conjures dark memories of school cafeterias, try the real thing. Because this dish is very rich — as is anything based on béchamel — serve it with something lean, like roasted chicken, low-fat fish, or maybe just saltines and a Dr. Pepper.

Variations on béchamel

Mornay sauce: Add grated cheese, like Gruyère or Parmesan, to the simmering béchamel, along with fish stock (optional) and butter.

Horseradish sauce: Add freshly grated horseradish to taste. Serve with game, fish such as trout, or long-braised sinewy cuts of beef from the shoulder and neck.

Soubise: Boil or steam yellow onions until they are soft; puree them in the blender and add to the sauce, seasoning to taste with salt and pepper. Slightly sweet from the onions, soubise sauce is suitable for many types of game, poultry, and meat.

You can use dozens of other ingredients commonly found in a well-stocked pantry or refrigerator to easily alter the flavor of béchamel. A short list of possibilities includes fresh tomatoes (skinned and finely chopped); sautéed mushrooms, shallots, onions, garlic, or leeks; ground ginger or curry powder; chopped fresh tarragon, dill, parsley or marjoram; paprika; grated lemon zest; white pepper; and Tabasco sauce. Add them to taste when the béchamel has almost finished cooking.

Creamed Spinach

Tools: *Large pot, colander, food processor or electric blender, two saucepans, wire whisk*

Preparation time: *About 15 minutes*

Cooking time: *About 8 minutes*

Yield: *3 to 4 servings*

8 cups fresh, trimmed spinach, about 10 ounces

1 cup milk

1 tablespoon unsalted butter

1 tablespoon flour

¼ teaspoon ground nutmeg

Salt and black pepper to taste

2 tablespoons grated Parmesan cheese

1 Wash spinach well. (Do not dry.) Immediately place the spinach in a large pot with just the water that clings to its leaves. Cover and cook over medium-low heat for about 2 minutes, or just until the leaves are wilted.

2 Place the cooked spinach in a colander and, using a wooden spoon, press down on the spinach to extract most of the water.

3 Put the spinach in a food processor or electric blender container and blend thoroughly. You should have about ¾ cup processed spinach.

4 Heat the milk almost to boiling in a small saucepan over medium heat.

5 Meanwhile, melt the butter in a medium saucepan over medium heat; add the flour, stirring with a wire whisk. Add the warmed milk, whisking rapidly. Add the nutmeg and salt and pepper to taste. Cook, whisking often, about 3 to 4 minutes or until the sauce thickens. Reduce heat to low, stir in the spinach and Parmesan cheese, and cook just until heated through. Taste for seasoning.

You can substitute a 10-ounce package of frozen chopped spinach for the fresh ingredient. (If you do, it isn't necessary to puree the spinach, so you can skip step 3.) Remember to squeeze out excess liquid after cooking. You need about ¾ cup, cooked and drained.

Velouté: A Variation on Béchamel

A *velouté* is essentially a béchamel made with a stock (fish or chicken) in place of the milk, which gives it extra flavor. Sometimes you enhance a velouté before serving by adding a little cream (for a smoother texture) or some fresh lemon juice (for a little tartness). It is wonderful with poached fish, poultry, veal, vegetables, and eggs. Following is a simplified version of a classic velouté; variations are endless after you get this technique down.

Velouté

Tools: *Medium saucepan, small saucepan, wire whisk, waxed paper*

Preparation time: *About 10 minutes*

Cooking time: *About 8 minutes*

Yield: *About 1¾ cups*

2 tablespoons butter

3 tablespoons flour

1½ cups homemade or canned chicken or vegetable stock

⅓ cup heavy cream or half-and-half

Salt and white pepper to taste

1 Heat the stock almost to boiling in a small saucepan over medium heat.

2 Melt the butter over medium heat in a medium saucepan (don't let it brown or burn). Add the flour and whisk until blended smooth. Reduce heat to low and cook for about 2 minutes, whisking constantly.

3 Raise the heat setting to medium and gradually add the hot chicken broth (watch out — it could splatter), whisking for about 1 minute or until the sauce thickens. Raise the heat and bring to a boil; immediately lower the heat to simmer and cook for about 2 minutes, whisking often.

4 Add the cream, salt, and pepper. Raise the heat and whisk constantly while bringing the mixture back to a boil. When it boils, immediately remove the saucepan from the heat and cover with waxed paper (to prevent a thin film from forming on the surface) until served.

If you forget to cover the velouté with waxed paper and a thin film or skin forms on the sauce's surface, simply whisk it back into the sauce. If the sauce cooks a little too long and gets too thick, add a little more stock or cream.

Brown Sauces

One major difference between white and brown sauce is that brown sauce is harder to get off your silk tie. Basic brown sauce derives from the nineteenth century Espagnole sauce, so called because a major ingredient was Spanish ham. It took two or three days to make, which is probably one reason why women's liberation did not catch on faster in Spain. That's all you need to know about the traditional Espagnole sauce — most modern chefs don't bother with it.

Most brown sauces today are based on a reduced stock of beef or veal. When we use the term *stock,* we mean a liquid that results from boiling bones, water, vegetables, and seasonings. The more you reduce the liquid, the stronger the flavor. Extra flavor also comes from browning the bones first in the oven.

If you reduce veal stock to a jelly consistency, it is sometimes called *demi-glace.* If you reduce the liquid so much that it coats a spoon, it is called simply *glace.* Note that, once they've chilled and set, you can cut demi-glace and glace into small pieces and freeze them for later use.

The following two recipes use the deglazing technique. Not sure what deglazing is? Do you ever have a casserole of macaroni and cheese and, when dinner is over, go over and pick at the little semi-burned nuggets of cheese and pasta that cling to the dish? Aren't they the best part?

Well, think of deglazing as more or less the same thing. When you sauté a steak or chicken in a hot pan, it leaves behind little particles that stick to the pan. These bits are packed with flavor, and you want to incorporate them into any sauce you make.

For example, when you remove a steak from the pan, you might deglaze the pan with red wine (you generally deglaze with wine or stock of some sort). As the wine or stock sizzles in the pan, you scrape the pan's bottom (preferably with a wooden spoon) to release those tasty little particles. That process is called *deglazing.* After you do that, you finish the sauce and serve.

Pork Chops with Rosemary Sauce

In this recipe, you make the sauce quickly in the same pan you use to brown the pork.

Tools: Chef's knife, large skillet or sauté pan, wooden spoon or rubber spatula

Preparation time: About 15 minutes

Cooking time: About 25 minutes

Yield: 4 servings

(continued)

4 loin pork chops, each about 8 ounces

Salt and black pepper to taste

1 tablespoon olive oil

2 tablespoons butter

2 large shallots, minced

½ cup homemade or canned beef stock

½ cup dry red wine

2 tablespoons chopped rosemary leaves, or 2 teaspoons crumbled, dried

1 Season the pork chops with salt and pepper. Heat the olive oil over medium-high heat in a sauté pan or skillet that is large enough to hold the chops in one layer. Cook the chops for about 20 minutes or until done, turning them occasionally. (Watch them carefully and reduce the heat to medium if they brown too quickly.) Set the chops aside on a platter and cover with foil to keep warm.

2 Pour off any accumulated fat and scrape off and discard only the very burned bits of food sticking to the bottom of the pan. Return the pan to medium heat. Add the butter. When it melts, add the shallots, stirring and scraping the pan until they wilt, about 2 to 3 minutes. Add the beef stock and stir. Add the red wine; stir for 1 minute. Add the rosemary.

3 Increase the heat to high and reduce the sauce, stirring until it evaporates slightly. Taste for seasoning, adding more salt and pepper, if desired. Add to the pan the chops and all of the juices that accumulated on the plate; heat a few seconds until warmed through. Place the chops on a serving platter and spoon the sauce over them.

Serve with buttered rice, noodles, or mashed potatoes see (Chapter 3 for recipes).

Sautéed capers give this dish a lively saline accent that is counterbalanced by the garlic, rosemary, and vegetables. Capers are the flower buds of a Mediterranean plant that are dried and then pickled in a vinegar and salt solution. You should rinse and drain them before adding them to a recipe. Capers can be found in any major supermarket or specialty food store.

Shallots

To paraphrase Mark Twain, shallots are onions with a college education. Buy them regularly, as you do onions and garlic. Shaped a little like garlic, shallots grow in clusters with individual bulbs. They are generally available year-round, although they are freshest in the spring. They have a flavor that is more delicate than onions and are less acidic, which makes them ideal for subtle sauces, raw vegetable salads, and vinaigrettes. To use shallots, remove their papery skin and thinly slice or mince the pale purple flesh, as you do an onion.

Chicken Breasts with Garlic and Capers

As in the last recipe, you make the sauce quickly in the same pan you use to brown the meat.

Tools: *Chef's knife, large sauté pan, wooden spoon*

Preparation time: *About 25 minutes*

Cooking time: *About 20 minutes*

Yield: *4 servings*

4 boneless, skinless chicken breast halves, about 1¼ pounds total

Salt and black pepper to taste

2 tablespoons olive oil

1 medium onion, chopped

1 tablespoon finely minced fresh rosemary leaves, or 1 teaspoon crumbled, dried

1 large clove garlic, chopped

⅔ cup homemade or canned chicken stock

1 tablespoon red wine vinegar

3 tablespoons capers, rinsed and drained

1 tablespoon plus 1 teaspoon tomato paste

2 tablespoons chopped parsley

1 Season the chicken breasts lightly with salt and pepper.

2 Heat the oil in a large sauté pan over medium-high heat. Add the chicken and sauté, turning occasionally, until lightly browned on both sides, about 7 minutes. Remove the chicken to a platter.

3 Over medium heat, add the onion, rosemary, and garlic to the pan. Cook, stirring, for 1 to 2 minutes or until the onion is wilted. (Be careful not to brown the garlic.)

4 Add the chicken broth and vinegar. Deglaze the pan by stirring and scraping with a wooden spoon for about 1 minute to dissolve the brown particles clinging to the bottom.

5 Add the capers and tomato paste and blend well. Return the chicken breasts and any juices on the plate to the pan. Bring to a boil, cover, and reduce heat to simmer 5 to 7 minutes or until cooked, turning the chicken once. (To test for doneness, cut into the thickest part of each breast. The meat should look white and juicy, with no trace of pink.)

6 Stir in the parsley and serve.

This recipe goes great with Couscous with Yellow Squash or White Beans with Tomato and Thyme (see Chapter 15).

Vinaigrette Sauces

Vinaigrette sauces, which are low in saturated fat, are worth knowing about. They are also quick. After you get the technique down, the possible modifications are endless.

You can make quick, sprightly sauces for grilled fish or meat by using oil and vinegar as a base. The following recipe is a variation of one of our favorite recipes from Wolfgang Puck's Spago in Los Angeles.

Grilled Swordfish with Cilantro and Cherry Tomatoes Vinaigrette

Tools: *Two baking pans, mixing bowl, wire whisk, blender or food processor, chef's knife*

Preparation time: *About 20 minutes, plus 1 hour to marinate fish*

Cooking time: *About 25 minutes*

Yield: *4 servings*

¾ pound cherry tomatoes, stems removed (or ripe plum tomatoes, cored and quartered)

6 sprigs cilantro, thick bottom of stems removed, leaves chopped

2 cloves garlic, peeled and crushed

½ teaspoon seeded and minced jalapeño pepper (optional)

¾ cup plus 2 tablespoons olive oil

Salt and black pepper to taste

2 tablespoons red wine vinegar

4 swordfish steaks, about 2 pounds total

1 Preheat oven to 400 degrees.

2 On a baking pan, arrange the cherry tomatoes, cilantro, garlic, and jalapeño pepper. Sprinkle 2 tablespoons of the olive oil over them and add salt and pepper to taste. Bake for 20 minutes. (The cherry tomatoes should begin to break apart.)

3 Scrape everything into the bowl of a food processor or electric blender container and puree well. Pour into a bowl.

4 Whisk in the vinegar and ½ cup of the olive oil. Taste for seasoning, adding salt and pepper, if desired. Cover and set aside.

5 Place the swordfish steaks on a baking pan. Rub all over with the remaining ¼ cup of olive oil and season generously with salt and pepper. Refrigerate for 30 minutes to 1 hour.

6 Brush the grill grate with vegetable oil and prepare a medium-hot fire in a charcoal or gas grill.

Dried versus fresh herbs

Unless you live in the southern or western regions of the United States, an area where fresh herbs are available year-round, you may need to substitute dry herbs. Dried herbs will generally do in these circumstances, but you must remember that they are three times as concentrated as fresh. So if a recipe calls for 1 tablespoon of fresh thyme, for example, use 1 teaspoon of the dried herb. (See Chapter 5 for herb and spice charts.)

7 When the grill is hot, cook the swordfish for about 2 to 4 minutes per side (depending on thickness) or until done. (To check for doneness, make a small incision in the center of each steak. It should look pale pink, not deeply salmon colored.) Transfer to warm plates. Spoon some of the vinaigrette onto the plate and set the fish over it.

Serve this swordfish with Baby Carrots in Cumin Butter (see Chapter 15), Couscous with Yellow Squash (see Chapter 15), or Grilled Peppers (see Chapter 6).

 If you'd rather, you can cook the entire recipe in your oven. After roasting the cherry tomato mixture, simply turn on the oven broiler to cook the swordfish for about 4 minutes per side or until done, while you're finishing the vinaigrette.

Egg-Based Sauces: Hollandaise and Mayonnaise

Hollandaise is the most common of all egg-based sauces. Your first introduction to hollandaise probably came at a fancy brunch with your parents where they served Eggs Benedict — hopefully not from the buffet steam table.

Hollandaise is a good exercise for beginners because if you blow it, you can repair it easily (see the following What If icon). The rich, lemon-tinged hollandaise has chameleonlike qualities: Add tarragon and chervil, and you have Béarnaise; add tomato, and you have Choron (good with steak); fold in lightly whipped heavy cream, and you have Chantilly; add dried mustard, and you have a fine accompaniment to boiled vegetables.

Hollandaise

Tools: *Whisk, bowl, double boiler, rubber spatula*

Preparation time: *About 10 minutes*

Cooking time: *About 10 minutes*

Yield: *About ¾ cup*

4 egg yolks, separated (see illustrated instructions for separating an egg in Chapter 8)

1 tablespoon cold water

½ cup (1 stick) room-temperature butter, cut into 8 pieces

2 tablespoons fresh lemon juice

Salt and white pepper to taste

1 In the top of a double boiler, whisk the egg yolks for about 2 minutes or until they are thick and pale yellow. Add the water, whisking for about another minute, until the mixture easily coats a spoon.

2 Set the top of the double boiler with the egg mixture into the bottom of the double boiler, over, but not touching, water that is almost boiling. Heat until just warm, about 3 minutes, stirring constantly with a rubber spatula or whisk.

3 Add the butter 2 tablespoons at a time, whisking vigorously until each batch is incorporated completely. Continue cooking, stirring and scraping the sides of the pot, until the sauce thickens enough to coat the back of a metal spoon. Add the lemon juice and salt and pepper to taste and cook about 1 minute more, or until the sauce is smooth and heated through.

You can make a double boiler by setting any heat-resistant bowl snugly into one of your saucepans. Be sure to allow 2 to 3 inches between the bottom of the bowl and the bottom of the pan, for the boiling water.

The most common foul-up that beginners make when preparing hollandaise is leaving the heat on until it curdles. If that happens, or if the sauce becomes too thick, beat in 1 to 2 tablespoons boiling water. Stir vigorously until the sauce becomes smooth. To avoid lumpy hollandaise, reduce the heat to simmer.

If your blender is not tied up on daiquiri patrol, you might try the following quick and quite satisfactory method of turning out hollandaise.

Blender Hollandaise

Tools: *Blender*

Preparation time: *About 10 minutes*

Cooking time: *1 to 2 minutes*

Yield: *About ⅔ cup*

4 egg yolks

2 tablespoons fresh lemon juice

Salt and white pepper to taste

½ cup (1 stick) heated, melted butter

In a blender container, combine the egg yolks, lemon juice, salt, and pepper; cover and blend for about 30 seconds at low speed. With the motor still running, add the hot butter in a very thin drizzle. As the sauce thickens, increase the speed gradually. Continue until the sauce is thick and smooth textured. Use immediately or keep warm in a double boiler until ready to serve.

Recipes that use raw eggs run a very small risk of transmitting salmonella bacteria. Please review Chapter 8 for more information.

Did you ever wonder why a refrigerated jar of mayonnaise has a life span longer than the life span of the average golden retriever? Does that seem natural to you? Of course not. All the more reason to make your own mayonnaise, which is infinitely better, not to mention that it is much cheaper than the commercial product. Try the following recipe and compare for yourself.

Mayonnaise

Tools: *Wire whisk, mixing bowl*

Preparation time: *About 10 minutes*

Cooking time: *None*

Yield: *About 1 cup*

1 egg yolk

1 tablespoon fresh lemon juice

1 teaspoon Dijon-style mustard

Salt and black pepper to taste

1 cup olive oil, not extra-virgin

1 tablespoon water (if needed)

(continued)

1 Place the egg yolk, lemon juice, mustard, salt, and pepper in a medium mixing bowl. Beat well with a wire whisk.

2 While continuing to whisk, add the oil in a thin drizzle. Continue until you use all the oil. If you do not use the mayonnaise immediately, whip in 1 tablespoon water to *stabilize* it (hold together all the ingredients).

 You can season mayonnaise in all sorts of ways as an accompaniment to cold vegetables, meats, and appetizers; add dill, chervil, basil, capers, lemon juice, anchovies, chopped watercress, mashed avocado (maybe with Tabasco sauce), and more. Fresh mayonnaise lasts several days when covered tightly and refrigerated. The type of oil you use also changes the flavor of mayonnaise. Extra-virgin olive oil might be overpowering. Olive oil and vegetable oils are fine; use an equal portion of each.

The American Egg Board has developed the following recipe for a mayonnaise that gently cooks the egg yolks over very low heat (thus eliminating potential health hazards).

Cooked-Egg Mayonnaise

Tools: *Small saucepan, wooden spoon, blender, rubber spatula*

Preparation time: *About 10 minutes*

Cooking time: *About 2 minutes, plus 4 minutes standing time*

Yield: *About 1¼ cups*

2 egg yolks	*1 teaspoon dry mustard*
2 tablespoons vinegar or fresh lemon juice	*½ teaspoon salt*
2 tablespoons water	*Pinch black pepper*
1 teaspoon sugar	*1 cup vegetable oil*

1 In a small saucepan, stir together the egg yolks, vinegar or lemon juice, water, sugar, mustard, salt, and pepper with a wooden spoon until thoroughly blended. Cook over very low heat, stirring constantly, until the mixture bubbles in 1 or 2 places.

2 Remove from the heat and let stand for 4 minutes. Pour into a blender container. Cover and blend at high speed.

3 While blending, very slowly add the oil. Blend until thick and smooth, occasionally turning off the motor to scrape down the sides of the container with a rubber spatula. Cover and chill if not using immediately.

Remoulade sauce, like the one in the following recipe, is really a mayonnaise sauce intensely flavored with shallots, pickles, garlic, capers, and other ingredients.

Remoulade Sauce

Tools: *Medium bowl, rubber spatula*

Preparation time: *About 15 minutes*

Cooking time: *None*

Yield: *About 1⅓ cups*

1 cup mayonnaise

2 large shallots, finely minced (or ¼ cup minced red or yellow onion)

3 tablespoons finely minced sweet pickles, well drained

1 tablespoon chopped tarragon

2 to 3 teaspoons Dijon-style mustard

2 teaspoons capers, well drained

2 teaspoons chopped fresh parsley

1 clove garlic, minced

1 teaspoon fresh lemon juice

Salt and black pepper to taste (optional)

In a medium bowl, combine all the ingredients. Chill and serve with cold meats, poultry, shellfish, or grilled foods.

This classic sauce can be altered to suit your taste in many ways. You can add a chopped, hard-cooked egg or a few minced anchovies. If you like it hot, shake in some Tabasco sauce to taste. It's quite good with grilled fish or chicken, or as a dressing for cold pork sandwiches.

Blender Sauces

For cooks in a hurry, the blender can be an invaluable tool. You can make blender sauces literally in minutes. And they can be more healthful, too, especially if bound with vegetables, low-fat cheeses (like ricotta), yogurt, and the like.

Although food processors are unsurpassed for chopping, slicing, and grating, blenders have an edge when it comes to liquefying and sauce-making. Their blades rotate faster, binding (or pulling together) liquids better. The two-level slicing blade on a food processor cuts through liquids instead of blending them, and its wide, flat work bowl is too large for mixing small quantities of sauce.

Blender sauces can be so quick that your dinner guests will suspect that Julia Child is hiding in the pantry. You can transform simple poached fish into something special by combining some of the poaching liquid with wine, fresh watercress, seasonings, and just a dab of cream or ricotta cheese. When mixed in the blender with several pats of butter, these ingredients create a savory and exceptionally smooth sauce. (Read more about the blender in Chapter 2.)

Certain fruit sauces for desserts also work better in a blender than in a food processor, whether it's a puree of raspberries spiked with *framboise* (French raspberry brandy) or of mango with lime and rum.

Following are two quick and terrific blender recipes.

Watercress sauce

This watercress sauce works with any smoked fish or meat, fresh vegetables, and omelets, or even as a thin and delicious sandwich spread.

TOQUE TIP

Even the pros use blenders these days

It may seem a minor historical irony that blenders have gained new respectability in the hands of leading French chefs and their American counterparts — the same people who abandoned the appliance two decades ago. Jean Banchet, chef and owner of Le Francais restaurant outside of Chicago, uses a blender to add smoother texture and subtle color to many of his sauces. "I first saw this when I was in France a few years ago visiting some restaurants, and I liked the way it worked," Banchet says. "Now I do most of my sauces in a blender."

Watercress Sauce

Tools: *Blender*

Preparation time: *About 15 minutes*

Cooking time: *None*

Yield: *About 1½ cups*

1¼ cups sour cream

1 cup loosely packed, rinsed, and dried watercress (including stems)

½ teaspoon Dijon-style mustard (optional)

Salt and black pepper to taste

1 Place the sour cream, watercress, and, if desired, the mustard in a blender container. Blend at low speed until the sour cream liquefies and begins to incorporate the watercress.

2 Turn the blender to high for several seconds; shut off the motor. Adjust seasoning with pepper and only enough salt to bring out the flavor of the watercress.

This sauce is delicious spooned over smoked salmon or trout, grilled or poached chicken or fish, or as a light dressing for potato or macaroni salads.

Pesto sauce

Pesto is a favorite summertime sauce that you can make easily in the blender. It goes beautifully with pasta, cold meats, and crudités (raw vegetables). Try swirling a bit of pesto into a sauce of summer tomatoes as a topping for broiled fish or chicken or pasta.

Pesto Sauce

Tools: *Blender, grater, rubber spatula*

Preparation time: *About 15 minutes*

Cooking time: *None*

Yield: *About 1 cup*

(continued)

2 cups lightly-packed fresh basil leaves, stems removed, about 2 ounces

½ cup extra-virgin olive oil

3 tablespoons pine nuts or walnuts

3 large cloves garlic, coarsely chopped

Salt and black pepper to taste

½ cup grated Parmesan cheese

1 tablespoon hot water

1 Rinse and pat dry the trimmed basil leaves.

2 Put the basil leaves in the container of a food processor or blender. Add the oil, pine nuts or walnuts, garlic, and salt and pepper. Blend to a fine texture but not a smooth puree, stopping the motor once to scrape down the sides of the blender container and to force the ingredients down to the blades.

3 Add the Parmesan cheese and water and blend just a few seconds more. Chill until served.

Compound Butters

Take fresh herbs, chop them, and then squish them, in your hands, into room-temperature butter, and you have *compound butter* (or simply *herb butter*). You can make these butters ahead of time and refrigerate. Compound butters are great with all sorts of foods. Compound butters can also be made with grated lemon or orange peel, assorted spices, capers, and other seasonings.

A dollop of herb butter atop a piece of grilled meat or fish adds a sprightly flavor. Herb butters also bring out the best in vegetables. (See Chapter 3 for steamed and boiled vegetable recipes.) And in combination with white wine or stock, herb butters are the foundations of quick, flavorful sauces for all kinds of foods.

You can prepare many herb butters without using a blender or food processor. Simply let the butter soften in a bowl until it's malleable but not too soft and then work in the seasonings with your hands or a spoon. Scoop the mixture onto a sheet of plastic wrap and cool the mixture slightly until you can mold it with your hands. Then roll the herb butter into a cylinder and wrap well. After chilling, slice off pieces as needed. It lasts for weeks in the refrigerator.

Herb butter combinations are as varied as the gardens to which you have access. A combination of finely minced parsley, thyme, and butter is a versatile garnish to have around the house. It is so tasty that you can use it as a table butter for toast and sandwiches. Tarragon, sorrel, basil, chives, garlic, sage, chervil, and shallots work well in various combinations. Try sorrel and parsley with fish; sage and shallots with fowl or game; and basil with tomatoes. Probably the best-known compound butter is *maitre d'hôtel,* which combines parsley, lemon juice, salt, and pepper. Maitre d'hôtel generally accompanies chicken or fish.

Compound butter sauces

With compound butters, you can make many quick butter sauces right in the same pan in which you cook meat or fish. For example, if you sauté a fillet of swordfish, take it out of the pan when it is cooked and add ¼ cup of melted butter (for 4 portions) and 2 tablespoons rinsed and drained capers. Set over medium heat. When the butter turns golden, add 1 tablespoon fresh lemon juice and a pinch of salt. Stir well, letting the butter sizzle but not brown. Pour over the swordfish fillet.

After you learn to make this quick pan sauce, you can do all sorts of variations. Instead of capers, add fresh dill, basil, thyme, minced garlic, Dijon mustard, shallots, grated orange zest, or tomato paste. The list is endless.

Orange butter?

You can have great fun experimenting with vegetable butters in all colors of the garden. We recently experimented with carrot butter and used it as a simple sauce for various vegetable dishes like mashed potatoes, steamed spinach, and boiled hard-shell squash. After you discover this simple technique, you may be tempted to make your refrigerator dairy section look like a Crayola box.

Simple carrot butter can be the highlight of a dinner party when served over steamed red new potatoes.

Carrot Butter

Tools: *Small saucepan, blender or food processor, rubber spatula*

Preparation time: *About 5 minutes*

Cooking time: *About 15 minutes*

Yield: *About ½ cup*

(continued)

*1 large carrot, peeted and cut into
6 pieces*

½ cup (1 stick) butter at room temperature

Dash of ground nutmeg

Salt and white pepper to taste

1 Put the carrot pieces in a small saucepan with lightly salted water to cover; bring to a boil and cook until tender, about 15 to 20 minutes. Drain and put them in a blender or food processor container.

2 Add the butter, nutmeg, salt, and pepper. Puree the mixture, stopping to scrape down the sides of the container if necessary. Put the mixture in a bowl and chill until needed. Use to season boiled or steamed potatoes, spinach, or squash.

Dessert Sauces

Many dessert sauces are so easy that you can make them during TV commercials. And you can vary almost all of them in innumerable ways.

Dessert sauces come in two basic types: cream based and fruit based. Cream-based recipes usually require cooking, but you can often make the fruit sauces right in a blender. In this section, you'll find some popular sauces and ways to modify them.

The following smooth and creamy vanilla sauce dresses up ice cream, fresh strawberries, pound cake, poached pears, soufflés, cold mousses, and more.

Keep in mind that when you're making this sauce, as well as custards and yeast breads, you scald milk primarily to shorten the cooking time. Without bringing it to a boil, heat the milk (or cream) in a saucepan over medium-low heat until it foams.

Be careful not to cook the following vanilla sauce too long. Also, maintain a low to medium-low heat setting to prevent the sauce from curdling. If the sauce curdles, whisk it quickly or whirl it in a blender container to cool it rapidly.

Vanilla Custard Sauce

Tools: *Electric mixer, heavy saucepan, mixing bowl, wire whisk, wooden spoon, sieve*

Preparation time: *About 15 minutes*

Cooking time: *About 25 minutes*

Yield: *2 cups*

1 cup heavy cream	*4 egg yolks*
1 cup milk	*¼ cup sugar*
2 vanilla beans, split lengthwise	

1 Place the cream, milk, and vanilla beans in a heavy medium saucepan. Scald the milk-cream mixture over medium-low (bring to a foam but do not boil). Remove from the heat and let sit for 15 to 20 minutes.

2 Using a handheld or standup mixer, beat the egg yolks and sugar in a bowl for several minutes. The mixture should be pale yellow and thick.

3 Return the cream mixture to the heat and scald it again. Pour about one-quarter of the hot cream mixture into the egg yolks and whisk vigorously. Pour the egg mixture into the saucepan that is holding the rest of the cream. Cook over low heat, stirring with a wooden spoon, about 4 to 5 minutes or until it thickens enough to coat the back of the spoon. Strain through a sieve into a bowl, discard vanilla beans, cover, and chill.

Add flavorings of your choice: rum, Grand Marnier, kirsch, or brandy. Three to 4 tablespoons should suffice.

Cracklin' Hot Fudge Sauce is a twist on regular chocolate sauce and is ideal for ice cream. Because it has butter in it, the sauce turns hard when poured over ice cream and forms a thin, cracklin' crust.

Many recipes for ice cream, custards, puddings, cakes, cookies, and chocolate desserts are flavored with vanilla. You can use either the whole vanilla bean or pure vanilla extract. While the whole beans are somewhat preferable, because they have much more of an intense flavor than the extract, they are also more expensive and less convenient. (In the following recipe, we call for using the more convenient and less expensive pure vanilla extract.) Never purchase "artificial" or "imitation" extract. Made mostly of paper-industry byproducts treated with chemicals, it has a nasty taste.

To split open vanilla beans, take a sharp knife and make an incision lengthwise to expose the tiny black seeds; then add the split bean to the recipe. Look for vanilla bean in the spice section of your supermarket.

Cracklin' Hot Fudge Sauce

Tools: *Sifter, heavy medium saucepan, chef's knife, wooden spoon*

Preparation time: *About 15 minutes*

Cooking time: *About 5 minutes*

Yield: *About 2 cups*

1 cup confectioners' sugar, sifted (see Chapter 2 for sifting instructions)

½ cup (1 stick) butter

½ cup heavy cream

8 ounces (8 squares) bittersweet chocolate, finely chopped (see the following Improvise icon)

2 teaspoons vanilla extract

1 In a heavy medium saucepan over medium-low heat, combine the powdered sugar, butter, and cream. Stir with a wooden spoon until the butter is melted and the mixture is smooth.

2 Remove the pan from the heat and add the chocolate, stirring until smooth. Then add the vanilla and stir to blend.

You can prepare this sauce up to a week ahead of time and keep it covered and refrigerated. Rewarm in a double boiler or in the microwave.

If you can't find bittersweet chocolate, substitute the more common semisweet chocolate and reduce the powdered sugar by 2 tablespoons.

Chop chocolate into pieces on a cutting board with a sharp knife or whirl the chocolate in the container of a blender or food processor for a few seconds.

You have no excuse for serving chemical tasting, aerosol whipped cream. The real thing is so easy and so good that everyone should know how to make it. Spoon sweetened, flavored whipped cream over pies, pudding, cakes, mousses, poached fruit, your cat's nose — anything!

Whipped Cream

Tools: *Chilled bowl, whisk or electric mixer*

Preparation time: *About 5 minutes*

Cooking time: *None*

Yield: *About 2 cups*

1 cup well-chilled heavy cream

3 teaspoons sugar, or to taste

1 teaspoon vanilla extract, or to taste

In a chilled bowl, combine the cream, sugar, and vanilla. Beat with a whisk or electric mixer on medium speed until the cream thickens and forms peaks. (Do not overbeat, or the cream will become lumpy.)

Add 1 tablespoon unsweetened cocoa powder before mixing; add 1 tablespoon instant coffee; or add 1 or 2 tablespoons Grand Marnier, Kahlua, Cointreau, Crème de Menthe, or other liqueur.

Caramel forms when the moisture is cooked out of sugar and the sugar turns dark golden. Caramel sauce is simply caramel thinned out with a little water, lemon juice, and cream so that it pours easily and has more flavor. It is delicious as a coating on meringue, vanilla cake, and ice cream.

Caramel Sauce

Tools: *Medium saucepan, wooden spoon, whisk*

Preparation time: *About 5 minutes*

Cooking time: *About 10 minutes*

Yield: *1 cup*

1 cup sugar

⅓ cup water

½ teaspoon fresh lemon juice

⅔ cup heavy cream

1 Combine the sugar, water, and lemon juice in a medium saucepan over medium-low heat. Stir with a wooden spoon, about 3 minutes, until the sugar dissolves.

(continued)

2 Increase the heat to medium-high and cook until the mixture reaches an amber color, about 3 to 4 minutes. (The mixture comes to a boil rather rapidly.)

3 If you want a medium-colored caramel, remove the mixture from the heat when it is still light golden because it continues to cook and darken off the heat. For darker, more flavorful caramel, remove when medium golden-brown. Remove the pan from the heat and gradually pour in the heavy cream, stirring with a wire whisk. (Be careful: The cream bubbles wildly as you do so.)

4 When all is incorporated, return the saucepan to medium-low heat and stir for 2 to 3 minutes or until the mixture is velvety. Serve warm. To rewarm it after it cools, place it in a microwave or over medium heat on the stove.

Quick sauces made with fresh, seasonal fruit could not be easier. The following technique also works for blueberries and raspberries. (When making raspberry sauces, strain the sauce through a fine sieve before serving to remove the seeds.) These sauces are wonderful as toppings for ice cream, fresh fruits, custards, and puddings.

Fresh Strawberry Sauce

Tools: *Paring knife, food processor or blender*

Preparation time: *About 10 minutes*

Cooking time: *None*

Yield: *About 2 cups*

1 quart fresh strawberries, hulled (stems removed) and washed

2 tablespoons confectioners' sugar, or to taste, depending on fruit's ripeness

1 tablespoon fresh lemon juice

Place all ingredients in the bowl of a blender or food processor; puree until smooth. Taste for sweetness and add more sugar, if desired.

Serve this sauce over ice cream, pound cake, custards, or a big bowl of mixed berries.

For extra flavor, add rum, kirsch, flavored vodka, or other liquor of choice. This sauce can also be made with thawed strawberries.

Part III
Expand Your Repertoire

The 5th Wave   By Rich Tennant

Bill and Irwin make vichyssoise

OK- take a leek...

Let me drink some water first.

In this part . . .

Here's where the music starts. You grab your culinary baton and start off slowly, executing the basics. From there, we tell you how to jazz things up — always in a harmonious way.

This part covers various categories of food — from sauces to soups and salads to desserts. We explain the foundations of each category and also give you some ideas for improvising.

After a little bit of practice, you'll be ready to invite volunteer diners over for a meal. Solicit their opinions, always starting with their praise. And keep an open mind.

Chapter 8

The Amazing Egg

In This Chapter

▶ Selecting fresh eggs

▶ Cooking eggs the "hard" way

▶ Scrambling around

▶ The Big Three: omelets, frittatas, and soufflés

▶ Don't throw out those extra whites

Recipes in This Chapter

↻ Easy Egg Salad

↻ Omelet with Herbs

↻ Frittata with Bell Peppers and Potatoes

▶ Classic Quiche Lorraine

↻ Gruyère Soufflé

Nothing helps scenery like ham and eggs.

— Mark Twain

Eggs are the Tiger Woods of the food world — they can do it all. What other food carries its main ingredient (the yolk) and a lightening agent (the white) all in the same convenient package?

Moreover, the repertoire of egg cooking embraces most of the techniques we stress in this book. Making eggs is a great way to start out, especially if your family is big on breakfast. And believe us, the first time a golden-brown soufflé comes out of the oven, with a golden puffed lid and an aroma that makes you weak-kneed, you'll be hooked.

Selecting Fresh Eggs

Freshness is of paramount concern for egg eaters. As an egg ages, the white breaks down and the membrane covering the yolk deteriorates. So if you cook an older egg, chances are greater that the yolk will break.

Consumers rely on the expiration date on the carton and on the *Julian date,* which indicates the day the eggs were actually packed in their carton. A Julian date of 002, for example, means that the eggs were packed on January 2, or the second day of the year. As a standard, you should use eggs within 4 to 5 weeks of their packed date.

Egg grading, sizing, and coloring

In the supermarket, you generally see two grades of eggs: AA and A. The differences between the grades are hardly noticeable to the average home cook. Purchase either grade.

Egg size is based on a minimum weight per dozen: 30 ounces per dozen for jumbo eggs, 27 ounces for extra large, 24 ounces for large, and 21 ounces for medium. Most recipes (and all of them in this book) call for large eggs.

Shell color is not related to quality.

Blood spots

Contrary to what most people believe, blood spots inside a raw egg are not a sign that the egg was fertilized. They are usually the result of a blood vessel rupturing on the surface of the yolk. The spot does not affect flavor, and the egg is perfectly safe to eat. You can remove the blood spot with the tip of a knife.

A short history of egg cookery

Egg cookery goes back at least to the Egyptians, who used eggs in bread-making, among other things. Western Europe didn't become acquainted with eggs on a wide scale until the nineteenth century.

In the mid-twentieth century, chicken-raising in the United States became high tech. Chickens weren't too keen on spending most of the day in a dark barn, but egg production exploded. The average factory-laying chicken today produces from 250 to 300 eggs per year. (Talk about a Type A personality.)

Concern about cholesterol in the diet has curtailed egg consumption slightly in the United States, but egg-eating is by no means nearing extinction.

Dollars for eggheads

Here's one to remember in case you are ever on a quiz show and the host says:

"For $500: By spinning an egg on a countertop, you can determine what?"

Tick . . . tick . . . tick . . .

"Okay, Vern! What's your answer?"

"Uh, the gravity in the room?"

"Is that your final answer? Sorry, Vern, the correct answer is whether it's cooked: A hard-cooked egg, which has a solid center, spins quickly and easily; a raw egg, because it has liquid swishing around inside, does not."

Raw Eggs

The American Egg Board, a marketing and research organization for the egg industry, does not recommend the consumption of raw or undercooked eggs, yet many recipes call for them. Salmonella, one of several types of bacteria that can cause food poisoning, has been found inside a small number of raw eggs — about 0.005 percent, or 1 in every 20,000 eggs. Though the odds of getting salmonella poisoning from raw eggs are low, it would be wise to use them only in recipes in which they are essential, like homemade mayonnaise and Caesar salad. A good substitution for raw eggs is pasteurized liquid egg substitute, which closely resembles fresh eggs.

You can't tell by looking at it whether an egg is infected. Bacteria is destroyed when the egg reaches a temperature of 140 degrees. Never eat an egg whose shell is cracked or broken. Cracked eggs become vulnerable to other types of bacteria, so you should throw them away.

Hard-Cooked Eggs

Eggs really should never be hard-*boiled* (in their shells), but rather hard-*cooked*; rigorous boiling causes eggs to jostle and crack, leaving the whites tough. The correct technique is to place the eggs in cold water, bring the water to a boil, and then immediately remove the pot from the heat, as in the following steps:

1. **Place the eggs in a saucepan large enough to hold them in a single layer. Add cold water to cover by about 1 inch.**

2. **Cover the saucepan and bring the water to a boil over high heat as fast as possible. Then turn off the heat.**

   If your stove is electric, remove the pan from the burner.

3. **Let eggs stand in the pan, still covered, for 15 minutes for large eggs, 18 minutes for jumbo, and 12 minutes for medium.**

4. **Drain the eggs in a colander and run cold water over them until completely cooled.**

Hard-cooked eggs have numerous uses. Slice them into tossed green salads or potato salads, make deviled eggs, or mash them for egg salad sandwiches.

Peeling a hard-cooked egg

The fresher the egg, the more difficult it is to peel. Use hard-cook eggs that have been refrigerated for a week to ten days or less. Then follow these steps to peel the eggs as soon as they are cool enough to handle:

1. **Tap each egg gently on a table or countertop to crackle the shell all over.**

2. **Roll the egg between your hands to loosen the shell.**

3. **Peel off the shell, starting at the large end of the egg.**

   Holding the egg under running water as you work makes peeling easier.

Egg salad for grown-ups

Egg salad is a classic for picnics and brown-bag lunches. And after you get the basic formula down, you can vary it in countless ways.

Let your taste buds and what's available in your refrigerator determine how you dress up this basic egg salad. You can add any number of ingredients to taste, such as flavored mustard, chopped pickles, minced onion, diced celery, fresh or dried herbs such as parsley, dill, or tarragon, sweet relish, or Tabasco sauce.

Easy Egg Salad

Tools: *Medium mixing bowl, fork*

Preparation time: *About 5 minutes*

Cooking time: *About 15 minutes*

Yield: *2 servings*

4 hard-cooked eggs, peeled

2 tablespoons mayonnaise (or more to taste)

Salt and black pepper to taste

Mash the hard-cooked eggs in a medium mixing bowl with a fork. Add the mayonnaise and season to taste with salt and pepper. Cover and refrigerate until ready to use.

Making Omelets in a Flash

A plain omelet is quick and easy and cooked on top of the range, whereas a soufflé omelet is lightened with stiff whites and beaten yolks and is finished in the oven.

You can serve the following basic omelet for breakfast, brunch, lunch, or dinner. Various garnishes, such as watercress, parsley, tarragon, or chives, make the omelet more eye-appealing.

If you cook the omelet properly, the skin is very smooth and the center is a little moist. You can change the herbs to suit seasonality or personal tastes. And fillings are unlimited: cheese, cooked vegetables, ham, hot peppers, and much more. (See the sidebar "Ten omelet variations" for suggestions.)

Omelet with Herbs

Tools: *Chef's knife, mixing bowl, 10-inch (preferably nonstick) omelet pan or skillet, wooden spoon*

Preparation time: *About 10 minutes*

Cooking time: *About 1 minute*

Yield: *1 serving*

(continued)

3 eggs

1 teaspoon chopped tarragon, or ¼ teaspoon dried

2 teaspoons chopped parsley, or ½ teaspoon dried

1 tablespoon chopped chives

Salt and black pepper to taste

2 teaspoons butter

1 Combine the herbs in a medium mixing bowl. Remove and set aside one teaspoon of the fresh herb mixture for garnish. (If you're using dried herbs, chop extra chives for garnish.)

2 Add the eggs to the bowl and beat with a fork, just enough to combine the whites and yolks.

3 Heat a 10-inch omelet pan or skillet over medium-high heat, then add the butter and melt it, turning the pan to coat evenly. Make sure that the butter is hot and foaming, but not browned, before you add the eggs. Pour in the egg mixture. It should begin to set at the edges immediately.

4 Using a wooden spoon, gently pull the cooked edges toward the center and tilt the pan so the runny mixture flows to the exposed bottom. When the mixture solidifies, remove the pan from the heat and let it rest for a few seconds. The center should be a little moist because the omelet continues to cook in the hot pan. (If you are making an omelet with a filling, add the filling at this point.)

5 Holding the pan so that it tilts away from you, use the spatula to fold about one-third of the near side of the omelet toward the center.

6 Firmly grasping the pan handle with one hand, lift the pan off the stove, keeping it tilted slightly down and away from you. (Be sure to use a pot holder!) Leave a little bit of the handle tip exposed. With the other hand, strike the handle tip two or three times with the side of your fist to swing up the far side of the pan. Doing so causes the far edge of the omelet to fold back on itself, completing the envelope. Use the spatula to press the omelet closed at the seam. Roll the omelet onto a warm dish, seam side down. Sprinkle the remaining herbs on the top. (See Figure 8-1 for illustrated instructions.)

For lunch or a light dinner, serve this omelet with a tossed green salad and Sautéed Cubed Potatoes (see Chapter 4), or the French Potato Salad in Chapter 10 and a chilled Beaujolais.

Another way to fold an omelet is the "half-moon" technique. Slide half the omelet onto a serving plate and turn the pan over to flip the omelet into a half-moon shape.

TIP

Making an omelet is easier in a pan with nonstick coating. Keep in mind, though, that a nonstick surface can give an omelet a thin "skin," which, to most people, is no big deal.

Folding an Omelet

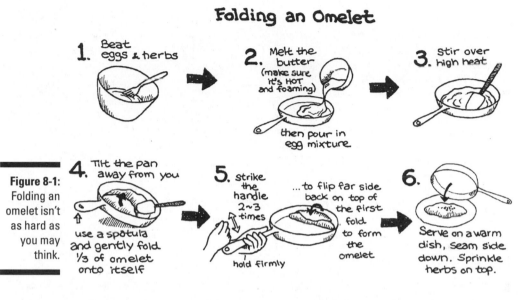

Figure 8-1: Folding an omelet isn't as hard as you may think.

1. Beat eggs & herbs

2. Melt the butter (make sure it's HOT and foaming) then pour in egg mixture

3. Stir over high heat

4. Tilt the pan away from you — use a spatula and gently fold ⅓ of omelet onto itself

5. Strike the handle 2~3 times — hold firmly ...to flip far side back on top of the first fold to form the omelet

6. Serve on a warm dish, seam side down. Sprinkle herbs on top.

WHAT IF?

If the butter burns before you add the egg mixture, carefully wipe the pan clean with paper towels and start again, being careful this time not to let the butter brown. Just let it heat up before adding the eggs. If the folding is too difficult or the omelet gets stuck in the pan, gently scrape the bottom free with a pancake spatula, and slide it out onto a platter. Then fold it in half.

Frittatas: All Dressed Up in No Time at All

The Italian frittata can get time-pressed cooks out of a jam in no time. Making a frittata is simple — and you can dress it up so that it looks great. The fundamental difference between an omelet and a frittata is that an omelet is made with eggs and seasonings, then filled with sundry ingredients, and then folded; a frittata incorporates the ingredients in the egg mixture. The result is sort of like a cake, slightly thicker and more firm than an omelet. Moreover, an omelet is cooked completely on top of the stove, while a frittata, according to most versions, is finished under the broiler or fully cooked in the oven.

Ten omelet variations

To alter the basic omelet recipe, omit the herbs and chives and use ½ cup of any of the following ingredients. There's no limit to the type and combination of ingredients, herbs, or seasonings that you can use to fill and flavor an omelet. Be sure to prepare your fillings before you start cooking the eggs.

Grated hard cheese, such as cheddar, Swiss, or Gruyère, and soft and semisoft cheese, such as mozzarella, goat, or Brie should be added to the egg mixture.

The following fillings are laid on the omelet a few minutes before folding:

✔ **Spanish:** Any combination of chopped tomatoes, green bell peppers, onions, and hot sauce, or a couple of tablespoons of salsa

✔ **Vegetarian:** Cooked, chopped asparagus, artichoke hearts, mushrooms, white or sweet potatoes, spinach, broccoli, or cauliflower; slices of avocado; grilled, sliced eggplant; and red peppers

✔ **Mediterranean:** Feta cheese, tomatoes, spinach, and onions

✔ **Seafood:** Smoked salmon or trout, crab meat, or cooked shrimp

✔ **Meat:** Cooked, crumbled bacon or sausage, diced cooked ham, or salami

✔ **Mixed greens:** Watercress, arugula, or spinach, with a dollop of sour cream

✔ **Mushrooms:** Sautéed button, portobello, crimini, or oyster mushrooms

Keep in mind that fresh herbs and dried herbs are similar in flavor but different in potency. Fresh herbs are more delicate; dried herbs are more concentrated. When a recipe calls for, say, 1 teaspoon of fresh thyme and you have only dried thyme, use roughly a third to a half of the quantity, and always taste.

A frittata makes a wonderful lunch main course, accompanied by a salad.

You can use an omelet pan or a nonstick, ovenproof skillet for this recipe.

Frittata with Bell Peppers and Potatoes

Tools: *Chef's knife, mixing bowl, 12-inch ovenproof nonstick skillet with lid, rubber spatula*

Preparation time: *About 20 minutes*

Cooking time: *About 20 minutes*

Yield: *4 servings*

8 eggs

2 tablespoons finely chopped basil or parsley, or 2 teaspoons dried

Salt and black pepper to taste

¼ pound Gruyère or Swiss cheese (or any hard, aged cheese), cut into small cubes

2 tablespoons vegetable oil

2 small red potatoes, thinly sliced, about ½ pound

1 medium red bell pepper, cored, seeded, and cut into ½-inch cubes

1 medium green bell pepper, cored, seeded, and cut into ½-inch cubes

1 small onion, chopped

1 tablespoon olive oil

1 Beat the eggs in a medium mixing bowl with the basil or parsley, salt, and pepper. Add the cheese and set aside.

2 Heat the vegetable oil in a 12-inch nonstick skillet over medium heat. Add the potatoes in a single layer and cook for about 4 minutes, turning them over and shaking the pan occasionally. Add the peppers and onion and cook for 5 to 7 minutes or until the vegetables are tender, stirring occasionally.

3 Raise the heat to medium-high. Add the olive oil and the egg-cheese mixture to the skillet and cook for about 1 minute, running a rubber spatula around the edges to make sure it does not stick. Cover and reduce the heat to medium. Cook for about 4 to 5 minutes or until the bottom is set and golden brown. The top should still be wet.

4 As the frittata cooks, preheat the broiler.

5 Uncover the skillet and place it under the broiler on the highest oven rack. Broil (with the oven door open) for 30 seconds to 1 minute or until the top is cooked solid and golden.

6 To serve, run a rubber spatula around the outside of the frittata. Invert a large, round serving plate over the pan and invert the pan and plate again quickly, letting the frittata fall onto the plate. It should be golden brown. Serve immediately or at room temperature.

Note: *To core and seed a pepper, first cut a circle around the stem with a paring knife and then twist and pull out the stem and core in one piece. Cut the pepper in half lengthwise and remove any remaining white fibers and seeds. (See Figure 4-2 for illustrated instructions.)*

For a brunch or lunch, serve this frittata with the Watercress, Endive and Orange Salad or the Roasted Pepper and Snow Pea Salad, both from Chapter 10.

Quiche seems to have been relegated to a carry-out food status, but the homemade version, warm from the oven, can be a real treat. This quick version uses a commercial pastry crust, which you can buy in the supermarket. Save any leftover quiche to eat the next day, either cold or reheated in a 325-degree oven for about 15 minutes.

Classic Quiche Lorraine

Tools: *Chef's knife, skillet, whisk, mixing bowl, baking sheet*

Preparation time: *About 20 minutes*

Cooking time: *About 50 minutes*

Yield: *4 servings*

3 strips bacon

1 small onion, diced

9-inch frozen, commercial pie crust

½ cup cubed Gruyère or Swiss cheese

2 tablespoons freshly grated Parmesan cheese (optional)

3 eggs, lightly beaten

½ cup heavy cream or half-and-half

½ cup milk

2 tablespoons minced parsley

¼ teaspoon ground nutmeg

¼ teaspoon salt, or to taste

⅛ teaspoon white pepper, or to taste

1 Place the oven rack in the lowest position and preheat the oven to 375 degrees.

2 Heat a medium skillet over medium heat, add the bacon strips, and cook for about 3 to 4 minutes or until crisp, turning frequently. Remove and drain on paper towels. Pour off all but 1 tablespoon of fat from the pan. (Pour the fat into a metal can — not down the sink where it can clog the drain.) In the same pan, cook the onions over medium heat until they wilt, stirring occasionally, for 2 to 3 minutes.

3 Crumble the bacon and sprinkle it over the pie crust along with the onion and the cheese.

4 In a bowl, whisk together the eggs, cream, milk, parsley, nutmeg, salt, and pepper. Pour this mixture over the bacon, onions, and cheese. Place on a baking sheet and bake for 45 to 50 minutes or until firm.

Replace the bacon with ⅓ to ½ cup of any of the following: cooked cubed zucchini, summer squash, okra, chopped spinach, roasted bell peppers, diced sautéed mushrooms, chopped sautéed leeks, cubed tomatoes sautéed with garlic and onions, cubed sautéed artichoke hearts, diced baked ham, or blanched asparagus.

Soufflé Savvy

Most home cooks are intimidated by soufflés, believing that if they look at one the wrong way, it will collapse like a house of cards, causing snickers among their guests. The truth is that soufflés are no more challenging than poached eggs.

After you learn the technique of making a soufflé — either sweet or savory — you can take off in many directions. All you do is decide on a main ingredient (in this recipe, cheese) and combine it with egg yolks and seasonings, and then you fold in whipped egg whites, which makes the soufflé rise. Savory soufflés often have a roux base (flour, butter, and milk) to give them muscle.

Soufflés are usually baked in round, straight-sided, ovenproof soufflé dishes. The straight sides allow the mixture to rise above the rim of the dish as it bakes. But you can substitute a straight-sided casserole dish as long as it is the correct size. If the dish is too big, the soufflé may not rise sufficiently above the rim. If the container is too small, the mixture may spill over onto the oven floor.

To make a soufflé, you need even, uninterrupted heat in the oven. So avoid the temptation to keep opening the door to peek in the oven.

Separating an egg

Soufflés require separated egg whites and yolks. Don't worry; separating an egg really isn't as difficult as it looks. Follow these steps, as illustrated in Figure 8-2, to separate an egg without breaking the yolk. (You don't want any yolk in your whites, or the whites will not beat stiff.)

1. **Hold the egg in one hand above two small bowls.**

2. **Crack the shell on the side of one bowl — just enough to break through the shell and the membrane without piercing the yolk or shattering the shell.**

   This step might take a little practice. Repeat on the other side if necessary.

3. **Pry open the eggshell with both thumbs and gently let the bulk of the white fall into one of the bowls.**

4. **Carefully pass the yolk back and forth from one shell cavity to the other, each time releasing more white.**

5. **When all the white is in the bowl, carefully transfer the yolk to the other bowl (it doesn't matter if the yolk breaks); cover and refrigerate, if not using right away.**

Figure 8-2:
Recipes often call for separated egg yolks or whites. Follow these steps to get only the part you want.

How to Separate an Egg

1. Hold the egg in one hand over two small bowls

2. Crack the shell on the side of one bowl

3. Let the white fall into one of the bowls

4. Pass the yolk back & forth, each time releasing more white

5. When all the white is in the bowl, drop yolk in the other bowl.

Beating egg whites

Beaten egg whites make soufflés rise. Before beating egg whites, make sure that your mixing bowl and beaters are clean and dry. Even a speck of dirt, oil, or egg yolk can prevent the whites from beating stiff. Beat the whites slowly until they are foamy; then increase the beating speed to incorporate as much air as possible until the whites form smooth, shiny peaks. (If you use a whisk, the same principle applies.) If you're making a sweet soufflé, start beating in the sugar after the whites form soft peaks.

If any of the yolk breaks and falls into the separated whites before you beat them stiff, be sure to remove the yolk by dabbing with a piece of paper towel. Also avoid using plastic bowls when beating whites. Fat and grease adhere to plastic, which can diminish the volume of the beaten whites.

If you overbeat the egg whites so that they lose their shine and start to look dry and grainy, add another egg white and beat briefly to reconstitute.

Folding egg whites into a soufflé base

To fold egg whites into a soufflé base, begin by stirring about one-quarter of the beaten whites into the yolk mixture. (This step lightens the batter somewhat.) Then pile the remaining egg whites on top. Use a large rubber spatula to cut down through the center of the mixture going all the way to the bottom of the bowl. Pull the spatula toward you to the edge of the bowl, turning it to bring some of the yolk mixture up over the whites. Give the bowl a quarter-turn and repeat this plunging, scooping motion about 10 to 15 times (depending on the amount of batter) until the whites and yolk mixture are combined. Be careful not to overblend, or the beaten whites will deflate. See Figure 8-3 for illustrated instructions of this technique.

How to Fold Egg Whites into a Soufflé Base

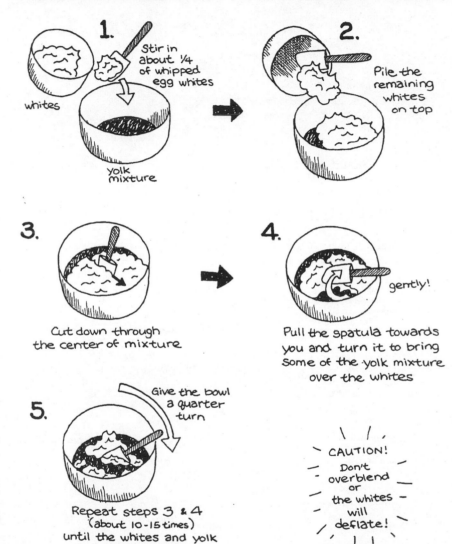

1. Stir in about ¼ of whipped egg whites

whites

yolk mixture

2. Pile the remaining whites on top

3. Cut down through the center of mixture

4. Pull the spatula towards you and turn it to bring some of the yolk mixture over the whites

gently!

5. Give the bowl a quarter turn

Repeat steps 3 & 4 (about 10-15 times) until the whites and yolk are Combined

CAUTION! Don't overblend or the whites will deflate!

Figure 8-3: Folding egg whites into a soufflé base involves a plunging, scooping motion.

TIP

The copper connection

We won't go into the scientific details of why copper bowls are best for whipping egg whites — just believe us. As far back as the mid-eighteenth century, this was common knowledge. Just remember that if you are making a meringue or other dish that requires whipped whites, whipping the whites in a copper bowl with a balloon whisk yields a more fluffy and stable foam.

A 10-inch copper bowl for whisking costs about $60. If you don't have a copper bowl, a pinch of cream of tartar, added to the egg white, can also stabilize the foam.

Basic cheese soufflé

Here is a recipe for a basic cheese soufflé (known as a *savory* soufflé, or one that is not sweet).

Gruyère Soufflé

Tools: *6-cup soufflé dish, chef's knife, mixing bowls, medium heavy-bottom saucepan, rubber spatula, electric mixer or wire whisk, grater, baking sheet*

Preparation time: *About 45 minutes*

Baking time: *About 30 minutes*

Yield: *4 servings*

4 tablespoons butter	*Pinch cayenne pepper (optional)*
6 eggs	*Salt and white or black pepper to taste*
2 tablespoons cornstarch	*4 ounces Gruyère or Swiss cheese (or any hard, aged cheese), cut into small cubes*
3 tablespoons water	
2 cups milk	*2 tablespoons grated Gruyère or Swiss cheese*
3 tablespoons flour	
⅛ teaspoon ground nutmeg	

1 Preheat the oven to 400 degrees.

2 Place a 6-cup soufflé dish in the refrigerator. When it is cool, take 1 tablespoon of the butter and thoroughly butter the bottom and sides of the dish, paying special attention to the sides. Return the dish to the refrigerator.

3 Separate the eggs, placing the yolks in one bowl and the whites in a larger bowl. (Refer to Figure 8-2 for instructions for separating eggs.)

4 Blend the cornstarch into the water and set aside. Heat the milk just to the point of boiling and then remove it from the heat.

5 Melt the remaining 3 tablespoons butter in a medium heavy-bottom saucepan over medium heat. Add the flour, stirring constantly with a wire whisk. Blend well, about 1 minute, but do not brown the flour. Gradually add the warmed milk, stirring rapidly with a wire whisk until the mixture is smooth and creamy, about 2 to 3 minutes. Add the nutmeg, cayenne (if desired), salt, and pepper. Raise the heat, bring to a boil, and cook for 30 seconds, whisking constantly.

6 Whisk the cornstarch-water mixture into the bubbling sauce. Lower the heat to medium and cook for about 2 minutes over medium heat, whisking. Add the egg yolks, whisking. Cook for about 1 minute, whisking. (Whisk constantly to avoid burning the egg yolk mixture.)

7 Spoon and scrape the mixture into a large mixing bowl. Add the cubed Gruyère, blend well with a wire whisk, and set aside.

8 With a balloon-shaped wire whisk or an electric mixer, beat the egg whites in a large mixing bowl until stiff and thick but not dry. (See "Beating egg whites," earlier in this chapter, for more information.) Add about one-quarter of the whites to the soufflé mixture and mix thoroughly. Add the remaining whites, folding them in quickly but gently with a rubber spatula. (See Figure 8-3 for illustrated instructions for folding whites into batter.)

9 Gently transfer the mixture into the buttered soufflé dish. The mixture should fit inside the dish to about ¼ inch from the top. With your thumb, create a channel around the edge of the mixture to allow for even expansion. Sprinkle the top with the grated Gruyère or Swiss cheese.

10 Place the dish on a baking sheet on the bottom rack of the oven and bake for about 30 to 35 minutes or until the crust is golden and the top is firm with a slight wobble in the center. Serve immediately, using a large spoon to scoop out portions of the soft interior and golden crust.

You could serve this soufflé for dinner, with Carrots in Cumin Butter (see Chapter 15) or Carrot Soup with Dill (see Chapter 9).

Or try one of these variations:

- **Salmon soufflé:** Substitute ¼ pound smoked, diced salmon for the cubed gruyére.

- **Ham soufflé:** Substitute ¼ pound minced boiled ham for the cubed gruyére.

Check out the following tips for making the perfect soufflé:

✔ A perfectly cooked soufflé is firm and crusty on the outside with a moist and somewhat creamy center. If you prefer a drier, denser center, leave it in the oven a few minutes longer than the recommended cooking time.

✔ Opening the oven door and letting in cold air can deflate the soufflé. If you must peek, do so only during the last 10 minutes of baking and only to check it for doneness.

✔ Have your diners seated at the table, waiting for the soufflé — it will deflate within a minute or two after it's removed from the oven.

Chapter 9

Soups

*N*o offense to the gastronomic wizards at major commercial soup companies, but most seven-year-olds with a recipe and a stepladder can make soup that is superior to the canned version. For one, canned soups are always overcooked — overcooking usually occurs in the sterilization process. What's more, the seasonings are toned down (except for salt, in most cases) so as to offend the smallest number of people — sort of like American beer.

Homemade soups are worth the minimal effort they take for many other reasons, too. For one, homemade soups can be awesomely nutritious. Secondly, they can be stunningly delicious. A soup can be a complete meal or a savory appetizer. In the winter months, a steaming bowl of soup can have a comforting, stick-to-the-ribs quality. In the summer heat, soup can be cold and refreshing. Need we say more?

Soups come in several categories: namely *clear,* as in consommé, certain vegetable soups, and broths; and *creamy,* as in New England-style chowder, vichyssoise (a creamy leek and potato soup), cream of tomato, cream of mushroom, cheesy soups, and so on. Soups that fall in-between include the cloudy Rhode Island Style Chowder, certain vegetable soups, onion soup, and so on. And then you have purees like gazpacho.

What am I eating? Soups defined

Bisque: A thick, rich, pureed soup usually made from shellfish (such as crab or lobster).

Broth: A clear, flavored liquid made from simmering together any combination of water, vegetables, herbs, meats, poultry, or fish bones. All the solids are strained out. Broth is often served as an appetizer with a garnish floating on the surface. The French word for broth is bouillon (which is not to be confused with what you get from a bouillon cube).

Chowder: A typically-thick and chunky fish soup, usually with vegetables.

Consommé: The "consummate" broth that's completely clear of grease and impurities. A mixture of egg whites, and sometimes finely chopped meat and vegetables, is simmered in the stock. The egg whites cook or solidify, trapping any impurities. After simmering an hour or more, the stock is strained through layers of cheesecloth, resulting in a very clear, pure consommé.

Court bouillon: A broth, usually strained, that simmers for only a short time — no more than 30 minutes — but long enough to draw out the flavor of the vegetables added to the broth. It's used as a poaching liquid for fish, seafood, and vegetables.

Fumet: A strained stock of fish bones, water, vegetables, and herbs. Fumet (French for "fish stock") cooks for about 30 minutes and is used as a flavoring base for soups and sauces.

Gumbo: A soup that typically combines assorted shellfish, poultry, vegetables, a long-cooked dark brown roux of flour and oil, okra, and filé powder (a seasoning made from ground sassafras leaves), which thicken and flavor the soup as it cooks. Gumbo is the African word for okra.

Pureed soup: A soup in which solid ingredients are whirled in a blender or food processor or forced through a food mill. Sometimes the puree is coarse, as in gazpacho (see the recipe later in this chapter). Other times the puree is creamy and velvety, as with a puree of cooked potatoes and leeks. Stock, cream, or a velouté is often added to the vegetable mixture for extra texture and flavor.

Stock: The foundation of countless soups. (Chapter 3 includes recipes for basic stocks.) In a brown stock, meat bones are browned in the oven before being added to a simmering pot of liquid, vegetables, and herbs. This browning gives the stock a rich caramel color and flavor.

Clean the Crisper and Make Some Soup

You may have the makings of a terrific soup at home and not realize it. Start by looking in the vegetable crisper. Do you have carrots and celery? Toss them in a pot of water along with a bay leaf and black peppercorns. If you have parsley, toss that in. An onion? All the better. What you've made is a vegetable stock. The longer you cook and reduce it, the more flavorful it becomes.

To this stock, you can add pieces of cooked chicken, turkey, or beef; noodles; rice; or whatever you have on hand. Just as with sauces, as long as you have a good base, you can build upon it. This chapter includes a cross-section of easy soup bases that show you how to carry on by yourself and improvise to your heart's content.

Making the following soup is a great way to use the remaining meat and bones of a turkey carcass. Adding inexpensive turkey is a good way to turn a soup into a nutritious meal. The cilantro garnish is a flourish that gives the soup an exotic Asian accent.

Turkey (or Chicken) Vegetable Soup

Tools: *Large saucepan or pot, chef's knife, vegetable peeler*

Preparation time: *About 25 minutes*

Cooking time: *About 30 minutes*

Yield: *4 to 6 servings*

2 tablespoons butter

1 large onion, chopped

4 leeks, about 1 pound, white and pale green parts only, cleaned and cut into ¼-inch slices

3 carrots, peeled and cut into ¼-inch rounds

3 boiling potatoes, about 1 pound, peeled and cut into ¼-inch cubes

1 parsnip, peeled and cut into ¼-inch cubes

4 cups homemade or canned chicken stock

4 cups water

Salt and black pepper to taste

1 pound boneless, skinless turkey or chicken breast (or 1 pound leftover cooked turkey or chicken), cut into ½-inch cubes

3 tablespoons chopped cilantro or parsley (optional)

1 In a large saucepan or pot over medium heat, melt the butter and add the onion, leeks, carrots, potatoes, and parsnip. Cook, stirring occasionally, until the onions and leeks wilt, about 5 minutes.

2 Add the chicken stock, water, salt, and pepper. Cover and bring to a boil; reduce heat and simmer, uncovered, for 30 minutes.

3 Add the turkey or chicken breast cubes and simmer for 20 to 30 minutes more, skimming with a large metal spoon any scum or fat that rises to the surface. Garnish each serving with cilantro or parsley, if desired.

For a light lunch, serve this soup with a Cherry Tomato and Feta Salad (see Chapter 10).

Skimming soups and stocks

When making soups or stocks, especially those that contain dried beans or lentils, meat, or poultry, you often need to use a long-handled spoon to skim the surface of the simmering liquid to remove and discard any scum or foam that rises to the surface. Try to skim the surface as soon as the foam forms. If you allow it to boil back into the broth, it affects the flavor. Also skim off any fat floating on the surface or refrigerate the soup to chill it and then lift off the congealed fat.

For a curry flavor, add l tablespoon curry powder to the sautéing vegetables in step 1.

Sometimes you want to thicken your soup so that it looks more luxurious and tastes richer. You can thicken soup in several ways:

- ✔ Take 1 tablespoon slightly softened butter and work it together with 1 tablespoon all-purpose flour. (The French call this a *beurre manié,* but don't worry about that — they have a different word for everything.) Scoop a cup or so of soup liquid into a small bowl and mix in the flour-butter mixture. Stir this back into the soup pot and cook over medium heat for about 5 minutes, until thickened.

- ✔ Blend 1 tablespoon all-purpose flour with 2 tablespoons soup broth. Stir, add about 1 cup more broth, stir again, and add to the soup.

Pureed Soups

Pureed soups use a blender or food processor to whirl the ingredients into a smooth texture. After you understand the pureeing technique, the variations you can make on this cooking theme are limitless. Asparagus, broccoli, corn, cucumber, mushrooms, parsnips, spinach, rutabaga, winter squash, pumpkin, turnip, and watercress are among the vegetables that puree to a rich and smooth consistency.

On a hot summer day, nothing is more refreshing than a bowl of this lovely cold soup.

Cream of Leek Soup

Tools: *Chef's knife, large saucepan or pot, wooden spoon or wire whisk, blender or food processor*

Preparation time: *About 20 minutes*

Cooking time: *About 25 minutes*

Yield: *4 appetizer servings*

4 medium leeks (white and pale green parts only), cleaned and trimmed (see following sidebar)

1 tablespoon butter

2 teaspoons olive oil

1 large clove garlic, finely minced

3 tablespoons all-purpose flour

2⅔ cups homemade or canned chicken or vegetable stock

½ cup milk

Generous pinch of nutmeg (optional)

Salt and black pepper to taste

½ cup heavy cream or half-and-half

4 small chervil sprigs, or 1 tablespoon chopped chives (optional)

1 Quarter the leeks lengthwise and cut into ½-inch-long pieces. You should have about 2½ cups.

2 In a large saucepan or pot, melt the butter with the olive oil over medium heat. Add the leeks and garlic. Cook for about 2 minutes, stirring often. Do not let the garlic burn.

3 Add the flour, blending well with a wooden spoon or wire whisk. Add the chicken or vegetable stock, milk, nutmeg, salt, and pepper. Stir well and bring to a simmer. Cook for about 15 to 20 minutes, stirring occasionally. Cool slightly. (See following warning.)

4 Spoon and scrape the mixture into a blender or food processor container and puree well.

5 To serve hot, warm the cream or half-and-half. Just before serving, add it to the soup and stir well. To serve cold, chill the soup and add the cold cream or half-and half-before serving. Always check seasonings before serving. Garnish each serving with chervil sprigs or chopped chives, if desired.

Serve with country bread and a vinaigrette-based salad like Roasted Pepper and Snow Pea Salad (see Chapter 10).

Cleaning and trimming leeks

Leeks look like overgrown green onions but are milder tasting. They can be added to soups and stews or sautéed in butter with tender vegetables like mushrooms.

The fine grains of sand trapped between the layers of leek must be thoroughly washed away before the leek is cooked. On a cutting board with a sharp knife, trim off the little roots shooting out from the bulb end. Then cut off the tough dark green portion of the tops, leaving about 2 inches of pale green stem. (The dark green portion of the stems should be discarded. You generally use only the white and pale green part of the leek. However, the dark green parts can be rinsed and used to make vegetable or chicken stock.) Slice the trimmed leeks in half lengthwise and rinse them under running cold water, opening up the layers with your fingers to wash away the grit and sand.

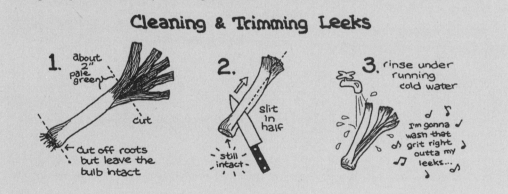

Cleaning & Trimming Leeks

1. about 2" pale green — cut — Cut off roots but leave the bulb intact

2. slit in half — still intact

3. rinse under running cold water — I'm gonna wash that grit right outta my leeks...

If you're going to puree a soup in a blender, let it cool slightly first. Otherwise, the trapped steam could explode and redecorate your ceiling.

This soup is as bland as an accountants' convention!

If your soup is bland, you may want to toss in a bouillon cube (chicken, beef, or vegetable, depending on the soup). But remember that bouillon cubes are loaded with salt and may overwhelm the other flavors of the soup. Start with half a cube and taste before adding the other half. Maybe the soup simply lacks salt and pepper. Or perhaps herbs can give it zip: Try rosemary, sage, savory, tarragon, or thyme. You also can add a little lemon juice or dry sherry.

Dill is a natural sidekick to carrots. The following pureed soup usually calls for heavy cream at the end; instead, we use low-fat ricotta, which works just as well at a fraction of the calories. Port adds a touch of sweetness.

Carrot Soup with Dill

Tools: *Deep saucepan or pot, chef's knife, paring knife, colander, blender or food processor*

Preparation time: *About 15 minutes*

Cooking time: *About 35 minutes*

Yield: *6 appetizer servings*

2 tablespoons butter

1 medium onion, finely chopped

1½ pounds carrots, peeled and cut into 1-inch-thick pieces

4 cups homemade or canned chicken or vegetable stock

2 cups water

Salt and black pepper to taste

½ cup low-fat ricotta cheese

2 to 3 tablespoons port (optional)

2 tablespoons chopped fresh dill, or 2 teaspoons dried

1 In a large, deep saucepan or soup pot over medium heat, melt the butter. Add the onion and cook, stirring often, until it softens. Add the carrots, stock, water, salt, and pepper. Cover and bring to a boil. Reduce the heat and simmer, uncovered, for 30 minutes, skimming off any foam that rises to the surface. Cool slightly.

2 Strain the mixture through a colander set over a second deep pan or pot and reserve the cooking liquid. Puree the remaining solids in a food processor or blender container along with the ricotta and 1 cup of the reserved cooking liquid. Add the puree to the pot holding the remaining cooking liquid. Stir well with a wooden spoon.

3 Bring the soup to a boil and add the port (if desired) and dill. Serve hot or cold.

This soup makes a smashing lunch with sandwiches or wraps, like Chicken and Grilled Vegetable Wrap (see Chapter 17).

 Always add fresh herbs to soups or sauces at the last minute before serving. That way, the herbs remain vibrant and alive with flavor.

You also can use ground ginger as the seasoner in this creamy carrot soup. Ginger is more intense than dill, so you need less. Omit the dill and instead add ½ to ¾ teaspoon ground ginger.

To turn this soup into a vegetable side dish, simply proceed as instructed, pureeing the cooked vegetables with the ricotta but adding only as much of the cooking liquid as necessary to produce a thick puree.

The following soup of chicken stock, spinach, and eggs, derived from the Italian classic Stracciatella, is ready in minutes for a quick lunch and is especially easy if you use canned chicken stock. For special occasions, this soup makes an elegant introduction to a rich meal, but you will probably want to prepare the stock. (Turn to Chapter 3 for our homemade chicken stock recipe.)

Spinach Cloud Soup

Tools: *Medium saucepan or pot, blender or food processor*

Preparation time: *About 10 minutes*

Cooking time: *About 5 minutes*

Yield: *6 servings*

6 cups homemade or canned chicken or vegetable stock

4 eggs

⅔ cup fresh spinach, rinsed, trimmed of stems, and chopped

¼ cup grated Parmesan cheese, plus more for serving

2 tablespoons fresh lemon juice

Salt and black pepper to taste

1 Bring the stock to a boil in a covered medium saucepan over high heat.

2 As the stock heats, combine the eggs, spinach, Parmesan cheese, 1 tablespoon of the lemon juice, salt, and pepper in a blender or food processor container. Whirl for a few seconds to form a smooth puree.

3 When the broth comes to a boil, stir in the remaining 1 tablespoon lemon juice and the spinach-egg mixture. Turn off the heat. Little cloudlike lumps of spinach and egg form immediately on the surface. Taste for seasoning. Serve with extra grated Parmesan cheese.

Like the carrot soup, this soup is superb with sandwiches or with a dinner of Roasted Chicken (see Chapter 6).

In step 1, add ½ cup cooked carrots, sliced into thin rounds.

Stock-Based Soups

"You can tell a good cook from a great cook by how they make a soup," says Bob Kinkead, chef and owner of Kinkead's in Washington, D.C. "The single most important factor for a great soup is a great stock. If you can't make one from scratch, then buy it at a specialty market. College Inn is good quality canned stock, but buy the low-salt version."

Lamb or beef soup

Lamb or beef soups derive much of their flavor from bones added to the cooking liquid. Notice how the lamb bones are cooked in the broth in this easy recipe — in a sense, you are making your stock at the same time you make this soup. Because you remove the meat from the bone, cut it into small pieces, and put it in the soup, nothing is wasted, and the soup absorbs every bit of flavor. Be sure to use cold water to cook the ingredients — doing so helps the bones and meat release their juices. This rich and hearty soup stands on its own as a main dish for a cold winter day.

Lamb Barley Soup

Tools: *Large pot, chef's knife, tongs or slotted spoon*

Preparation time: *About 20 minutes*

Cooking time: *About 2 hours*

Yield: *8 to 10 servings*

4 lamb shanks, cracked (or a meaty bone from a leg of lamb)

1 cup pearl barley, washed (see following note)

1 cup green split peas, washed (following note)

2 medium onions, peeled and chopped

3 large cloves garlic, chopped

3½ quarts water

3 to 4 teaspoons salt

Black pepper to taste

7 medium carrots, sliced

(continued)

1 Place all ingredients except the carrots in a large soup pot. Cover and bring to a boil. Reduce the heat and simmer for 1 hour and 40 minutes partially covered, stirring occasionally and skimming the surface as necessary.

2 Add the carrots and simmer for another 20 minutes.

3 Taste for seasoning. Remove the bones with tongs or a slotted spoon and let them cool slightly. When the bones are cool enough to handle, trim off the meat and add it to the soup.

Note: Rinse grains and dried beans thoroughly in a large pot of cold water to wash off soil particles. Discard any small stones or stray pieces that rise to the surface before adding the grains or beans to the cooking water or broth.

 Soups that contain grains or dried beans (or other legumes) have relatively long cooking times, so you can soak them in water overnight to shorten the cooking time, or add them near the beginning of cooking. Add any "garnish" vegetables, like the carrots in the preceding recipe, toward the finish of the dish so that their flavors do not completely cook away before the soup is done.

 When simmering thick soups like the preceding one, occasionally stir and scrape the bottom of the pot with a wooden spoon to prevent the mixture from sticking and burning. Add more water, if necessary. If you do burn food, transfer the unburned portion to another pot.

Black bean soup

The secret to good black bean soup is a strong stock to give it that lingering flavor. Here we recommend homemade chicken stock, but if you don't have time, use a good brand of frozen or canned stock. The vegetables and slab bacon — available at any good butcher — provide a lot of flavor.

You can make the soup as spicy as you like. Black bean soup is best if made a day ahead of time, chilled, and then reheated. The recipe makes enough for a small army, but you can freeze leftovers for another day.

Note: The recipe is a little labor intensive, but trust us: This soup is worth the effort.

ESSENTIAL SKILL

Freezing and reheating soup

If you cook up a big batch of soup and find that you can't eat it all at once, chill it in the refrigerator and skim off any fat that rises to the surface before freezing. Freeze soup in an airtight plastic container.

Reheat frozen soups in a microwave oven or in a heavy saucepan over low heat. Heat only until warmed through to avoid overcooking starchy ingredients, such as potatoes, pasta, and rice.

Black Bean Soup

Tools: *Chef's knife, large pot or heavy saucepan, colander, ladle*

Preparation time: *About 30 minutes if using prepared stock*

Cooking time: *About 2 hours and 15 minutes*

Yield: *8 to 12 servings*

½ pound smoked slab bacon with rind (see following note)

2 medium onions, finely chopped

2 stalks celery, finely chopped

2 large carrots, peeled and finely diced

3 large cloves garlic, minced

1 bay leaf

2 tablespoons finely chopped oregano, or 2 teaspoons dried

2 tablespoons ground cumin

1 teaspoon black pepper

1¼ teaspoons dried thyme

3 tablespoons tomato paste

4 quarts (16 cups) homemade or canned chicken stock

1 pound dried black beans, about 3 cups

½ cup finely chopped fresh cilantro leaves

¼ teaspoon Tabasco sauce, or to taste

¼ teaspoon cayenne pepper, or to taste

Salt to taste

Salsa for garnish (see following recipe)

Sour cream for garnish (optional)

1 Slice off and reserve the rind of the bacon. Cut the bacon into ¼-inch cubes.

2 Put the bacon cubes and the rind into a stock pot or large, heavy saucepan and cook over medium heat, about 10 minutes, stirring often, until the bacon rinds are brown and crisp.

(continued)

3 Add the onions, celery, carrots, garlic, bay leaf, oregano, 1 tablespoon of the cumin, black pepper, and thyme. Stir to blend and cover the pot. Cook for about 5 minutes over moderately low heat, stirring occasionally. Do not allow the mixture to burn.

4 Add the tomato paste and stir briefly. Add the chicken stock, increase the heat to high, cover, and bring to a boil.

5 Rinse and drain the beans. Reduce the heat, stir in the beans, and simmer, uncovered, for about 2 hours, stirring and skimming the surface occasionally to remove any scum with a large metal spoon as it rises to the top. The soup is ready when the beans are soft and some of them have disintegrated into the soup.

6 Stir in the cilantro, Tabasco sauce, cayenne pepper, salt, and remaining cumin. Remove and discard the bacon rind and bay leaf.

7 Ladle the soup into soup bowls. Serve salsa and sour cream, if desired, on the side.

Note: Slab bacon comes in thick rectangles and has less fat than regular American bacon. If you use fatty bacon, trim most of the fat before browning it. American bacon crisps and browns in about 5 minutes over medium heat.

Black Bean Soup can be a meal in itself with bread. It also goes well with The Perfect Hamburger (see Chapter 6).

You can use this salsa fresh, but it tastes better after it sits in the refrigerator for about an hour.

Salsa

Tools: *Chef's knife, small mixing bowl*

Preparation time: *About 20 minutes*

Cooking time: *None*

Yield: *About 2½ cups*

2 large tomatoes, peeled, seeded, and cut into ¼-inch cubes

1 medium onion, finely chopped

¼ cup finely chopped cilantro or parsley

2 tablespoons fresh lime juice

1½ teaspoons seeded and finely chopped jalapeño peppers, more to taste

Salt to taste, if desired

Combine all the ingredients in a bowl and stir to mix well. Refrigerate until ready to serve. Taste for seasoning before serving.

You can add one ripe, chopped avocado to the salsa and serve it as an appetizer with yellow or blue corn chips.

Jalapeño pepper oils can burn your eyes as badly as tear gas. Take care not to accidentally rub your eyes after chopping and seeding them. You may want to wear rubber gloves when working with them. To seed and chop a jalapeño, slice the pepper lengthwise in half, discarding the stem and core. Scrape away the seeds; then mince or dice. (Then go wash your hands!)

Flavor from pork fat

Pork products, like the slab bacon in the preceding Black Bean Soup recipe, are often used to flavor soups, stews, and long-simmering casserole dishes. Chef Bob Kinkead of Kinkead's in Washington, D.C., says that the most important step in making a great soup is to first "render the bacon fat," which means cooking it until the fat melts away.

Here's a list of common cooking products available from pork:

✔ **Back fat:** Taken right from under the pig's skin, back fat has no meat at all, and is sold fresh and salted as a cooking fat. Sometimes it is also tied around roasts or used to line meat terrines. It can usually be found in butcher shops.

✔ **Canadian bacon:** Made by curing the boneless center-cut loin of pork in the same fashion as bacon. Canadian bacon needs no further cooking at home but is delicious warmed in a skillet with eggs or chopped into scrambled eggs and omelets. It's also much leaner than other pork products.

✔ **Crispy pork skin (cracklings):** Produced from fried or roasted pork skin, crispy pork skin is considered a delicacy by some. In the southern United States, it is used to flavor cornbread and vegetable dishes.

✔ **Fresh pork belly:** An important ingredient in sausages and for flavoring vegetables. If salted or cured, fresh pork belly becomes salt pork. Bacon is pork belly that has been both smoked and salted. Most bacon is sold presliced, but some butcher shops still carry unsliced or slab bacon that you can cut into chunks or cubes for flavoring soups, stews, and chowders. Slab bacon comes with the rind or skin intact and has a smoky-salty character all its own.

✔ **Lard:** Pure, clarified pork fat — free of all skin or other protein. It is especially good as a shortening for biscuits and baked goods because it produces a very light and flaky pastry.

✔ **Pancetta:** Italian bacon, cured with salt and spices, but not smoked like American bacon. Pancetta usually comes in a sausage-shaped roll and is thinly sliced for flavoring sauces, pasta dishes, stuffings, breads, and omelets.

The best way to extract the juice from limes, lemons, oranges, and other citrus fruits is to use a manual or electric juicer that separates the juice from the seeds. Rolling the fruit on a counter, or between your palms, for a few seconds helps to break up the juice sacks and makes juicing easier.

Seafood Soup

Seafood soups of all kinds are quick and easy to make. Fish cooks in minutes, so you have to get your timing right. The following version adds mussels, but you also can use clams or scallops.

Seafood Soup

Tools: *Chef's knife; large, heavy saucepan or pot*

Preparation time: *About 35 minutes*

Cooking time: *About 25 minutes*

Yield: *4 servings*

1 pound lean skinless fish, such as monk-fish, cod, tilefish, halibut, or any combination

2 tablespoons olive oil

1 medium onion, chopped

1 large leek, trimmed, rinsed, and finely chopped, white and pale green parts only

1 medium red bell pepper, cored, seeded, and cut into small cubes

1 medium green bell pepper, cored, seeded, and cut into small cubes

3 large cloves garlic, finely chopped

2 cups water

1 cup dry white wine

1 cup canned crushed tomatoes

1 sprig fresh thyme, or ½ teaspoon dried

1 bay leaf

1 teaspoon anise seed (optional)

¼ teaspoon red pepper flakes (optional)

Salt and black pepper to taste

20 mussels, well scrubbed and with beards removed (see following instructions)

¼ cup finely chopped basil or parsley

1 loaf Italian or French bread

1 Cut the fish into 1-inch cubes and remove any small bones.

2 Heat the oil in a heavy pot over medium heat. Add the onion, leek, red and green bell peppers, and garlic. Cook, stirring often, until the onion and peppers wilt, about 5 minutes.

3 Add the water, wine, tomatoes, thyme, bay leaf, anise seed (if desired), red pepper flakes (if desired), salt, and pepper to taste. Bring to a boil and then reduce heat to simmer for 10 minutes.

4 Add the fish and the mussels, stir gently, and bring to a boil. Cover and simmer over low heat for about 5 to 10 minutes or until the fish is cooked through and the mussels open. (Discard any mussels that do not open.) Check for seasoning.

5 Remove the thyme sprig (if you used a fresh sprig) and bay leaf. Sprinkle individual servings with the basil or parsley and serve with sliced Italian or French bread.

Fish soup makes a fine lunch with a side dish of Watercress, Endive, and Orange Salad (see Chapter 10).

Be sure to remove any small bones before adding the fish to the stew.

Cleaning mussels

See the following figure for an illustration of each step.

1. Using a butter knife or scouring pad, scrape any barnacles off the shells.

2. Pull off the beardlike strands.

3. Place the mussels in a large pot and cover with cool, fresh water by about 2 inches. Agitate the mussels with your hand in the water in a washing machine motion.

4. Drain and discard the water.

5. Repeat several times until the water is clear.

6. Drain once more and, if not using them immediately, chill the mussels until you're ready to use them. (Just be sure to use them soon after they are cleaned.)

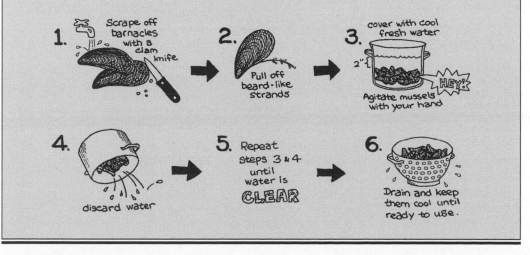

If you goofed with the salt, don't dump the soup. If the soup tastes too salty, the simple solution is to add water. If you don't want to add water and thin the soup, try adding paper-thin slices of potato. Cook them until translucent — they tend to soak up salt. Leave them in the soup if you like. Tomatoes, either fresh or canned (but unsalted!), do the same thing.

Gazpacho

Gazpacho is a puree of raw vegetables (generally based on tomatoes) with citric accents. No two recipes are ever the same. At home, making gazpacho in a food processor or blender is a cinch. Don't overblend, though, because you want the soup to have a chunky texture. If you like your gazpacho spicier, simply add more jalapeño pepper to taste. Lemon or lime juice adds a refreshing touch.

Whenever you make a cold soup, be sure to use only the freshest, ripest vegetables or fruits. Gazpacho is an excellent choice as a summer soup when juicy, locally grown tomatoes are abundant.

Fresh Tomato Gazpacho

Tools: *Chef's knife, paring knife, vegetable peeler, food processor or blender, medium bowl*

Preparation time: *About 30 minutes*

Cooking time: *A few seconds to puree and about 1 hour to chill*

Yield: *6 appetizer servings*

3 pounds ripe tomatoes, peeled, seeded, and chopped (see Chapter 11 for instructions on seeding tomatoes)

1 large onion, chopped

1 large red bell pepper, cored, seeded, and chopped

6 tablespoons coarsely chopped cilantro or parsley

¼ cup olive oil

3 tablespoons red wine vinegar

3 tablespoons fresh lime or lemon juice

3 large cloves garlic, chopped

2 teaspoons seeded and chopped jalapeño pepper, or to taste

Salt and black pepper to taste

1 medium cucumber, peeled, seeded, and cut into ¼-inch cubes

1 Combine all ingredients except for 2 tablespoons of the cilantro or parsley and the cucumber in a food processor or blender (if necessary, blend in batches). Blend to a semicoarse (still chunky) texture. Pour and scrape the mixture into a bowl. Cover with plastic wrap and refrigerate until cold.

2 Just before serving, stir in the cucumber, adjust the seasoning with salt and pepper if needed, and sprinkle with the remaining 2 tablespoons cilantro or parsley.

To remove the seeds from a cucumber, cut the cucumber in half lengthwise and scrape away the layer of seeds with a spoon.

Dressing Up Your Soups

You can make soup look sensational in many ways. A garnish should complement a soup without masking its basic character. There's only one cardinal rule: Complex-tasting soups that have lots of flavor call for simple garnishes, and simple soups call for more assertive garnishes.

Try chopped fresh herbs, a slice of lemon or lime, a dollop of sour cream, a grating of Parmesan, a sprig of watercress, chopped green onions, hard-cooked egg, cooked shrimp, or assorted chopped and sautéed wild mushrooms.

You also can try these garnishes:

- **Julienned vegetables:** Thinly sliced and parboiled root vegetables, such as carrots and parsnips. In a brunoise garnish, the same thin strips are cut into tiny cubes.

- **Chiffonade:** Roll spinach or sorrel leaves lengthwise like a cigar and slice widthwise into thin, lacy strands. Drop into clear broths just before serving.

- **Croutons:** Season toasted bread cubes with garlic and toss with grated cheese before dropping into hot soups. (See the following recipe for Garlic Croutons.)

- **Gremolata:** Toss together chopped garlic, chopped parsley, and grated lemon zest — also wonderful on broiled steak, chicken, or pork.

- **Pistou:** Similar to pesto sauce. Pound fresh basil leaves, garlic, Parmesan cheese, and olive oil into a creamy paste.

✔ **Salsa:** Chopped fresh tomatoes, garlic, onion, and hot chili peppers. (See the Salsa recipe earlier in this chapter.) Endless variations exist.

✔ **Fancy garnishes:** Carve a little man out of a carrot and place him on a tarragon leaf "surfboard." Blow to make waves in the soup.

Many soups benefit from tasty little croutons. Homemade croutons are much better than store-bought ones, and you can make them in minutes.

Garlic Croutons

Tools: Serrated knife, chef's knife, skillet, metal spatula

Preparation time: About 5 minutes

Cooking time: About 3 minutes

Yield: 6 servings

4 slices white or whole wheat bread

2 large cloves garlic, peeled

¼ cup vegetable or olive oil

Black pepper to taste

1 Stack the bread slices and use a serrated knife to trim off the crusts. Cut the slices into ¼-inch cubes. You should have about 2 cups.

2 Set the garlic cloves on a cutting board and use the side of a chef's knife to press or crush the cloves flat.

3 Heat the oil in a large skillet over medium-high heat. Add the crushed garlic and cook while stirring, for about 1 minute, or until very lightly browned. (Do not let it burn.) Discard the garlic. Add the bread and cook for about another 2 minutes, using a metal spatula to toss the cubes so that they brown on all sides. Remove from the skillet and drain on paper towels. Season with pepper, if desired.

Chapter 10

Salads

· ·

In This Chapter

▶ Making vinaigrettes and creamy dressings

▶ Checking out oils and vinegars

▶ Foraging for greens

▶ Ten quick and easy salads

· ·

T ossing together a salad is easy if you have fresh ingredients; what you put *on* the salad makes the difference. For simplicity's sake, we break down dressings into two categories: vinaigrette and creamy (or mayonnaise-based). When you're making a salad, the first thing to consider is which kind of dressing you want.

Gentlemen, Choose Your Dressing: The Two Types

Vinaigrette goes with all sorts of salad greens and grilled vegetables. A creamy dressing can enhance various greens as well as cold shellfish, meat, and poultry. Both types are simple to prepare. The advantage of vinaigrette-based dressing is that you can make a large quantity and store it, sealed, in an old wine bottle or mason jar. Mayonnaise-based dressings should be used within a week or so.

Following are two basic dressing recipes and suggestions for varying them.

Vinaigrette Dressing

The proportions in this vinaigrette recipe are only approximations. You must taste it as you go along to balance the vinegar and olive oil flavors.

Tools: *Small bowl, whisk*

Preparation time: *Less than 5 minutes*

Yield: *4 to 6 servings (about ½ cup)*

2 tablespoons red or white wine vinegar   *⅓ cup olive oil*

1 teaspoon Dijon-style mustard   *Salt and black pepper to taste*

Place the vinegar and mustard in a bowl. Whisk to blend well. Add the olive oil in a stream while whisking. Season with salt and pepper to taste.

Following are some variations on this basic vinaigrette:

- ✔ In the recipe above, you can replace 2 tablespoons of the olive oil with 2 tablespoons of walnut or hazelnut oil to give the vinaigrette a distinctive, nutty flavor. Serve with mixed green salads or salads with grilled poultry.

- ✔ Add 1 teaspoon drained capers and 1 tablespoon chopped fresh chervil, tarragon, basil, or lemon thyme. This herby vinaigrette really enlivens a cold pasta salad.

- ✔ Specialty shops and even supermarkets sell all kinds of flavored vinegars. Tarragon and other herb vinegars add a nice touch to salads.

- ✔ Place one small ripe tomato in a blender or food processor container with the rest of the dressing and blend well.

- ✔ To thicken the vinaigrette, combine it in a blender with 1 to 2 tablespoons of ricotta cheese. Low-fat ricotta enriches just like cream, with far fewer calories.

- ✔ Substitute 2 tablespoons fresh lemon juice for the vinegar.

We add sour cream to the following mayonnaise dressing because it adds a nice, sharp edge. You can use all mayonnaise if you prefer.

Herbed Mayonnaise Dressing

Tools: *Chef's knife, bowl, citrus juicer, whisk*

Preparation time: *About 5 minutes*

⅓ cup mayonnaise

3 tablespoons sour cream

2 tablespoons minced chives

2 tablespoons minced parsley

1½ tablespoons fresh lemon juice

Salt and black pepper to taste

Combine all ingredients in a bowl and whisk well. Taste for seasonings.

This flavorful mayonnaise is great as a sauce with smoked fish, cold chicken, or any cold meats.

Try jazzing up this dressing in any of the following ways:

- ✔ For a seafood salad, add 1 tablespoon drained capers and 1 tablespoon (or to taste) minced tarragon, or 1 teaspoon dried.

- ✔ For a cold meat dish, chicken or shrimp salad, make a curry dressing by adding 1 teaspoon curry powder (or to taste).

- ✔ For cold vegetable salad, crumble ½ cup or more blue cheese or Roquefort and blend it with the dressing.

- ✔ For cold meats, add 1 teaspoon horseradish (or to taste) and mix well.

Every chef has his or her secret when it comes to making salad dressings. "Use a flavored oil and a good quality vinegar," recommends Annie Somerville, chef of Greens Restaurant, a famous vegetarian restaurant in San Francisco, "and don't use too much oil in proportion to the vinegar. Our standard at the restaurant is one part vinegar to three parts oil, unless the vinegar is balsamic — then you can use a little more vinegar because it's sweeter."

Olive and Other Salad Oils

Buying olive oil in the supermarket has become as confusing as ordering coffee at Starbucks, what with all the nationalities and fancy labels and terminology in baffling languages. The most important thing to look for in olive oil is its *grade,* which is usually printed right on the front of the bottle. In ascending order of quality, you'll find *pure, virgin,* and *extra-virgin.*

The grade has to do with the oleic acid content of the oil, with the finest oils having the least acidity. All three varieties of olive oil come from the olive's first *pressing* (the crushing process that releases the oil from the olives), but extra-virgin is the highest quality. Extra-virgin olive oil usually has the richest aroma and strongest flavor. Pure olive oil can come from both the first and second pressing of the tree-ripened olives and may be blended with 5 to 10 percent virgin olive oil to enrich its flavor.

Don't be misled by olive oil sold as "light." The "light" has nothing to do with its fat content; instead, it refers to its pale color and extremely bland flavor, a result of the way it's processed. One tablespoon of any oil contains the same 120 calories.

Other salad oils include walnut, hazelnut, sesame, corn, peanut, safflower, and soy. The neutral flavors of corn, peanut, and safflower oils can be mixed with equal amounts of olive or nut oils. Walnut, hazelnut, and sesame oil are strong, so use them sparingly.

Fancy food markets and gourmet shops are increasingly stocking oils flavored with herbs, lemon, peppercorns, and sun-dried tomatoes. These oils can add just the right seasoning touch to a tossed green salad, and they are delicious drizzled over pizza, French bread, goat cheese or Brie, roasted vegetables, or toasted croutons.

The shelf life of oil depends on its variety. Olive oils should keep for up to a year if tightly capped and stored out of the sun in a cool, dark place. But nut oils last only a few months, so purchase them in small quantities.

Vinegars

Oil in a salad dressing needs an acidic counterpoint — a tart ingredient that stimulates the palate and cuts through the richness of oil. In most cases, vinegar is the choice, but fresh lemon juice also carries a pungent bite.

Balsamic: The world's most expensive vinegar

Traditional balsamic vinegar is a dark, sweet, syrupy, aged liquid that is worth its weight in gold. The real thing is made in the area around Modena, Italy, and nowhere else (the word "Modena" should be on the label). Virtually all those large bottles of balsamic vinegar you see in supermarkets are imitations — some aged, some not — made to look like the real thing. This "fake" balsamic vinegar is not necessarily bad, just different.

Recognizing real balsamic vinegar is easy: You start to hyperventilate upon seeing the price. Real balsamic vinegar is sold only in little bulb-shaped bottles — they look like perfume. It is usually more than 25 years old and costs $100 and up for a tiny portion. Such rarefied vinegar is not to be tossed around in salads. Italians use it for sauces or just drizzle some on fresh fruit (strawberries are best).

Although red or white wine is the most common liquid base, anything that ferments can be used to make vinegar:

- **Cider vinegar:** Made from apples, this strong, clear, brown vinegar holds up well with pungent greens and is especially good sprinkled on meat, fish, or fruit salads. Also excellent with ginger or curry dressings.

- **White vinegar:** Colorless and sharp, white vinegar is distilled from assorted grains, and it's terrific in cold rice or pasta salads.

- **Red or white wine vinegar:** Made from any number of red or white wines, this vinegar is full bodied and perfect for dressing pungent, dark greens.

- **Rice vinegar:** Common to Japan and China, rice vinegars are less tart than white vinegars and combine well with sesame oils. They are also good in seafood salads.

Salad Days: Vinaigrette-Based Recipes

A delicious, low-fat potato salad hinges on a good vinaigrette. The following version is relatively lean, and is delicious warm or chilled.

French Potato Salad

Tools: *Chef's knife, medium saucepan, small bowl, serving bowl, whisk*

Preparation time: *About 15 minutes*

Cooking time: *About 30 minutes*

Yield: *4 to 6 servings*

2 pounds red potatoes, well scrubbed	*¼ cup finely chopped parsley*
Salt to taste	*1 large clove garlic, finely chopped*
6 tablespoons olive oil	*Salt and black pepper to taste*
1 tablespoon white vinegar	*¼ cup dry white wine at room temperature*
½ cup red onion, chopped	

1 In a medium saucepan, cover the potatoes with lightly salted cold water and bring to a boil. Boil for 20 minutes or until the potatoes are tender when pierced with a knife, but not until they fall apart. Drain and let stand until cool enough to handle. (You should assemble the salad while the potatoes are still warm.)

2 As the potatoes cook, make the dressing. Whisk together the oil and vinegar in a small bowl. Whisk in the red onion, parsley, garlic, salt, and pepper.

3 Peel the cooked potatoes and cut them into ¼-inch slices. (Or leave the skins on for more color.) Layer the slices in a shallow serving bowl, sprinkling the wine between the layers.

4 Pour the dressing over the potatoes and gently toss to blend well. Let the salad stand about 30 minutes to blend the flavors. Stir from the bottom before serving, either chilled or at room temperature.

This potato salad is a natural for picnics because it doesn't spoil in heat the way a mayonnaise-based salad can. It would go well with sandwiches, gazpacho (see Chapter 9), or Sautéed Chicken Breasts with Tomatoes and Thyme (see Chapter 4).

Add ¼ cup minced green onions; 2 tablespoons chopped herbs like rosemary, chervil, or basil; or 1 cup diced, roasted bell peppers.

Cold pasta salads are handy to have around for quick lunches or for entertaining. You can make them with just about any ingredients that go into hot pasta. In the following recipe, note that you cook the pasta in the same broth as the zucchini for extra flavor (and nutrition).

Bow-Tie Pasta Salad with Mussels

Tools: *Small bowl, whisk, chef's knife, large saucepan or pot, colander, slotted spoon, 2 large bowls*

Preparation time: *About 30 minutes*

Cooking time: *About 20 minutes*

Yield: *4 appetizer servings*

2 tablespoons red or white wine vinegar

1 tablespoon Dijon-style mustard

Salt and black pepper to taste

¾ cup extra-virgin olive oil

3 tablespoons finely chopped shallots or green onions

2 large cloves garlic, finely chopped

Pinch cayenne pepper

3 pounds mussels, well scrubbed, with beards and barnacles removed (see Chapter 9 for illustrated instructions)

½ cup dry white wine

2 quarts water

2 small zucchini, about ¾ pound, cut into ½-inch rounds

½ pound bow-tie pasta

2 ripe tomatoes, about ¾ pound, peeled and cut into ½-inch dice

½ cup coarsely chopped basil leaves or parsley

1 Combine the vinegar, mustard, salt, and pepper in a small bowl. Beat the mixture with a wire whisk while slowly adding the oil. After all the oil is incorporated, add the shallots or green onions, garlic, and cayenne pepper and blend well. Set aside.

2 Place the mussels in a large saucepan and add the wine. Cover and cook over high heat, gently shaking the pan occasionally to redistribute the mussels, for about 4 minutes or until the mussels open. Discard any mussels that do not open.

3 Remove the mussels with a slotted spoon, put them in a large bowl, and set them aside to cool. Pour the cooking liquid through a fine sieve or into a colander that is lined with a paper towel and set over another large bowl to strain and reserve the broth. When the mussels are cool enough to handle, remove the meat and discard the shells, leaving the meat in the large bowl.

4 Place the strained broth and the 2 quarts water in a large saucepan or pot. Bring to a boil and add the zucchini. Cook for 3 minutes and then remove the zucchini with a slotted spoon, and add them to the bowl with the mussels.

5 Bring the water back to a boil, add the pasta to the pot, stir, and cook for about 10 to 12 minutes, until the pasta is tender but still firm (al dente). Drain well and let cool slightly.

(continued)

6 Add the tomatoes and pasta to the bowl with the zucchini and mussels. Add the dressing and basil and toss well. Adjust the seasoning with more salt and pepper, if desired. Serve chilled or at room temperature.

> *Cold pasta is best served with other cold items, like Avocado and Tomato Salad (see Chapter 16).*

You can vary this recipe in many ways:

✔ Use different pastas, such as shells, penne, fusilli, or tortellini. (See Chapter 11 for explanations of the different types of pastas.)

✔ Toss the cold pasta with al dente-cooked vegetables tossed in vinaigrette, perhaps with fresh herbs.

✔ Substitute clams for the mussels.

✔ Roast three types of bell peppers (red, green, and yellow), remove skins and seeds, and cut them into ¼-inch cubes (see Roasted Pepper and Snow Pea Salad recipe in this chapter for more specific instructions). Dress the pasta with herb vinaigrette and toss in the peppers.

The following colorful salad combines the pungency of watercress and endive with sweet orange, a refreshing combination. You also can add black olives or Niçoise-style olives for a salty flavor.

Watercress, Endive, and Orange Salad

Tools: *Chef's knife, salad or mixing bowl, whisk*

Preparation time: *About 25 minutes*

Yield: *4 servings*

1 bunch watercress, washed and drained	*½ cup chopped red onion*
2 Belgian endive	*Salt and black pepper to taste*
2 teaspoons Dijon-style mustard	*1 medium navel orange, peeled and sectioned (see following Essential Skill icon)*
2 tablespoons red wine vinegar (or to taste)	*2 tablespoons chopped parsley*
¼ cup olive, vegetable, or corn oil	

1 Trim and discard the stems of the watercress. Trim the base of the endive and cut them crosswise into 2-inch lengths.

2 To make the dressing, put the mustard in a salad or mixing bowl. Whisk in the vinegar followed by the oil. Add the red onion and season with salt and pepper. Blend well.

3 Add the watercress, endive, orange sections, and parsley. Toss well and serve.

The sweetness of orange makes this salad especially good with Mustard-Brushed Barbecued Chicken Breasts (see Chapter 6).

To keep a mixing bowl from moving as you whisk, set it over a folded dish towel.

To section an orange, use a sharp knife to peel it and then divide the sections along the membranes. If you want to eliminate the stringy, white membrane that holds each section in place, cut along each side of the membrane, working the knife down toward the center of the fruit. (See Figure 10-1.)

Adding orange, lemon, or lime zest is a simple way to enhance the flavor of a salad dressing. Grate the fruit against the smallest holes of a hand grater, taking care to remove only the colored portion of the skin. The white, underneath layer tends to be bitter.

Sectioning an Orange to Eliminate Membranes

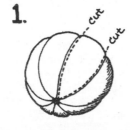

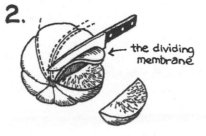

Figure 10-1:
Sectioning
an orange.

Roasted Pepper and Snow Pea Salad

Tools: *Baking sheet, paper bag, chef's knife, paring knife, colander, large skillet, whisk, small bowl, tongs*

Preparation time: *About 20 minutes*

Cooking time: *About 30 minutes*

Yield: *4 servings*

2 red or yellow bell peppers, cored

¾ pound snow peas, rinsed

1 small red onion, halved, and cut into thin slices

2 tablespoons red wine vinegar

1 tablespoon Dijon-style mustard

½ teaspoon ground cumin

Salt and black pepper to taste

¼ cup olive oil

¼ cup finely chopped parsley

8 leaves Bibb or Boston lettuce, rinsed and dried

1 Preheat the broiler. Place the peppers on a baking sheet and place under the broiler, 4 to 6 inches from the heat. As one side of each pepper blackens, rotate with tongs until all sides of the peppers are blackened. Remove the peppers from the broiler and place in a paper bag; then close the bag and set aside for about 5 minutes to loosen the skin.

2 Remove the peppers from the bag and peel away the skin with your fingers or a paring knife. Slice the peppers lengthwise into ¼-inch strips, discarding the seeds.

3 Trim the snow peas by snapping off the stem ends and pulling off the string that runs across the top of the pod. Put about 2 inches of lightly salted water in a large skillet or pot and bring to a boil. Add the snow peas and cook for 2 minutes. Drain. Run cold water over the peas to cool them quickly and drain again. Put the snow peas, pepper strips, and red onion in a salad bowl.

4 Combine the vinegar, mustard, and cumin in a small bowl and add salt and pepper. Whisk vigorously while slowly adding the oil. Stir in the parsley. Pour the dressing over the vegetables and toss. Place 2 lettuce leaves on each of 4 serving plates and spoon equal portions of the salad in the center.

This colorful salad is wonderful with Grilled Swordfish Steaks with Lemon and Thyme (see Chapter 6).

Try varying this recipe in any of the following ways:

- ✔ Use different-colored peppers.
- ✔ Place around the plate halved cherry tomatoes and thinly sliced fresh *fennel,* a faintly licorice-tasting root vegetable.
- ✔ Garnish with cooked asparagus spears.
- ✔ Place cooked pasta shells, tossed in herbed vinaigrette, in the center of the salad under the peppers and snow peas.

Warm Shrimp Salad with Spinach

Tools: *Shrimp deveiner, chef's knife, large skillet*

Preparation time: *About 25 minutes*

Cooking time: *About 4 minutes*

Yield: *4 servings*

1¼ pounds large shrimp

4 cups loosely packed fresh spinach leaves

4 thin slices of red onion, broken into rings

6 tablespoons olive oil

2 red or yellow bell peppers, cored, seeded, and cut into ½-inch strips or cubes

Salt and black pepper to taste

2 large cloves garlic, finely chopped

3 tablespoons red wine vinegar

½ cup chopped basil leaves or parsley

½ teaspoon grated lemon peel

1 Peel and devein the shrimp and set aside. (Turn to Chapter 12 for instructions.)

2 Trim off any tough stems of the spinach leaves. Rinse well and pat dry. Arrange the spinach leaves on 4 dinner plates.

3 Arrange an equal portion of the onion rings in the center of each plate.

4 Heat the oil in a large (preferably nonstick) skillet over medium-high heat. Add the shrimp, bell peppers, salt, and pepper. Cook, stirring often, for about 2 minutes or until the shrimp are almost evenly pink. Add the garlic and cook, stirring often, for 1 minute more. (Do not let the garlic brown.) Add the vinegar; cook and stir for 45 seconds. Remove from the heat.

(continued)

5 Add half the basil or parsley and all the lemon zest and toss well. Spoon the shrimp and sauce equally over the onion rings and spinach. Sprinkle with the remaining basil or parsley. Taste for seasoning, adding more salt and pepper if desired. Serve immediately.

Warm salads are usually served alone with bread. You could, though, follow this salad with Broiled Skirt Steak, Cajun Style (see Chapter 16) or Grilled Brochettes of Pork with Rosemary (see Chapter 6).

A Glossary of Greens

A salad demands the freshest greens and herbs and the tastiest vegetables you can find. If at all possible, buy produce that is in season, and then speed home with your lights flashing. Better yet, grow some in your yard, if you have one.

Greens range in taste from mild to pungent and even bitter. Mild greens like iceberg, Boston, and Bibb lettuce should be used as a base for more assertive, full-strength ingredients and seasonings. Use greens like radicchio, arugula, and escarole sparingly as a contrasting accent. Composing a salad of tart radicchio with a sharp vinaigrette is like catching baseballs without a glove — ouch! You may prefer counterbalancing pungent greens with cream-style dressings.

Supermarkets and produce markets carry an array of greens 12 months of the year, allowing you to combine different types in one bowl. Don't limit yourself to a bland iceberg lettuce. The more variety of greens in the bowl, the better.

Our favorite salad greens, some of which are pictured in Figure 10-2, include those listed in the following sections.

Don't overdress

A common mistake with salads is overdressing them, which is like overdressing for dinner. Drizzle just enough dressing over the greens to lightly coat them when tossed well. And when you toss, really toss. Don't just phlegmatically move the greens around the bowl. Pretend that you're conducting the Boston Pops and go to it.

Figure 10-2: Our favorite salad greens.

Mild greens

- **Bibb (or limestone lettuce):** Tender, rippled leaves form a small, compact head. Bibb has the mildness of Boston lettuce, but more crunch. It tends to be expensive, but a little makes a big impression.

- **Boston:** Buttery textured, this lettuce looks like a green rose. Mixes well with all varieties and stands well alone topped with sliced, ripe summer tomatoes.

- **Iceberg:** The white bread of the salad world, iceberg is common to salad bars and political banquets. Iceberg has more texture than flavor, and, if wrapped, can be used for foul-shot practice.

  To remove the core of iceberg lettuce, smash the head (core side down) on a cutting board or countertop. The hard core should then twist out easily.

- **Loose-leaf lettuce:** Also called red leaf or green leaf lettuce, depending on its color. Its long, curly leaves are buttery and almost sweet. Add the red leaf variety to green salad for an elegant contrast or mix red and green leaf together in one bowl.

- **Romaine:** The emperor green of Caesar salad, romaine has dark-green exterior leaves with a pale-yellow core. Mixes well with other greens. One advantage of romaine is that it keeps well for up to a week in the refrigerator. Like other dark, leafy greens, romaine is a good source of vitamin A.

- **Red oak leaf lettuce:** Named for the oak tree leaves it resembles, this green is sweet and colorful. Good mixed with Boston or Bibb lettuce. Also makes a pretty plate garnish.

Pungent greens

- **Arugula:** You can practically taste the iron in arugula's dark green leaves. The peppery flavor mixes well with any mild lettuce or toss with grilled, portobello mushrooms, red onions, along with a lemon vinaigrette.

- **Belgian endive:** Its pale yellow and white leaves are packed tightly together, in a cigar-like shape. This green has lots of crunch and a slightly bitter taste. Pull the leaves away from the base and tear them into pieces in green salads, or use an entire leaf as a serving base for various cheese and vegetable spreads and fillings.

- **Cabbage:** Red or green, cabbage is a great salad addition and amazingly inexpensive. Tear or shred leaves with a knife and toss with other greens to add color and texture. A long-storage vegetable and a good source of vitamin C.

- **Curly endive (sometimes called chicory):** Similar to escarole in flavor, but with very curly leaves.

- **Dandelion:** A green that you can probably harvest off your front lawn (if you don't have dogs), dandelion leaves arrive on the market in the spring. Italians cherish its bitter, crunchy qualities. (Young, tender leaves are used; the older ones are too bitter and tough.) Toss in a mixed green salad with chopped, hard-cooked eggs and a vinaigrette dressing. A good source of vitamin C and calcium.

- **Escarole:** A green that you can consume raw in salad or sauté in olive oil and garlic. A member of the endive family, escarole is also rather tart and stands up to strong-flavored dressings.

- **Frisée:** Mildly bitter, this pale-yellow green also has prickly-shaped leaves. Mix it sparingly with other greens for contrasting texture and taste. Similar to curly endive in appearance, but with a more delicate taste.

- **Mesclun (pronounced *mess-clan*):** A salad mix that usually contains frisée, arugula, radicchio, red leaf lettuces, mustard, and other delicate greens. Mesclun is very expensive, so purchase only if it appears very fresh, or the greens will wilt before you get home. It's best to buy a small amount to mix with other less expensive salad greens.

- **Radicchio:** A small, tightly wound head with deep magenta leaves that can add brilliant splashes of color to a bowl of greens. Radicchio is extremely pungent and comparatively expensive. Use it sparingly. Keeps well in the refrigerator (up to two weeks), especially if wrapped in moist paper towels. Like cabbage, radicchio also may be grilled, baked, or sautéed.

- **Spinach:** Deep green, slightly crumpled leaves that are full of iron. Discard the thick stems. The leaves of baby spinach are smaller, oval shaped, smooth, and buttery. Rinse all spinach thoroughly to rid the leaves of sand. Dry well. Mix with milder greens like Boston, Bibb, or loose-leaf.

- **Watercress:** Its clover-shaped leaves lend peppery crunch to any salad. Snap off and discard the tough stems and be sure to rinse well. Watercress makes a pretty soup or plate garnish.

Depending on where you live, different greens are better than others at different times of the year. If you see dark green arugula leaves in the market, try mixing them with other greens like romaine, red leaf, or chicory (curly endive). Arugula has a nice, tart snap that enlivens any salad. It can be sandy, so rinse it well.

Here is a simple, well-balanced salad combining snappy arugula and mild Boston or red leaf lettuce.

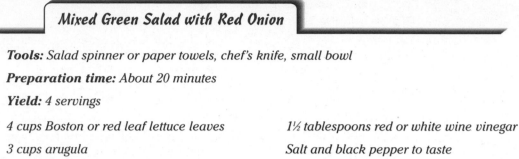

Mixed Green Salad with Red Onion

Tools: *Salad spinner or paper towels, chef's knife, small bowl*

Preparation time: *About 20 minutes*

Yield: *4 servings*

4 cups Boston or red leaf lettuce leaves

3 cups arugula

⅓ cup coarsely chopped red onion

2 tablespoons finely chopped parsley

1½ tablespoons red or white wine vinegar

Salt and black pepper to taste

¼ cup olive oil

1 Rinse the greens in a large pot of cold water or in the sink. (Change the water several times, rinsing until no sand remains and the greens are thoroughly cleaned.) Pick over the leaves, removing tough stems. Spin the greens in a salad spinner or lay them flat on paper towels and pat dry. (Greens may be washed and dried ahead of serving time and stored in plastic bags in the refrigerator.)

2 Tear the greens into bite-sized pieces and put them in a salad bowl. Add the onion and parsley.

3 Put the vinegar in a small bowl and add salt and pepper. Start beating while gradually adding the oil. Pour the dressing over the salad and toss to evenly coat.

This salad is a fine all-around first course.

The following variations to this recipe are tasty, too:

- ✔ Substitute balsamic vinegar for the red wine vinegar.

- ✔ Whisk 2 teaspoons Dijon-style mustard into the vinaigrette.

- ✔ Add 2 teaspoons mayonnaise, yogurt, or sour cream for a creamy vinaigrette.

- ✔ Mix up the lettuce, adding romaine, Bibb, or radicchio.

- ✔ Add 1 teaspoon of minced garlic.

- ✔ Add minced herbs, such as tarragon, thyme, basil, chervil, sage, or savory, to taste.

- ↙ Add 1 tablespoon of rinsed and drained capers.

- ↙ Crumble goat cheese or blue cheese over the greens.

- ↙ Make garlic croutons (see recipe in Chapter 9) and sprinkle them over the greens.

Buying and Storing Greens

When buying greens, avoid those that are wilted or limp. A fresh head of romaine should look like a bouquet of green leaves, clumped tightly together without any rust-colored edges or signs of decay. Pass up the watercress if its leaves are yellowing. Brown spots on iceberg lettuce indicate rot. Greens sold in bunches, such as arugula and dandelion, are especially delicate and prone to quick decay; consume them within a few days of purchase. And don't believe (just because you watched your mother do it) that wilted greens revive when plunged into cold water.

Store rinsed and dried greens in the extra-cold crisper drawer of the refrigerator, wrapped in damp paper towels. You can place bunches of watercress, arugula, parsley, and other fresh herbs in a full glass of water, stem ends down, like fresh-cut flowers. Greens are not long-storage items, so consume them within a few days of purchase.

Now that pre-buttered rolls and pre-grilled chicken are commonly available at supermarkets, you should not be surprised to find prepackaged salad greens complete with dressings, croutons, and other "instant" salad ingredients. Although these bagged salads save you time, they are comparatively expensive and do not offer, in our opinion, the same fresh taste of loose greens.

Washing and drying lettuce

Did you ever fall asleep at the beach with your mouth open and the wind blowing sand in your direction? Well, that's what unwashed salad can taste like. To make sure that you get all the sand out of lettuce, remove the leaves and soak them briefly in cold water, shaking occasionally. Then run them under the tap, being careful to rinse the root ends thoroughly.

Drying lettuce completely is critical, or else the dressing slides right off. Towel-drying works, but it's a nuisance. The easiest method is to use a salad spinner (see Chapter 2) that dries with centrifugal force.

Ten Quick Salads . . . So Easy You Don't Need a Recipe

Simply follow the advice of your taste buds to create your own salads from these simple combinations:

- **Tomato, red onion, and basil salad:** Slice ripe, red tomatoes ¼ inch thick and layer on a platter with diced red onion and 4 or 5 large chopped fresh basil leaves. Drizzle with oil and vinegar and season with salt and pepper.

- **Bell pepper rice salad:** Combine about 3 cups cooked white rice with 1 cup cooked green peas and 2 cups seeded, cored, and chopped red, green, or yellow bell peppers (or any combination of colors). Toss with enough herb-vinaigrette dressing to moisten the ingredients sufficiently, add salt and black pepper to taste, and chill before serving.

- **Cucumber-dill salad:** Toss peeled, sliced, and seeded cucumbers in a dill-flavored vinaigrette. (See the recipe for Vinaigrette Dressing in this chapter for a starting point.)

- **Cherry tomato and feta cheese salad:** Toss 1 pint cherry tomatoes, rinsed and sliced in half, with 4 ounces crumbled feta cheese and ½ cup sliced, pitted black olives. Season with vinaigrette dressing to taste (see the recipe for Vinaigrette Dressing in this chapter).

- **Orzo medley salad:** Combine about 2 cups cooked *orzo* (a rice-shaped pasta) with ½ cup chopped, sun-dried tomatoes. Season lightly with oil, vinegar, and black pepper to taste.

- **Garbanzo bean toss:** Combine 1 13-ounce can drained garbanzo beans, ½ cup chopped red onion, 1 or 2 cloves crushed garlic, and the grated zest of 1 lemon. Toss with lemon-vinaigrette dressing. (See the recipe for Vinaigrette Dressing in this chapter for a starting point.)

- **Layered cheese and vegetable salad:** Arrange alternating thin slices of ripe tomatoes and mozzarella cheese on a round platter. Fill the center with slices of avocado sprinkled with fresh lemon juice to prevent discoloration. Drizzle with olive oil and lemon juice; garnish with fresh basil.

- **Grilled vegetable platter with fresh pesto:** Arrange any assortment of grilled vegetables (see Chapter 6) on a platter. Serve with spoonfuls of fresh pesto (see Chapter 7).

✔ **Fruit salsa:** Combine 1 ripe, peeled, pitted, and chopped avocado, 2 ripe, peeled, seeded, and chopped papayas, ½ cup chopped red onion, and 1 teaspoon seeded, chopped jalapeño pepper with a dressing of 1 table-spoon honey and the grated zest and juice of 1 lemon. Serve as a side salad with broiled hamburgers, chicken, or fish.

✔ **Three-berry dessert salad:** Combine 2 pints rinsed and hulled strawber-ries, 1 pint rinsed blueberries, and 1 pint rinsed raspberries in a bowl. Toss with a dressing of ½ cup heavy cream sweetened with confection-ers' sugar to taste.

Steamed Lobsters
with Orange-Lemon
Butter and Steamed
Red Potatoes with
Dill (both in
Chapter 3)

Sautéed Chicken Breast with Tomatoes and Thyme (Chapter 4)
and Roasted Pepper and Snow Pea Salad (Chapter 10)

Mediterranean Seafood Stew (Chapter 5)

Standing Rib Roast of Beef and Crispy Roasted Root Vegetables (both in Chapter 6)

Frittata with Bell Peppers and Potatoes (Chapter 8)

Grilled Tuna with Niçoise Dressing (Chapter 6) and
Watercress, Endive, and Orange Salad (Chapter 10)

Carrot Soup with Dill and Cream of Leek Soup, both with Garlic Croutons (all in Chapter 9)

**Warm Shrimp Salad
with Spinach (Chapter 10)**

Penne with Broccoli Rabe (Chapter 11)

Mediterranean-Style
Chicken (Chapter 15) with orzo

Shepherd's Pie (Chapter 12)

Clockwise from top left:
Roasted Chicken (Chapter 6); Chicken, Avocado, and Red Onion Salad (Chapter 17); Chicken and Grilled Vegetable Wrap (Chapter 17)

Bean and Sausage Casserole and Avocado and Pear Salad with Mixed Greens (both in Chapter 19)

Thanksgiving centerpiece: Roasted Turkey with Cornbread, Sausage, and Apple Stuffing and Madeira Pan Gravy (all in Chapter 20)

At the table (clockwise from top of plate): Roasted Turkey; Rum-Baked Sweet Potatoes; Fresh Cranberry Relish; Green Beans with Shallots, and Cornbread; Sausage, and Apple Stuffing (all in Chapter 20)

Clockwise from top left: Chocolate Cake with Walnuts and Cinnamon (Chapter 13); Old-Fashioned Chocolate Chip Cookies (Chapter 13); Lemon Bars (Chapter 13); and Red, White, and Blue Berry Shortcake (Chapter 18)

Chapter 11

Pastamania

● ●

In This Chapter

▶ "Don't watch the pot" and other secrets of successful pasta-making

▶ Alfredo: Tony Bennett's tailor or classic pasta sauce?

▶ Classic pasta recipes: Spaghetti with fresh tomato sauce, penne with cheese, lasagna, and more

● ●

No man can be wise on an empty stomach.

—George Eliot

A ncient Greeks ate foods that resembled today's pasta, and so did the Romans. In the late thirteenth century, Marco Polo returned from China toting a variety of noodles, although it's a wonder that he didn't scarf them down with tomato sauce on the long trek home. Today, people in dozens of nations eat pasta of one kind or another. Few people argue, though, that the Italians would take home the gold in a pasta Olympics.

Pasta is a complex carbohydrate, which means that the human body can draw upon its energy for a long time. Simple carbohydrates, such as sugar and honey, shoot energy but not nutrients into our systems. Put it this way: If you're on a diet high in simple carbohydrates, stick to short-distance sprints. The pasta guys can run the distances. Moreover, 2 ounces of pasta contains only 211 calories and about 1 gram of fat. One big ladleful of Alfredo sauce can easily destroy that, but don't blame us.

Dried Pasta versus Fresh Pasta

America's attics and closets must be jammed with pasta-making machines. In the late 1970s and early 1980s, anyone who knew how to boil water wanted to make fresh pasta. Somehow — maybe through a conspiracy of glossy food magazines — people started believing that if you didn't roll your own pasta, you were somehow unpatriotic. Young couples spent weeknights in the kitchen with flour flying all over, eggs spilling, and dough falling on the floor. They cranked and cranked and cranked some more. Then they hung the pasta overnight to dry on chairs, books, tables, and lampshades.

This trend didn't last long. But you can always spot the lapsed pastamaniacs — they're the ones who always remark in Italian restaurants, "Oooh, fresh pasta. We love making fresh pasta, but the kids like dried."

The truth is that fresh pasta is not inherently better than dried; it's just different. Many fine dried pastas are available, and the choice between fresh and dried is really a matter of personal taste. Homemade pasta — that is, well-made homemade pasta — is definitely lighter and more delicate. Dried pasta tastes more substantial — and because a wide range of flours are used, flavors vary. The better dried pastas use semolina flour, made from nutritious durum wheat. (Homemade pasta is usually made from plain white flour.)

Interviews with several of the finest Italian chefs in the country produced the following list of their favorite imported and domestic brands of pastas. Imported pastas that are available throughout the United States included De Cecco, Delverde, and Barilla. American pastas cited for excellence were Antoine's and Al Dente. Many excellent domestic pastas are available only locally.

Specialty food markets sell fresh pasta in the refrigerator section. Fresh pasta is good, but you pay a premium. For purposes of this chapter, we concentrate on dried pasta because it is widely available. In any case, the sauce is what really elevates pasta from ordinary to sublime.

Is the Pasta Ready Yet?

Al dente is not the name of an Italian orthodontist. It is a sacred term in Italy that means "to the tooth" or "to the bite." In cooking, al dente means slightly firm to the bite. Almost all nations outside Italy cook pasta longer. When pasta cooks too long, it absorbs more water and becomes mushy.

Tips for cooking pasta

✔ **Use a lot of water and an 8-quart pot (5 to 6 quarts of water for a pound of pasta).** Pasta, like tango dancers, needs room to move. If you don't have a pot large enough to hold that much water and still be three-fourths full or less, splitting pasta into two pots of boiling water is better than overloading one pot. An overloaded pot will splash boiling water all over the stovetop.

✔ **Salt the water to add flavor and to help the pasta absorb the sauce.** As a general guideline, 4 quarts of water takes about 2 teaspoons of salt, and 6 quarts of water calls for 1 tablespoon of salt.

✔ **Oil is for salads, not pasta water.** You don't need to add oil to the water if you use enough water and stir occasionally to prevent sticking. *Be sure to stir the pasta immediately and thoroughly* after adding it to the water.

✔ **Cover the pot to hasten heat recovery.** After you add pasta to the water, the water ceases to boil. When the water begins boiling again, remove the lid and finish cooking.

✔ **Save a cup of the cooking liquid when the pasta is done.** You can use some of the liquid to add moisture to the sauce. The starch in the water binds the sauce, helping it adhere to the pasta.

✔ **Do not rinse pasta.** When the pasta is al dente (tender but firm), pour it gradually into a colander. *Do not rinse!* You want starch on the pasta to help the sauce adhere to it. The only exception is if you are making a cold pasta salad.

✔ **After draining it, you may want to place the pasta in the pan in which the sauce is cooking and stir well.** This method coats the pasta better than spooning the sauce on top. Serve from the saucepan.

✔ **Never combine two types or sizes of pasta in the same pot of water.** Fishing out the type that is done first is a real nuisance.

✔ **Don't try to speak broken Italian when you serve your pasta.** "Bonissimo! Perfectamente mia amigas, Mangia, Mangia!" You will sound silly and irritate your guests.

The time-tested method for checking pasta for doneness is still the best: Scoop out a strand or two with a fork, take the pasta in hand, jump around and toss the scorching pasta in the air, and then taste it. (You don't really have to toss it in the air, but it makes the process more fun.)

Making Perfect Pasta and Sauce

The basic principles of making sauce for pasta are the same as those for making the other kinds of sauces described in Chapter 7. The main difference is that the quantities for the pasta sauces in this chapter are often larger.

Piero Selvaggio, owner of the famous Valentino in Los Angeles, offers these general tips for cooking perfect pasta: "Use a wooden, not a metal spoon, to stir the pasta right after it's dropped into the boiling water. Add the pasta to the water all at once and don't break up long pasta strands — it's a sin! If you absolutely cannot have salt, add a little lemon juice to the cooking water. It adds a pleasant little tartness."

Timing is everything: Adding the sauce

Cooked pasta needs to be sauced immediately after it's drained or it becomes stiff and gluey. So always have the sauce ready and waiting before the pasta is cooked. Then all you need to do is drain the pasta, add the sauce, toss well, and serve.

Note: In many of the recipes in this chapter, we have you work on the sauce as the water for the pasta boils or the pasta cooks. This way, you can ensure that your pasta and sauce will be ready at about the same time. Then all you need to do is drain the pasta (or add the pasta to the pan holding the sauce) and toss well.

Choosing the right amount and type of sauce

"The pasta sauce must be the right consistency, neither too thin, nor too thick, so it coats all of the pasta, leaving it perfectly moist. Too much sauce, and the pasta is mushy. Too little, and it is dry," says Lidia Bastianich, owner of Felidia restaurant in New York City.

Bastianich recommends changing pasta sauces to suit the seasons of the year:

- ✔ In the spring, serve pasta with fresh herbs and tender vegetables.
- ✔ In the summer, serve pasta with light fish sauces.
- ✔ In the fall, serve pasta with wild mushrooms or meat.
- ✔ In the winter, serve pasta with root vegetables or meat.

When pulling together a pasta sauce, always think in terms of a hierarchy of flavors. By *hierarchy,* we mean that one assertive ingredient should dominate; the dominant ingredient should not have to duke it out with other ingredients. Other elements of sauce should enhance and complement that main ingredient.

For example, if you have beautiful wild mushrooms in the fall, combining them in a sauce with powerful gorgonzola is a folly. The cheese you use, if any, should be mild and smoky to support the mushroom's flavor.

Picking perfect tomatoes

Nothing can compare with a vine-ripened summer tomato. But locally grown summer tomatoes are available only a few months of the year in most parts of the United States. One alternative is the hot-house varieties that are picked green, gassed to a pale shade of pink, and then marketed by commercial growers from far away. For making most soups, sauces, and stews, canned Italian plum tomatoes are superior. If a recipe calls for fresh tomatoes when regular tomatoes are not good, look for plum or Italian tomatoes. Named for the fruit they resemble, plum tomatoes usually ripen fully within a day or two of purchase and are perfect for quick skillet sauces laced with fresh basil and garlic. In the off-season, use canned plum tomatoes, which have lots of flavor.

The best way to ripen tomatoes is to place several in a brown paper bag for one or two days, thereby trapping their natural ripening gases. To hasten the ripening even more, place a banana in the bag. For a quick lesson on peeling and seeding tomatoes, turn to the recipe for Spaghetti with Quick Fresh Tomato Sauce, later in this chapter.

Name That Pasta: Pasta Types and Cooking Times

Italian pasta comes in two basic forms: macaroni and spaghetti.

Macaroni has distinctive shapes, hollows, and curves. *Spaghetti,* which means "little strings," is pasta cut into delicate strands. Sometimes linguine and fettuccine noodles are identified apart from spaghetti because their strands are flattened. Figure 11-1 depicts some common pasta shapes, also described in the following sections.

Macaroni

Also known as *tubular pasta,* macaroni is served with thick, rich sauces. Table 11-1 describes the different types of tubular pastas and tells you how to cook and sauce them.

Figure 11-1:
Various
shapes of
pasta.

Table 11-1		The Macaroni Family
Italian Name	*Translation*	*Description and Approximate Cooking Time*
Cannelloni	"Large reeds"	Stuffed with meat or cheese and baked smothered in sauce. Cooks in 7 to 9 minutes.
Ditali	"Thimbles"	Smooth and short. Used in soups and cold pasta salads. Cooks in 8 to 10 minutes.
Penne	"Quills"	Best coated all over with rich sauces. Cooks in 10 to 12 minutes.
Rigatoni	"Large grooves"	Large, wide tube that is excellent with tomato, meat, and vegetable sauces. Cooks in 10 to 12 minutes.
Ziti	"Bridegrooms"	Narrow tube shape that is excellent in rich, baked casseroles with thick tomato sauces. Cooks in 10 to 12 minutes.

Strand pasta

Strand pasta is best served with thin, flavorful sauces that are rich in oil, which keep the very thin pasta from sticking together. Table 11-2 shows the best way to cook each type of strand pasta.

Table 11-2		The Spaghetti Family
Italian Name	*Translation*	*Description and Approximate Cooking Time*
Capelli d'angelo	"Angel hair"	The thinnest pasta of all, Capelli d'angelo is good in soups. Excellent with thin cream or tomato sauces. Cooks quickly in 3 to 4 minutes.
Cappellini	"Little hairs"	Slightly thicker than angel hair. Cooks in 4 to 5 minutes.
Spaghetti	"Little strings"	Long, medium-thick strands. Cooks in 10 to 12 minutes.
Vermicelli	"Little worms"	Thin strands. Cooks in 5 to 6 minutes.

Flat ribbon pasta

Flat ribbon pasta is excellent with rich, creamy sauces such as Alfredo or simple butter sauces with fresh sautéed vegetables. To find out the best way to cook different types of flat ribbon pasta, see Table 11-3.

Table 11-3		Flat Ribbon Pastas
Italian Name	*Translation*	*Description and Approximate Cooking Time*
Fettuccine	"Small ribbons"	Flat strands. Cooks in 8 to 10 minutes.
Linguine	"Little tongues"	Long, thin ribbons. Cooks in 8 to 10 minutes.
Tagliatelle	"Little cuts"	Like fettuccine, but a bit wider. Cooks in 7 to 8 minutes.

Stuffed pasta

Filled with meat, cheese, fish, or vegetables, stuffed pastas are best coated with simple tomato or light, cream-based sauces. The dough is often flavored and tinted with spinach, tomato, mushrooms, or *saffron,* a fragrant spice. Table 11-4 gives the cooking times for frozen, stuffed pastas.

Table 11-4		Stuffed Pastas
Italian Name	*Description*	*Stuffing and Approximate Cooking Time*
Agnolotti	Half-moon shaped	Stuffed with meat or cheese. Cooks in 7 to 9 minutes.
Ravioli	Little square pillows	Stuffed with meat, cheese, fish, or vegetables. Cooks in 7 to 9 minutes.
Tortellini	Ring-shaped little twists	Stuffed with meat or cheese. Cooks in 10 to 12 minutes.

Sundry other shapes

Table 11-5 lists a grab bag of other pastas that don't quite fit into any of the other categories.

Table 11-5		**Miscellaneous-Shaped Pastas**
Italian Name	*Translation*	*Great Accompaniments and Approximate Cooking Time*
Conchiglie	"Shells"	Wonderful with a simple butter-basil sauce and a grating of Parmesan cheese. Cooks in 10 to 12 minutes.
Farfalle	"Butterflies"	Pretty tossed into cold salads with fresh vegetables. Cooks in 10 to 12 minutes.
Fusilli	"Twists"	Corkscrew shaped and good with chunky sauces. Cooks in 10 to 12 minutes.
Orecchiette	"Little ears"	Wonderful in chicken soups and clear broths. Cooks in 7 to 9 minutes.
Orzo	"Barley"	Rice-shaped pasta, good in dishes like cold-chicken-and-sun-dried-tomato salad with vinaigrette. Cooks in 8 to 10 minutes.
Rotelle	"Small wheels"	Fun-shaped favorite of children. Cooks in 8 to 10 minutes.

Pasta Sauces You Should Know About

Italian pasta sauces are as inventive and varied as pasta shapes. We briefly describe the classic ones, so the next time you dine at an expensive trattoria where the puttanesca is $24 a plate, you'll know what you're paying for.

- **Ragù alla Bolognese:** A long-simmered sauce of meat (usually ground beef, veal, or pork) and tomatoes, named for the city of Bologna, where it was invented. For a true Bolognese, you brown the meat lightly and then cook it in a small amount of milk and wine before adding tomatoes.

- **Primavera:** A mixture of sautéed spring vegetables, such as sweet red pepper, tomatoes, asparagus, and snow peas, and fresh herbs.

- **Fettuccine all'Alfredo:** A rich sauce of cream, butter, Parmesan cheese, and freshly ground black pepper tossed over fettuccine.

- **Carbonara:** Crisply cooked bacon (usually Italian pancetta) combined with garlic, eggs, Parmesan cheese, and sometimes cream.

- **Spaghetti alle Vongole:** Spaghetti tossed with clams, olive oil, white wine, and herbs.

- **Puttanesca:** A pungent sauce of anchovies, garlic, tomatoes, capers, and black olives.

- **Pesto:** Fresh basil leaves, pine nuts, garlic, Parmesan cheese, and olive oil blended to a fine paste.

Getting Started with Pasta

Following are some simple pasta recipes that you can vary after you feel more confident.

Pasta sauce 101

You can use this quick sauce as the foundation for endless enhancements with herbs, vegetables, meat, and more.

In this book, pasta is intended to be dry pasta (as opposed to fresh), unless otherwise indicated.

Spaghetti with Quick Fresh Tomato Sauce

Tools: *Paring knife, chef's knife, large pot, colander, saucepan or skillet, grater*

Preparation time: *About 15 minutes*

Cooking time: *About 15 minutes*

Yield: *3 to 4 servings*

5 to 6 ripe plum tomatoes, about 1½ pounds	2 teaspoons peeled and minced garlic, about 2 large cloves
Salt and black pepper to taste	3 tablespoons grated Parmesan cheese
¾ pound spaghetti or other pasta of your choice	2 tablespoons coarsely chopped fresh basil leaves
3 tablespoons olive oil	

1 Core the tomatoes and peel them by dropping into boiling water for about 10 to 15 seconds. Remove with a slotted spoon and plunge into a bowl of ice water to cool them quickly. After the tomatoes are cool enough to handle, peel them with a paring knife and remove their seeds. Cut them into ½-inch cubes. (See Figure 11-2 for an illustration of this procedure.)

2 Bring 4 to 5 quarts lightly salted water to a boil over high heat in a large, covered pot. Add the spaghetti, stir thoroughly with a long fork to separate the strands, and cook, uncovered, for about 8 minutes or just until al dente.

3 While the spaghetti cooks, heat the oil in a saucepan or skillet over medium heat. Add the garlic. Cook and stir about 30 seconds with a wooden spoon. Do not brown the garlic. Add the cubed tomatoes and salt and pepper to taste. Cook, crushing the tomatoes with a fork and stirring often, for about 3 minutes.

How to Peel, Seed, and Chop Tomatoes

1. Insert paring knife diagonally — Cut out stem

2. Cut a shallow "x" on the bottom

3. Drop into boiling water for about 10 seconds or so

4. Remove with a long-handled fork — Immerse in cold water

5. Starting at the "x," peel off the skin. Easy! (Peel peaches and apricots the same way.)

6. cut in half

7. Squeeze! Seeds ooze out

8. chop into desired size.

Figure 11-2: Dropping tomatoes in boiling water for a few seconds makes peeling them much easier.

4 Just before the pasta is done, carefully scoop out and reserve ¼ cup of the cooking liquid. When the pasta is ready, drain it and return it to the large pot. Add the tomato sauce, cheese, basil, and ¼ cup reserved cooking liquid to the pasta. Toss well over low heat for a few seconds. Serve immediately.

IMPROVISE You can omit the Parmesan cheese and add a small can of drained, flaked tuna. Or keep the cheese and toss in some sliced black olives and cooked artichoke hearts. A few sautéed shrimp and asparagus spears, or even sautéed chicken livers, also work with this classic sauce.

A saucy freeze-for-all

You can make this slow-cooked, intensely flavored marinara sauce in large quantities, as we do here, and freeze it in individual portions for later use. Omit the cheese until you thaw the sauce base. Or use it all at once in the Family Lasagna recipe later in this chapter.

Marinara Sauce

Tools: *Chef's knife, heavy saucepan, wooden spoon, food processor or blender, grater*

Preparation time: *About 15 minutes*

Cooking time: *About 1 hour*

Yield: *About 5 cups*

¼ cup olive oil	½ cup water
1 cup peeled and minced onion, about 1 large onion	2 teaspoons chopped fresh thyme, or 1 teaspoon dried
1 tablespoon peeled and minced garlic, about 3 large cloves	2 teaspoons chopped fresh oregano, or 1 teaspoon dried
35-ounce can Italian plum tomatoes	Salt and black pepper to taste
6-ounce can tomato paste	⅓ cup grated Parmesan or Romano cheese
⅓ cup dry red wine	

1 In a heavy saucepan over medium heat, heat the olive oil. Add the onion and garlic and sauté until wilted, about 3 to 4 minutes, stirring frequently. (Do not let the garlic brown.) Add all remaining ingredients except the cheese and simmer, partially covered, for about 1 hour, stirring occasionally. Let stand at room temperature to cool slightly.

2 Carefully transfer the sauce to the container of a blender or food processor (in batches, if necessary), secure the lid tightly, and puree until semi-smooth. (Leave the sauce a little grainy.)

3 Return the sauce to the saucepan and keep it warm over very low heat. Taste for seasoning, adding cheese to the sauce now or at the table.

Note: *Calling for Italian plum tomatoes should not be taken as an unpatriotic act. It's just that Italian tomatoes have more flavor, but domestic canned tomatoes will also work.*

Five cups of sauce is enough for about 2 pounds of pasta or for a large casserole of lasagna (see the Family Lasagna recipe later in this chapter). You can freeze extra sauce in an airtight container for up to 6 months.

A large pot of boiling water is one of the most dangerous elements in any kitchen. Use a pot with short handles that cannot be tipped easily and set it to boil on a back burner, away from small and curious hands.

Pasta on the run

Sometimes you can forgo a formal sauce and just whip together a quick cheese garnish for pasta, as in the following recipe.

Penne with Parmesan Cheese and Basil

Tools: *Large pot, chef's knife, grater, colander*

Preparation time: *About 10 minutes*

Cooking time: *About 20 minutes*

Yield: *3 to 4 servings*

Salt to taste

½ pound penne

2 tablespoons olive oil

1 tablespoon butter

¼ cup grated Parmesan or Romano cheese

¼ cup chopped fresh basil or Italian parsley

⅛ teaspoon freshly grated or ground nutmeg

Black pepper to taste

1 Bring 3 to 4 quarts lightly salted water to a boil in a large, covered pot over high heat. Add the penne, stir thoroughly to separate the macaroni, and return to a boil. Cook, uncovered, for about 10 minutes or until the pasta is al dente.

2 Just before the penne is done, carefully scoop out ¼ cup of the cooking liquid. When the penne is ready, drain it and return it to the pot. Add the olive oil and butter and toss a bit to coat; then add the cheese, basil, nutmeg, pepper, and the reserved cooking liquid.

3 Toss and blend over medium-high heat for 30 seconds. If necessary, add salt. Serve immediately.

Branching out

After you can make basic pasta dishes with relative ease, you can begin experimenting with different ingredients. Before you dash down to the store and buy Virginia ham and star fruit to toss into the pan, think first about food pairings. You don't want a single sauce ingredient to bully all the others — turnips, for example, overpower many food combinations. Think of it this way: If you can imagine the ingredients combined and served as part of a nonpasta dinner, then they probably work in a pasta sauce as well.

Eggplant and summer squash

Following is an example of a vegetable pasta that harmonizes flavors. Eggplant has a distinctive texture and a slightly tart but sweet flavor. Let the eggplant be the dominant ingredient. Subtle summer squash adds lovely color, enhanced by sweet tomatoes.

Rigatoni with Eggplant and Summer Squash

Tools: *Chef's knife, grater, large pot, 2 large saucepans or sauté pans, colander*

Preparation time: *About 25 minutes*

Cooking time: *About 30 minutes*

Yield: *4 to 6 servings*

4 tablespoons olive oil

2 teaspoons peeled and finely chopped garlic, about 2 large cloves

1½ pounds ripe tomatoes, cored, peeled, and chopped, or 28-ounce can crushed tomatoes

¼ cup chopped fresh Italian parsley

2 teaspoons dried oregano

½ teaspoon sugar

½ teaspoon red pepper flakes (optional)

Salt and black pepper to taste

1 medium eggplant, ends trimmed, peeled, and cut into 1-inch cubes, about 1 pound (see Figure 11-3 for illustrated instructions for dicing)

½ pound yellow summer squash or zucchini, ends trimmed, halved lengthwise, cut into ½-inch thick semicircles

1 pound rigatoni, ziti, fusilli, or shells

⅓ cup grated Parmesan or Romano cheese, plus more for serving

¼ cup coarsely chopped fresh basil

1 Heat 1 tablespoon of the olive oil in a large saucepan or sauté pan over medium heat and then add the garlic. Cook, stirring constantly, for about 1 minute, without browning the garlic. Add the tomatoes, parsley, oregano, sugar, pepper flakes (if desired), salt, and pepper. Stir to blend, bring to a boil, reduce heat, and simmer for 15 minutes, partially covered.

2 As the sauce simmers, heat the remaining 3 tablespoons olive oil over high heat in a separate large skillet. When the oil is very hot, add the eggplant, squash, and salt and pepper to taste. Cook over medium heat, tossing occasionally, about 5 to 7 minutes or until nicely browned and tender. After the tomato sauce simmers for 15 minutes, stir in the eggplant and zucchini mixture and simmer for 15 minutes more.

3 Meanwhile, bring a large, covered pot with 5 quarts lightly salted water to a boil over high heat.

4 Add the pasta to the boiling water, stir thoroughly to separate the macaroni, and cook according to package instructions or until al dente. Just before draining the pasta, use a measuring cup to carefully scoop out ½ cup of the cooking liquid and add it to the sauce.

5 When it's ready, drain the cooked pasta and return it to the pot in which you cooked it. Add the sauce, cheese, and basil. Toss and serve hot with extra cheese.

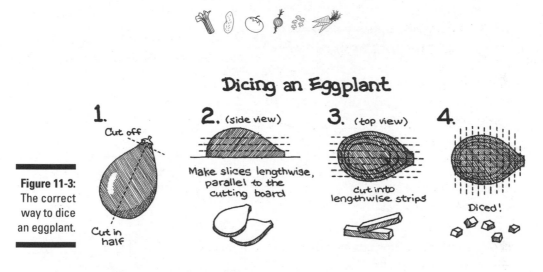

Dicing an Eggplant

1. Cut off

Cut in half

2. (side view) Make slices lengthwise, parallel to the cutting board

3. (top view) cut into lengthwise strips

4. Diced!

Figure 11-3: The correct way to dice an eggplant.

This thick and hearty sauce stands up to the addition of a savory meat like sweet Italian sausage or ground pork. For example, you can coarsely chop and then cook in a small skillet ½ pound mild Italian sausage. Add the cooked sausage to the tomato sauce along with the eggplant and squash mixture. For roasted flavor, brush the eggplant and summer squash pieces with oil and grill them, or roast them in the oven until tender and then add to the tomato sauce.

Broccoli rabe

Broccoli rabe is a staple with pasta in Italy. Its slightly bitter flavor contrasts beautifully with heady garlic and aromatic olive oil. The following pasta dish takes advantage of the sharp, almost peppery quality of broccoli rabe. Rosemary and oregano give the sauce an extra dimension. (If you cannot find fresh herbs, use one-third to one-half the quantity of dried herbs, which are more potent.)

Many people confuse broccoli rabe with turnip or mustard greens. Unlike other greens, though, broccoli rabe has distinctive little buds, which you consume along with the tender leaves and stalks. One thing broccoli rabe has in common with turnip and mustard greens is that it is a powerhouse of vita-mins and minerals, particularly vitamin C and iron.

We use a bare minimum of water in this next recipe to gently steam the broc-coli rabe, thereby retaining most of its nutrients and flavor. For a delicious side dish, omit the penne and Parmesan and serve with an entrée of chicken, fish, pork, veal, or lamb.

Penne with Broccoli Rabe

Tools: *Large pot, tongs or slotted spoon, large saucepan or sauté pan, chef's knife, grater, colander*

Preparation time: *About 25 minutes*

Cooking time: *About 25 minutes*

Yield: *4 servings*

1 pound broccoli rabe, trimmed and cut into 2- to 3-inch pieces (see following note)

4 tablespoons olive oil

1 tablespoon peeled and finely chopped garlic, about 3 large cloves

1 teaspoon chopped fresh rosemary, or ½ teaspoon dried and crumbled

1 teaspoon chopped fresh oregano, or ½ teaspoon dried

¼ to ½ teaspoon dried red pepper flakes, according to taste

¼ cup water

¾ pound penne or rigatoni

⅓ cup grated Parmesan cheese

Salt and black pepper to taste

1 Rinse the broccoli rabe and place it in a large bowl with the water clinging to its leaves.

2 In a large skillet or sauté pan, heat 3 tablespoons of the olive oil over medium heat. Add the garlic, rosemary, oregano, and red pepper flakes, and cook for about 30 seconds stirring occasionally. Do not let the garlic brown.

3 Add the broccoli rabe, with any water in the bowl, and toss it in the oil-garlic mixture. (Salad tongs work well as a tossing tool.) Add the ¼ cup water. Cover and cook over medium heat about 8 to 10 minutes, or until the thin stalks are crisp-tender, stirring occasionally. Remove from the heat and set aside, covered.

4 Bring 4 to 5 quarts water to a boil in a large pot over high heat. Add the pasta and cook according to package directions, or until al dente. When the pasta is cooked, drain well and return it to the large pot.

5 Add the broccoli rabe mixture, the remaining 1 tablespoon olive oil, and the Parmesan cheese. Stir well to combine. Check for seasoning, adding more salt and pepper to taste, and serve immediately.

Note: Trim about 3 inches off the bottom of the stems of the broccoli rabe before rinsing in cold water. As you cut the broccoli into bite-sized pieces, be sure to leave the little buds intact.

Crumble sharp, dried rosemary needles between your fingertips before adding them to sauces, soups, and dressings.

Goat cheese and asparagus

Fresh goat cheese has a lovely, creamy texture and a faint, tangy aftertaste. It pairs naturally with pasta and fresh vegetables.

Fettuccine with Goat Cheese and Asparagus

Tools: *Large pot, large skillet, colander, grater*

Preparation time: *About 15 minutes*

Cooking time: *About 20 minutes*

Yield: *4 servings*

1¼ pounds fresh asparagus	*4 ounces goat cheese, room temperature*
4 ripe plum tomatoes	*¼ cup coarsely chopped fresh basil leaves*
¾ pound fettuccine	*Salt and black pepper to taste*
2 tablespoons olive oil	*Freshly grated Parmesan cheese (optional)*
2 tablespoons butter	
2 teaspoons peeled and finely chopped garlic, about 2 large cloves	

1 Bring 4 to 5 quarts lightly salted water to a boil in a large, covered pot over high heat.

2 Meanwhile, remove the woody base of the asparagus with a knife or by snapping at the natural breaking point (about 2 inches from the thick, woody end). Slice the spears diagonally, creating ½-inch pieces. Rinse and drain well.

3 When the water boils, carefully drop in the tomatoes for 10 to 20 seconds. Remove them from the water with a slotted spoon. (You are cooking them only long enough to loosen the skins.) When they are cool enough to handle, peel off the skins with a paring knife. Remove the core and seeds. (Refer to Figure 11-2 for illustrated instructions.) Chop the tomatoes coarsely and set aside.

(continued)

4 Bring the water to a boil again and add the fettuccine. Stir thoroughly to separate the strands and cook, uncovered, for about 8 minutes or just until al dente.

5 As the pasta cooks, heat the oil and butter in a large skillet and add the asparagus, tomatoes, and garlic. Cook over medium heat for 4 to 5 minutes, stirring often, until the asparagus is crisp-tender. Reduce heat to very low to keep warm.

6 Before draining the pasta, use a measuring cup to carefully scoop out and reserve ¼ cup of the cooking liquid. When it's ready, drain the pasta and return it to the large pot.

7 Add the vegetable mixture, goat cheese, basil, salt, and pepper to the pasta. Toss well over medium heat just until warmed through. If the sauce needs extra liquid, pour in some of the reserved cooking water. Serve immediately with Parmesan cheese on the side, if desired.

Oriental seasonings

Now you can get daring. Oriental seasonings have pervaded Western cooking in recent years as chefs discover how vibrant (and healthful) they are. Ginger root is one such ingredient. Its snappy flavor is particularly invigorating with shrimp. Thus shrimp and ginger are the dominant flavors in this recipe.

Fresh ginger root, sold in the produce departments of most supermarkets and all Asian produce stores, tastes nothing like ground ginger. You cannot substitute one for the other. Look for ginger root that has no signs of softness or decay. Use a vegetable peeler to remove the root's thin layer of skin before chopping or grating. Ginger root should be wrapped in plastic wrap and stored in the refrigerator, where it keeps for several weeks.

In this recipe, ginger root gives the pasta a pleasant bite. After you trim and cut the vegetables, assembling this recipe is easy.

Fettuccine with Ginger Shrimp

Tools: *Pasta pot, chef's knife, large skillet or sauté pan, colander*

Preparation time: *About 15 minutes (25 minutes if cleaning shrimp)*

Cooking time: *About 25 minutes*

Yield: *3 servings*

Salt to taste

½ pound fettuccine

4 tablespoons olive oil

1 cup peeled and coarsely chopped red onion, about 1 medium onion

1 pound small zucchini, rinsed, trimmed, and cut into ½-inch cubes

2 medium red bell peppers, cored, seeded, and cut into ½-inch cubes

Black pepper to taste

1¼ pounds medium shrimp, peeled and deveined (see instructions in Chapter 12)

6 ripe plum tomatoes, cored and cut into ½-inch cubes

1 tablespoon peeled and finely chopped garlic, about 3 large cloves

1 tablespoon peeled and finely chopped fresh ginger root

¼ teaspoon red pepper flakes

¼ cup chopped fresh basil

1 tablespoon red wine vinegar

1 Bring 4 to 5 quarts lightly salted water to a boil in a large, covered pot over high heat. Add the fettuccine, stir thoroughly to separate the strands, and cook, uncovered, according to package instructions. The pasta should be al dente.

2 Start to make the sauce as the water boils. Heat 2 tablespoons of the olive oil in a large skillet or sauté pan. Add the onion, zucchini, red peppers, salt, and pepper. Cook, stirring often, over medium-high heat until the vegetables are tender, about 3 to 4 minutes. Add the shrimp, tomatoes, garlic, ginger root, and red pepper flakes. Cook and stir often about 3 to 4 minutes longer, or just until the shrimp are evenly pink and cooked through. Add the remaining 2 tablespoons olive oil, basil, and vinegar and stir to blend well.

3 Just before draining the pasta, use a measuring cup to carefully scoop out and reserve ¼ cup of the cooking liquid. When it's ready, drain the pasta and return it to the large pot. Add the shrimp-tomato sauce to the pasta and toss well. If the sauce needs more moisture, add the reserved cooking liquid. Serve immediately.

Buying shrimp

Unless you live within eyeshot of fishing boats, chances are that the shrimp sold in your supermarket has been frozen in transit.

Much shrimp comes from the Gulf states or the Deep South. Flash-frozen shrimp (which is plunged into a super-deep freeze upon harvest) can be excellent when handled and stored properly. Its shelf life is about six months when well wrapped.

Always buy shrimp in the shell and not pre-cooked. After you remove the shell, pick out the thin, blackish vein that runs down the back, which can have a bitter flavor. (Turn to the sidebar in Chapter 12 for detailed instructions on cleaning and deveining shrimp. Or ask your fish merchant to devein your shrimp when you purchase it.)

Family cooking

Lasagna is easy to make, especially if you use a good bottled sauce, as we do in this next recipe. You can customize the dish by adding ingredients such as ground beef, spinach, mushrooms, or chopped chicken to the sauce. Our simple version feeds at least eight. Reheat leftovers, covered with foil, in a 350-degree oven for about 20 minutes, or in a covered skillet, with a little water, over low heat. You can microwave leftovers as well.

You can make this recipe the day before, refrigerate it, and then bake it for about 1 hour before serving.

Family Lasagna

Tools: *Large pot, colander, 9-x-13-x-3-inch pan, chef's knife, grater*

Preparation Time: *About 20 minutes, if using bottled sauce (longer if making sauce)*

Cooking Time: *About 1 hour*

Yield: *8 servings*

12 lasagna noodles

1 pound mozzarella cheese (reduced-fat variety, if desired)

2 cups (one 15-ounce container) ricotta cheese (reduced-fat variety, if desired)

⅓ cup, plus 2 tablespoons grated Parmesan or Romano cheese

5 cups, more or less, homemade (see the Marinara Sauce recipe in this chapter) or favorite brand tomato sauce (two 26-ounce jars)

Salt and black pepper to taste

1 Bring an 8-quart pot filled with about 6 quarts of lightly salted water to a boil over high heat.

2 When the water is boiling, add the lasagna noodles a few at a time. Cover the pot to bring the water back to a boil, then cook uncovered, according to package directions, until barely tender but not so soft that they tear easily.

3 As the noodles cook, preheat the oven to 375 degrees.

4 Cut the mozzarella cheese into ½-inch cubes. In a small bowl, combine the ricotta, ⅓ cup of the Parmesan cheese, and 1 tablespoon of water taken from the boiling pasta pot. Season the mixture with salt and pepper to taste and set aside.

5 When they are cooked, gently drain the noodles in a colander in the sink, and run cold water over them.

6 To assemble the lasagna, spread a heaping cup of the tomato sauce on the bottom of a 13-x-9-x-3-inch ovenproof lasagna pan. Place three noodles over the sauce so that they completely cover the bottom of the pan (the noodles should touch but not overlap). Spread (or dot by heaping teaspoonfuls) one third of the ricotta mixture evenly over the noodles. Sprinkle one third of the mozzarella cheese cubes over the ricotta. Ladle and spread a heaping cup of the sauce over this layer. Season, if desired, with salt and pepper.

7 Continue making layers, ending with a thin layer of sauce. Sprinkle top layer evenly with remaining 2 tablespoons Parmesan cheese.

8 Bake in the preheated oven, checking after 30 minutes. If the top layer appears to be dry, cover with foil. Bake for another 20 to 25 minutes, or until the lasagna is piping hot and bubbly. Let stand, covered, for 15 minutes before cutting into squares and serving.

You can make lasagna unique by adding a variety of ingredients to the essential layers of noodles, cheese, and sauce. For example, combine ¼ to ⅓ cup cooked, chopped, drained, fresh or frozen spinach or broccoli with the ricotta cheese mixture. Or, sprinkle the layers with ⅓ to ½ pound cooked ground beef or cooked shredded chicken or turkey. Or, sprinkle the layers with 1 cup cooked chopped vegetables like mushrooms, zucchini, or carrots. You can dress up bottled sauces by adding a little red wine to taste, or fresh herbs like chopped oregano, marjoram, or basil. For a spicy version, add to the sauce chopped, seeded jalapeño or crushed red pepper to taste.

If you don't have a lasagna pan, you can purchase an inexpensive, disposable, aluminum lasagna pan at most supermarkets.

Chapter 12

One-Pot Meals

*W*hy use two pots (or more) when one will do? For families, singles, and party animals, one-pot meals can be a lifesaver. Every culture has its own one-pot specialties: *pot au feu* (chicken in a pot with vegetables) in France, the seafood stews of Spain, the squab pies of Morocco, and even the jambalaya of Louisiana.

Why Casserole Dishes Are for You

Casseroles may seem old-fashioned, but they come in handy. Here are some reasons why:

➤ **Casseroles take advantage of the economies of scale.** Two pounds of black beans cost little more than one pound. Go ahead, invite the neighbors!

➤ **Casseroles save time and effort.** You can drink and chat and drink some more with your dinner guests while the casserole is cooking and then coolly saunter into the kitchen. Five minutes later, voilà! Dinner.

➤ **Casseroles make great leftovers.** If you come home late and ravenous, you can excavate a casserole and zap it in the microwave.

➤ **Casseroles are classics.** You can boast that your one-pot meal is an old family recipe, even if you got it from us!

Strata: Rock Formation or Family Meal?

A *strata,* great for Sunday brunch, is essentially a custard baked around layers of different ingredients, including bread, vegetables, cheese, and seasoning.

Stratas need to "set" a few minutes before baking so that the bread can absorb the custard mixture. If it's convenient, prepare and refrigerate the dish before heading out for work in the morning. Be sure to let the casserole sit out of the refrigerator for about 10 minutes to take off the chill before baking. Then just place the casserole in a preheated 350-degree oven about 30 to 45 minutes before you're ready to eat.

Bacon and Cheese Strata

Tools: *10-x-12-inch ceramic or glass shallow baking dish, mixing bowl, chef's knife, skillet*

Preparation time: *About 25 minutes, plus 15 minutes standing time*

Cooking time: *About 35 minutes*

Yield: *4 to 6 servings*

Butter for baking dish	*5 eggs*
8-ounce loaf of seedless Italian bread	*2 cups milk*
5 slices bacon	*2 tablespoons tomato-based salsa*
1½ cups grated Gouda, Gruyère, or Italian fontina cheese	*Salt and black pepper to taste*
½ cup rinsed, chopped, packed spinach or sorrel leaves	

1 Butter the bottom and sides of a 2½- to 3-quart shallow baking dish. (Use a rectangular dish that allows the bread slices to fit snugly in one layer.)

2 Trim and discard about 1 inch off of each end of the loaf of bread and cut it into about 16 slices. If the bread is fresh, dry the slices in a 175-degree oven for about 15 minutes. Arrange the slices in the baking dish, overlapping the edges so the slices fit in the dish.

3 Sauté the bacon in a large skillet over medium-high heat, about 5 minutes, or until crisp, turning occasionally. Drain on paper towels. When it's cool enough to handle, crumble it into small pieces.

4 Sprinkle the crumbled bacon over the bread slices and top with the cheese and spinach or sorrel.

5 In a medium bowl, beat together the eggs, milk, salsa, salt, and pepper. Pour the mixture over the layers of bread, bacon, cheese, and spinach. Using a fork, press the bread slices down to soak them in the egg mixture. Let it set for about 15 minutes.

6 Preheat the oven to 350 degrees.

7 Bake the strata, about 35 minutes or just until the custard mixture is firm and lightly browned. Do not overbake, or the custard will be dry. Remove from the oven and serve immediately, cutting into squares.

Serve this rich dish with a simple salad like the Mixed Green Salad with Red Onion in Chapter 10.

 With a few changes, you can bake this strata in a 9-x-13-inch glass baking pan. Instead of overlapping the bread slices, lay them flat, using only enough bread to cover the bottom of the pan. (You will have 2 or 3 slices of the 16 remaining. Use them to make bread crumbs.) Bake in a 350-degree oven for about 30 minutes, or just until the custard sets. Cut into squares and serve immediately.

 You can vary a strata almost as much as an omelet filling. Substitute cooked, ground meat or ham for the bacon. Use slices of challah (an egg-enriched bread) for the Italian bread. Omit the spinach and add ½ cup cooked broccoli florets, chopped onion, or sautéed mushrooms.

Shepherd's Pie

In Ireland, the classic Shepherd's Pie is made with beef, not lamb. We prefer the more distinctive flavor of lamb, so we're giving you the following lamb recipe. If you want to try it with beef, simply substitute the same amount of meat.

Shepherd's Pie

Tools: *Chef's knife, large pot, potato masher or ricer, large skillet, oval gratin dish*

Preparation time: *About 45 minutes*

Cooking time: *About 35 minutes*

Yield: *4 to 6 servings*

(continued)

2½ pounds baking potatoes

4 tablespoons butter

About 1 cup milk

Salt and black pepper to taste

1 tablespoon vegetable oil

1 medium onion, chopped

2 large cloves, peeled and chopped

1½ pounds cooked, chopped lamb (or raw, ground lamb)

1 tablespoon all-purpose flour

½ cup homemade or canned beef or chicken stock

1 tablespoon chopped thyme or sage, or 1 teaspoon dried

1 tablespoon chopped rosemary leaves, or 1 teaspoon dried

Dash ground nutmeg

1 Preheat the oven to 350 degrees.

2 Peel and quarter the potatoes. Put the potatoes in a large pot of lightly salted water and bring to a boil. Cook, covered, until the potatoes are tender, about 20 minutes. Drain well and return the potatoes to the pot.

3 Mash the potatoes with a masher or ricer along with 2 tablespoons of the butter and enough milk to make them smooth and fluffy. Season with salt and pepper and set aside.

4 Heat the oil in a large skillet over medium-low heat. Add the onion and garlic and cook, stirring often, until the onion is soft and wilted. (Be careful not to let the garlic brown.) Turn up the heat to medium and add the lamb. Cook about 5 minutes, stirring. (If using raw ground lamb, cook over medium heat, stirring often, for about 10 minutes or until it is well browned.) Pour off and discard any fat in the pan.

5 Add the flour and cook, stirring often, for about 2 to 3 minutes. Add the stock, thyme, rosemary, nutmeg, salt, and pepper. Reduce the heat to low and simmer, stirring occasionally, for about 15 minutes. Remove from the heat and let cool slightly.

6 Transfer the lamb mixture to an oval gratin dish (about 13 inches long). Spread the mashed potatoes over everything. Dot with the remaining 2 tablespoons butter (which simply means to break up the butter into several small pieces and distribute it evenly) and bake for 45 minutes or until nicely browned. Let cool for 5 minutes before serving.

This dish needs only a salad, like the Tomato, Red Onion, and Basil Salad in Chapter 10.

Meat Loaf

This slightly untraditional meat loaf (made partly with turkey to cut down on fat) can be a jumping-off point for other creations. If you like, try mixing in a little ground pork or ground veal instead of turkey. Lamb is a nice addition, too. The essential technique is the same for any ground meat.

Beef and Turkey Meat Loaf

Tools: *Chef's knife, medium skillet, large bowl, 5- to 6-cup loaf pan, whisk*

Preparation time: *About 30 minutes*

Cooking time: *About 1½ hours, plus 10 minutes standing time*

Yield: *6 servings*

2 tablespoons olive oil

1 large onion, chopped

3 large cloves garlic, finely chopped

¾ cup milk

2 eggs

1½ cups fresh bread crumbs

1 pound ground turkey

1 pound lean ground beef

2 tablespoons chopped thyme, or 2 tea-spoons dried

2 tablespoons chopped savory, or 2 tea-spoons dried

2 tablespoons finely chopped parsley

¼ teaspoon ground nutmeg

Salt and black pepper to taste

1 Preheat the oven to 350 degrees.

2 Heat the oil in a medium skillet over medium heat. Add the onion and cook, stirring occasionally, for about 3 minutes or until the onion begins to wilt. Add the garlic and cook, stirring often, about 2 minutes more. Do not let the garlic brown. Remove the pan from the heat and set aside.

3 In a large bowl, beat together the milk and eggs with the whisk; stir in the bread crumbs and let stand for 5 minutes. Add the remaining ingredients and the sautéed onion and garlic. Combine the mixture thoroughly by using your hands or a wooden spoon.

4 Mold the mixture into a 5- to 6-cup loaf pan. Bake, uncovered, about 1½ hours, draining off any excess grease if necessary. Let the meat loaf stand for about 10 minutes at room temperature before slicing from the pan.

You can serve this meat loaf with a quick tomato sauce, spicy salsa, mustard sauce, or even a jazzed-up sauce of ketchup flavored with Tabasco sauce and Worcestershire sauce. A great side dish is Braised Cabbage with Apple and Caraway (see Chapter 16).

A bulb baster is a handy tool for siphoning off undesired grease that can collect in a roasting pan. If you don't have a baster, a large metal spoon also works; carefully tip the pan and use the spoon to scoop out the grease.

Chicken Pot Pie

 In Colonial America, many foods, such as game, birds, and poultry, were served in pies. Pies were hearty one-dish meals that were easy to re-serve. The recipe hasn't changed much, unless you go to some hip new restaurant, where they may put fennel or fiddlehead ferns in it.

The following recipe, although not difficult to execute, takes time to make right. Steps include poaching the chicken, making a white sauce, chopping vegetables, and rolling out fresh biscuits for the pie's top. But the result is worth it.

Chicken and Biscuit Pot Pie

Tools: *Chef's knife, 4-quart pot with lid, colander, small saucepan, mixing bowl, 2-quart shallow baking dish, whisk, rolling pin*

Preparation time: *About 30 minutes*

Cooking time: *About 40 minutes*

Baking time: *About 25 minutes*

Yield: *6 servings*

2 to 2¼ pounds chicken breasts with skin and bones

3 cups homemade or canned chicken stock

1 medium onion, halved

1 celery stalk, trimmed of leaves and cut into 2-inch slices

2 cloves garlic, peeled

3 carrots, trimmed, scraped, and sliced into 2-inch pieces

1 medium boiling potato, peeled and quartered

6 tablespoons butter

3 tablespoons all-purpose flour

¼ cup heavy cream

¼ teaspoon ground nutmeg

Salt and black pepper to taste

1 cup fresh or frozen peas

1 tablespoon sherry (optional)

1½ cups packaged dry biscuit mix, plus additional mix for dusting work surface

½ cup milk

1 Combine the chicken breasts, stock, onion, celery, and garlic in a 4-quart pot. Add water to just cover the chicken and vegetables. Cover the pot and bring to a boil. Uncover, reduce heat, and simmer for 15 minutes.

2 Add the carrots and potato. Bring the stock back to a boil and then lower the heat and simmer 15 minutes more or until the chicken and vegetables are just tender. Let cool for about 5 minutes in the liquid.

3 Slowly and carefully, pour the broth with the chicken and vegetables into a large colander set over a larger pot to catch and reserve the chicken-vegetable stock. Let cool for about 10 minutes, or until the chicken is cool enough to handle.

4 Remove the meat from the chicken and slice it into bite-sized pieces. Discard the skin and bones, celery, and garlic. Coarsely cube the onion, carrot, and potato into ½-inch pieces and set them aside.

5 Skim the fat from the reserved stock. Pour 2 cups of the stock into a small saucepan. (Reserve any remaining stock for other uses, or, if necessary, add additional water to make 2 cups.) Heat the stock to just below the point of boiling.

6 Melt 3 tablespoons of the butter in a pot or large saucepan over medium heat. (You can use the same pot that you used to make the stock.) Add the flour and cook, whisking constantly, for about 1 minute. Stir in the 2 cups of hot stock, whisking occasionally and cooking about 2 to 3 minutes until the sauce comes to a boil and thickens. Add the cream and nutmeg. Adjust the seasoning with salt and pepper.

7 Stir the chicken, diced vegetables, peas, and, if desired, sherry into the sauce. Spoon the mixture into a 2-quart shallow baking dish.

8 Preheat the oven to 425 degrees.

9 Combine the biscuit mix and the remaining 3 tablespoons butter in a medium bowl. Using a fork or your fingers, blend the butter into the biscuit mix until the mixture resembles coarse crumbs.

10 Stir in the milk and blend the mixture into a soft dough. Transfer the dough to a well-floured wooden board or countertop. (You can use a little of the biscuit mix or regular flour.) The dough should be very soft. Before you attempt to roll or press out the dough with your hands, add more dry biscuit mix to your work surface and sprinkle the mound of dough with a little more dry mix. Also, dust your hands and the rolling pin (if you are using one) with the dry mix. You want to make the dough just firm enough to roll or press out into a square about ½-inch thick.

11 Using a knife, cut the dough into 9 or 10 triangles or rounds. Arrange the dough shapes on top of the chicken mixture and bake for about 25 minutes, or until the biscuits are lightly browned. Serve immediately.

This is a meal in itself, perhaps served with the Carrot Soup with Dill in Chapter 9.

Let's Party: Shrimp Appetizers

Shrimp make great party food. You can serve them as an appetizer or a meal along with rice, noodles, or a vegetable. (See Chapter 3 for rice and vegetable recipes.)

Shrimp are sized and priced according to how many shrimp are in a pound. Although the number can vary from one market to the next, medium shrimp usually contain about 40 to 50 per pound, large shrimp about 30 to 35, extra-large 25 to 30, jumbo 20 to 25, and colossal 15 to 18 per pound. The price of shrimp generally increases with its size, with colossal the most expensive and medium the most reasonable. For this recipe, you want shrimp that are big enough to hold a fair amount of the stuffing.

Baked Shrimp with Green Onion Bread Crumbs

Tools: *Shrimp deveiner, paring knife, chef's knife, medium skillet, baking sheet, pastry brush*

Preparation time: *About 30 minutes*

Cooking time: *About 12 minutes*

Yield: *4 servings*

1 pound extra-large or jumbo shrimp, shelled and deveined (see Figure 12-1 for instructions)

2 tablespoons butter

½ cup finely chopped green onions

¼ cup finely chopped red bell pepper

¼ cup finely chopped celery

2 large cloves garlic, finely chopped

¾ cup fresh bread crumbs (see following sidebar)

2 teaspoons fresh lemon juice

1 teaspoon chopped marjoram or chervil, or ½ teaspoon dried

1 teaspoon chopped thyme, or ½ teaspoon dried

½ teaspoon paprika

Salt and black pepper to taste

1 tablespoon olive oil

4 lemon wedges

1 Preheat the oven to 500 degrees.

2 Prepare the shrimp by slicing them (without cutting all the way through) with a paring knife from head to tail, along the back side, about three-fourths of the way into the flesh, so they open up and lay flat, resembling a butterfly.

3 In a medium skillet, melt the butter over medium heat. Add the green onions, red pepper, celery, and garlic. Cook, stirring, over medium heat, about 3 or 4 minutes, or until the vegetables begin to wilt. Add the bread crumbs, lemon juice, marjoram, thyme, and paprika. Blend well, remove from the heat, and season with salt and pepper.

4 On a lightly oiled baking sheet, lay the shrimp in rows, split side up. Spoon equal amounts of the stuffing onto the top of each butterflied shrimp. Press down lightly to smooth it. (The shrimp coil slightly around the stuffing as they bake.)

5 Brush the stuffing mixture lightly with the olive oil. Bake for about 8 minutes or until the shrimp are cooked and evenly pink. Serve immediately with the lemon wedges.

Any of the following would complement this dish: Orzo Medley (see Chapter 10), Converted Rice (see Chapter 3), or Garlic and Goat Cheese Tartines (see Chapter 16).

Cleaning and Deveining Shrimp

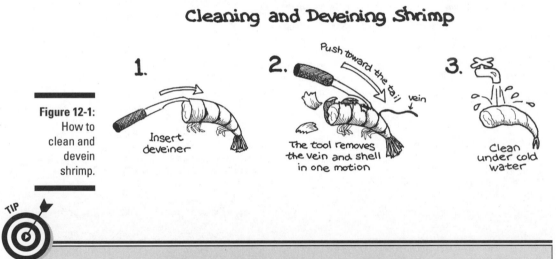

Figure 12-1:
How to
clean and
devein
shrimp.

TIP

Making fresh bread crumbs

You don't need to waste your money by buying bread crumbs. Instead, make your own and store them in an airtight jar.

Lightly toast six slices of bread. Tear the bread into pieces and place in a food processor or blender; then blend to the consistency of coarse crumbs.

Variation: Add dried herbs of your choice to the blender, or rub the slices of bread with cloves of peeled and sliced garlic before whirling the bread into crumbs.

Pasta Paradise

This next recipe is a classic and simple version of macaroni and cheese, which you can alter in many ways. You can substitute all kinds of pasta for the elbow macaroni, such as penne, ziti, or shells. Mozzarella or Gruyère can replace the fontina or cheddar, or you can use the cheeses in any combination. You can make a spicy version by adding more Tabasco sauce or even crushed red pepper flakes. Add sautéed onion and red bell pepper or cooked broccoli florets and mushrooms to the cheese sauce for a vegetable version. Or sprinkle the top with cooked, crumbled bacon, shredded ham, or Parmesan cheese instead of the bread crumbs.

American Macaroni and Cheese

Tools: *4- or 5-quart pot, two saucepans, whisk, grater, colander, chef's knife, deep 2- to 3-quart casserole dish with lid*

Preparation time: *About 25 minutes*

Cooking time: *About 25 minutes*

Yield: *4 servings*

2 cups elbow macaroni	*2 cups grated sharp cheddar cheese*
2½ cups milk	*Salt and black pepper to taste*
5 tablespoons butter	*½ cup cubed Italian fontina cheese*
3 tablespoons all-purpose flour	*1 cup fresh white bread crumbs (see preceding sidebar)*
½ teaspoon paprika	
Generous dash Tabasco sauce, or to taste	

1 Preheat the oven to 350 degrees.

2 Bring a 4- or 5-quart pot of lightly salted water to a boil. Add the macaroni and cook for about 6 to 8 minutes or until just tender. (Be careful not to overcook. The macaroni softens even more when it's baked.)

3 As macaroni cooks, make the cheese sauce. Heat the milk almost to the boiling point in a small saucepan over medium-low heat.

4 Melt 3 tablespoons of the butter in a large saucepan over medium heat. Add the flour and whisk constantly over low heat for 1 to 2 minutes. Do not let it brown.

5 Gradually whisk in the hot milk, and then add the paprika and Tabasco sauce. Cook over medium heat for 2 to 3 minutes or until the sauce thickens, whisking occasionally. Whisk in the grated cheddar cheese and remove from the heat. Season with salt and pepper.

6 Drain the elbow macaroni as soon as it is done and add it to the cheese sauce. Add the cubes of fontina and stir well to blend. (If the macaroni cooks before you finish making the sauce, drain and set it aside.)

7 Use 1 tablespoon of the butter to grease a deep, 2- to 3-quart casserole dish fitted with a lid. Add the macaroni and cheese mixture. Cover and bake for 20 to 25 minutes until hot.

8 As the casserole bakes, melt the remaining tablespoon of butter in a small skillet. Add the bread crumbs and sauté over low heat, stirring constantly, until they are moistened but not browned.

9 Carefully remove the casserole from the oven. Raise the oven temperature to broil; spread the bread crumbs evenly over the macaroni and cheese. Return the casserole to the oven, uncovered, and broil for 1 to 2 minutes, or until the crumbs are crisp and browned. Serve immediately.

All this dish needs is a colorful salad, like the Roasted Red Pepper and Snow Pea Salad in Chapter 10.

Chapter 13

Desserts

• •

In This Chapter

▶ Whipping up some pleasing puddings for all occasions

▶ Into the deep freeze with ice creams and granités

▶ Baking some (relatively) guilt-free desserts: cooked fruits and cobblers

• •

*1*n this chapter we walk down sweet memory lane, with soothing images of cinnamon-scented wobbly puddings, old-fashioned cobblers, and luscious baked fruits. Even if your mother's idea of a homemade dessert was Twinkies drenched with Hershey's chocolate syrup, you probably enjoyed puddings and cobblers in diners or family-style restaurants, where they were regally displayed in glass-fronted refrigerated cases — mouth watering and irresistible.

You can return to those heady days by spreading this book out on the kitchen counter and bringing those dusty memories to life. Don't procrastinate. Memories are made every minute.

As you dabble in this chapter, you discover all sorts of techniques that will make you a stellar dessert chef. You become familiar with the marvelous egg and its myriad uses, particularly in puddings. We introduce you to the technique of cooking egg-based puddings in a water bath, which prevents them from curdling. Imagine how you'll impress your friends — and yourself — with this technique!

In the fruit cobbler section, you discover the importance of precision in baking. What's more, you'll figure out how to make a simple dessert look great. We even show you how to make your own ice cream. Think about it. Why should you make the people at Haagen Daz rich when you can easily make a better product at home? Desserts are great crowd-pleasers, so if you want to make a good impression on your family and friends, try your hand at one of the recipes in this chapter. And just sit back and wait for the adoration.

Puddings, Creams, and Granités

This yummy, easy, and versatile dessert cream is most commonly used to stuff Italian cannoli — a deep-fried Sicilian pastry shaped like a thick cigar. But it is also delicious enough to serve on its own as a sweet sauce over ripe berries. Or you can spoon some over pound cake and garnish with sweetened fruit. This recipe also makes a great topping for waffles or pancakes, and it's wonderful as a cake layer filling as well.

Low-fat ricotta cheese can be used in all kinds of desserts, often as a substitute for heavy cream.

Ricotta Dessert Cream

Tools: *Food processor, mixing bowl or small glass serving bowl*

Preparation: *10 minutes*

Cooking time: *None*

Yield: *About 2 cups, or 4 servings*

2 cups whole milk ricotta cheese

¼ cup granulated sugar

1 tablespoon confectioners' sugar

1 teaspoon vanilla extract

1 teaspoon grated orange zest

1 Place all of the ingredients in a food processor container and pulse until the cheese mixture is smooth.

2 Transfer to a mixing bowl or small glass serving bowl; cover and refrigerate until chilled, 1 to 2 hours. Serve over fresh fruit or pound cake.

For a different flavor, increase the granulated sugar to ⅓ cup and add ½ cup sliced strawberries or whole raspberries to the container before processing. Or stir into the smooth ricotta mixture 1 ounce (1 square) of finely chopped, semisweet chocolate, or ½ cup mini-chocolate chips.

When grating citrus peel, be sure to remove only the colored portion of the skin, called the *zest*. The white portion underneath, called the pith, is bitter.

If possible, don't use imitation vanilla extract. Buy pure extracts that, although more expensive, make a big difference.

Rice pudding is one of those all-American dishes that you find in roadside diners across the country. It has many incarnations: Sometimes it's firm and custardy, other times creamy and rich. The recipe below falls on the rich and creamy side, with a nice sharp bite from cinnamon.

Homey Rice Pudding

Tools: Grater, saucepan, whisk, 2 mixing bowls, oval baking dish (approximately 14-x-8-x-2 inches), large baking dish

Preparation time: About 10 minutes

Cooking time: 1 hour

Yield: 8 servings

5 cups milk	*¾ cup raisins*
1 cup heavy cream	*3 egg yolks*
1 vanilla bean, split lengthwise so the inner seeds are exposed (or 1 teaspoon vanilla extract)	*1 tablespoon grated lemon zest*
	1 tablespoon butter for greasing the pan
1 cup converted rice	*1 teaspoon cinnamon*
1¼ cups sugar	

1 Pour the milk and cream into a heavy-bottomed saucepan and add the vanilla bean or extract. Bring the mixture to a boil and stir in the rice and sugar — stir from the bottom to keep the rice from sticking. Reduce the heat to low and simmer, stirring occasionally, until the rice is tender and most of the milk is absorbed, about 30 minutes. Set aside.

2 Meanwhile, put the raisins in a bowl and pour boiling water over them. Let them stand until the rice is cooked.

3 In another bowl, whisk the egg yolks and then blend in the lemon zest. When the rice is cooked remove it from the heat and slowly whisk in the egg mixture.

4 Preheat the oven to 400 degrees.

5 Drain the raisins and add them to the cooked rice.

6 Grease an oval baking dish measuring 14-x-8-x-2 inches (approximately). Pour the rice mixture into the dish, sprinkle with cinnamon, and place in a larger ovenproof dish with sides (like a casserole). Pour boiling water into the exterior dish about 2 inches up the sides. Bake for about 30 minutes or until the custard is set (you can tell it's set when a toothpick inserted into the center of the pudding comes out clean).

Smell the spices that have been sitting on your shelf for months or years. If they've lost their enticing fragrance, throw them out and treat yourself to new ones.

Think of a water bath as a backyard kiddie pool for pots and pans. It's essentially any large, high-sided baking dish or roasting pan that can be partially filled with water, and in which you set another pan. When making delicate sauces or custards, the dish holding the ingredients is set in the larger, bottom container, which holds the water. When you put the pot holding the ingredients inside the larger pan of boiling water, instead of putting it directly on the stove, you prevent it from getting too hot and curdling. The French call this method a *bain marie,* which translates as "Marie's bath."

This recipe comes from friends who live in southwestern France, land of orchards, sunflowers and foie gras. It's a quick, home-style dessert that is both light and delicious. Use a quality red wine in the recipe, and you'll be pleased with the result.

Baked Apples with Red Wine

Tools: *Paring knife, bread knife, baking sheet*

Preparation time: *10 minutes*

Cooking time: *20 to 30 minutes*

Yield: *4 servings*

Butter, for greasing aluminum foil	*¼ cup red wine*
4 thick slices country bread	*6 tablespoons sugar*
4 apples (Granny Smith, or any preferred apple)	*½ cup vanilla ice cream, more to taste*

1 Preheat the oven to 375 degrees.

2 Grease very well a double-thick sheet of aluminum foil that is large enough to hold the four slices of bread. Lay it over a baking sheet. Arrange the bread slices over the foil.

3 With a paring knife, cut a hole in the top of the apples, about ¾ inch in diameter, and deep enough to go about halfway down into the apple. (You want the hole large enough to hold a small scoop of ice cream.) Slice across the bottom of the apples, just enough so that they will stand upright on top of the bread slices. Carefully sprinkle the red wine over the bread slices so that they are thoroughly moistened but not soggy. Sprinkle evenly with 4 tablespoons of the sugar.

4 Place the cored apples on top of the bread slices. Sprinkle the remaining sugar into the hollow cores. Place the apples in the oven for 20 to 30 minutes, or until the apples are soft. Use a spatula to carefully remove the apples and bread to a serving plate. Serve with a tablespoon or so of vanilla ice cream placed in the hollow cores, adding a little on top.

Put away your packaged pudding mixes forever. This pudding is so rich and delicious it will be everyone's favorite. You can dress it up by spooning it into a tall wine or parfait glass between layers of sweetened whipped cream. Or forget the cream and just indulge in the pure chocolate flavor alone.

Double Chocolate Pudding

Tools: *Medium saucepan, chef's knife, small mixing bowl, wooden spoon, 3- to 4-cup capacity serving bowl or individual serving cups, plastic wrap or wax paper*

Preparation time: *10 minutes*

Cooking time: *6 to 8 minutes*

Yield: *4 servings*

¼ cup water

2½ tablespoons cornstarch

½ cup sugar

⅓ cup unsweetened cocoa powder

Pinch of salt

⅓ cup milk, heated just to warm

2 ounces (2 squares) semisweet chocolate, coarsely chopped

2 cups heavy cream

1¼ teaspoons vanilla extract

Sweetened whipped cream, optional garnish

Chopped pecans or almonds, lightly toasted, optional garnish (see Essential Skill icon after this recipe for instructions on toasting nuts)

1 In a small bowl, stir together the water and the cornstarch thoroughly until the cornstarch is dissolved and the mixture is smooth. Set the mixture aside.

2 In a heavy, medium saucepan mix together the sugar, cocoa, and salt. Using a wooden spoon, stir in the warm milk to make a smooth paste. Place the saucepan over medium heat and bring the mixture to a boil while stirring constantly, about 2 to 3 minutes. Add the chopped chocolate and stir until it completely melts.

(continued)

3 Gradually stir in the heavy cream. Stir the cornstarch mixture a few times to be sure it's completely dissolved, then stir it thoroughly into the chocolate mixture. Continue stirring over medium heat for about 5 minutes, or until the pudding begins to thicken and boil. (Be sure to sweep the spoon along the bottom and sides of the pan to prevent the pudding from getting lumpy or burning.)

4 Reduce the heat to low and cook for about 1 minute more while stirring constantly.

5 Remove the saucepan from the heat and stir in the vanilla.

6 Pour the pudding into a serving bowl or individual serving cups. To prevent a skin from forming lay a piece of plastic wrap or wax paper directly on the surface of the pudding. Refrigerate for several hours or until chilled before serving. If desired, garnish each serving with a dollop of sweetened whipped cream and a sprinkling of chopped nuts.

For a mocha flavored pudding, substitute 1 tablespoon (or to taste) coffee liqueur (like kahlua) for the vanilla extract.

Toasting nuts lightly before tossing into doughs or batters greatly improves their flavor. Simply spread them out on a baking sheet and toast in a 350-degree oven for about 10 minutes or until lightly browned.

Overbeating cream and other ingredients can cause problems, including the following:

✔ **If you overbeat cream it turns to butter.** Be sure to start with very cold cream, cold beaters, and a cold bowl. Start beating slowly and gradually increase the speed. Don't strive for stiff cream but rather soft, floppy peaks. Always refrigerate whipped cream immediately unless you're serving it right away.

✔ **Overbeating egg whites causes them to dry out.** Beat them so they form peaks that stand on their own. Start beating fairly vigorously and increase to higher speed, adding other ingredients, like sugar. Be sure your beaters and bowls are free of any fat or grease, which makes it more difficult to reach soft peaks.

✔ **Overbeating doughs, pie crusts, and batters toughens them, too.** Beating triggers the protein in flour and forms gluten — a toughening agent. The more you knead or beat the dough or batter the tougher it becomes. (Kneading dough is necessary for properly developing the dough of yeast breads, but not for making delicate desserts.) Therefore, use a light touch when making any pastry dough, biscuits, cakes, and cookies. Beat until the liquid and dry ingredients are blended, no more.

The following dessert is assembled and baked in just minutes, and doesn't require the skills of a pastry chef. It's the perfect sweet ending to a family dinner. It's also a very popular dessert; there may be two or three people in America who don't like chocolate mousse, but we've never met them. Simple and festive, you can make it days in advance.

Chocolate Mousse

Tools: *Stainless steel 2 quart bowl, saucepan, whisk, electric handheld mixer, spatula*

Preparation time: *About 10 minutes*

Cooking time: *About 10 minutes (plus several hours chilling)*

Yield: *10 to 12 servings*

8 ounces bittersweet chocolate

6 eggs, separated

3 tablespoons water

2 cups cream, well chilled

6 tablespoons sugar

Whipped cream for garnish (or grated bittersweet chocolate)

1 Chop the chocolate coarsely. Place the chocolate pieces in a saucepan or pot and set the pot over a larger pot holding barely simmering water. Cover the pot containing the chocolate.

2 Meanwhile, put the egg yolks in a saucepan and add the water. Place the saucepan over *very* low heat while whisking vigorously. When the yolks thicken slightly (to a light sauce consistency), remove the saucepan from the heat.

3 Check the chocolate. When it is melted, stir well with a whisk. Add the melted chocolate to the egg mixture and blend thoroughly. Scrape the mixture into a large mixing bowl.

4 With a handheld electric mixer, beat the cream in a chilled bowl until it forms soft peaks, adding 2 tablespoons of the sugar toward the end. Fold this into the chocolate mixture.

5 With a handheld electric mixer, beat the egg whites until they form soft peaks. (Wash the mixer thoroughly to remove the cream, before proceeding.) Beat in the remaining sugar and continue beating until the egg whites form stiff peaks. Fold this into the mousse mixture.

6 Spoon the mousse into a serving bowl and chill thoroughly before serving. Garnish with whipped cream or grated semisweet chocolate.

Our good friend and mentor, the late Pierre Franey, used to pour about ¼ cup of amaretto or Grand Marnier into the egg-yolk and chocolate mixture just before it thickened.

Also, you may want to garnish the mousse with strawberries, toasted almonds, hazelnuts, or walnuts.

What's special about the following ice cream, aside from its wonderful citric flavor, is the ease of preparation. You don't need an ice cream maker to prepare it. You simply combine all of the ingredients and freeze them until solid. It's creamy, refreshing, and so rich that a small serving is all that's needed.

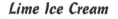

Lime Ice Cream

Tools: *Grater, knife, large bowl, 8- or 9-inch square metal cake pan*

Preparation time: *5 to 10 minutes*

Cooking time: *None (several hours to freeze it)*

Yield: *About 3 cups, or 4 servings*

2 cups heavy cream	*2 teaspoons grated lime zest*
1 cup sugar	*⅓ cup fresh lime juice*

1 In a large bowl, combine the cream and sugar; stir the mixture until the sugar is dissolved. Stir in the lime zest and juice. The mixture will start to thicken slightly.

2 Pour the mixture into the pan. Cover with foil and freeze until firm, about 4 hours. Scoop or spoon into individual serving bowls with sliced fruit, such as mango, blueberries, kiwi, or strawberries.

Grated citrus peel, also referred to as zest, has the unpleasant tendency of clinging to the holes of the grater. To loosen these pieces, brush the holes with a pastry brush so the grated peel falls onto a cutting board or right into the dish you're preparing.

Granité is the French word for flavored ices. Aside from being pure, healthful, and delicious, they require no fancy equipment beyond a fork and a little elbow grease. Essentially, granités are flavored and sweetened water — you can use all kinds of fruits to flavor them — that are frozen in ice cube trays. Every once in a while during the freezing process, you scrape the ice with a fork to create little crystals. That's it!

Orange Granité

Tools: *Medium saucepan, shallow pan or metal ice cube trays without dividers*

Preparation time: *10 minutes*

Cooking time: *None (freezing time of 90 minutes)*

Yield: *6 servings*

¾ *cup freshly squeezed orange juice*

1 cup water

6 tablespoons sugar

Fresh fruit, such as blueberries, strawberries, kiwis, and pitted cherries

1 In a saucepan, combine the orange juice, water, and sugar. Stir well. Bring to a boil, and remove from the heat.

2 Pour the mixture into a shallow pan or ice cube trays without dividers. Place in the freezer.

3 After about 30 minutes, remove the trays from the freezer and, using a fork, scrape back and forth over the ice, eventually reaching the bottom of the container. Return the mixture to the freezer. Repeat twice more at 30 minute intervals. You should not see any big chunks of ice. Serve in chilled bowls, with fresh fruits around it.

Fresh mint, which grows profusely in the summer months, is our favorite flavor of granité. Combined with a little lemon and orange, it evokes a sunny summer day around the pool. Any leftover mint can be used in mint juleps, but that's another book.

Fresh Mint Granité

Tools: *Medium saucepan, shallow pan or metal ice cube trays without dividers*

Preparation time: *10 minutes*

Cooking time: *None (freezing time of 90 minutes)*

Yield: *6 to 8 servings*

(continued)

¾ cup loosely packed fresh mint leaves

4 cups water

1 cup sugar

Grated zest of 1 lemon

Grated zest of 1 orange

1 In a saucepan, combine all of the ingredients. Stir well. Bring to a boil and remove from the heat.

2 Strain and pour the mixture into a shallow metal pan or ice cube trays without dividers. Place in the freezer.

3 After about 30 minutes remove the tray from the freezer and, using a fork, scrape back and forth over the ice, eventually reaching the bottom of the container. Return the mixture to the freezer. Repeat twice more at 30 minute intervals. You should not see any big chunks of ice. Serve on chilled plates with fresh fruits around it.

You can make terrific granités with all kinds of fresh fruits, including blueberries, strawberries, Concord grapes, watermelon, cantaloupe, apple juice, lemons, limes, and more. Just extract all of the juice either with a reamer (in the case of citrus) or by putting peeled and pitted fruit in a blender, then straining the juice into the saucepan along with the sugar and water. Fibrous fruits (mangos, apricots, plums, figs, bananas, and papayas, for example) do not work as well for granités.

When making granités, select the ripest fruit you can find; it can even be a tad overripe. You want as much flavor from the fruit as possible.

Poached and Baked Fruits

This section is primarily about fruits and their various uses in desserts. Two of America's earliest desserts are featured here: cobblers and crisps. You may be thinking, "What's the difference between a cobbler and a crisp?" A cobbler is a deep-dish fruit dessert baked with a thick biscuit crust; in a crisp, the fruit is baked under a crumbly topping, usually made with flour, butter, and sugar, and sometimes oats, nuts, and spices. Both are terrific in the fall, when apples are in season.

We also cover poached fruits in this section. The basic poaching liquid is a syrupy solution of one part sugar to three parts water. But many recipes add flavors like vanilla bean, orange and lemon zest, honey, white or red wine, fresh ginger, whole cloves, star anise, fresh herb sprigs (rosemary is especially good with pears), and even whole black peppercorns.

Fruit for poaching should be ripe but still a little firm. Underripe fruit has little sweetness. Overly ripe fruit, on the other hand, may fall apart and become soggy.

Poached Pears

The most attractive way to serve poached pears is standing upright with the stems intact; however, if you like, they can also be halved or quartered, which makes them cook more quickly.

Tools: *Vegetable peeler or paring knife, large deep saucepan (to hold 4 pears upright), citrus juicer, chef's knife, slotted spoon*

Preparation time: *5 to 10 minutes*

Cooking time: *15 to 25 minutes (depending on ripeness and size of the pears)*

Yield: *4 servings*

1 large navel orange

2 cups water

1 cup dark rum

½ cup granulated sugar

½ cup dark brown sugar, packed

2 tablespoons diced crystallized ginger, or 1 cinnamon stick

4 medium ripe but firm Bosc pears

2 cups vanilla ice cream, optional

1 Using a vegetable peeler or a paring knife, remove a strip of zest from the orange, about 4 to 5 inches long and about 1 inch thick. Squeeze out the orange juice (a simple juicer is the easiest tool to use for squeezing out the juice) and add it to a saucepan that is just large enough to hold 4 whole pears. Add the orange zest strip, water, dark rum, sugars, and ginger or cinnamon stick.

2 Bring to a boil, covered. Reduce heat and simmer, covered, about 2 to 3 minutes or until sugars are completely dissolved.

3 As the syrup simmers, carefully peel the pears, leaving them whole with their stems intact. Use a melon baller or paring knife to remove the core from the bottom of each pear. If necessary, slice across the bottom so the pears stand upright.

4 Immediately place the pears in the syrup and poach over low heat, covered, turning occasionally to expose all sides to the cooking liquid. Cook just until tender, anywhere from 15 to 25 minutes. A sharp knife should be able to easily pierce through to the center of each.

5 With a slotted spoon remove each pear to an individual serving dish.

(continued)

6 Bring the poaching liquid to a boil over medium-high heat and cook, uncovered, about 5 to 10 minutes to concentrate the syrup. To serve, spoon some of the poaching liquid over each pear. Add a scoop of vanilla ice cream, if desired, to each dish. To serve chilled, return the pears to the concentrated syrup and refrigerate for several hours or until ready to serve, turning them occasionally so they color evenly. They will keep in the refrigerator for several days.

Add a pinch or two of black pepper or nutmeg to the concentrated liquid for a spicy, exotic touch.

To keep a box of brown sugar from hardening after opening, place the box in a resealable, airtight, plastic bag and refrigerate.

Like some of the other dessert classics in this chapter, this one has been slightly altered — we've added pears to the apple mixture and splashed the fruit with a little brandy. The dish can be assembled before dinner and baked while you are eating. The vanilla ice cream or sweetened whipped cream is optional, but we recommend it.

Apple-Pear Crisp

Tools: *Apple corer or paring knife, medium mixing bowl, pastry blender or table knives (for stirring), 2-quart glass or ceramic baking dish*

Preparation time: *About 20 minutes*

Cooking time: *40 to 45 minutes*

Yield: *6 servings*

3 large Granny Smith apples

2 large firm-ripe pears

2 to 3 tablespoons brandy or dark rum (optional)

¾ cup flour

⅔ cup granulated sugar

2 tablespoons brown sugar, packed

Grated zest of ½ lemon

¼ teaspoon salt

½ teaspoon ground cinnamon

¼ teaspoon ground nutmeg

½ cup (1 stick) cold butter, cut into small pieces

½ cup toasted chopped almonds or pecans

Vanilla ice cream or whipped cream (optional garnish)

1 Position a rack in the lower third of the oven. Preheat the oven to 375 degrees.

2 Peel and core the apples and cut them into 1-inch chunks (for illustrated instructions on coring apples, see Figure 16-4 in Chapter 16). Core the pears and cut them into 1-inch chunks. Spread the fruit evenly over the bottom of an unbuttered, shallow, 2-quart baking dish. If desired, sprinkle the fruit with the brandy or rum.

3 In a medium mixing bowl, combine the flour, sugars, lemon zest, salt, and spices. Using a pastry blender, two knives, or your fingertips, cut the butter into the dry ingredients until the mixture resembles coarse bread crumbs. Mix in the chopped nuts.

4 Spread the topping evenly over the fruit. Bake for 40 to 45 minutes, or until the fruit is tender and the crust is lightly browned. Serve warm, if desired, with vanilla ice cream or sweetened whipped cream (see the recipe for whipped cream in Chapter 7).

 If desired, add half a cup of fresh, rinsed cranberries to the apple-pear mixture before spreading on the sugar topping. Or, for a summer crisp, substitute peaches and nectarines for the apples and pears.

 Throughout this book, we call for unsalted butter (and no margarine), and with good reason — margarine doesn't taste as good as butter. Salt (in salted butter) can affect the delicate sweetness of many baked goods. Sometimes, however, margarine is used in combination with butter to add a light and flaky quality to pie crusts (see Chapter 16 for a great pie crust recipe, and notice that we specifically call for butter *and* margarine).

Cobblers are deep-dish desserts in which sweetened fruits (fresh berries are the traditional choice) are topped with a biscuit dough before baking. Almost any type or combination of fruits can be used, and just about any kind of baking dish — round, square, oval, or rectangular.

For best results be sure the fruit is very close to fully ripe. Taste the sweetened fruit mixture before covering it with the biscuit dough. If the fruit is not quite ripe (or tart), you may need to sprinkle on a little more sugar. Some recipes call for removing the skins of the peaches by blanching them in boiling water for 1 minute, then peeling them off. However, we don't think it's necessary. And note that nectarine skins, which are thinner than peach skins, do not need to be removed.

Peach-Blueberry Cobbler

Tools: *Chef's knife, grater, large mixing bowl, 2-quart glass baking dish, fork, rolling pin, biscuit cutter or cookie cutter, medium mixing bowl, electric mixer*

Preparation time: *35 to 40 minutes*

Cooking time: *45 minutes*

Yield: *6 to 8 servings*

2 pounds firm, ripe nectarines or peaches (or a combination of both)

1 cup blueberries or blackberries, rinsed, picked over, and stemmed

⅓ cup (or according to taste and ripeness of fruit) plus 2 tablespoons granulated sugar

2 tablespoons light brown sugar, packed

1½ cups plus 2 tablespoons all-purpose flour

½ teaspoon cinnamon

Grated zest and juice of ½ lemon

7 tablespoons cold butter, cut into small pieces

2 teaspoons baking powder

½ teaspoon salt

1 teaspoon fresh lemon juice

8 to 10 tablespoons heavy cream or half-and-half, plus ¾ cup heavy cream, well chilled

Confectioners' sugar to taste

½ teaspoon vanilla extract

1 Preheat the oven to 375 degrees.

2 To make the fruit filling, cut the peaches or nectarines in half and remove the pits. Cut each half into 4 to 5 wedges and place in a large mixing bowl. Add the blueberries, ⅓ cup granulated sugar, light brown sugar, 2 tablespoons flour, cinnamon, and grated zest and juice of half a lemon. Toss to mix well. Taste the fruit and see if it is sweet enough. If necessary, add more sugar. Turn the fruit mixture into a 2-quart, 2-inches-deep baking dish. Dot the top of the fruit with 1 tablespoon butter, and bake for 10 minutes.

3 As the fruit bakes, prepare the topping. In a medium mixing bowl, toss together 1½ cups flour, 2 tablespoons sugar, baking powder, and salt. Add 6 tablespoons butter and, using a pastry blender, 2 knives, or your fingertips, cut the butter into the dry ingredients until the mixture resembles coarse bread crumbs. Sprinkle the mixture with the 1 teaspoon lemon juice.

4 Using a fork, wooden spoon, or rubber spatula, gradually stir in just enough of the 8 to 10 tablespoons of heavy cream or half-and-half to moisten the dough so that it holds together and can be rolled or patted. Gather the dough into a ball and place it on a lightly floured work surface. Roll out or pat the dough with your hands so it is about ½ inch thick and roughly matches the shape of the top of the baking dish.

5 Using either a biscuit cutter, a round cookie cutter, or a knife, cut the dough into 2½-inch circles. (You should have 9 to 10 circles.) Alternatively, you can gently roll small pieces of the dough into balls and flatten each into ½-inch-thick rounds.

6 After 10 minutes, remove the fruit from the oven. Place the dough on top of the fruit.

7 Return the cobbler to the oven and bake 30 to 35 minutes more, or until the topping is golden brown and the fruit is bubbling around the edges.

8 As the cobbler bakes, make the sweetened whipped cream. Pour ¾ cup heavy cream into a medium mixing bowl. Using an electric mixer, beat the cream just until it starts to thicken. Add the confectioners' sugar, to taste, and the vanilla, and continue beating until soft peaks form. Refrigerate until ready to use.

9 To serve, spoon the warm cobbler into shallow bowls. Spoon some of the cream over each serving; drizzle some of the fruit juices over the cobbler and serve.

Substitute other summer fruits for the peaches and blueberries, such as plums, raspberries, apricots, or blackberries. Add other spices like allspice, ginger, or nutmeg, or sprinkle fruit with a fruit liqueur. Substitute vanilla or lemon ice cream for the sweetened whipped cream.

When a recipe calls for fresh lemon juice, as this one does, never use the bottled reconstituted liquid kind; it tastes more like furniture polish than lemon juice.

Drop Cookies and Bar Cookies

In this section, don't confuse "drop" cookies with "dropped" cookies. Dropped cookies are what the dog scarfs up off the floor. Drop cookies are made from cookie dough that is literally dropped onto a baking sheet. In these recipes, we stress the importance of timing, because every oven is different. Always check the cookies a few minutes before they are supposed to be done.

The same rule about timing applies to brownies, which should be moist in the center. The most unusual recipe here is for a lemon bar. Imagine super-thick lemon pie that is attacked with a chef's knife and chopped into small pieces. That's a lemon bar. Trust us — it's great!

A chocolate chip cookie manufacturer once told us that the secret to his famous cookie dough was a little bit of grated lemon peel. It makes sense. Lemon zest, loaded with rich, lemony oil and without a trace of sourness, is frequently used by bakers to heighten the flavors of cookies and other sweet desserts. In this next recipe, the grated lemon zest punches up the flavor of the chocolate chips, and a little heavy cream in the dough gives the cookie a pleasant, melt-in-your-mouth softness. These cookies freeze very well in covered, plastic containers; they also keep for a week at room temperature in an airtight tin.

For a more traditional-tasting chocolate chip cookie without a hint of lemon flavor, omit the grated lemon peel.

Old-Fashioned Chocolate Chip Cookies

Tools: *Medium mixing bowl, electric mixer, grater, chef's knife, wooden spoon or rubber spatula, metal spatula, baking sheet (preferably nonstick)*

Preparation time: *About 20 minutes*

Cooking time: *8 to 10 minutes*

Yield: *About 36 cookies*

1 cup plus 2 tablespoons all-purpose flour

½ teaspoon baking powder

½ teaspoon grated lemon zest

¼ teaspoon salt

½ cup (1 stick) butter, softened

⅓ cup plus 2 tablespoons light brown sugar, packed

⅓ cup plus 2 tablespoons granulated sugar

1 egg

2 tablespoons heavy cream or half-and-half

½ teaspoon vanilla extract

1 cup (6-ounce package) semisweet chocolate chips

⅓ cup coarsely chopped walnuts or pecans (optional)

1 Preheat the oven to 375 degrees.

2 In a medium mixing bowl, stir together the flour, baking powder, lemon zest, and salt.

3 Using an electric mixer at medium speed, cream the butter with the brown and white sugars, about 3 minutes. ("Creaming" means making a soft paste out of butter so it absorbs flavors better.) Beat in the egg, heavy cream, and vanilla until well blended. (Turn off the mixer and scrape the sides of the bowl when necessary.)

4 Using a wooden spoon or a rubber spatula, stir the flour mixture into the butter mixture until well blended. Stir in the chocolate chips and nuts.

5 Drop heaping teaspoons of the batter onto a greased baking sheet (nonstick is best), about 1 to 2 inches apart. Bake one sheet at a time, until the cookies are lightly golden on the top with slightly browned edges, about 8 to 10 minutes. Rotate the sheet 180 degrees halfway through baking to ensure even browning. Remove the baking sheet to a wire rack and let the cookies cool for about 2 minutes, or until slightly firm. Using a metal spatula, carefully remove the cookies from the baking sheet and slide them onto a wire rack to cool completely.

You don't need to re-grease baking sheets after you've removed one batch of baked cookies, especially if you use a nonstick sheet.

Many cooks, even good ones, would not consider making brownies from scratch, because so many great commercial mixes are available. But we believe that homemade is almost always better than the mix. So, we give you this classic brownie recipe that's easy, rich, moist, and better (we guarantee it!) than any boxed mix you can buy. Plus, they freeze well, so you can bake them ahead of time and save them for an upcoming event.

Divine Brownies

Tools: *Chef's knife, 9-x-13-inch baking pan, saucepan, large mixing bowl, wooden spoon or rubber spatula*

Preparation time: *25 minutes*

Cooking time: *About 30 minutes*

Yield: *24 brownies*

1 cup (2 sticks) butter

1 ounce (1 square) unsweetened chocolate, coarsely chopped

2 cups sugar

¾ cup unsweetened cocoa powder

4 eggs

2 teaspoons vanilla extract

1⅓ cups flour

½ cup chopped walnuts or pecans (optional)

(continued)

1 Preheat the oven to 375 degrees. Grease and flour a 9-x-13-inch baking pan.

2 In a small, heavy saucepan, over very low heat, melt the butter and unsweetened chocolate, stirring occasionally until the mixture is smooth. Set the mixture aside to cool slightly.

3 In a large mixing bowl, combine the sugar and the cocoa powder; add the melted chocolate-butter mixture and stir well to combine. Add the eggs, one at a time, stirring with a wooden spoon or rubber spatula, only until well blended. Stir in the vanilla. Add the flour, in three batches, stirring after each addition, just until the ingredients are blended. If desired, stir in the walnuts. Do not overmix.

4 Scrape the batter into the prepared pan, spreading it evenly and to the edges. Bake in the top half of the preheated oven for 20 to 25 minutes until the center is firm to the touch when lightly pressed. Remove the pan to a rack and let stand until completely cool before cutting into squares.

This lemon bar recipe is a Sunkist Growers classic that we've altered just a bit by decreasing the sugar and adding flaked coconut. The results are perfectly chewy bars with intense lemon flavor.

Lemon Bars

Tools: *Chef's knife, citrus juicer, 13-x-9-inch nonstick baking pan, medium mixing bowl, large mixing bowl, whisk or electric mixer, wooden spoon*

Preparation time: *15 minutes*

Cooking time: *About 35 minutes*

Yield: *24 bars*

½ cup butter, softened

6 tablespoons plus 1½ cups sugar

Grated zest of 1 lemon

1½ cups plus 3 tablespoons all-purpose flour

4 eggs

¼ teaspoon baking powder

¾ cup sweetened flaked coconut

6 tablespoons freshly squeezed lemon juice (about 2 lemons)

1 teaspoon vanilla extract

1 Preheat the oven to 350 degrees.

2 Line a 13-x-9-inch baking (nonstick is best) pan with aluminum foil so the ends extend over the two 9-inch sides of the pan. Butter the foil lining the pan. Set the pan aside. (Lining the pan with foil allows you to lift the baked dessert easily from the pan before cutting into squares. See Figure 13-1 for an illustration.)

3 To make the crust, in a medium mixing bowl cream together the butter, 6 tablespoons of the sugar, and half of the lemon zest, using an electric mixer. Gradually stir in 1½ cups of the flour to form a soft, crumbly dough. (If necessary, use your fingers or a pastry blender to work the butter into the flour mixture.) Turn the dough into the foil-lined pan and press it evenly into the bottom. Bake for 12 to 15 minutes or until the crust is firm and lightly browned.

4 Prepare the filling as the crust bakes. In a large mixing bowl, use an electric mixer or a wire whisk to beat the eggs well. Add 1½ cups of the sugar, 3 tablespoons of the flour, and the baking powder, and beat well to combine. Stir or whisk in the coconut, the lemon juice, the remaining half of the lemon zest, and the vanilla, just until blended.

5 Using a rubber spatula, spread the filling over the hot, baked crust, being sure to evenly distribute the coconut throughout the filling. Return the pan to the oven and bake for about 20 minutes, or until the top is lightly golden and the filling is set. Set the pan on a wire rack to cool completely. Lift the foil by the ends to lift out the bar cookie; then set it on a cutting board. It will come out easily in one piece. Gently loosen the foil along all the sides. With a long, sharp, wet knife, cut into squares. Refrigerate squares until ready to serve.

Use nonstick baking equipment, which makes removing things like cookies, breads, cakes, and other baked desserts much easier

Line Your Pan with Foil!

Figure 13-1:
Lining a baking pan with aluminum foil.

Line a 13×9 inch baking pan with foil so the ends extend over the two 9 inch sides of the pan.

Butter the foil lining pan. Set the pan aside. (Lining the pan with foil allows you to lift the baked dessert easily from the pan before cutting squares.)

The foil should cover all 4 sides of the pan, but hang longer over the 9 inch sides.

ready to cut! easy!

Cakes, Tarts, and Tiramisù

In this section, we introduce you to several kinds of cakes: pudding cake, shortcake, chocolate cake, and that oh-so-trendy tiramisù. Each is quite different, but they all include valuable cooking techniques. Probably the most American of the lot is strawberry shortcake, which dates back to the 1700s. The base is a biscuit pastry, which eighteenth-century cooks called "shortcake." It is a lovely, seasonal dessert that is easy to make.

The fruit tart recipe is really a template for any kind of dessert tart you desire. After you master making the pastry, you're ready to try it with any kind of fruit filling. The same can be said of the recipe for chocolate cake. We experimented with many versions of chocolate cake and found this one to be the hands-down best. Tiramisù, which was originally a simple Italian dessert of lady fingers or biscuits soaked in coffee and topped with sweetened mascarpone cheese, has metamorphosized, at least in the United States, into a bloated, cloying, chocolate cream cake. Here we give you the authentic, Italian recipe.

The following recipe is a two-layered dessert, with a firm, cake-like top and a soft, custardy bottom. Lots of fresh lemon flavor and the dual textures make this quite a delightful surprise. Serve it warm or cold, topped with fresh, sliced, slightly sweetened strawberries.

Lemon Pudding Cake with Fresh Berries

Tools: 2-quart, 11-x-7-inch ceramic or glass baking dish, medium and large mixing bowls, electric mixer, rubber spatula, grater, large baking pan

Preparation time: 20 to 25 minutes

Cooking time: About 50 minutes

Yield: 6 servings

Butter for greasing the baking dish	¼ teaspoon salt
3 tablespoons butter, softened to room temperature	1 cup milk
	Grated zest of 1 lemon
4 eggs, separated	1 pint strawberries, rinsed, hulled, and sliced
¾ cup sugar	
¼ cup freshly squeezed lemon juice	2 tablespoons confectioners' sugar, or to taste
3 tablespoons all-purpose flour	

1 Preheat the oven to 325 degrees. Heat a tea kettle of water to boiling to help with Step 6 of this recipe.

2 Lightly butter a shallow, 2-quart, 11-x-7-inch ceramic or glass baking dish. Set aside.

3 In a large bowl with an electric mixer, beat the 3 tablespoons of butter and egg yolks until well combined. Gradually add ½ cup of the sugar, beating until well blended, about 3 to 4 minutes. Stop the mixer and scrape down the sides of the bowl. Add the lemon juice, flour, and salt; using a wooden spoon or rubber spatula, stir to combine. Gradually blend in the milk and lemon zest. Set aside.

4 In a clean, medium-sized, glass or metal mixing bowl, beat the egg whites until foamy. Gradually add the remaining ¼ cup granulated sugar, and continue beating until soft peaks form.

5 Gently fold the beaten egg whites into the lemon mixture (see Chapter 8 for illustrated instructions for folding egg whites into a batter).

6 Pour the batter into the buttered baking dish. Set the dish in a shallow baking pan filled with ½ inch of hot water. (See instructions for making a bain marie, or water bath, earlier in this chapter.) Bake, uncovered, for 45 to 55 minutes, or until the top is lightly browned and firm to the touch.

7 As the pudding-cake bakes, toss the sliced strawberries with the confectioners' sugar. Set aside.

8 Spoon the pudding cake, warm or cooled, onto individual serving plates; top each serving with a heaping spoonful of the sweetened strawberries.

Did you forget to bring the butter to room temperature? Just grate it on the largest holes of a box grater. It will soften quickly.

Instead of strawberries, substitute 2 to 2½ cups of other soft fruits, like blackberries, sliced kiwi, mango, papaya, or blueberries. Or sprinkle one or two tablespoons of a sweet fruit liqueur, such as Cointreau over the fruit. For a more elegant presentation, spoon the pudding cake into tall wine glasses, then top with the fruit.

Rolling out and fitting pie pastry into a pie plate can be a tricky task for the novice cook (see illustrated instructions in Chapter 16). This next recipe avoids that step; you simply place the pastry on a large baking sheet. Sliced nectarines and peaches, or a combination of both, are then arranged on the dough and coated with a fruit jam. The open-faced tart is baked until the fruit is tender and the pastry is crisp. We call for less sugar than traditionally used to bake a pie in order to allow the flavors of the fruit to shine through. But if you prefer something sweeter, simply increase the sugar until the fruit slices taste just right to you.

This sweet French pastry combines the richness of an egg yolk with the sweet-ness of a little sugar to make a rich cookie-like dough that's easy to roll out.

Free-Form Fresh Fruit Tart

Tools: *Grater, medium mixing bowl, pastry blender, nonstick baking sheet, rolling pin, knife, small saucepan, 2 mixing bowls, metal spatula, pastry brush*

Preparation time: *About 30 minutes*

Cooking time: *10 to 15 minutes (plus 30 minutes refrigeration for the pastry)*

Yield: *6 servings*

7 tablespoons butter, softened

¼ cup plus 1½ tablespoons (or more to taste) sugar

1 egg yolk

Grated zest of ½ lemon

¼ teaspoon vanilla extract

1 cup all-purpose flour

Pinch salt

4 to 6 ripe, medium peaches or nectarines, or a combination of both

3 tablespoons apricot or peach jam

1 tablespoon Cointreau, or other fruit liqueur (optional)

2 tablespoons finely chopped almonds

¼ cup blueberries or raspberries, rinsed, drained, and stemmed

Vanilla ice cream or whipped cream (see instructions for making whipped cream in Chapter 7), optional

1 To make the pastry, in a medium mixing bowl, use a wooden spoon to blend 6 table-spoons of the butter, ¼ cup of the sugar, egg yolk, lemon zest, and vanilla extract. Add the flour and salt. Use your fingers or a pastry blender to lightly work the butter-egg mixture into the dry ingredients until they form a smooth dough. Press the dough into a ball; enclose in plastic wrap and chill for about 30 minutes.

2 Preheat the oven to 425 degrees. Butter a large, flat baking sheet, preferably nonstick.

3 On a lightly floured counter, use a floured rolling pin to roll out the dough into a free-form rectangle, about 9 inches by 12 inches. Carefully drape the dough over the rolling pin and transfer it to the buttered baking sheet. Fold up and lightly crimp the edges of the dough all around to form a neat rim. Set aside.

4 Halve and pit the fruit; slice each half into 4 to 5 thin wedges. Starting at one corner, arrange the fruit slices side by side on the dough, overlapping and fitting them snuggly, until the surface of the pastry is completely covered (see Figure 13-2 for an illustration of this technique).

5 In a small saucepan over low heat, combine the jam and 1 tablespoon of the butter, stirring. Cook a few minutes, stirring constantly, until the butter is melted and the jam is runny. Remove the saucepan from the heat and, if desired, stir in the Cointreau. Using a pastry brush, coat the fruit slices with the jam-butter mixture.

6 In another small mixing bowl, combine 1½ tablespoons of the sugar and almonds. Sprinkle the blueberries or raspberries randomly over the top of the fruit slices and then sprinkle the sugar-almond mixture evenly over the fruit. (Sprinkle with a little more sugar to taste, if desired.)

7 Bake the tart for about 25 to 30 minutes or until the dough is crisp and golden and the fruit is tender.

8 Cut the tart into six pieces. Using a metal spatula, transfer each piece to an individual serving plate. Serve warm or cold, with a little whipped cream or vanilla ice cream if desired. If baked ahead, the tart can be reheated in a 375-degree oven for about 10 to 15 minutes.

 If desired, substitute ripe plum slices for some of the peaches and/or nectarines.

Figure 13-2:
Arrange fruit in an attractive manner over the bottom of the pan, slightly overlapping the fruit slices.

Free-Form Fresh Fruit Tart

On a lightly floured counter, use a floured rolling pin to roll out the dough into a free-form rectangle (about 9×12 inches).

Carefully drape dough over the rolling pin and transfer to a buttered baking sheet. Fold up and crimp edges of dough all around to form a neat rim.

Halve and pit the fruit. Slice each half into 4 or 5 thin wedges. Start at one corner, arrange slices side by side on dough, overlapping + fitting them snugly, until the surface is completely covered.

cozy...

 Most kinds of nuts quickly go stale or rancid if left exposed to air at room temperature. To prevent this, wrap them well in foil or plastic wrap (or place in a tightly sealed container or a resealable plastic bag) and store them in the freezer. (You do not need to defrost them before using.)

The following recipe for classic American chocolate cake comes from our buddy Bill Yosses, the pastry chef of Bouley Bakery in New York City (and the coauthor, with Bryan Miller, of *Desserts For Dummies,* published by IDG Books Worldwide, Inc.). The cake is enhanced with walnuts (for added texture) and a little cinnamon. You can leave out both, if you wish.

The recipe also calls for you to use parchment paper, which is a thick, durable paper that is heat-proof. It is used to line cake pans and the like. Parchment paper also prevents cakes and cookies from sticking to metal pans. (You can even use it to make cool Halloween masks.)

Chocolate Cake with Walnuts and Cinnamon

Tools: *Mixing bowls, rubber spatula, electric mixer, double boiler or two pots to simulate double boiler, whisk, 9-inch cake pan, parchment paper, sieve*

Preparation time: *About 15 minutes*

Cooking time: *About 30 minutes*

Yield: *8 to 10 servings*

6 ounces bittersweet chocolate (Lindt, Valrhona, and Callebaut are the best brands)

½ cup butter (1 stick)

5 eggs, separated

½ cup sugar

½ teaspoon cream of tartar

½ cup chopped walnuts

¼ cup flour, sifted

1 teaspoon ground cinnamon

2 tablespoons unsweetened cocoa powder or confectioners' sugar, optional

1 Preheat the oven to 350 degrees. Line the bottom of a 9-inch cake pan with a circular piece of greased parchment paper. Then grease the sides of the pan.

2 To make a double-boiler, fill one pot halfway with water and bring to a boil. Place a second pot on top of the first (they should fit snugly). Place the chocolate and the butter in the top pot and turn off the heat, leaving the pots on the stove. Stir to blend the chocolate and butter together.

3 Meanwhile, using an electric mixer, beat the egg whites, 1 teaspoon of the sugar, and the cream of tartar until nearly stiff. Slowly add the remaining sugar while mixing. Set aside.

4 Beat the egg yolks in a medium bowl. Remove the chocolate mixture from the stove, then whisk the egg yolks into the chocolate. Add the walnuts, sifted flour, and cinnamon and blend well.

5 Fold the egg white mixture into the chocolate. Pour the mixture into the cake pan. Smooth the top with a spatula.

6 Bake for 25 minutes, or until a knife or toothpick inserted into the middle comes out clean. Let the cake cool in its pan.

7 When the cake is cool enough to handle, place a serving plate over the cake pan and then invert them both so the plate is on the bottom. Tap gently to unmold the cake. Using a wide spatula and your hand, reverse the cake again so the top side is up.

8 If desired, decorate the cake with the cocoa powder or confectioners' sugar. Shake either topping through a sieve, dusting the surface of the cake evenly.

 Sometimes cakes develop a bulge on the top from uneven cooking. To prevent this bulge, use "cake strips," which are essentially strips of aluminum-coated cloth that you wet and place around the outside of the cake pan (they come with pins to secure them in place). You can also use strips of old denim to accomplish the same thing. The wet strips slow the heat transfer around the perimeter, thus preventing the bulging.

 Baking is the most precise and scientific part of cooking. Doughs must have the right proportion of liquids to solids to perform correctly when baked; and cakes must have the right flour-liquid-sugar-leavening ratio. Always measure dry and wet ingredients precisely. Level off the tops of dry measuring cups with the flat edge of a knife. Also do this when using measuring spoons to measure dry ingredients like baking powder, flour, or baking soda. Check out Chapter 2 to read more about the differences between dry and liquid measuring cups.

 A fuss-free way to decorate a layer cake without using frosting is to sprinkle it with a layer of confectioners' sugar. Place the sugar in a fine mesh sieve, hold it over the top of the cake and tap the strainer lightly with your hand, distributing the sugar evenly over the cake. You can also place a decorative (self-made or store-bought) stencil on the cake, perhaps one with a heart or flower pattern. Sprinkle the sugar over the stencil, then remove it to reveal the design. Powdered semisweet cocoa also works nicely.

 Always check the temperature of your oven when baking. If a cake looks soupy when the timer has gone off, your oven may not be not working correctly. Buy an oven thermometer (the mercury type is best) to determine if it's accurate; if it is not, adjust the temperature dial as necessary each time you bake. Or better, call your range serviceperson and have it fixed.

This coffee-flavored confection is arguably one of the top three desserts in American restaurants. Over the years what originally was a simple little treat has been altered, so that the one often served in the United States is a bloated, over-sweetened, and creamy chocolate cake. Tiramisù comes from Italy where, as the story goes, older ladies used to play cards in the afternoon, and, after their card games were finished, they made a sweet treat called tiramisù, which means "pick me up." They would take out some biscuits or cookies and drench them with espresso, then slather some mascarpone cheese on top. And tiramisù was born.

Our recipe, which comes from our friend Bill Yosses, the wizard pastry chef at four-star Bouley Bakery in New York City, calls for a combination of sweetened whipped cream, sour cream, and mascarpone cheese (if you can't find mascarpone use whipped cream and sour cream). The hallmark of a good tiramisù is a strong coffee flavor. You don't need to make espresso; instant coffee does the trick just fine.

Tiramisù

Tools: *Metal spatula, fine sieve, rubber spatula, whisk or electric mixer, wooden spoon, 10-inch circular plate or 9-x-9-inch serving dish, 2 mixing bowls*

Preparation time: *About 20 minutes (plus 2 hours refrigeration)*

Cooking time: None

Yield: *About 8 servings*

3 heaping tablespoons instant coffee	*¼ cup confectioners' sugar*
3 tablespoons granulated sugar	*2 teaspoons vanilla extract*
1 cup water	*⅓ cup mascarpone cheese*
2 6-ounce packages of ladyfingers	*2 heaping tablespoons sour cream*
1 pint heavy cream, well chilled	*1 tablespoon unsweetened cocoa powder*

1 In a small bowl combine the instant coffee and granulated sugar. Bring the water to a boil and pour it over the coffee mixture, stirring. Set aside and let cool to room temperature.

2 Place about half of the ladyfingers on the bottom of a 9- or 10-inch square or round serving dish.

3 Using a tablespoon, drizzle half of the coffee mixture evenly over the ladyfingers in the serving dish. Set aside.

4 In a bowl, combine the cream, confectioners' sugar, and vanilla. With a whisk or an electric mixer, whip the mixture until it forms soft peaks. Refrigerate for at least 1 hour.

5 In another bowl, combine the mascarpone and sour cream. Using a wooden spoon, stir the mixture until smooth.

6 Fold half of the whipped cream mixture into the cheese and cream mixture until well blended. Then fold in the rest, being sure not to overmix.

7 Using a metal spatula or spoon, spread half of the mixture over the ladyfingers, and place another layer of ladyfingers, curved side down, over it. Drizzle these ladyfingers with the remaining coffee and cover them with the other half of the cream mixture. Using a sieve, sprinkle the cocoa powder evenly over the top. Refrigerate for 2 hours before cutting into pieces to serve.

Note: *The width and length of ladyfingers vary from brand to brand. Therefore, the number of cookies to complete a layer in a 9-x-9-inch pan will also vary. In general, 2 6-ounce packages will complete two layers.*

Part IV
Now You're Cooking! Real Menus for Real Life

The 5th Wave   By Rich Tennant

"I'm trying to be more creative with herbs, so I sprinkled some pipe tobacco in the sauce for a smoky flavor."

In this part . . .

Contrary to what most cookbooks assume, cooking is not done in a vacuum — that is, you may have to contend with limited time, ringing phones, leaking washing machines, traumatized tots, and begging dogs.

We don't offer any help with the dogs or the washing machine, but we do address the critical element of time. Recipes in this part are designed for real-life situations: when you're trying to plan what to feed your family for the coming week or when you have guests coming in an hour and need to put together a meal, for example. We also offer some tips for becoming a savvy shopper so that you can make a good meal from what you have on hand — both quickly and inexpensively.

Chapter 14

The Bare Necessities: A Pantry List

*Y*ou could probably survive for quite some time on a diet of peanut butter, canned tuna, and saltines, but eventually you would get bored. This chapter helps to alleviate the boredom of stocking your pantry. Shopping thoughtfully not only cuts down on trips to the market, but it also saves you money — those 8 p.m. dashes to 7-Eleven for grated cheese add up quickly. And when you don't have time to make it to the market, what's for dinner often depends on the ingredients you have in the fridge and cupboard.

Following are a series of checklists of pantry basics. Foods such as milk, cheese, eggs, and bread are obvious items to keep stocked. Less common staples such as sun-dried tomatoes, fruit chutney, dry sherry, anchovies, and artichoke hearts are important, too, because they can instantly impart flavor and dress up everyday dishes like tossed salads, omelets, and pasta.

Dry Goods

You will probably consume these foods at least once a week, so buy them in bulk to save on packaging costs:

- ✔ **Assorted coffees:** You can freeze ground or whole beans for long storage.

- ✔ **Cold and hot cereals:** Always tightly reseal cereal boxes after opening to keep them fresh.

- ✔ **Assorted breads and English muffins:** All breads can be frozen. Yeast breads freeze well for 6 to 8 months. Quick breads (baked with baking powder or soda) freeze without losing flavor for 2 to 4 months.

- ✔ **Dry beans and grains:** See Chapter 15 for more information about the various types.

- ✔ **Herbal and regular teas:** Store in a sealed canister in a cool, dry place.

- ✔ **Macaroni and other pasta:** See Chapter 11 for a complete pasta chart.

- ✔ **White and brown rice, wild rice, and Arborio (an Italian rice used for making risotto):** See Chapter 3 for more information about the various types of rice.

Dry Herbs, Spices, and Seasonings

Herbs and spices are essential flavoring ingredients. Herbs are produced from the leaves and stems of a variety of plants; spices can come from a plant's roots, seeds, bark, buds, or berries. See Chapter 5 for a complete herb and spice chart. Here are the herbs, spices, and seasonings you should stock regularly:

- ✔ **Dry herbs:** Basil, bay leaves, dill, marjoram, oregano, rosemary, sage, tarragon, thyme, and parsley

- ✔ **Salt and pepper:** Table salt, black peppercorns, whole or ground white pepper, and red pepper flakes

- ✔ **Spices:** Allspice, chili powder, cinnamon, whole and ground cloves, ground cumin, curry powder, ginger, dry mustard, nutmeg, and paprika

Purchase dried herbs and spices in small quantities. After a year or so of storage, their potency diminishes drastically. Keep all dried herbs and spices tightly sealed and away from direct heat (don't store them near the stove) and sunlight.

To get the most flavor from dried herbs, crush them briefly between your fingers before adding them to a dish. Whole spices, such as peppercorns and nutmeg, have much more aroma and flavor than those sold pre-ground, so try grinding or grating them yourself as needed.

Bottled and Canned Goods

Obvious items include canned tuna, jellies and jams, peanut butter, and assorted canned soups. Always stock the following essentials:

- ✔ **Assorted oils and vinegars:** See Chapter 10 for a complete list.

- ✔ **Tomato paste:** Buy it in cans or the more convenient tube (which you can store in the refrigerator after opening). For flavoring stews and sauces.

- ✔ **Wines:** A dry white and a dry red wine, for adding to sauces, stews, and long-simmering casseroles and soups. Dry sherry, port, and Madeira are nice to have, too.

Following are other items that can help make your cooking more inspired:

- ✔ **Anchovies:** For salad dressings and simple sauces, anchovies can lend subtle depth of flavor. They also enhance store-bought Boboli and pizza. (See Chapter 16 for more information about anchovies.)

- ✔ **Artichoke hearts marinated in olive oil:** Great tossed into green salads, marinated vegetable salads, and even cooked pasta.

- ✔ **Beans:** Kidney, garbanzo, and baked beans for soups, salads, and quick side dishes. Refried beans for tacos, burritos, nachos, omelet fillings, and side dishes come in handy, too.

- ✔ **Canned clams and clam juice:** For quick pasta sauce or as a substitute for homemade fish stock.

- ✔ **Canned stock:** For when you run out of your homemade stock. Purchase beef and chicken (or vegetable for vegetarians), preferably salt-free.

- ✔ **Capers (pickled flower buds of the caper bush):** For making quick, tangy sauces for meats and poultry.

- ✔ **Cranberry sauce:** Serve with grilled meats and poultry or use as a basting sauce.

- ✔ **Hoisin sauce:** A favorite of Chinese cuisine that is made from soybeans, garlic, chile peppers, and spices. Terrific in marinades and with spareribs, roast duck, or poultry.

- ✔ **Olives:** Green, black, and stuffed for appetizers and slicing into salads and pasta dishes. (See the Mediterranean Pasta recipe, later in this chapter.)

- ✔ **Roasted peppers:** For adding to marinated vegetables, tossed green salads, and creamy dips.

- ✔ **Tomatoes:** Italian plum tomatoes and crushed tomatoes for making pasta sauces when fresh tomatoes are pale and tasteless.

Condiments

Having quality condiments and sauces — mustards, chutneys, salsas, hot sauces, barbecue sauce, and more — is always wise. Make sure to stock the following:

- **Dijon-style mustard:** Good for adding to salad dressings, dips, and sauces and for garnishing hot or cold meats and sandwiches. To produce a flavored mustard, add herbs or spices, citrus juice or zest, or a little honey to the Dijon base.

- **Ketchup:** For hamburgers and as an ingredient in fish and barbecue sauces and baked beans.

- **Mayonnaise:** Because you can't always make your own. (You can find a recipe in Chapter 7.)

These items are handy to keep on hand, too.

- **A good bottle of mango or tomato chutney:** Chutney is a sweetened fruit condiment for broiled chicken, lamb, pork, or duck. Try using it as a basting sauce for roasting meats or poultry or for spreading on cold sandwiches of hard-cooked eggs, tuna, chicken, or turkey. Also good in yogurt-based dips and in omelet fillings.

- **Assorted relishes:** Relishes such as corn, tomato, cranberry, and onion are good for spreading on cold sandwiches and grilled and roasted meats.

- **Dill and sweet pickles:** For serving with sandwiches and also for chopping into potato, chicken, and egg salads. *Cornichons* are crisp, tiny pickles made from small gherkin cucumbers. Serve them with cheeses, roasted meats, and pâtés, or chop them into vinaigrettes or creamy dressings.

- **Horseradish:** For sandwiches, salad dressings, roast beef, ham sandwiches, raw oysters and clams, and certain cream and tomato-based sauces.

- **Pesto (jarred, or homemade and frozen):** For pasta, grilled meats, fish, poultry, or vegetables.

- **Salsa:** With grilled meats and fish, omelets and other egg dishes, salads, and traditional Mexican foods.

- **Soy sauce (dark and light, Chinese and Japanese):** For marinades, salad dressings, stir-fries, sushi, and sauces. Chinese soy sauce is stronger and saltier than the Japanese variety. Light soy sauces are for seasoning shrimp, fish, and vegetables, such as stir-fried snow peas or broccoli. Dark soy sauce, flavored with caramel, is delicious with broiled meats.

✔ **Sun-dried tomatoes in olive oil:** Enhance sauces (especially for pasta), tossed salads, and dressings.

✔ **Tabasco sauce:** For adding flavor and heat to savory dishes. Use in omelets, on steaks and French fries, and in marinades, soups, stews, and casseroles.

✔ **Worcestershire sauce:** For hamburgers, steak, marinades, sauces, baked clams, and Bloody Marys.

Condiments such as relishes, jellies, pickles, mayonnaise, mustard, and jars of salsa keep for months in the refrigerator after you open them. Steak sauce, peanut butter, oil, vinegar, honey, and syrup do not require refrigeration after you open them and can be stored on a shelf or in a cool cabinet for months, away from heat and sunlight. When in doubt, always follow the storage instructions on the product's label.

Baking Items

No one expects you to bake a cake when you get home from work at 7:30 p.m. But sometimes you need a quick dessert or sweet and have the zeal to do it yourself. Having the ingredients on hand makes it so much easier. Always keep these items in stock:

✔ **All-purpose flour (5-pound bag):** For dredging meats, fish, and poultry, and for pancakes, biscuits, and waffles, as well as baking. Store flour in a tightly covered canister, where it stays fresh for months.

✔ **Baking powder:** A leavening agent used in some cake, cookie, and quick bread recipes to lighten texture and increase volume. Check the sell-by date to ensure that the powder is fresh before buying. (Baking powder loses its effectiveness sitting on the shelf.) Buy a small container and keep it tightly sealed. To test whether powder is still potent, mix 1 teaspoon baking powder with ⅓ cup warm water. The solution fizzes if the powder is good.

✔ **Baking soda:** Used as a leavening agent in baked goods and batters that contain an acidic ingredient such as molasses, vinegar, or buttermilk. Also good for putting out grease fires and flare-ups in the oven or on the grill. Keep an open box in the refrigerator to absorb odors. (Change the box every 6 months, or it may become one of the foul odors.)

✔ **Granulated sugar (5-pound bag):** An all-purpose sweetener. Store in a canister with a tight-fitting lid.

Having the following items increases your range of possibilities:

- ✔ **Chocolate:** Unsweetened and bittersweet squares, semisweet chips, and cocoa powder for chocolate sauces, chocolate chip cookies, and hot chocolate. (Recipes for chocolate sauces are in Chapter 7.)

  When the temperature climbs above 78 degrees, chocolate begins to melt, causing the cocoa butter to separate and rise to the surface. If the cocoa butter separates, the chocolate produces a whitish exterior called *bloom*. Though it looks a little chalky, bloomed chocolate is perfectly safe to eat. To prevent bloom on chocolate, store it in a cool, dry place (not the refrigerator), tightly wrapped.

- ✔ **Confectioners' sugar (l-pound box):** For sprinkling over baked goods and cookies or for quick frostings.

- ✔ **Cornmeal:** Yellow or white for corn muffins and quick bread toppings for stews and baked casseroles. Keep in a canister or tightly sealed bag.

- ✔ **Cream of tartar:** For stabilizing egg whites.

- ✔ **Dark and light brown sugars:** For baking and making barbecue sauces and glazes for ham and pork. Dark brown is more intense in flavor than light. To keep brown sugar soft after you open it, store the whole box in a tightly sealed plastic bag. If it hardens, place half an apple in the bag for several hours or overnight and then remove the apple. This little trick softens the brown sugar.

- ✔ **Gelatin:** Unflavored and powdered for molded salads and cold dessert mousses.

- ✔ **Honey:** For sweet glazes, dressings, and syrups. To thin crystallized honey, set the bottle in a pan of hot tap water.

- ✔ **Muffin mixes in assorted flavors:** For when you don't have time to make them from scratch.

- ✔ **Vanilla and almond extract:** For flavoring whipped cream, desserts, and baked goods. (Other handy extracts include orange, lemon, and hazelnut.) Don't buy imitation vanilla extract. It's a poor substitute for the real thing.

- ✔ **Vanilla bean:** For dessert sauces and vanilla sugar. (See the Vanilla Sauce recipe in Chapter 7.) To store, wrap tightly in plastic wrap, place in an airtight container, and refrigerate. It will keep for about 6 months.

Refrigerated and Frozen Staples

Following are a few essential items to stock in the refrigerator or freezer:

- **Eggs:** Never be without them for omelets, breakfast foods, and quick dinners. (See Chapter 8 for handy egg recipes and other egg tips.) Store in the shipping carton to keep them from picking up odors and flavors from other refrigerated foods. Raw eggs keep in the refrigerator for at least 4 weeks beyond their pack date.

- **Milk:** We make our recipes with whole milk, which has about 3.5 percent butterfat. If you prefer, use 1 percent or 2 percent low-fat milk or skim (nonfat) milk, with the understanding that the recipe may not have as creamy a consistency. Whole milk keeps for about a week after the store expiration date. Skim milk has a shorter shelf life. Some markets sell sterilized milk in vacuum packages that last for months unrefrigerated. After you break the seal, however, vacuum-packed milk is just like any other milk and must be refrigerated.

- **Pastas:** Stock various stuffed pastas like ravioli in the freezer for quick dinners. You can wrap fresh pasta in freezer bags and store it for 6 to 8 months. Do not defrost before cooking. Simply drop frozen pasta into boiling water and cook until al dente.

- **Sweet (unsalted) butter:** Use sweet butter in all recipes so that you can control the amount of salt. Butter has a refrigerator shelf life of about 2 to 3 weeks and can be frozen for 8 to 12 months.

These items are nice to have, too:

- **Bagels and other specialty breads:** For breakfasts and sandwiches. All bread products can be frozen in freezer bags. Thaw on the counter, in the microwave, or in the oven at 300 degrees.

- **Cottage cheese, ricotta, and cream cheese:** For adding to dressings and dips, snacking, spreading on bagels or toast, and for cheesecakes. Store in the original, covered container or foil wrapping and consume within 1 to 2 weeks.

- **Hard and semi-hard cheeses:** Mozzarella, Parmesan, cheddar, and blue for salads, casseroles, omelets, white sauces, and sandwiches, to grate into pasta, and just to eat. (See the sidebar "Cheese: Milk gone to heaven" for more cheese choices.)

  Wrap all cheese in foil or plastic wrap after opening. Trim off any mold that grows on the outside edges of hard cheeses. Depending on its variety, cheese keeps in the refrigerator for several weeks to months.

  Don't buy pre-grated Parmesan or Romano cheese. It quickly loses its potency and absorbs the odors of other refrigerated foods. Instead, keep a piece of cheese for grating in the fridge to use as needed.

- **Heavy cream, light cream, or half-and-half:** For making quick pan sauces for fish, poultry, and pasta. Use within a week of purchase or freeze for longer storage. Heavy cream (not half-and-half or light cream) is used for making whipped cream.

✔ **Ice cream or frozen yogurt:** Instant dessert; for eating guiltily in bed at midnight. After you open it, you should eat ice cream within 2 weeks. You can freeze unopened containers for up to 2 months.

✔ **Pie crusts:** Keep frozen shells in the freezer for up to 6 to 8 months to fill with fresh fruits and pudding fillings when you need a dessert in a hurry, or to make a quick quiche. (See Chapter 8 for a recipe for Classic Quiche Lorraine.)

✔ **Sour cream:** You can use standard (18 percent fat), low-fat, and nonfat interchangeably in recipes. As with all dairy products, buy the container with the latest store expiration date. Sour cream should keep for about 2 weeks.

✔ **Plain yogurt:** Good for quick dips and low-fat sauces, especially if mixed with dry mustard and various herbs. Also makes pancake batters lighter. Follow expiration date on package.

Cheese: Milk gone to heaven

Compared to most European countries, America is not a major cheese consumer. That is, cheese is not routinely part of a meal, either in addition to or in place of dessert. But if you get to know your cheeses, eating it can be a tantalizing change of pace, especially with wine.

Cheese is a perfect after-dinner course, especially if you don't have time to fuss with dessert. Serve it with fruit or with neutral crackers that don't interfere with the flavor. Let cheese reach room temperature before serving.

Trying to define which cheeses are best for dessert is sort of like saying which cars are best for driving to the supermarket — most of them can do the job; it's just that some do it with more style. Foremost, think of what is harmonious with the meal. For example, you don't want to serve a very potent blue cheese after a subtle dinner of grilled chicken breasts and summer vegetables.

Wine also is a consideration. For example, sharp cheddars and tart goat cheeses go best with assertive red wines (Bordeaux, California Cabernet Sauvignons, Zinfandels, ports, and even bitter beer). You want a wine that can stand up to the potent cheese. Light cheeses like Gouda, Havarti, Monterey Jack, and Muenster call for equally delicate wines so that you have a balanced taste: Beaujolais, lighter Côtes-du-Rhône, and Barbarescos. For more information about wines, see *Wine For Dummies*, 2nd Edition, by Ed McCarthy and Mary Ewing-Mulligan (IDG Books Worldwide, Inc.)

When buying cheese, remember that there's a big difference between aged cheese and old cheese. Old cheese looks fatigued, has discoloration, maybe a cracked rind, and signs of overdryness. Old cheese makes your car smell like a locker room. If cheddars look darker around the periphery than at the center, they probably are dried out. Inspect these cheeses extra carefully. Your best bet is to go to a store that sells a large volume of cheese because the inventory changes quickly and the selection is better and fresher.

✔ **Brie:** Almost a cliché because it was the first "gourmet" cheese for many American palates, spawning wine-and-cheese cocktail parties across the land. This soft, creamy cheese is generally mild tasting and goes well with most light red wines.

✔ **Camembert:** French, from Normandy. A creamy cheese not unlike Brie. When ripe, it oozes luxuriously.

✔ **Cheddar:** One of the world's most popular cheeses. Made all over the world, but originally from England, where much of the best cheddar comes from. The flavor of this semi-firm cheese ranges from rich and nutty to extremely sharp.

✔ **Fontina Val d'Aosta:** Italian cow's milk cheese, semi-firm, subtle, nutty, and rich.

✔ **Goat cheese (chèvres in France):** Goat cheese ranges from mild and tart when young to sharp and crumbly when aged.

✔ **Gorgonzola:** From the Lombardy region of Italy. This blue-veined cheese is extremely popular in the United States. Gorgonzola is rich and creamy yet pleasantly pungent. Creamier than Roquefort.

✔ **Gruyère:** Sort of a more gutsy version of Swiss cheese, from Switzerland. Faint nuttiness. The classic fondue cheese.

✔ **Mascarpone:** An Italian cow's milk cheese

that has the consistency of clotted cream. Often used in cooking but can be seasoned with fresh herbs and used as a delicious dip. The cheese used in authentic tiramisù.

✔ **Monterey Jack:** A California cow's milk cheese in the cheddar family that is semisoft, smooth, and very mild when young, and sharper when aged.

✔ **Mozzarella:** Familiar to all from pizza and lasagna fame. Mozzarella is often breaded and fried for an appetizer, called *Mozzarella in Carozza.* It is also great in salads or layered with sliced tomatoes and basil.

✔ **Pecorino Romano (or Romano):** A sheep's milk Italian cheese (all sheep's milk cheese in Italy is called pecorino). Pecorino Romano is soft and mild when young with a touch of tartness. Quite tart when older, mostly grated over pasta.

✔ **Roquefort:** Made from ewe's milk and aged in the famous caves of Roquefort, France. Roquefort is among the most intense of all blue-veined cheeses. Has a creamy texture at its best.

Kiwi Anyone? Storing Fruits and Vegetables

Have on hand potatoes, onions, garlic, carrots, salad greens, parsley, and a few other fresh herbs like basil and dill. You also may want to stock cucumbers, green onions, assorted citrus, mushrooms, red and green peppers, and celery for slicing and eating raw or for flavoring sauces, soups, salads, and stews. Keep an assortment of fresh fruits — apples, oranges, grapes, bananas, or whatever is in season — for snacking, slicing into cereals, or making quick dessert sauces.

It's best to keep unripe melons and tree fruits like pears, peaches, and nectarines at room temperature so that they can ripen and grow sweeter. Once fully ripe, they can be stored in the refrigerator for several more days. Fruits like cherries and berries are quite perishable and should always be refrigerated. For best flavor, consume them the same day you purchase them.

✔ Bananas can go in the refrigerator to slow down their ripening. Their peel continues to darken, but not their flesh.

✔ Tomatoes have more flavor at room temperature. Keep in a cool, dark place or in a paper bag to ripen fully. Refrigerate them after they ripen to keep them from spoiling. Then return to room temperature before eating. (See Chapter 11 for more information about tomatoes.)

✔ Citrus fruits, such as lemons, grapefruits, and oranges, do not ripen further after they are picked and are relatively long-storage fruits. They keep for up to 3 weeks or more if refrigerated.

✔ Avocados, papayas, kiwis, and mangoes should be kept at room temperature until fully ripened and then refrigerated to keep for several more days.

✔ Most vegetables are quite perishable and require refrigeration, with the exception of onions, potatoes, garlic, shallots, and hard-shelled winter squash, which keep at room temperature for several weeks to a month. Keep garlic and shallots in a small bowl within reach of your food preparation area. Store onions, potatoes, and winter squash in a cool, dry, dark drawer or bin.

Here are some storage tips for specific fresh fruits and vegetables:

✔ **Apples:** Refrigerate or store in a cool, dark place. Keep for several weeks.

✔ **Artichokes and asparagus:** Refrigerate and use within 2 to 3 days of purchase.

✔ **Bell peppers:** Store in the refrigerator for up to 2 weeks.

✔ **Broccoli and cauliflower:** Refrigerate and consume within a week.

✔ **Cabbage:** Keeps for 1 to 2 weeks in the refrigerator.

✔ **Carrots:** Keep in the refrigerator for several weeks.

✔ **Celery:** Keeps for 1 to 2 weeks in the refrigerator.

✔ **Corn:** Refrigerate and use the same day of purchase. After corn is picked, its sugar immediately begins converting to starch, diminishing its sweetness.

✔ **Cucumbers and eggplant:** Keep for 1 week in the cold crisper drawer of the refrigerator.

✔ **Grapes:** Keep in the refrigerator for up to a week.

✔ **Green beans:** Refrigerate and use within 3 to 4 days of purchase.

✔ **Leaf greens (beet tops, collards, kale, mustard greens, and so on):** Very perishable. Refrigerate and consume within 1 to 2 days.

- **Mushrooms:** Store in a paper bag in the refrigerator. Use within a week.

- **Pineapple:** Does not ripen after it's picked, and is best if eaten within a few days of purchase. Keep at room temperature, away from heat and sun, or refrigerate whole or cut up.

- **Salad greens:** Rinse thoroughly, trim, and dry completely before storing wrapped in paper towel or in plastic bags in the refrigerator crisper drawer. Keep for 3 to 4 days. (See Chapter 10 for more information.)

- **Spinach:** Trim, rinse, and dry thoroughly before storing in the refrigerator for 2 to 3 days.

- **Summer squash (zucchini and yellow squash):** Store in the refrigerator for up to a week.

Buying and Storing Meat, Poultry, and Fish

Meat, poultry, and fish are highly perishable foods that need to be stored in the coldest part of your refrigerator. Keep them tightly wrapped, preferably in their own drawer, to prevent their juices from dripping onto other foods.

Always check expiration dates (avoid items that are older than your car's last oil change). And never allow meat, poultry, or fish to thaw at room temperature, where bacteria can have a field day. Always thaw them in the refrigerator, which takes more time (and planning), but is by far the safest method.

Beef

Beef is rated according to the animal's age, the amount of fat, or *marbling*, in the cut (the more marbling, the more moist and tender), as well as its color and texture. *Prime* meat is the highest grade and the most expensive. In general, the most tender and flavorful meat falls under this category. But aging has a lot to do with it. Years ago, all beef aged "on the hoof," or the whole carcass, before it was shipped. Today, most meat is cut up and shipped in vacuum-sealed Cry-O-Vac containers. The aging takes place in the wrapping. Buy from butchers in your area who still age their own beef. You pay a little more, but it's worth the price. Aged meat is more tender and has more flavor.

Choice is the second tier of meat grading, leaner than prime. *Select* meats are best for stewing and braising.

The more tender cuts of meat include steaks such as porterhouse, sirloin, shell, New York strip, Delmonico, and filet mignon as well as roasts like rib, rib eye, and tenderloin. Tender meats are usually cooked by the dry heat methods of roasting, broiling, grilling, and sautéing. (See Chapter 6 for roasting, broiling, and grilling recipes and Chapter 4 for sautéing recipes.)

Less tender cuts that have more muscle tissue and less fat are usually cooked by braising and stewing. (See Chapter 5 for braising and stewing recipes.) Tougher cuts include brisket, chuck, shoulder, rump, and bottom round. Figure 14-1 illustrates where the various cuts come from.

Figure 14-1:
Various cuts
of meat
come from
different
parts of a
steer.

Look beyond ratings to judge meat. Meat should look bright red, never dull or gray. Excess juice in the package may indicate that the meat has been previously frozen and thawed — do not purchase it. Boneless, well-trimmed cuts are slightly more expensive per pound but have more edible meat than untrimmed cuts so, in the long run, can cost about the same.

Store meat in the meat compartment or the coldest part of the refrigerator. Keep raw meat away from ready-to-eat foods. To freeze, rewrap in aluminum foil, heavy-duty plastic wrap, or freezer bags, pressing out as much air as possible and dating all packages. Freeze ground meat for a maximum of 3 months; freeze other cuts for up to 6 months. Defrost in the refrigerator or microwave.

Chicken

The tenderness and flavor of fresh poultry vary somewhat from one commercial producer to the next, so you should buy and taste a few different brands to determine which you like. Grade A poultry is the most economical because it has the most meat in proportion to bone. Skin color is not an indication of quality or fat content. A chicken's skin ranges from white to deep yellow, depending on its diet.

Most supermarkets carry five kinds of chicken:

- **Broiler/fryer:** A 7- to 9-week-old bird weighing between 2 and 4 pounds. Flavorful meat that is best for broiling, frying, sautéing, or roasting. A whole broiler/fryer is always less expensive than a precut one.

- **Roaster or pullet:** From 3 to 7 months old and between 3 and 7 pounds. Very meaty, with high fat content under the skin, which makes for excellent roasting.

- **Capon:** A 6- to 9-pound castrated male chicken. Excellent as a roasting chicken because of its abundance of fat. Just to be sure, pour off or scoop out excess melted fat as the chicken roasts — especially if you do not have an exhaust fan — or your kitchen will resemble the *Towering Inferno*. Not widely available in supermarkets (it usually needs to be special-ordered).

- **Stewing chicken:** From 3 to 7 pounds and at least 1 year old. Needs slow, moist cooking to tenderize. Makes the best soups and stews.

- **Rock Cornish game hen:** A smaller breed of chicken weighing 1 to 2 pounds. Meaty, moist, and flavorful for roasting.

Remove the package of giblets (the neck, heart, gizzard, and liver) in the cavity of a whole bird and then rinse under running cold water before cooking it. Also trim away excess fat. After preparing poultry, wash your hands and work surfaces (counters and cutting boards) with soap and water to avoid bacteria.

You should consume whole or cut-up poultry within 1 to 2 days of purchase. A whole, raw chicken may be wrapped and frozen for up to 12 months; parts can be frozen for up to 9 months. Defrost in the refrigerator, never at room temperature. Be sure to place the thawing package in a pan or on a plate to catch any dripping juices. A 4-pound chicken takes 24 hours to thaw in the refrigerator; cut-up parts between 3 and 6 hours. If you use your microwave to defrost poultry, do so on a very low setting and be sure to cook the poultry immediately after thawing it.

How free is free range?

Compared to cooped-up, hormone-blasted, sunshine-deprived regular chickens, free-range chickens have a pretty cozy life. But *free range* is a bit of exaggeration in most cases. These privileged chickens do not pack lunches and take daily outings across the vast countryside, stopping for a couple of pecks in fields of clover on the way home. Most free-range chickens are enclosed in fenced areas with very limited room to maneuver. They do get some sunshine, at least, and a little exercise. And in most cases, they are chemical-free.

Fish

Fish falls into two broad categories: lean and oily. Lean fish include mild-tasting sole, flounder, snapper, cod, halibut, and haddock. Oily fish have more intense flavor and generally darker flesh and include bluefish, mackerel, salmon, swordfish, and tuna. In general, you should purchase fillets of oily fish with the skin intact. That way, the fish holds together better during cooking. You usually purchase lean fish skinless.

Here are some of the more reasonably priced types of fish that you can try in lieu of expensive gray sole, swordfish, and the like. Always ask your fish dealer what is most fresh that day.

- **Bluefish:** Rich flavor, especially when fresh and under 2 pounds. Bake or broil.
- **Catfish:** Dense, relatively mild fish. Usually cooked in a strong sauce or deep-fried.
- **Cod:** Mild-flavored, white, firm flesh. Can be broiled, baked, fried, or braised.
- **Haddock:** Meaty, white flesh, mild flavor. Good pan-fried or braised.
- **Porgy:** Firm, low-fat, white-fleshed fish with delicate flavor. Excellent grilled or broiled.
- **Whiting (Silver Hake):** Fine, semi-firm white flesh. Subtle and delicious when broiled or pan-fried.

Freshness is the most important factor in purchasing fish. Learn to recognize it. In a whole fish, the eyes should be bright and clear, not cloudy. The gills of fresh fish are deep red, not brownish. The skin should be clear and bright with no trace of slime. Fish get slimy if they are not properly iced.

TOQUE TIP

How do you tell whether the fish is fresh? "Put your nose close to the fish to find out," says Eric Ripert, executive chef of Le Bernardin in New York. "Fresh fish doesn't smell like fish. It might smell like the ocean, but it will never smell fishy."

If possible, have your fishmonger cut fresh fillets from whole fish while you wait. Purchase precut fillets only if they are displayed on a bed of ice, not sealed under plastic, which can trap bacteria and foul odors. Fillets should look moist and lay flat, with no curling at the edges. Fresh fish and seafood should be consumed as soon as possible and ideally on the day of purchase. Freshly caught and cleaned fish may be frozen for 2 to 3 months if wrapped well in 2 layers of freezer wrap. Never refreeze fish after thawing it.

Shellfish should be firmly closed and odorless when purchased. If clams or mussels do not close when tapped on the counter, toss them. Eat fresh clams, oysters, and mussels as soon as possible. Store for no more than 24 hours in the refrigerator in a plastic bag poked with small holes, allowing air to circulate. It's best to purchase shrimp in the shell. Eat shrimp the same day you purchase it. Most of all, never overcook shellfish because it gets rubbery.

Cooking in a Well-Stocked Kitchen

The payoff for keeping a well-stocked kitchen — with only enough perishables that you can eat in a week — is that you can whip up satisfying meals on short notice. Here are just a few dishes to get you started.

Onion Soup

Tools: *Chef's knife, heavy-bottomed large saucepan or pot, wooden spoon, grater*

Preparation time: *About 15 minutes*

Cooking time: *About 1 hour*

Yield: *4 servings*

3 tablespoons butter

3 medium onions, thinly sliced

2 tablespoons all-purpose flour

2 cups homemade or canned beef, chicken, or vegetable stock

2 cups water

Salt and black pepper to taste

4 slices French bread, toasted

½ cup grated Gruyère or Parmesan cheese

(continued)

1 Melt the butter in a heavy-bottomed saucepan or pot over medium heat. Add the onions and cook for about 5 minutes or until the onions wilt, stirring often. Reduce the heat to low and cook for about 20 to 25 minutes or until the onions are well-browned, stirring often.

2 Sprinkle the flour over the onions and cook for about 2 minutes, stirring constantly and scraping the bottom of the pan with a wooden spoon.

3 Gradually stir in the broth and water. Cover the pan and bring to a boil over high heat. Reduce the heat and simmer for 30 minutes, stirring occasionally. Season with salt and pepper.

4 Ladle the soup into a *tureen* (a large soup serving bowl) or 4 individual soup bowls. Float the toasted bread slices in the hot soup and sprinkle each bowl evenly with the cheese.

If you follow our pantry-stocking instructions, you can turn out the following two pasta recipes without leaving the house.

Mediterranean Spaghetti

Tools: *Chef's knife, large pot, large saucepan or sauté pan, colander*

Preparation time: *About 20 minutes*

Cooking time: *About 15 minutes*

Yield: *4 servings*

¼ cup olive oil

1 small onion, diced

4 anchovy fillets packed in olive oil, drained and chopped (optional)

3 large cloves garlic, chopped

¼ teaspoon red pepper flakes, or to taste

28-ounce can Italian plum tomatoes, drained and diced

12 pitted black olives, halved

2 tablespoons capers, rinsed and drained

¼ teaspoon dried thyme

½ cup chopped parsley

Salt and black pepper to taste

1 pound spaghetti

1 Heat the oil in a large saucepan or sauté pan over medium heat. Add the onion, anchovies (if desired), garlic, and red pepper flakes. Cook for 1 to 2 minutes or until the garlic is golden, stirring often. Do not let the garlic brown.

2 Add the tomatoes, olives, capers, and thyme to the pan. Stir to blend well. Bring to a boil; then reduce the heat and simmer, partially covered, for about 5 minutes. Stir in the parsley, season with salt and pepper, and set aside.

3 Bring about 5 quarts lightly salted water to boil in a large pot over high heat. Add the spaghetti and cook about 8 minutes, or just until al dente.

4 Just before the pasta is done, carefully scoop out and reserve ½ cup of the cooking liquid. Then drain the pasta, returning it to the same pot. Add the sauce and toss well, adding a little of the reserved cooking liquid to moisten the mixture, if necessary. Serve immediately.

 TOQUE TIP Francesco Antonucci, cookbook author and exuberant chef of Remi Restaurant in New York City, says that his mother used to make the following recipe for dinner whenever she was running late and had no time to visit the market. "I also make this dish after a long day in the restaurant because it is so practical and delicious — not to mention that it reminds me of my youth in Venice," says Antonucci. From the ingredients you have on hand, you can make this dish, too.

Francesco Antonucci's Spaghetti with Tuna

Tools: *Large pot, grater, small bowl, colander*

Preparation time: *About 5 minutes*

Cooking time: *About 15 minutes*

Yield: *3 to 4 servings*

8 ounces spaghetti

6½-ounce can tuna packed in olive oil

2 tablespoons freshly grated Parmesan cheese

2 tablespoons extra-virgin olive oil

2 teaspoons butter

Salt and black pepper to taste

(continued)

1 Bring 4 quarts lightly salted water to boil in a large pot over high heat. Add the spaghetti and cook according to package directions, just until al dente.

2 As the pasta cooks, drain the can of tuna. Mash the tuna in a small bowl with a fork to break it into small pieces.

3 Before draining the pasta, scoop out and reserve about ¼ cup cooking liquid. When it's ready, drain the pasta and return it to the large pot.

4 Add the tuna, Parmesan, olive oil, butter, and just enough of the reserved cooking liquid to moisten the pasta. Toss well, season to taste, and serve immediately.

A boiling pot of water is one of the most dangerous elements in any kitchen. Use pots with short handles that cannot be easily tipped and set them to boil on back burners, away from small and curious hands.

Cuban, Mexican, and much of South American cuisine is built around highly seasoned rice dishes — from *arroz y pollo* (chicken and rice) and black bean and rice dishes of Brazil to the fish and rice casseroles of the Mexican coast. If you have long-grain rice in the pantry (see Chapter 3 for more on rice), you can turn out dozens of spontaneous, economical dishes like the following one.

Red Beans and Rice

Tools: *Chef's knife, large sauté pan with lid*

Preparation time: *About 20 minutes*

Cooking time: *About 20 minutes*

Yield: *4 servings*

1 tablespoon olive oil	*2½ cups homemade or canned chicken stock*
4 slices bacon, coarsely chopped	*14-ounce can red kidney beans, drained*
1 medium onion, diced	*1 bay leaf*
2 large cloves garlic, peeled and chopped	*¼ teaspoon red pepper flakes, or to taste*
1½ cups white rice	*2 tablespoons dry sherry (optional)*
½ teaspoon turmeric	*Salt and black pepper to taste*
½ teaspoon ground coriander	*2 tablespoons chopped parsley*
8-ounce can diced tomatoes	

1 Heat the olive oil in a sauté pan over medium heat. Add the bacon and onion and cook for 2 to 3 minutes or until the bacon is crisp, stirring often. Add the garlic and cook for 1 minute, stirring often. Do not let the garlic brown.

2 Add the rice, turmeric, and coriander, stirring to coat the rice grains with the oil. Add the tomatoes with their juice, chicken stock, beans, bay leaf, and red pepper flakes. Stir well.

3 Bring to a boil. Cover and simmer over low heat for about 17 minutes or until most of the liquid is absorbed. (If adding sherry, stir it into the rice mixture about 2 minutes before the rice is tender.) Before serving, adjust seasoning with salt and pepper, if desired. Remove the bay leaf and sprinkle with the chopped parsley.

This dish goes well with The Perfect Hamburger (see Chapter 6), Chicken Breasts with Garlic and Capers (see Chapter 7), or Poached Salmon Steaks with Herb Vinaigrette (see Chapter 3).

Other ways to season rice include the following:

- **Pilaf:** Melt butter in a pan, add chopped onion and garlic, and cook, stirring. Add the rice and stir to coat grains in the oil; then add the stock, parsley, thyme, salt and pepper, and a bay leaf. Bring to a boil, cover, and simmer for about 17 minutes or until the rice is tender.

  Note: For most of the following variations, the technique is the same as pilaf; you simply change the seasoning as indicated.

- **Turmeric rice:** Add chopped onion, minced garlic, turmeric, rice, chicken stock, thyme, and a bay leaf.

- **Sweet rice:** Add chopped onion, minced garlic, raisins, rice, stock, and pine nuts or almonds just before serving.

- **Creole rice:** Cook the rice and set aside. Place butter and chopped onion in a sauté pan and cook until the onion wilts. Add diced tomatoes and salt and pepper, cooking and stirring for 1 to 2 minutes. Add the cooked rice to the tomato mixture with chopped fresh basil, 1 tablespoon fresh lemon juice, and ½ teaspoon grated lemon zest.

- **Curried rice:** Cook chopped onions in butter in a skillet. Add the rice and chicken or vegetable stock, 2 teaspoons curry powder (or to taste), salt and pepper, and ½ cup raisins, if desired. Cover and cook until done.

Potatoes are one of four or five vegetables that no kitchen should be without. You can almost make a meal of this simple potato side dish — it's that rich and satisfying. If you like the mellow, nutty taste of baked garlic, add a few more crushed cloves.

Potatoes Layered in Cream and Cheese

Tools: *Chef's knife, 2½-quart glass or ceramic shallow baking dish, grater, mixing bowl*

Preparation time: *About 20 minutes*

Baking time: *About 1 hour and 15 minutes*

Yield: *4 servings*

Butter for baking dish

2 large cloves garlic, peeled

1¼ cups light cream or half-and-half

⅛ teaspoon cayenne pepper, or to taste

⅛ teaspoon nutmeg

Salt and black pepper to taste

4 medium baking potatoes, about 1½ pounds

1 cup grated, tightly packed Swiss or Gruyère cheese

1 Preheat oven to 350 degrees.

2 Butter the sides and bottom of a 2½-quart shallow baking dish.

3 Place a garlic clove on a wooden cutting board or other firm surface and use the broad side of a chef's knife to crush or press the clove flat. Repeat with the second clove.

4 Combine the garlic cloves, cream, cayenne, nutmeg, salt, and pepper in a bowl or measuring cup. Set aside.

5 Peel and slice the potatoes thinly. They should be about ¼-inch thick or slightly less.

6 Place a layer of half of the potato slices on the bottom of the baking dish so that their edges overlap slightly. Pour over about half the cream mixture and then sprinkle about half the cheese on top. Repeat with another layer of potatoes, cream mixture, and cheese.

7 Bake for 1 hour and 15 minutes or until the potatoes are tender and the top is golden brown.

You can serve this rich and creamy potato side dish with a simple piece of grilled chicken (see Chapter 6) and a steamed green vegetable like broccoli or brussels sprouts (see Chapter 3) or with scrambled eggs (see Chapter 2).

Here are a few more suggestions for dishes you can make from your pantry:

✔ Omelet with Herbs, Frittata with Sweet Peppers and Potatoes, or Gruyère Soufflé (see Chapter 8)

✔ Spaghetti with Quick Fresh Tomato Sauce (substitute canned tomatoes for fresh — see Chapter 11)

✔ Penne with Cheese (see Chapter 11)

✔ American Macaroni and Cheese (see Chapter 12)

✔ Bacon and Cheese Strata (see Chapter 12)

Chapter 15

Champagne Meals
on a Beer Budget

In This Chapter

▶ Tell them it's filet mignon: Delicious meals from secondary cuts

▶ Beans, greens, and cheap proteins

▶ Thrifty cooking made easy

To understand how much money the average shopper wastes every week, just stand around any supermarket checkout counter. Instead of flipping through the intellectual journals on sale ("Liz to Marry an Alien; Honeymoon on Pluto"), take an inventory of customers' shopping carts. Even discounting the usual fatty snack food, you'll find that the average cart is loaded with high-priced (for what you get) frozen dinners, sugared-up prepared sauces, prebuttered bread, precut vegetables, frozen pizzas, boxed croutons (stale bread!), and more.

In an experiment done several years ago, a Tennessee newspaper gave $10 to noted chef and cookbook author Jacques Pépin and asked him to prepare a dinner for four. Not only did he pull it off, but he served beef and came back with 35 cents in change. The meal consisted of salad; flank steak in red wine sauce; sautéed cabbage; mashed potatoes; and poached pear with orange sauce — and yes, he even bought a bottle of wine.

Of course, preparing that meal takes great skill. But by rethinking your shopping habits and getting acquainted with less common cuts of meat, poultry, and fish — and with beans, legumes, and seasonal fresh vegetables — you can approximate this economic approach, and eat better, too.

Remember, frugality is no reason to forgo elegance, as the recipes in this chapter demonstrate.

Big Dishes for Small Bucks

Whether you're using inexpensive cuts of beef, dirt-cheap chicken legs, or a weekly special at the supermarket, a little attention to detail and presentation can make any meal fit for a, well, family.

All the main dish recipes in this section also make delicious leftovers — a blessing for busy cooks. Consider the following advice from Jacques Pépin:

"A good cook never apologizes about leftovers. The common mistake is to try to re-serve them in their original form. A roasted chicken is good only when fresh. Reheated, it tastes like a leftover, with all the word's pejorative connotations. But if it is served in a hash or in a cream sauce or is transformed into a salad, it will taste as it should — like a freshly made dish."

Chili

Few words spark gastronomic brouhaha like chili, whether it is rich Texas-style chili con carne, fiery Arizona-style chili, or one of the myriad variations in between. Maybe it's not a glamorous meal, but chili is a real crowd-pleaser, and you'd be surprised how festive you can make it look with some thought to presentation. And you can feed your whole football team for about ten bucks.

Chili is generally agreed to have originated in Texas more than 100 years ago, in the days of cowboys. Chili made sense for these hard-riding buckaroos because it was quick, filled with protein, and cheap — beef was not exactly scarce for the herders. The degree of fire in the form of hot peppers became a matter of cowboy competition.

In New Mexico, another state famous for chili, it was made with lamb or mutton rather than beef, and red beans were popular.

You can make endless variations on chili. Many champion chilis in competitions around the United States combine beef and pork, one for flavor and the other for texture, as in the following recipe. If you like, you can add lamb, too. Vegetarians can increase the amount of vegetables and skip the meat altogether.

Stoke the chili as much as you want with extra red pepper flakes and chili powder. Be careful, though, because pepper flakes intensify as they cook.

If the chili gets too dry while cooking, add a little more beef stock or water, or even some liquid from the canned kidney beans.

Southwestern Chili

Tools: *Chef's knife, deep pot or Dutch oven, wooden spoon*

Preparation time: *About 25 minutes*

Cooking time: *About 35 minutes*

Yield: *4 servings*

1 tablespoon olive oil

1 large onion, finely chopped

1 small green bell pepper, seeded, cored, and finely chopped

2 large cloves garlic, finely chopped

½ pound lean ground beef

½ pound lean ground pork

1 tablespoon chili powder, or to taste

1 teaspoon ground cumin

½ teaspoon ground coriander

2 cups ripe, diced tomatoes, or 14½-ounce can diced tomatoes

¾ cup homemade or canned beef stock

½ cup red wine or water

2 teaspoons tomato paste

¼ teaspoon red pepper flakes, or to taste

Salt and black pepper to taste

15-ounce can red kidney beans, drained

4 cups cooked long-grain rice (optional)

Sour cream or chopped cilantro or parsley for garnish (optional)

1 Heat the oil in a large, deep pot or Dutch oven. Add the onion, pepper, and garlic and cook for 2 to 3 minutes over medium heat, stirring occasionally.

2 Add the ground meat and cook for another 3 minutes or until browned, stirring to break up any lumps. Add the chili powder, cumin, and coriander. Stir well.

3 Stir in the tomatoes, beef stock, wine (or water), tomato paste, red pepper flakes, salt, and pepper. Bring to a boil, reduce heat to a simmer, and then cook for 25 to 30 minutes, stirring often. Add the drained kidney beans and cook 5 to 10 minutes more. If desired, serve over rice (see Chapter 3), and garnish with sour cream and cilantro or parsley.

Note: *If you have a plastic squeeze bottle (available in restaurant supply stores), you can squirt flavored sour cream in the shape of Texas or Cleveland. You can really get carried away with this idea.*

Chili calls for colorful side dishes like Avocado and Tomato Salad (see Chapter 16), or Watercress, Endive, and Orange Salad (see Chapter 10).

This chili recipe can be doubled or even tripled to serve 8 or 12.

Chicken

Following is an inexpensive, quick-cooking chicken and vegetable stew with sunny Mediterranean flavors of garlic, green olives, and tomatoes.

Mediterranean-Style Chicken

Tools: *Chef's knife, large sauté pan, tongs*

Preparation time: *About 25 minutes*

Cooking time: *About 40 minutes*

Yield: *4 servings*

3½- to 4-pound chicken, cut into 8 serving pieces and trimmed of excess fat

Salt and black pepper to taste

2 tablespoons olive oil

1 large onion, finely chopped

2 large cloves garlic, finely minced

1 tablespoon all-purpose flour

1½ cups homemade or canned chicken stock

½ cup dry white wine or water

2 medium red bell peppers, cored, seeded, and coarsely chopped

1½ cups coarsely chopped ripe or canned tomatoes

1 tablespoon tomato paste

1½ teaspoons dried rosemary leaves, minced well

¼ teaspoon red pepper flakes

1 bay leaf

2 small zucchini, ends trimmed and cut into rounds

16 small, pitted green olives (optional)

1 Rinse the chicken pieces and pat dry with paper towel. Season on all sides with salt and pepper. Heat the oil in a large sauté pan. Add the chicken pieces, skin side down, and cook over medium-high heat, about 7 to 10 minutes or until browned all over, turning frequently with tongs.

2 Remove the chicken from the pan and drain on paper towels. Spoon off all but about 1 tablespoon of fat from the pan. Add the onion and garlic and cook for 2 to 3 minutes over medium heat, stirring. Add the flour and cook for 1 minute, stirring and scraping the bottom of the pan.

3 Gradually pour in the chicken stock and wine or water. Raise the heat and bring to a boil, stirring constantly. Add the red peppers, tomatoes, tomato paste, rosemary, red pepper flakes, and bay leaf.

4 Return chicken pieces to the skillet. Cover, reduce the heat to medium-low, and simmer for about 10 minutes. Add the zucchini and olives (if desired), cover, and cook for about 5 minutes. Uncover and cook for about 10 minutes more or until the chicken is cooked (the juices should run clear and there should be no trace of pink near the bone) and the zucchini is tender. Season with salt and pepper to taste. Remove the bay leaf before serving.

This herby broth is terrific with Couscous with Yellow Squash (see following recipe) or any kind of rice (see Chapter 3).

Super Sidekicks

Inviting side dishes are another great way to dress up your meals. Following are some inexpensive but tasty recipes.

Couscous

If you have never tried couscous, this recipe will be an eye-opener. Couscous is a wonderful alternative to rice or noodles.

Made from finely ground semolina (coarse durum wheat) grains, couscous originated in North Africa and is especially popular in Morocco, Algeria, and Tunisia. Couscous can also refer to a stew (of chicken or lamb, vegetables, chick peas, and raisins), in which semolina is steamed atop a pot holding the stew. This two-tiered pot is called a *coucoussière*.

Precooked couscous, which doesn't require special equipment, is available in supermarkets. It comes in a box, like rice. In addition to saving a lot of time, it's quite good. Couscous is a fine alternative to rice or noodles when simply seasoned with butter and salt and pepper. Although experts say that even precooked couscous should be steamed for the best texture and flavor, it is still exceptionally tasty when you cook it in a flavorful stock, stirring well to keep the grains fluffy. We add onions, garlic, yellow squash, and coriander. Zucchini and eggplant are fine substitutes for the yellow squash.

Couscous with Yellow Squash

Tools: *Chef's knife, medium saucepan with a lid*

Preparation time: *About 15 minutes*

Cooking time: *About 10 minutes*

Yield: *4 servings*

1 tablespoon butter

1 tablespoon olive oil

1 small yellow squash, cut into ¼-inch cubes

1 small onion, finely chopped

1 large clove garlic, finely chopped

2 cups homemade or canned chicken or vegetable stock

1 cup precooked couscous

¼ cup coarsely chopped cilantro

Salt and black pepper to taste

1 Heat the butter and oil in a medium saucepan over medium heat. Add the squash, onion, and garlic. Cook, stirring often, over medium heat, until the onion wilts, about 2 to 3 minutes.

2 Add the chicken or vegetable stock and bring to a boil. Add the couscous and blend well. Cover tightly, remove from the heat, and let stand for 5 minutes. Stir in the cilantro with a fork. Season to taste with salt and pepper.

This type of couscous goes best with dishes that have a lot of juice or sauce, such as Mediterranean-Style Chicken (earlier in this chapter), Osso Buco (see Chapter 16), or Mediterranean Seafood Stew (see Chapter 5).

You can substitute 1 cup fresh or frozen corn kernels or peas for the yellow squash.

Cumin-flavored carrots

Cumin, a spice most often associated with Middle Eastern and Indian cooking, has an affinity with sweet carrots, as the following recipe demonstrates. These exotic-tasting carrots are best paired with a mild-flavored dish, such as Roasted Chicken (see Chapter 6) or Salmon Steaks with Red Pepper Sauce (see Chapter 4).

Carrots in Cumin Butter

Tools: *Chef's knife, medium saucepan*

Preparation time: *About 10 minutes*

Cooking time: *About 15 minutes*

Yield: *4 to 6 servings*

1 pound carrots, peeled and cut in 1-inch pieces

Salt to taste

2 tablespoons butter

¼ teaspoon ground cumin

2 tablespoons chopped cilantro or parsley

1 Put the carrots in a saucepan and add cold salted water to cover. Bring to a boil and simmer until the carrots are tender, about 15 minutes.

2 Drain the carrots and return them to the saucepan. Add the butter, cumin, and cilantro or parsley and toss well. Serve immediately.

Dried beans

We find it rather amazing that Americans don't cook more with dried beans, which are so inexpensive, healthful, and delicious. You can use dried beans in a side dish, as in the following recipe, or as part of a main course. Whether or not you are cooking on a tight budget, becoming familiar with all kinds of legumes, each of which has a special texture and flavor, is definitely worthwhile. Table 15-1 lists several common types of dried beans.

Before cooking dried beans, sort and rinse them. Look over the beans carefully, picking out and discarding any that are withered. Rinse them thoroughly in cold water until the water runs clear, removing any beans or other substances that float to the surface.

White Beans with Tomatoes and Thyme

Tools: *Chef's knife, large pot, large skillet or sauté pan, colander or strainer*

Preparation time: *About 20 minutes, plus time to soak beans*

Cooking time: *About 50 minutes*

Yield: *4 servings*

1 cup dried white beans (such as Great Northern or baby limas), rinsed

2 medium onions

2 whole cloves

1 quart water

3 slices bacon

1 large carrot, peeled and cut in half lengthwise

2 sprigs fresh thyme, or ½ teaspoon dried

1 bay leaf

Salt and black pepper to taste

2 teaspoons butter or oil

1 large clove garlic, minced

1 teaspoon chopped thyme, or ½ teaspoon dried

14½-ounce can diced tomatoes, drained

2 tablespoons chopped parsley

1 Place the beans in a large pot and add cold water to cover by about 1 inch. Soak overnight or boil for 2 minutes and then let stand for 1 hour. (See note at the end of this recipe.)

2 Stick the cloves into one onion, and chop the other onion finely.

3 Drain the beans and return them to the pot. Add 1 quart water, the onion stuck with cloves, the bacon, carrot, thyme, bay leaf, salt, and pepper. Cover the pot and bring to a boil over high heat. Reduce the heat to medium-low, and simmer, partially covered, for 45 minutes to 1 hour or until the beans are tender. (Different varieties require different cooking times.)

4 Remove the bacon strips and chop them into small pieces.

5 Heat the butter or oil in a large skillet or sauté pan over medium heat and sauté the chopped bacon until golden brown, stirring. Add the chopped onion, garlic, and thyme and cook for about 2 to 3 minutes or until the onions wilt. Add the tomatoes and cook for 2 to 3 minutes, stirring frequently. Remove from the heat.

6 Remove and discard the carrot, onion with cloves, and bay leaf from the pot of beans. Carefully scoop out and reserve ½ of the bean liquid and drain the beans. Add the beans to the tomato mixture and stir gently. If the mixture seems dry, add a little of the reserved liquid. Adjust seasoning with salt and pepper. Serve the beans hot, sprinkled with the chopped parsley.

Note: You soak most dried beans before cooking to shorten the cooking time, which is important if you cook them with other ingredients. If you don't have time to soak the beans overnight, use this shortcut: Place the beans in a deep pot covered with lots of water. Bring to a boil and cook for 2 minutes. Remove pot from the heat, cover, and let stand for 1 hour.

Pair these aromatic beans with dishes like Mustard-Brushed Barbecued Chicken Breasts (see Chapter 6) or Grilled Swordfish Steaks with Lemon and Thyme (see Chapter 6).

Table 15-1	Dried Beans
Bean	*Description*
Black beans	Often used in South American and Caribbean dishes and mixed with rice and spices. Sweetish flavor.
Black-eyed peas	Traditional ingredient in the cooking of the American South — black-eyed peas and collard greens, black-eyed peas with ham. Earthy.
Borlotto beans	Large, speckled beans. Mostly pureed and turned into creamy dips.
Boston beans	See "White beans (Boston beans), small."
Chickpeas	Large, semi-firm beans sold dried and canned. Used in casseroles, soups, and stews. Pureed and seasoned in Middle Eastern cuisine. Also known as *garbanzo beans.*
Kidney beans/ red beans	The traditional beans used in chili and other earthy casserole dishes and soups. A white kidney bean, called *cannellini,* is used in many northern Italian dishes. A staple in Mexican cooking as well. Faintly sweet.
Lentils	A tiny legume. Boiled with vegetables and other seasonings for side dishes, soups, and stews. No soaking is required before cooking.
Lima beans	Eaten as a side dish with mild seasonings. Also good in casseroles, especially with ham. Sweet flavor.
Pinto beans	The base of Mexican refried beans. Frequently used in highly spiced dishes. Earthy, mild flavor.
Split peas	Often used in soups, especially with ham. Sweet. Like lentils, no soaking is required.

(continued)

Table 15-1 (continued)

Bean	Description
White beans, large	Used in stews and casseroles. Often simmered with ham bones or other flavorful stocks. Neutral flavor.
White beans, small (Navy and Pea)	Foundation of Boston baked beans and the French *cassoulet.* Neutral flavor.

The sweet edge of the balsamic vinegar performs magic on the nutty flavored lentils in the following recipe. Unlike many other dried beans, lentils don't require soaking and boil tender in 20 to 25 minutes.

Lentils with Balsamic Vinegar

Tools: *Chef's knife, large pot or saucepan, large sauté pan*

Preparation time: *About 20 minutes*

Cooking time: *About 30 minutes*

Yield: *4 servings*

1½ cups lentils, rinsed

1 quart water

Salt to taste

2 small onions

2 cloves

1 bay leaf

2 sprigs fresh thyme, or ½ teaspoon dried

1 tablespoon butter

1 tablespoon olive oil

1 large carrot, peeled and finely diced

1 large clove garlic, finely chopped

1 tablespoon balsamic (or red wine) vinegar

Black pepper to taste

1 Put the lentils in a large pot or saucepan. Add the water and salt to taste. Cover and bring to a boil over high heat. Stick the cloves into one onion and chop the other onion finely. Add the onion with cloves to the saucepan along with the bay leaf and thyme. Reduce heat, and simmer, partially covered, for about 20 minutes or until the lentils are tender.

2 Before draining the lentils, carefully scoop out and reserve ½ cup of the cooking liquid. Drain the lentils. Remove and discard the onion with cloves, bay leaf, and thyme sprigs.

3 Heat the butter and olive oil in a large sauté pan or skillet over medium-high heat. Add the carrot, chopped onion, and garlic. Cook, stirring often, until the onion wilts, about 3 to 4 minutes. (Do not brown the garlic.) Add the vinegar and the reserved ½ cup cooking liquid. Cover, reduce heat, and simmer for about 5 minutes or until the vegetables are tender.

4 Stir the lentils into the vegetable mixture, cover, and cook over medium heat for about 2 minutes more, just to blend flavors. Season with salt and pepper and serve.

Lentils are ideal with Grilled Brochettes of Pork with Rosemary (see Chapter 6) or Chicken Breasts with Garlic and Capers (see Chapter 7).

 Recommending specific heat settings in a recipe is a little tricky. Medium-low heat on one stovetop may be medium on another. And, depending on the metal they are made of, pots and pans conduct heat differently. Use common cooking sense and modify a stovetop heat setting as necessary.

Seasonal vegetables

Most seasonal vegetables tend to be a relative bargain (except for exotic and imported produce), and certain types are incredibly cheap. And like the less expensive cuts of meat, vegetables are terrific when prepared properly. Kale, a hearty, iron-packed member of the cabbage family that is available year-round, is one of those vegetables. Other relatively inexpensive veggies include collard greens, mustard greens, squashes of all kinds, turnips, rutabagas, cabbage, and zucchini (in season).

Following is a down-home recipe for kale, one of the most nutritious vegetables. Southerners traditionally combine kale with sausage or bacon.

Homestyle Kale

Tools: *Chef's knife, sauté pan*

Preparation time: *About 15 minutes*

Cooking time: *About 15 minutes*

Yield: *4 servings*

1 ½ to 2 pounds kale	*½ cup water*
4 slices bacon, diced	*1 bay leaf*
1 medium onion, finely chopped	*Salt and black pepper to taste*
3 large cloves garlic, minced	*4 lemon wedges*

(continued)

1 Wash the kale thoroughly in a sink full of cold water or a large pot. Do not dry. Strip the leaves from the tough center ribs (discarding the ribs) and cut out any blemished areas.

2 In a sauté pan, cook the bacon over medium heat for about 4 to 5 minutes. Add the onions and cook until the bacon is lightly browned. Add the garlic, kale leaves, water, bay leaf, salt, and pepper. Cover and steam for 15 minutes or until tender, stirring occasionally. Discard the bay leaf and serve with lemon wedges.

Money-saving kitchen tips

Being economical in the kitchen has nothing to do with cutting quality — in fact, just the contrary. Making every ounce count takes skill and respect for food. Here are some ways to begin:

✔ **Don't let leftovers ossify in the refrigerator.** Think ahead and use them the next day in omelets (see Chapter 8), chili, soups (see Chapter 9), stir-fries, casseroles like macaroni and cheese (see Chapter 12), and salads (see Chapter 10).

✔ **Develop knife skills.** Cutting up your own chicken and boning your own meat saves considerable money. Plus, you have bones for making stock. Whole vegetables are cheaper than cut-up ones, too.

✔ **Develop delicious recipes with high-protein dried beans and less-expensive vegetables like squash, kale, collard greens, and potatoes.**

✔ **Use your freezer intelligently.** Take advantage of supermarket sales. Buy in bulk ground meat, chicken breasts and other poultry parts, steaks, and chops. Wrap and save leftovers from large casseroles such as baked lasagna (see Chapter 11), meat from a roasted leg of lamb (see Chapter 6), or a baked ham. And date everything you put in the freezer. To discover some great ways of turning leftovers into delicious meals, see Chapter 17.

✔ **If possible, grow an herb garden, even if in a window box.** So many packaged fresh herbs go to waste because you don't use them often enough. Plus, they're rather expensive and the cost adds up over time.

✔ **Make your own versions of foods that you routinely buy in the supermarket.** You'll spend less money and get better quality. Examples include croutons (see Chapter 9), salad dressings (see Chapter 10), garlic bread, and chicken stock.

✔ **Buy less-expensive cuts of meat and learn to tenderize them by braising and stewing.** (See Chapter 5.)

✔ **Discourage children from bringing friends home for dinner. And visit friends and relatives around mealtime and compliment them on how delicious the kitchen smells.**

Chapter 16

The Clock Is Ticking . . . and the Guests Are on Their Way!

Noncooks think it's silly to invest two hours' work for two minutes' enjoyment; but if cooking is evanescent, well, so is the ballet.

— Julia Child

Picture yourself in this situation: In a foolish moment of bravado at an office cocktail party, you invite two couples to dinner Friday evening a week hence, 7:30 p.m. When the dreaded day arrives, you dart out of the office at 5:45 with no idea what to prepare for dinner. After running several red lights on the way to the grocery store — all the while thinking, "I'll get inspired by what looks good in the market" — you arrive to find that the lettuce looks as if it has been used for batting practice and the only items left in the picked-over meat section are beef tongue and tripe.

So you frantically buy boxes of pasta, tomato paste, sweet peppers, garlic, broccoli, leeks, a turnip, pre-washed lettuce, Ben and Jerry's Ambulance Vanilla ice cream, and some beef tongue — just in case.

Judging by the traffic on your way home, you would think that the Super Bowl had been transferred to your suburb this evening. You listen to a talk show on the radio. The topic: "The Joys of Summer Entertaining." After what seems like an eternity, you pull into the driveway only to see a strange car parked there. Even more disturbing, people outside the house are looking into your windows.

"What the heck do you think you're doing?" you shout, realizing in mid-sentence that the suspected burglars are, in fact, your guests. Yikes!

This little scene goes to show that cooking is not always done under ideal conditions. Even Julia Child's washing machine sometimes goes haywire right in the middle of a stuffed goose recipe.

Cooking by the Clock

When you plan a vacation, what is the first consideration: Cost? Distance? Exoticism? Not at all. The first consideration is *time*. If you have only one week, doing a flora tour of Australia's outback hardly makes sense — the flight alone takes five days (well, almost).

The same philosophy applies to cooking for company. Think about how much time you realistically have. If you are lucky enough to have all day Saturday to prepare for a dinner party, indulge in it. We give you some great ideas for that luxury.

But if you have only one hour — or less — the type of foods you prepare by necessity are totally different, which does not mean that they are not as good. Rather than making a braised shoulder of pork that takes three hours to cook, for example, you might serve Mustard-Brushed Barbecued Chicken Breasts, which take about 20 minutes. (See Chapter 6 for the recipe.)

Regardless of how much time you have, the important thing is to use it well. With the right scheduling strategies and planning, you can whip up a dinner party and still be composed when your guests arrive. The trick is in getting the techniques down and then planning your menus accordingly.

If You Have All Day

If you have all day, relax. Enjoy yourself. You may want to try something different. But don't lose track of the clock. The danger with having plenty of time on your hands is forgetting that you still have a schedule and a deadline (the guests *are* going to show up eventually). Go ahead and run errands while the main dish roasts, but don't forget to be back in time to adjust that oven temperature or stir that side dish. And make a list before you start so that you don't find yourself at the end of a day's happy cooking without a crucial part of your menu that you forgot all about. If you plan your day's cooking, at least roughly, before you get started, you'll be sure to have a leisurely day in the kitchen, and everything you want to serve will be ready by dinnertime.

One nice menu planning option, if you have time, is to start your meal with an appetizer that involves marinating, such as the spectacular salmon infused with ginger and coriander in the following recipe.

 Marinating fish can be tricky business. The acid in the marinade — which comes from the lime and vinegar — actually "cooks" the fish. Be sure not to leave it in the marinade too long. (This marinade does not have the same effect on dense cuts of meat or poultry.) This dish calls for marinating for four to five hours, so you can put everything together in the early afternoon and have it for dinner.

Salmon Marinated in Ginger and Cilantro

Tools: Chef's knife, grater, large non-reactive bowl (glass, plastic, or ceramic, but not metal)

Preparation time: About 25 minutes

Marinating time: 4 to 5 hours

Yield: 6 to 8 appetizer servings

2 pounds skinless salmon fillets (have your fishmonger remove the skin and bones)

½ cup fresh lime juice

1 large onion, thinly sliced

3 tablespoons white wine vinegar

3 tablespoons olive oil

2 tablespoons chopped cilantro

1 tablespoon grated fresh ginger

¼ teaspoon red pepper flakes

Salt and black pepper to taste

Lettuce for garnish

1 Using a pair of tweezers or your fingers, remove any small bones (called pin bones) in the salmon fillets.

2 Slice salmon thinly (¼ inch or less) widthwise, leaving strips about 2 inches long. Place the strips in a large bowl.

3 Add the onion, lime juice, vinegar, oil, cilantro, ginger, red pepper flakes, salt, and pepper. Stir gently and cover with plastic wrap. Refrigerate for 4 to 5 hours. Taste for seasoning. (You may need more salt; if so, blend it in thoroughly.)

4 Line small serving plates with lettuce of your choice and place a serving of salmon over the lettuce.

In some cases, we give a dried substitute for a fresh herb. However, substitutions don't work with a few ingredients. You cannot substitute dried cilantro for fresh, or powdered ginger for fresh ginger root. The fresh ingredient tastes entirely different from the dried one. Dried parsley is another herb that has its limitations. Always use fresh, chopped parsley when sprinkling it on a dish as a garnish.

Other starter dishes

Another way to go if you have the luxury of time is to start the meal with a light vegetable soup. This type of vegetable soup — and you can vary the cast of characters — is a perfect prelude to the hearty main course of Osso Buco that we tackle next. You don't want to serve a full-bodied soup like black bean or cheesy onion before a lusty main course (unless you are cooking in a lumberjack camp).

Notice how the soup's garnish of chopped tomatoes, basil, garlic, and olive oil, first sits and marinates a bit before you stir it into the simmering soup. You may want to accompany this dish with a loaf of hot and crusty French bread.

Spring Vegetable Soup

Tools: *Medium pot or saucepan, chef's knife, paring knife, vegetable peeler, small bowl*

Preparation time: *About 45 minutes*

Cooking time: *About 35 minutes*

Yield: *6 to 8 servings*

1 tablespoon vegetable oil

1 large onion, diced

1 large carrot, peeled and diced

4 cups water

2 cups chicken or vegetable stock

2 medium baking potatoes, peeled and diced

1 large leek (white and light green parts only), washed and diced (see Chapter 9 for illustrated instructions)

1 small zucchini, rinsed, trimmed of ends, and diced

1 cup green beans, trimmed and cut into ½-inch pieces

2 large ripe tomatoes, peeled, seeded, and chopped

2 tablespoons finely chopped basil

2 large cloves garlic, minced

1 tablespoon olive oil

Salt and white or black pepper to taste

1 Heat the vegetable oil in a medium pot or saucepan over medium heat. Add the onion and cook for about 3 minutes, stirring occasionally.

2 Stir in the carrot and cook for 1 minute. Stir in the water and chicken or vegetable stock. Raise the heat to high and bring to a boil; then reduce the heat to low and simmer for 10 minutes, uncovered.

3 Peel the potatoes and cut into small cubes. Add to the pot the potatoes, leek, zucchini, and green beans. Cover, raise the heat to high, and bring to a boil. Then uncover, reduce the heat to low, and simmer 25 minutes, skimming the surface when necessary to remove any foam.

4 While the soup simmers, place the chopped tomatoes in a small bowl. Stir in the basil, garlic, and olive oil. Set aside.

5 Just before serving, stir in the tomato-basil mixture and the salt and pepper. Serve hot or at room temperature.

 You can make a pasta and vegetable version of this soup by omitting the potatoes and adding ½ cup small-shaped pasta (elbows or shells) 6 to 7 minutes before the soup finishes cooking. Replace the green beans with 1½ cups of coarsely chopped cabbage.

If you have time, you also can try one of these first courses:

- ✔ Fresh Tomato Gazpacho (see Chapter 9)
- ✔ Black Bean Soup (see Chapter 9)
- ✔ Cream of Leek Soup (see Chapter 9)
- ✔ Warm Shrimp Salad with Spinach (see Chapter 10)
- ✔ Bow-Tie Pasta Salad with Fresh Mussels (see Chapter 10)

Main dish choices

One of the long-cooked main courses we recommend for entertaining is Osso Buco, a glorious dish of braised veal shank with garlic, tomato, and other ingredients. The meat on the shank is exceptionally succulent, and the sauce that simmers in the meat juices is packed with herbal flavors and lemon.

Many cooks don't know it, but one traditional ingredient in Osso Buco is anchovies. Their intense saltiness, when added in moderation, adds a special flavor. If you are one of those people who pick anchovies off pizza, simply omit them from the recipe.

TOQUE TIP

Anchovies

On the culinary hit parade, anchovies fall somewhere at the bottom, between brussels sprouts and tripe. A staple of Mediterranean cooking, anchovies have never had widespread appeal among American home cooks — although professional chefs use them frequently.

Fresh anchovies, which are superb when grilled over charcoal, are rarely available in the United States. Typically, they are sold salted in jars or cans, yielding a product that has little relation to fresh anchovies, although you can put the salted ones to good use in many ways.

Todd English, chef and owner of Olives restaurant in Charlestown, Massachusetts, says, "There are many interesting ways to season a dish. I use anchovies a lot. . . . I know that lots of people don't like them, but they add an element, a depth of flavor that tastes nothing like an anchovy. Often, you can't even tell they are in the dish."

Ideally, Osso Buco should be made a day or two in advance, chilled, and then reheated — the flavors meld and intensify that way. Because you have all day to make this meal, you can prepare it at midday, cool it, and then reheat it for the dinner party.

Osso Buco

Tools: *Chef's knife, grater, Dutch oven (cast-iron is best)*

Preparation time: *About 40 minutes*

Cooking time: *1 hour and 30 minutes*

Yield: *4 servings*

4 meaty slices of veal shanks cut across the bones (each about 2 inches thick), about 3½ pounds total

Salt and black pepper to taste

½ cup all-purpose flour for dredging

2 tablespoons olive oil

1 large onion, finely chopped

2 to 3 large carrots, peeled and chopped

1 stalk celery, chopped

3 large cloves garlic, finely chopped

4 canned anchovy fillets, drained and mashed with a fork (optional)

½ teaspoon dried marjoram

2 sprigs fresh thyme, or 1 teaspoon dried

1½ cups canned crushed tomatoes

1 cup dry white wine

1 bay leaf

1 teaspoon finely grated lemon peel

1 teaspoon finely grated orange peel

¼ cup finely chopped parsley

1 Sprinkle the veal shanks with salt and pepper and then roll them in the flour to give them a light coating, patting to remove excess flour. (This technique is called *dredging*.)

2 Heat the oil over medium-high heat in a heavy Dutch oven large enough to hold the veal shanks in one layer with the bones upright. Brown the veal all around, turning often, about 10 minutes. Remove shanks from the pan and reserve them on a plate.

3 Lower the heat to medium and add the onion, carrots, and celery to the pan. Cook, stirring often, until the onions wilt, about 2 or 3 minutes. Add the garlic, mashed anchovies (if desired), marjoram, and thyme. Stir and add the tomatoes, wine, bay leaf, and salt and pepper to taste. Return the veal shanks to the pan with any juices that have accumulated in the plate. Cover, reduce heat to low, and simmer for about 1 hour or until the meat is tender. (The meat should easily separate from the bone when prodded with a fork.)

4 Sprinkle the orange and lemon zest over the veal and stir to blend. Cover and cook about 15 minutes more. Remove the bay leaf, spoon some of the vegetable mixture on each serving plate, then place a veal shank on top; sprinkle with chopped parsley.

You can serve this dish with garlic mashed potatoes, buttered rice (see Chapter 3), or couscous (see Chapter 15).

Following is another stick-to-the-ribs style of cooking that is perfect for entertaining. In this ancient French country recipe (also found in the Spanish repertoire), you first brown a loin of pork on the stovetop to sear in the moisture and then braise it slowly in sweet onions and milk for three hours. The milk gives the pork a rich and velvety texture that is out of this world. You set aside the pan juices to form the base of a gravy and then finish the roast in the oven.

Pork Loin Braised with Milk and Onions

Tools: *Chef's knife, Dutch oven, roasting pan, sieve, small saucepan*

Preparation time: *About 20 minutes*

Cooking time: *About 2 hours and 50 minutes*

Yield: *6 servings*

(continued)

3-pound boneless loin of pork	1 quart milk
Salt and black pepper to taste	¼ cup heavy cream or half-and-half (optional)
1 tablespoon olive oil	
12 small white pearl onions, peeled, about 1 pound	

1 Rub the pork with salt and pepper.

2 Heat the oil in a Dutch oven over medium heat until hot, about 1 minute. Brown the pork well in the oil on all sides for about 10 minutes. Remove the meat to a platter. Add the onions to the Dutch oven. Stir and brown them for about 5 minutes.

3 Carefully drain off all the fat. Return the pork to the Dutch oven, pushing the onions to the sides. Add the milk and cover. Raise the heat to high and bring to a boil. Reduce the heat to low and simmer for 1 hour, turning the roast over after 30 minutes.

4 Remove the lid and simmer over medium-low heat for another 1½ hours (turning the roast every 30 minutes), or until about 2 cups of the simmering liquid remains in the pan.

5 Preheat the oven to 425 degrees.

6 Place the roast on a lightly oiled roasting pan and cook about 10 minutes until brown.

7 As the pork cooks in the oven, strain the sauce into a saucepan. (Discard the solids left in the strainer.) Add the cream, if desired, to the sauce and heat just to a simmer.

8 Slice the pork and serve, spooning 2 to 3 tablespoons of sauce over each slice.

You tie butcher's string around a boned roast to preserve its shape. Remove the string with a sharp knife or kitchen shears just before slicing.

If you have time, you also can try any of these main dishes:

- Poached Salmon Steaks with Herbed Vinaigrette Sauce (see Chapter 3)
- Old-Fashioned Beef Stew (see Chapter 5)
- Braised Lamb with White Beans (see Chapter 5)
- Pot Roast with Vegetables (see Chapter 5)
- Mediterranean Seafood Stew (see Chapter 5)
- Any of the roasting recipes from Chapter 6
- Fettuccine with Ginger Shrimp (see Chapter 11)

✔ Family Lasagna (see Chapter 11)

✔ Chicken and Biscuit Pot Pie (see Chapter 12)

✔ Shepherd's Pie (see Chapter 12)

Side dishes

A perfect side dish for all roasts is mashed potatoes — chefs today like to call them "pureed potatoes," as if they are something more sophisticated. But how can you improve on something so basic and so delicious? Serve mashed potatoes with baked garlic, found in Chapter 3. Mashed potatoes can be enhanced in many ways. You can add to the mix mashed parsnips, carrots, or turnips or chopped green onions, minced yellow onions, or fresh herbs.

The slight crunch of cabbage also goes particularly well with roasted pork. You can make cabbage ahead of time and reheat it before serving. The following recipe brings the lowly cabbage to life, giving it a sweet personality with apples and a bit of spice with caraway.

Braised Cabbage with Apple and Caraway

Tools: *Chef's knife, paring knife, large skillet or sauté pan with lid, wooden spoon*

Preparation time: *About 25 minutes*

Cooking time: *About 25 minutes*

Yield: *4 servings*

3 tablespoons vegetable oil

1 medium onion, coarsely chopped

1 large clove garlic, minced

1 medium apple

1 small head cabbage, about 1½ pounds, halved, cored, and coarsely shredded

½ cup homemade or canned chicken or vegetable stock

1 tablespoon white vinegar

1 teaspoon caraway seeds

Salt and black pepper to taste

1 Heat the oil in a large skillet or sauté pan over medium heat. Add the onion and garlic and cook, stirring often, until the onion is wilted, about 2 to 3 minutes; remove from heat. (Do not brown the garlic.)

2 Peel, core, and cut the apple into thin slices. Add the apple, cabbage, chicken or vegetable stock, vinegar, caraway seeds, salt, and pepper to the skillet.

(continued)

3 Raise the heat to high and bring to a boil. Cover, reduce the heat to low, and simmer for 15 to 20 minutes or until the cabbage is crisp-tender, stirring occasionally. Uncover. If a lot of liquid is still in the pan, raise the heat to high and cook, stirring, for about 1 to 2 minutes or until most of the liquid is evaporated.

These side dishes also go well with any of the main courses in this chapter:

- ✔ Basic Wild Rice (see Chapter 3)
- ✔ Flavored Brown Rice (see Chapter 3)
- ✔ Risotto (see Chapter 3)
- ✔ Crispy Roasted Root Vegetables (see Chapter 6)
- ✔ Sautéed Cubed Potatoes (see Chapter 4)
- ✔ Creamed Spinach (see Chapter 7)
- ✔ Assorted Potato Purees (see Chapter 3)

Desserts

Okay, dessert time. Without getting involved in stratified layer cakes or chocolate concoctions that resemble a nuclear power plant, you can make plenty of easy desserts that are suitable for entertaining. Knowing how to make a basic sweet pastry crust is always a good idea. Make the recipe over and over again until you can make it in your sleep. Then when fresh fruit is in season, or when you want to make a lemon or chocolate mousse pie, all you have to concentrate on is the filling. And that's a cinch.

All you have to know about a basic pastry crust is that butter makes it sweet and shortening (like Crisco) makes it flaky. Many cooks split it down the middle and use equal amounts of butter and lard to make the dough.

"Typical pie dough pastry calls for you to cut the butter and shortening into the flour with a pastry blender until the mixture resembles coarse cornmeal, but we do it just the opposite at Campanile," says Nancy Silverton, owner and chef of this famous Los Angeles bakery-restaurant. "We've found the texture of the pastry to be lighter and flakier when the butter and shortening are first creamed together and then the dry ingredients are worked in.

"We also bake our pies in a very hot, preheated 450-degree oven for about 15 minutes and then turn the heat to 350 degrees for the remainder of the baking time," says Chef Silverton. "The hot oven helps to 'set' the crust and gives it a nice brown color.

"Be sure to use really cold water, chilled with ice cubes, to hold together the dough," she says.

See how you like this pastry dough and then modify it, if you want, with suggestions that follow this recipe.

Basic Pastry Crust

Tools: *Food processor or mixer, wire pastry blender (if making by hand), rolling pin, 9-inch pie pan*

Preparation time: *About 1½ hours (includes time to chill dough)*

Yield: *Enough pastry for a 9-inch double-crust pie*

⅓ cup plus 1 tablespoon cold butter, cut into small pieces

⅓ cup plus 1 tablespoon vegetable shortening (like Crisco or margarine)

2 cups all-purpose flour

¾ teaspoon salt

4 to 5 tablespoons ice water

1 In the bowl of a food processor, cream the butter and shortening. (Stop the motor as necessary to push the mixture with a rubber spatula toward the blade.) Add the flour and salt and process just a few seconds until the dough resembles coarse cornmeal. With the motor running, add the cold water a little at a time, just enough to hold together the dry ingredients. (The exact amount of water required depends on the humidity of the day.) Do not overblend or the dough will get tough. Shape the dough into a ball.

To make the dough without a food processor, as shown in Figure 16-1, cream the butter and shortening in a large bowl with an electric mixer. Add the flour and salt. Using a pastry blender or your fingers, work the flour mixture into the butter and shortening, making a dough that resembles coarse cornmeal. Sprinkle enough ice cold water to form soft but not sticky dough. Shape the dough into a loose ball.

2 Divide the dough into two equal halves, wrap both in plastic, and refrigerate for at least 1 hour. (As the dough is chilling, prepare the filling from the following Apple Pie recipe.)

3 When ready to make your pie, preheat the oven to 450 degrees.

4 Lightly flour a large cutting board or counter and roll out one dough ball into a circle that is a few inches larger in diameter than the pie plate — that is, about 11 inches. (See Figure 16-2 for illustrated rolling instructions.)

5 Loosely drape the dough around the rolling pin and transfer it to the pie plate. Unroll the dough flat onto the bottom and gently press it against the sides and rim of the pie plate. Trim off any excess dough with a knife. Lightly press any excess dough into the remaining ball. (Fill the pie shell, or, if the recipe calls for it, bake the pie shell before filling it. For an apple pie filling, see the following recipe.)

(continued)

6 Roll out the second ball of dough the same way and lay it over the filled bottom crust, leaving an overhang of about ½ inch. Tuck the overhang under the lower crust to form a neat edge; crimp firmly by pressing the tines of a fork all around the edge. Prick the top a few times with a fork before baking. (See the following Apple Pie recipe for baking instructions.)

Figure 16-1:
How to make pie dough by hand.

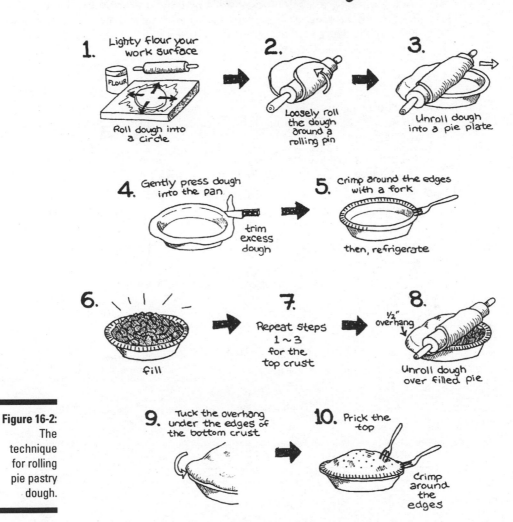

How to Roll Dough

1. Lighty flour your work surface — Roll dough into a circle

2. Loosely roll the dough around a rolling pin

3. Unroll dough into a pie plate

4. Gently press dough into the pan — trim excess dough

5. Crimp around the edges with a fork — then, refrigerate

6. fill

7. Repeat steps 1~3 for the top crust

8. ½" overhang — Unroll dough over filled pie

9. Tuck the overhang under the edges of the bottom crust

10. Prick the top — Crimp around the edges

Figure 16-2:
The technique for rolling pie pastry dough.

Variations to this pastry crust include the following:

- **Nuts:** Add ¼ cup ground pecans, hazelnuts, almonds, or walnuts to the flour mixture before you process or blend by hand.
- **Spice:** Add some cinnamon, allspice, or ground ginger to the flour.
- **Citrus:** Add 2 teaspoons of finely grated lemon or orange zest to the flour.
- **Sweet:** Add 1 tablespoon sugar to the flour-salt mixture.

✓ **Single-crust pie:** If you are making a recipe that calls for prebaked crust (usually custard or other soft fillings), cover the pie shell with aluminum foil and pour dried beans or other weights inside, as shown in Figure 16-3. Bake the crust for 15 minutes in a 400-degree oven; then lower the heat to 350 degrees and bake another 10 minutes. Be careful that the crust does not get too brown.

Remember these tips for rolling pastry dough:

✓ Work on a lightly floured counter or board. Dust the rolling pin and your dough *lightly* with flour, using a little more flour *only* if the dough sticks to the counter or the pin.

✓ Roll the dough from its center out to the edges and turn it frequently (about one quarter turn) to keep it from sticking to the counter.

✓ Try to work quickly so that the dough remains chilled. Room temperature dough is more difficult to roll, which is why it's important to chill dough thoroughly before rolling out.

✓ If the dough sticks to the counter, run a long metal spatula underneath to loosen it.

✓ Do not stretch the dough when transferring it from the counter to the pie plate.

For a Single Crust

Figure 16-3:
Preparing dough for a single crust.

1.
Follow "How to Roll Dough," steps 1~5

2. Prick the bottom & sides with a fork

and/or line the pan with aluminum foil filled with dry beans as weight

Rolling dough is a skill that takes a little practice. Don't be discouraged if, after your first try, your pie crust looks like a relief map of Antarctica.

If, while rolling, your pastry starts to break apart at the edges, overlap the pieces a little bit. Then gently roll over the overlapping edges until smooth, moistening them first with a drop of water. If that doesn't work, reshape the pastry into a ball and roll again. But remember, the more you handle the pastry dough, the tougher it becomes.

The taste and texture of a homemade crust is superior to any packaged mix. But when you don't have the time to make the pastry yourself, using a box of pie crust mix or frozen pie shells is better than having no pie at all.

Apple Pie

Tools: *Paring knife, large bowl, 9-inch pie plate*

Preparation time: *About 30 minutes, plus time to prepare pie crust dough*

Cooking time: *About 1 hour*

Yield: *6 to 8 servings*

6 medium apples (tart style is best; see the nearby sidebar for information on which apples are best for baking), peeled, cored, and sliced about ½-inch thick (see Figure 16-4)

¾ cup sugar

2 tablespoons all-purpose flour

1 tablespoon fresh lemon juice

¾ teaspoon cinnamon

½ teaspoon grated lemon zest

⅛ teaspoon nutmeg

9-inch pie plate covered with pastry dough plus 1 uncooked sheet of pastry dough, about 11 inches in diameter (see preceding recipe)

1 tablespoon butter

About 2 tablespoons milk or water (optional)

About 1 teaspoon sugar (optional)

1 Preheat oven to 450 degrees.

2 Combine apples, sugar, flour, lemon juice, cinnamon, lemon zest, and nutmeg in a large bowl. Toss gently to evenly coat apples with sugar and seasonings.

3 Fill the uncooked pie shell with the apple mixture. Dot with butter. Fit the top crust over the apples, trim off excess, and crimp edges firmly, as in Figure 16-2.

4 Prick the top crust several times with a fork to provide a vent for steam to escape. (For a shiny crust, use a pastry brush to brush the crust lightly with milk or water and then sprinkle sugar over it.)

5 Bake for 15 minutes. Reduce the heat to 350 degrees and bake another 45 minutes or until the pie crust is golden-brown. Cool the pie for at least 20 minutes before serving.

TIP

Which apples are best for baking?

Tart, crisp apples that hold their shape are best for pie-making. Fall or early winter is the ideal time to bake an apple pie because the apple crop is fresh. With the exception of Granny Smiths (tart, green apples that are available all year), apples found in markets in the spring and summer have been stored since the fall harvest and do not have the same taste or texture as fresh apples.

The following varieties are among the best for baking in pies: Baldwin, Cortland, Granny Smith, Gravenstein, Jonathan, Macoun, Newtown Pippin, Northern Spy, Rhode Island Greening, Rome Beauty, and Winesap.

Peeling and Coring an Apple

Figure 16-4:
You peel and core apples before slicing them into a pie.

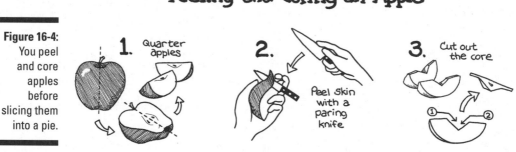

IMPROVISE

You can substitute fruits such as peaches, strawberries, apricots, and berries. You may want to vary the seasonings, but the idea is essentially the same. Pick a fruit and think about how to enhance it. For example, you may want to toss peaches with sugar, vanilla extract, and maybe a touch of rum. For pears, you can use sugar, cinnamon, maybe clove, and, if you like, vanilla extract. A dash of rum or brandy doesn't hurt, either. Adding ¼ cup brown sugar gives the filling a slightly caramelized flavor.

You also can use the basic pie crust for individual ramekins (single-serving, porcelain baking dishes) and fill them with fruits. The cooking time is less, of course — approximately half the cooking time for a 9-inch pie.

If You Have One Hour

One hour is actually a good chunk of time in which to put together a meal — that is, if you are organized, have all the shopping done, and can focus without out interruptions. One phone call can throw off your pace.

So don't be tempted to run out to the mailbox, and do think in advance about how long each dish needs at each stage so that one doesn't burn while another is still cold, and they all make it to the table on cue.

Starter dishes

You can take a lot of heat off the situation by starting with a good mixed salad. A balanced vinaigrette is the fuel that energizes a salad, as in the following recipe.

This slightly tart combination of endive and radicchio is a refreshing starter. You can jazz it up with other lettuce or roasted sweet peppers.

Mixed Summer Salad with Balsamic Vinegar Dressing

Tools: *Chef's knife, small mixing bowl*

Preparation time: *About 25 minutes, plus 1 hour (more or less) to let dressing stand*

Yield: *4 servings*

½ cup olive oil

⅓ cup finely chopped shallots

3 tablespoons balsamic vinegar

1 clove garlic, peeled and cut crosswise in half

Salt and black pepper to taste

20 Belgian endive leaves (about 2 large heads), rinsed and dried

4 radicchio leaves, rinsed and dried

4 cups rinsed, dried, loosely packed arugula leaves

Balsamic Vinegar Dressing

Combine the oil, shallots, vinegar, garlic pieces, salt, and pepper in a bowl. Before serving, discard the garlic pieces and vigorously blend the dressing with a fork.

Salad

1 Arrange 5 endive lettuce leaves, spoke-fashion, on each of 4 large dinner plates. Arrange 1 radicchio leaf in the center of each plate.

2 Put equal portions of arugula leaves in the center of the radicchio leaves. Spoon as much salad dressing as desired over the leaves and serve.

Coarsely chop 1 large ripe tomato and divide among the plates, or add 4 to 5 cooked shrimp to each serving.

Here's another simple, colorful salad that you can serve if you have one hour to prepare a meal.

Avocado and Tomato Salad

Tools: *Chef's knife, paring knife, salad bowl*

Preparation time: *About 25 minutes*

Cooking time: *About 15 minutes*

Yield: *4 servings*

2 ripe avocados

4 ripe plum tomatoes

2 hard-cooked eggs, peeled and quartered (optional)

1 small red onion, thinly sliced

¼ cup coarsely chopped cilantro

2 large cloves garlic, finely chopped

6 tablespoons olive oil

2 tablespoons red wine vinegar

½ teaspoon ground cumin

Salt and black pepper to taste

1 Halve and pit the avocados. Peel away the skin and cut each half into 4 lengthwise slices and then across into large cubes.

2 Core the tomatoes and cut them into 1-inch cubes.

3 Toss the cubes of avocado and tomato with all the remaining ingredients in a salad bowl and serve.

Or you may want to try one of these starter dishes if you have an hour or less:

- Garlic-Grilled Mushrooms (see Chapter 6)
- Layered Cheese and Vegetable Salad (see Chapter 10)
- Carrot Soup with Dill (see Chapter 9)
- Baked Shrimp with Green Onion Bread Crumbs (see Chapter 12)
- Watercress, Endive, and Orange Salad (see Chapter 10)

TIP

Making and storing dressings

To save the time and effort of making a vinai-grette every time you need one, make a large batch and store it in empty wine bottles. In a mixing bowl, combine 1 tablespoon or more of Dijon-style mustard with lots of salt and freshly ground black pepper. Add about ½ cup olive oil in a slow stream while whisking. Gradually whisk in vinegar (roughly a 5-to-2 ratio of oil to vinegar). Taste constantly. When you like the results, pour the dressing into the bottle with a funnel. If you like, add fresh herbs or minced garlic to the bottle. Shake, seal with a cork, and refrigerate.

Main dish choices

These recipes are enhanced with the anise-flavored aperitifs called Ricard and Pernod.

Snapper Fillets with Tomatoes and Fennel

Tools: *Chef's knife, paring knife, medium saucepan, sauté pan with lid*

Preparation time: *About 30 minutes*

Cooking time: *About 15 minutes*

Yield: *4 servings*

2 tablespoons olive oil

5 plum tomatoes, peeled, seeded, and chopped

1 large leek, white and light green part only, finely chopped

½ cup chopped fennel bulb

2 large cloves garlic, finely chopped

1 teaspoon turmeric

Salt and black pepper to taste

½ cup dry white wine

½ cup fish stock or bottled clam juice

1 bay leaf

4 sprigs fresh thyme, or 1 teaspoon dried

⅛ teaspoon Tabasco sauce

4 snapper fillets with skin on, or other white-fleshed fish, about 6 ounces each

2 tablespoons Ricard, Pernod, or other anise-flavored liquor

2 tablespoons chopped basil or parsley

(continued)

1 In a medium saucepan over medium heat, combine 1 tablespoon of the olive oil and the tomatoes, leeks, fennel, garlic, and turmeric. Season with salt and pepper. Cook, stirring often, about 3 minutes. Add the wine, broth, bay leaf, thyme, and Tabasco. Bring to a boil, reduce heat, and simmer for 5 minutes.

2 In a large sauté pan, add the remaining tablespoon of oil and arrange the fillets of fish in one layer, skin side down. Season with salt and pepper. Pour the leek-tomato mixture evenly over the fish fillets. Sprinkle the Ricard or Pernod, cover, and cook over medium heat for about 5 minutes until the fish is opaque in the center. (The exact cooking time depends on the thickness of the fillets.) Discard the bay leaf and sprinkle with basil or parsley before serving.

This zesty skirt steak dish is an alternative to flank steak. Adjust the seasonings to taste.

Broiled Skirt Steak, Cajun Style

Tools: *Chef's knife, mixing bowl, broiler or grill*

Preparation time: *About 35 minutes, including marinating time*

Cooking time: *About 10 minutes, including standing time*

Yield: *4 servings*

4 skirt steaks, ½ pound each	*½ teaspoon dried thyme*
Salt to taste	*¼ teaspoon cayenne pepper*
2 tablespoons olive oil	*¼ teaspoon black pepper*
1 teaspoon chili powder	*2 tablespoons butter*
½ teaspoon ground cumin	*2 tablespoons finely chopped fresh parsley*

1 Half an hour before broiling or grilling, sprinkle the steaks with salt. In a small bowl, combine the oil, chili powder, cumin, thyme, cayenne, and black pepper and stir well to mix. Brush this mixture all over the steaks. Cover the steaks with plastic wrap but do not refrigerate.

2 Preheat the broiler or set a charcoal or gas grill to medium-high.

3 If broiling, arrange the steaks on a rack and place under the broiler about 6 inches from the heat source. Broil for 3 minutes with the door partly open. Turn the steaks and continue broiling, leaving the door partly open. Broil for about 3 minutes more, for medium-rare, or to the desired degree of doneness. To check for doneness, make a small incision with a sharp knife into the center or thickest part of the steak. Medium-rare meat is bright red and juicy; medium has a light pink center with light brown edges and less juice.

If grilling, put the steaks on a medium hot, oiled grill and cover. Cook for 3 minutes. Turn the steaks, cover, and cook about 3 minutes more, for medium-rare, or to the desired degree of doneness.

4 Transfer the steaks to a hot platter and dot with butter. Let them stand in a warm place for 5 minutes to redistribute the internal juices, which accumulate as the steaks stand.

5 Sprinkle with parsley and serve with the accumulated butter sauce.

When you are trying to get everything together within an hour, you may want to serve a dish that finishes in the oven while you are doing other things, like panicking.

You also can try one of these main dishes if you have an hour:

- ✔ Grilled Brochettes of Pork with Rosemary (see Chapter 6)
- ✔ Frittata with Sweet Peppers and Potatoes (see Chapter 8)
- ✔ Rigatoni with Eggplant and Summer Squash (see Chapter 11)
- ✔ Sautéed Chicken Breasts with Tomatoes and Thyme (see Chapter 4)
- ✔ Sautéed Peppered Filet of Beef (see Chapter 4).

TIP

Skirt steak

Skirt steak, formerly unknown to home cooks and now a fashionable cut of meat in restaurants, goes by many names, including hanger steak, oyster steak, and butcher steak. The last name arose because butchers traditionally kept these exceptionally juicy and flavorful cuts for themselves.

If you know how to cook a skirt steak, it can be delicious and far less expensive (and leaner) than sirloins or fillets. The skirt steak comes from the pad of muscle that runs from the rib cage toward the loin (see beef chart in Chapter 14). It is usually sold in sections of about 12 ounces each and has a thin, silvery membrane that the butcher should remove.

Because skirt steak contains a lot of moisture, it should be cooked very fast over high heat to sear. For that reason, you should let the steak reach room temperature before broiling or grilling. Also let the cooked steak sit for several minutes before slicing, so the juices can settle. Cut the steak on a bias across the fibrous muscle on a cutting board that can catch the runoff. (*Cutting on a bias* means slicing the meat at about a 45-degree angle to the cutting board — not perpendicular to the board as you would with a loaf of bread. Cutting on a bias gives you a larger, thinner slice for each portion.) Pour the juice back over the steak when serving, or use it in your sauce.

Side dishes

The following colorful combination goes perfectly with steak. The dish is so easy and appealing that it could tempt anyone to flirt with vegetarianism. You can substitute summer squash, or even thin slices of eggplant, for the zucchini.

Roasted Zucchini and Tomatoes with Summer Herbs

Tools: *Chef's knife, medium saucepan or skillet, shallow gratin baking dish*

Preparation time: *About 25 minutes*

Cooking time: *About 40 minutes*

Yield: *4 servings*

3 tablespoons olive oil

1 large onion, thinly sliced

3 large cloves garlic, minced

1 tablespoon chopped sage, or 1 teaspoon dried

1 tablespoon chopped rosemary, or 1 teaspoon dried

2 teaspoons chopped basil, or 1 teaspoon dried

1½ pounds zucchini, trimmed and sliced into ¼-inch rounds

Salt and black pepper to taste

3 large ripe red tomatoes, sliced ¼-inch thick

⅓ cup freshly grated Parmesan cheese

1 Preheat the oven to 375 degrees.

2 In a medium saucepan or skillet over medium heat, add 2 tablespoons of the olive oil, the onion, garlic, and half the herbs. Cook, stirring often, for about 3 minutes (do not let the garlic brown). Remove the mixture to a shallow baking dish.

3 In the same skillet, add the remaining tablespoon of olive oil, the zucchini, remaining herbs, salt, and pepper. Cook, stirring occasionally, for about 5 minutes.

4 Place the zucchini in the baking dish and blend well with the onions. Lay the tomatoes over the zucchini in a decorative fashion. Sprinkle the Parmesan cheese over the tomatoes.

5 Cover with aluminum foil and bake for about 20 minutes. Remove cover and bake 10 minutes more.

This exotic-tasting rice goes well with any steak or poultry dish as long as the sauce does not contain the same seasonings.

Ginger Rice with Cilantro

Tools: *Chef's knife, medium saucepan or sauté pan, grater*

Preparation time: *About 15 minutes*

Cooking time: *About 20 minutes*

Yield: *4 servings*

2 tablespoons butter

¼ cup finely chopped onion

1 teaspoon grated fresh ginger

¼ teaspoon red pepper flakes, or to taste

1 cup converted rice

1¾ cups homemade or canned chicken or vegetable stock, heated to just below boiling

Salt to taste

3 tablespoons finely chopped cilantro or parsley

1 Heat the butter in a saucepan over medium heat. Add the onion and cook, stirring often, until the onion is wilted, about 2 to 3 minutes. Add the ginger and pepper flakes. Cook, stirring constantly, for about 30 seconds. Stir in the rice, coating the grains in the melted butter. Carefully add the hot chicken stock. Season with salt, if desired.

2 Cover and simmer over low heat for 20 minutes or until the rice is tender. Stir in the cilantro or parsley and taste for seasoning just before serving.

Desserts

This warm blueberry sauce goes well with ice cream, pastries, or even a simple pound cake. This basic technique works for all fresh berries.

Warm Blueberry Sauce

Tools: *Paring knife, saucepan, whisk*

Preparation time: *About 10 minutes*

Cooking time: *About 7 minutes*

Yield: *4 servings*

(continued)

⅓ cup granulated sugar

1 tablespoon cornstarch

Pinch salt

¾ cup water

2 teaspoons fresh lemon juice

1 cup ripe blueberries, rinsed and stems removed

2 tablespoons butter, softened

¼ teaspoon ground cinnamon, or to taste

1 In a saucepan, thoroughly combine the sugar, cornstarch, and salt. Add the water and lemon juice and cook over medium-high heat, whisking frequently, until the mixture thickens, about 3 to 5 minutes.

2 Add the blueberries and lower the heat to medium, whisking frequently, for 1 minute. Remove the pan from the heat and add the butter and cinnamon. Stir well. Keep warm in a double boiler until ready to serve. Stir well before serving.

If You Have 30 Minutes

What can you do in 30 minutes? Half an aerobics class? Almost wash the car? Watch the first part of *60 Minutes*? Not much fun, huh? But you can prepare a meal in this time if you follow our approach.

The good news is that you don't have to worry too much about orchestrating your time; the bad news is that's because you'll be doing everything at once. Before you dive in, give some thought to what tasks, if any, you can combine. Chop all the vegetables together, for example. Do two of your dishes call for celery? Prepare enough for both at one time. Another key time-saver is to have all your materials out and ready before you begin so that you don't get thrown off track mid-menu trying to locate the darn marjoram.

Putting a meal on the table in 30 minutes also often means that you have to rely on certain store-bought goods for help and give your timesaving gadgets in the kitchen a real workout. But in the end, you have a real meal.

The following recipes are meant to steer you into a certain way of thinking when the clock's incessant ticking is following you all over the house and your guests will be arriving in no time.

Starter dishes

In France, tartines are open-faced sandwiches that can be topped with cheese, meats, fish, or whatever. This tasty version calls for goat cheese and olive oil and couldn't be easier. These tidbits are superb with red wine. (See *Wine For Dummies,* 2nd Edition, by Ed McCarthy and Mary Ewing-Mulligan (IDG Books Worldwide, Inc.) for more information about pairing food with wine.)

Garlic and Goat Cheese Tartines

Tools: *Toaster oven (optional), bread knife*

Preparation time: *About 10 minutes*

Cooking time: *Less than a minute*

Yield: *6 to 8 servings*

½ loaf French or Italian bread, cut into ¼- to ½-inch slices

3 cloves garlic, peeled and halved

About ¼ cup olive oil

Salt and black pepper to taste

8 ounces fresh goat cheese

1 to 2 tablespoons finely chopped fresh chives, thyme, or basil (or all three combined to make 1 to 2 tablespoons)

1 In a toaster oven or preheated 400-degree oven, toast the bread slices until they just begin to turn golden, no more. Let the bread cool.

2 Rub the bread on both sides with the cut side of the garlic. Drizzle about ½ teaspoon olive oil over one side of each slice. Lightly salt and pepper the same side.

3 Spread goat cheese over the slices and garnish with chopped fresh herbs.

And with a little practice, you can knock off any of these appetizers in minutes:

- ✔ **Hummus dip:** Whirl in a blender until smooth a 16-ounce can of drained chickpeas, 1 clove garlic, ¼ cup sesame seeds, the juice and grated zest of 1 lemon, ½ cup water, with salt and black pepper to taste. Serve on triangles of toasted pita or with assorted raw vegetables.

- ✔ **Sweet mustard chicken kebobs:** Thread thin strips of boneless chicken and cherry tomatoes on skewers (preferably metal, which cook the meat faster and, unlike wooden skewers, don't require presoaking); grill or broil about 2 minutes a side or until done, brushing at the last minute with store-bought honey mustard. Serve hot.

- **Guacamole:** Mash in a small bowl the flesh from 2 medium, ripe avocados. Add 1 small, finely chopped onion, 1 ripe finely chopped tomato, 2 tablespoons chopped cilantro, half a jalapeño chili, seeded and minced, and the juice and grated zest of half a lemon. Season with salt and black pepper and serve with blue or white corn chips.

- **Sun-dried tomato spread:** Whirl sun-dried tomatoes, garlic, and onions in a food processor or blender container with enough oil to moisten into a coarse spread. Season with white pepper. Serve on Melba toast rounds.

- **Smoked chicken slices with coriander sauce:** You can buy smoked chicken and slice it into bite-sized strips, serving the strips over thin slices of French or Italian bread. Brush with a basic vinaigrette seasoned with chopped cilantro, and, if you like, a dash of Tabasco sauce.

Main dish choices

If you have only about 30 minutes, you also can try any of these main dishes:

- Salmon Steaks with Red Bell Pepper Sauce (see Chapter 4)
- Steamed Lobsters with Orange-Lemon Butter (see Chapter 3)
- Sautéed Chicken Breasts with Tomatoes and Thyme (see Chapter 4)
- Mustard-Brushed Barbecued Chicken Breasts (see Chapter 6)
- Chicken Breasts with Garlic and Capers (see Chapter 7)
- Omelets or Frittatas (see Chapter 8)
- Spaghetti with Quick Fresh Tomato Sauce (see Chapter 11)
- Sautéed Peppered Filet of Beef (see Chapter 4)

Desserts

As for dessert, you can serve fresh fruit and ice cream. Or, you can make a nice, quick ice cream sauce with frozen strawberries (or fresh, of course, if they're in season). See Chapter 7 for a recipe for Fresh Strawberry Sauce. The Caramel Sauce and Cracklin' Hot Fudge Sauce from Chapter 7 are also great with ice cream.

If you have only 30 minutes, you also can try sweetened Whipped Cream (see Chapter 7) to add on top of fresh fruit or ice cream.

TIP

Shop and platter: The art of antipasto

When you barely have time to shop, much less prepare a full meal, knowing how to buy and assemble various foods into an attractive spread is an invaluable skill. As a source of inspiration, we recommend an Italian approach that calls for serving an array of cheeses, meats, breads, olives, and vegetables on a large platter.

Assembling an Italian *antipasto* is 50 percent presentation. Think about how the tastes and colors contrast. Antipasto is traditionally served as the appetizer course, but there's no reason you can't make a meal of it. Here is an incomplete list of choices for an antipasto platter that you can purchase about half an hour before your guests arrive — that is, if you catch all the green lights on the way home from the market.

- Mozzarella, provolone, Fontina, Parmesan, or goat cheese (cubed or thinly sliced)

- Thinly sliced ham, prosciutto, and Genoa salami

- Rounds of pepperoni or sopressata salami

- Thin slices of *mortadella* (a garlic-flavored bologna) or *capicola* (made from cured pork)

- Cooked shrimp (best if tossed in a vinaigrette dressing)

- Canned anchovies, sardines, or tuna packed in olive oil

- Canned chickpeas tossed in vinaigrette dressing (you need to make the dressing)

- Sun-dried tomatoes in oil

- Marinated artichoke hearts, roasted red peppers, and capers

- Assorted black and green olives

- Assorted fresh vegetables like radishes with tops; carrot, celery, cucumber, and pepper sticks; pieces of fennel; green onions; and whole red or yellow cherry tomatoes

- Arugula, basil leaves, and radicchio for garnishing

- Sliced ripe pears, melon, figs, or small bunches of grapes

- Flavored breads, breadsticks, flatbreads, and warmed Boboli (a brand of flat bread that resembles a thick pizza crust)

Chapter 17

Cook Once, Eat Thrice

· ·

In This Chapter

▶ Making one recipe last several days

▶ Figuring out how to stir-fry like a pro

· ·

*N*o matter how crazy about cooking you become as you read this book, you will undoubtedly be too busy to cook from time to time. Long work days, the kids' Little League games, social commitments, running out of gas on the way home, and so on all contribute to make your life the hectic mess it sometimes is. This chapter addresses those inevitabilities. You can save the day by cooking one large meal — say, twice as large as needed. Then, on following days, you can toss together quick meals using the leftovers. If you want, you can freeze some of the next days' meals until you need them.

Take a look at the following sections for menu suggestions to take you and your family through the next two or three days.

Porkathon

The first group of meals we recommend starts with a great pork recipe:

✔ Meal 1: Pork with Winter Vegetables

✔ Meal 2: Smoked Pork Hash

✔ Meal 3: Pasta and Bean Soup

Pork, which is lean (with today's breeding techniques), versatile, and delicious, lends itself to this multiple cooking technique.

Pork shoulder, for some anatomically illogical reason, is also sold by the name "pork butt." The pork shoulder (or pork butt) is the upper part of a hog's shoulder. It's firm, rosy, and well-marbled meat that is used often for making pâtés and sausages. Pork shoulder is usually sold trimmed and tied to hold its shape while cooking.

The following recipe can be used as a dinner to serve 8, with no leftovers. Or, you can make it for 4 people, with plenty of leftovers to make the two follow-up dishes we recommend: a pork and vegetable hash, and a delicious pasta and bean soup.

Smoked Pork with Winter Vegetables

Tools: *Chef's knife, vegetable peeler, large pot, slotted spoon*

Preparation time: *10 minutes (plus 5 minutes for soaking)*

Cooking time: *1½ hours*

Yield: *8 servings (or 4 servings, with enough left over for the following dishes)*

3 pounds boneless smoked pork shoulder (also called smoked pork butt)

1 large onion, peeled and halved

2 bay leaves

10 black peppercorns

6 carrots, peeled and quartered crosswise

6 medium baking potatoes, peeled and quartered

3 large parsnips, peeled and quartered crosswise

½ head green cabbage, cut into 3 to 4 wedges

¼ cup chopped parsley (for garnish)

Salt and black pepper to taste

1 stick softened butter (for the vegetables)

Dijon-style mustard, to taste (for the meat)

1 Remove the netting from the pork butt and soak the meat in warm water for about 5 minutes to remove excess salt.

2 Place the pork, onion, bay leaves, and peppercorn in a large pot; add cold water to cover. Cover the pot and bring the water to a boil; reduce the heat and simmer for 1 hour and 10 minutes, adding more water if necessary to keep the pork immersed in the liquid.

3 Remove the onion and bay leaves with a slotted spoon and discard. Add the carrots, potatoes, and parsnips to the pot and bring the liquid to a boil again; reduce the heat and simmer for 10 minutes. Add the cabbage and return to a boil; reduce the heat and simmer for another 10 to 15 minutes or until the pork and vegetables are tender.

4 Remove the meat from the simmering liquid and slice it into serving portions; arrange the slices on a serving platter. Remove the vegetables with a slotted spoon and arrange them around the meat. (Reserve the cooking liquid to make the Pasta and Bean Soup later in this section.) Sprinkle the meat and vegetables with chopped parsley. Season the vegetables with salt and pepper. Serve with small bowls of butter, to mash into the steaming vegetables, and mustard, for the pork.

We wrote this recipe so that the pork and vegetables are cooked at the same time. However, if the potatoes start to fall apart in the broth, remove them with a slotted spoon to a buttered baking dish. Cover the dish with foil and keep warm in a 200-degree oven until you need them.

If you can't find smoked port butt in your supermarket, you can make this recipe with a 3-pound boneless smoked ham.

After you've served the Smoked Pork with Winter Vegetables, you can use the leftovers to make the following dish. This recipe stands on its own as a light supper, perhaps with a green salad and bread; or you can make it a country breakfast by adding fried eggs and serving with toasted cornbread muffins.

Smoked Pork Hash

Tools: *Chef's knife, large skillet (cast-iron is best), metal spatula*

Preparation time: *About 10 minutes*

Cooking time: *About 15 minutes*

Yield: *4 servings*

3 tablespoons vegetable oil

1 cup chopped onion

2 cups cubed cooked smoked pork butt, trimmed of excess fat

2 to 3 cups drained, cubed, leftover vegetables, excluding the cabbage, from Smoked Pork with Winter Vegetables

Salt and black pepper to taste

3 tablespoons chopped parsley for garnish

1 In a large skillet, heat the oil over medium heat; add the onion and cook, stirring often, until translucent, about 2 to 3 minutes.

(continued)

2 Gently stir in the cooked pork and the vegetables so they are well mixed; adjust seasoning with salt and pepper to taste. Using a metal spatula, press down on the hash to compress it against the bottom of the skillet. Cook, without stirring, until the bottom is well browned, 10 to 15 minutes. (If desired, place the skillet under the broiler, about 6 inches from the heat, for 3 to 4 minutes, to brown the top.) Using a metal spatula lift and invert the hash onto individual serving plates. Garnish with chopped parsley.

Round out this great meal by pairing the hash with Scrambled Eggs (see Chapter 2) or a Mixed Summer Salad with Balsamic Vinegar (see Chapter 16).

A well-seasoned cast-iron skillet will give hash a deep brown crust. You can use a nonstick skillet and reduce the oil to 2 tablespoons from 3 because the coating on the pan keeps the crust from burning. But the crust on the hash will be lighter.

You can really let your creative cooking side go wild and dress up this hash with different seasonings and ingredients:

✔ Add 1 to 2 chopped, seeded, jalapeño or other chili peppers along with the onions.

✔ Add 1 large seeded and chopped green or red bell pepper to the onions.

✔ Add 1 cup of cooked frozen or canned corn with the vegetables.

✔ Add 1 tablespoon chopped fresh herbs, such as rosemary, thyme, or marjoram, with the cooked vegetables.

✔ Sprinkle some hot sauce, like Tabasco, over the cooking vegetables.

Few kitchen tasks are more satisfying to a home cook (or a professional chef, for that matter) than making a delicious soup using rich, homemade broth derived from another dish. The smoked pork butt adds just the right salty, meaty tones to this soup's broth. Pasta and Bean Soup is one dish that tastes even better the next day.

Pasta and Bean Soup

Tools: *Chef's knife, vegetable peeler, grater, large pot, ladle*

Preparation time: *10 minutes*

Cooking time: *25 minutes*

Yield: *8 servings*

¼ cup olive oil

1 medium onion, peeled and chopped

2 carrots, peeled and diced

1 stalk celery, diced

1 large clove garlic, peeled and chopped

1 14½-ounce can diced tomatoes

7 to 8 cups broth saved from Smoked Pork with Winter Vegetables

1 tablespoon chopped fresh basil, or 1 teaspoon dried

1 teaspoon chopped fresh thyme, or ½ teaspoon dried

1 15-ounce can cannellini or red kidney beans, rinsed and drained

1 bay leaf

1 cup small dried pasta, such as elbow macaroni

Salt and black pepper to taste

Grated Parmesan cheese for garnish

1 In a large, heavy-bottomed soup pot or saucepan, heat the oil over medium heat. Add the onion and cook, stirring occasionally, until wilted, about 5 minutes. Stir in the carrots, celery, and garlic and cook over medium-high heat another 5 minutes, or until the vegetables are softened, stirring often.

2 Add the diced tomatoes with their juice, 7 cups of the broth, the basil, and thyme; cover the pot, bring to a boil, then reduce the heat and simmer gently for 20 minutes.

3 Carefully ladle 1½ to 2 cups of the soup into a blender container; pulse for just a few seconds. Stir the mixture back into the soup.

4 Add the cannellini or kidney beans, and the bay leaf; cover the pot and simmer another 5 minutes.

5 Add the macaroni and cook, partially covered, only until al dente, or firm to the bite; stir occasionally. If, after cooking the pasta, too much of the liquid has evaporated and the soup seems a little thick, add enough of the remaining broth to thin to a desired consistency.

6 Remove the bay leaf. Adjust seasoning with salt and pepper to taste. Ladle soup into bowls; sprinkle each with grated cheese.

A salad and bread always go well with a substantial soup. Try the Mixed Green Salad with Red Onion (see Chapter 10).

 You could add to this soup 1 cup of cooked, chopped cabbage; 1 cup cooked, diced potatoes; or ½ to 1 cup cooked, diced pork — all from the Smoked Pork with Winter Vegetables recipe in this section.

Here are a few other ideas for using leftover cooked pork shoulder or butt:

- ✔ Use the cold, sliced pork for sandwiches, along with mustard, chutney, or relish.
- ✔ For a hearty breakfast, cook pork slices in a small, buttered skillet and serve with eggs.
- ✔ Make a main course salad by adding chopped cooked pork to a bowl of salad greens, perhaps with Swiss cheese and hard-boiled eggs. Toss in a mustard-vinaigrette dressing.

On the Lamb

In this section, we give you three dishes, based on a roasted leg of lamb.

- ✔ Meal 1: Roasted Leg of Lamb (see Chapter 6 for the recipe)
- ✔ Meal 2: Lamb Curry
- ✔ Meal 3: Sliced Lamb Sandwiches with Red Onion and Mango Chutney

A large roasted leg of lamb often has lots of meat left around the bone. This curry is a perfect way to use it. The flavors intensify if the curry is refrigerated overnight.

Lamb Curry

Tools: *Chef's knife, grater, large saucepan*

Preparation time: *About 15 minutes*

Cooking time: *About 45 minutes*

Yield: *3 to 4 servings*

1 tablespoon olive oil

½ tablespoon butter

1 large onion, chopped

1 medium red bell pepper, cored, seeded, and diced

2 teaspoons seeded and minced jalapeño or other hot chili pepper (optional)

1 clove garlic, minced

1 tablespoon peeled, grated fresh ginger

1 tablespoon curry powder

½ teaspoon ground cumin

1½ cups homemade or canned beef stock

¼ cup plus 2 tablespoons canned coconut milk

1 tablespoon tomato paste

2½ to 3 cups 1-inch cubed cooked lamb, trimmed of excess fat

⅓ cup golden raisins

Salt and black pepper to taste

4 cups cooked long-grain rice

Optional accompaniments: mango chutney, chopped dry-roasted peanuts, chopped parsley or cilantro

1 In a large, deep saucepan heat the oil and butter over medium-high heat. Add the onion, red pepper, jalapeño pepper (if desired), and garlic, and cook for about 4 to 5 minutes, stirring often, until the vegetables begin to soften. Stir in the ginger, curry powder, and cumin; cook about 1 minute, stirring.

2 Stir in the beef stock, coconut milk, and tomato paste; bring to a boil. Stir in the lamb. Reduce the heat, cover, and simmer for 20 minutes. Add the raisins and simmer for another 20 minutes. Season to taste with salt and pepper. Serve over rice with suggested accompaniments, if desired.

Lamb curry is an assertive dish, packed with flavor, so you should pair it with something mild, such as a Cucumber-Dill Salad (see Chapter 10) or White Rice (see Chapter 3).

Another way to use leftover lamb is in sandwiches. Make the sandwiches with the cold sliced lamb and a slathering of chutney.

A good chutney tastes both sweet and savory at the same time with flavors more complex than a jam or jelly. A mixture of fruits, onions, sugar, and vinegar, chutney makes a great sandwich condiment to strong-tasting meats like pork or beef tenderloin, lamb, or a grilled hamburger. The ingredients for chutney are extremely flexible. In the following recipe you could try substituting firm peaches for the mangoes, or add dark raisins, or chopped green pepper, if you like.

Red Onion and Mango Chutney

Tools: *Medium saucepan, wooden spoon, chef's knife*

Preparation time: *About 20 minutes*

Cooking time: *About 25 to 30 minutes*

Yield: *About 2 cups*

(continued)

2 tablespoons vegetable oil

1 cup chopped red onion

1 to 2 (or to taste) jalapeño peppers, or other hot chili pepper, seeded and minced

2 teaspoons peeled, minced fresh ginger

1 clove garlic, minced

½ cup plus 2 tablespoons packed brown sugar

½ cup cider vinegar

2 large ripe mangoes, peeled and cut into ¼-inch cubes (see Figure 17-1 for instructions)

Salt and black pepper to taste (optional)

1 In a medium saucepan, heat the oil over medium heat; add the onion and sauté for 4 to 5 minutes, or until slightly browned, stirring often. Add the jalapeño, ginger, and garlic, and cook for 1 minute more, stirring. (Do not let the garlic brown.)

2 Remove the saucepan from the heat; stir in the brown sugar and vinegar. Return the saucepan to the heat; bring the mixture to a boil. Reduce the heat and simmer for 3 to 4 minutes. Stir in the mango.

3 Raise the heat and bring the mixture to a boil. Reduce the heat and simmer, partially covered, for 15 to 20 minutes, or until the mango is tender. (Exact cooking time may vary, depending on the ripeness of the mango.) Taste and adjust seasoning, if desired, with salt and pepper. Chill and serve as a condiment on lamb sandwiches. It's also good with grilled chicken or beef.

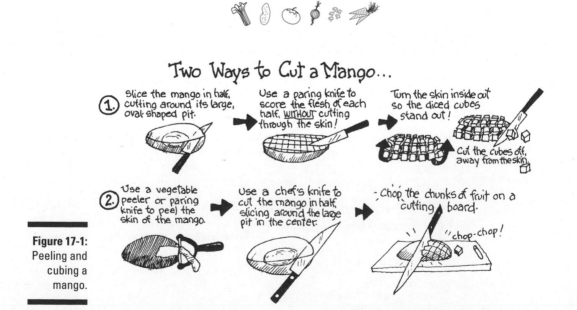

Two Ways to Cut a Mango...

① Slice the mango in half, cutting around its large, oval shaped pit.

Use a paring knife to score the flesh of each half, WITHOUT cutting through the skin!

Turn the skin inside out so the diced cubes stand out!

Cut the cubes off, away from the skin.

② Use a vegetable peeler or paring knife to peel the skin of the mango.

Use a chef's knife to cut the mango in half, slicing around the large pit in the center.

Chop the chunks of fruit on a cutting board.

"chop-chop!"

Figure 17-1: Peeling and cubing a mango.

A ripe mango is slightly soft to the touch, with at least half of its otherwise green skin tinged with orange, yellow, or red coloring.

Chicken

If you roast or poach a large chicken (for example, 4 or 5 pounds), you will have enough leftovers to make the following three recipes. You may even want to roast two chickens while you're at it!

- ✔ Meal 1: Roasted Chicken (see Chapter 6)
- ✔ Meal 2: Chicken, Avocado, and Red Onion Salad
- ✔ Meal 3: Chicken and Grilled Vegetable Wrap

This chicken salad uses leftover roasted chicken from the recipe in Chapter 6. However, if you don't have 3 cups of leftover chicken, simmer a whole chicken breast (or less depending on what you need) in chicken broth (or in water, seasoned with salt, pepper, and lemon juice) for about 10 minutes, or until the chicken is fully cooked (you can tell the chicken is fully cooked when you slice it in the center and see no pink).

The dressing for this colorful salad is first used as a marinade for the cooked and diced chicken. Use generous amounts of salt and pepper in the dressing and on the salad ingredients to pull out the flavors of the fresh vegetables.

Chicken, Avocado, and Red Onion Salad

Tools: *Chef's knife, medium mixing bowl*

Preparation time: *20 to 25 minutes*

Cooking time: *None (30 minutes refrigeration time)*

Yield: *4 servings*

2 tablespoons cider vinegar

2 tablespoons fresh lemon juice

1 teaspoon Dijon mustard

½ cup olive oil

2 tablespoons chopped fresh herbs, such as basil, tarragon, and/or marjoram, or to taste (or 2 teaspoons dried herbs)

2 cloves garlic, minced

Salt and black pepper to taste

3 cups cubed cooked chicken

6 cups spinach, rinsed and torn into bite-size pieces

2 cups Boston lettuce, rinsed and torn into bite-size pieces

(continued)

2 ripe avocados, peeled, pitted, and cut
into ½-inch cubes

½ cup crumbled blue cheese (or other
favorite cheese)

8 slices bacon, cooked and broken into
small pieces

16 cherry tomatoes, stemmed and halved

1 small red onion, chopped

1 In a medium mixing bowl, whisk together the vinegar, lemon juice, and mustard. Slowly add the olive oil, whisking constantly to incorporate it into the vinegar-lemon juice mixture. Stir in the herbs, garlic, salt, and pepper. Add the chicken and toss well. Refrigerate for at least 30 minutes.

2 Divide the salad greens among four individual plates. Place equal amounts of the chicken on top of the greens. Reserve the small amount of vinaigrette that remains in the bottom of the mixing bowl.

3 Arrange an equal amount of the avocado, blue cheese, bacon, cherry tomatoes, and red onion around the chicken on each plate; drizzle the remaining marinade over everything. If desired, adjust seasoning with salt and pepper; serve immediately.

Toasted corn muffins are the perfect accompaniment to this salad. You could also serve this salad with a side dish of Garlic Grilled Mushrooms (see Chapter 6).

Roasted Chicken can be served with any kind of salad, grilled or roasted vegetables, or potatoes. Our suggestions include Mashed Potatoes (See Chapter 3), Roasted Zucchini with Summer Herbs (See Chapter 16), and Homestyle Kale (Chapter 15).

You can substitute 16 to 20 pitted black olives for the cherry tomatoes. You can also add 4 chopped, hard-cooked eggs to the base of the greens, or use other types of mixed greens entirely.

When buying an avocado, feel the skin; it should be slightly soft but not mushy. If you want to ripen the avocado quickly at home, place it in a paper bag along with an orange, close the bag, and let it sit overnight. Oranges emit a gas called ethylene, which causes other fruits — apples, melons, tomatoes, bananas — to ripen quickly. In fact, avocados, bananas, and tomatoes are usually shipped hard and then placed in rooms filled with ethylene.

A *wrap* is a sandwich made with flatbreads, such as flour tortillas, that roll around a filling of vegetables, poultry, meat, or fish. Unlike a sandwich, the fillings in a wrap are usually diced, shredded, or thinly sliced. In this next recipe, we've designed a wrap using leftover cooked chicken, grilled vegetables, and a sour cream-yogurt dressing.

Chicken and Grilled Vegetable Wrap

Tools: *Chef's knife, charcoal or gas grill, brush for oiling the grill grates, baking sheet, large mixing bowl, blender, small pitcher*

Preparation time: *About 15 minutes*

Cooking time: *10 to 15 minutes*

Yield: *4 to 5 servings*

½ small eggplant (about ½ pound), cut lengthwise into ½-inch thick slices

1 red or yellow bell pepper, cored, seeded, and quartered

1 green bell pepper, cored, seeded, and quartered

1 medium red or yellow onion, cut into ½-inch slices

1 medium zucchini or yellow squash, cut lengthwise into ½-inch-thick slices

Oil for coating the vegetables and the grill

2 cups cooked chicken, cut into ½-inch cubes

¼ cup chopped basil or parsley

Salt and black pepper to taste

¾ cup sour cream

¼ cup low-fat yogurt

5 large 8- to 9-inch flour tortillas

1 Prepare a medium-hot fire in a charcoal or gas grill.

2 As the grill preheats, brush the vegetables with the oil, coating all sides. Brush the grill grate with the oil. Place the eggplant, peppers, onion, and zucchini or squash on the grill grate; grill, turning often, until the vegetables are lightly browned on both sides, about 10 to 15 minutes. Remove the vegetables to a baking sheet and let them stand until they are cool enough to handle.

3 Chop all the vegetables into ½-inch-thick pieces. Transfer the vegetables to a large mixing bowl; add the chicken and 2 tablespoons of the chopped basil or parsley and toss well. Season to taste with salt and pepper.

4 In a blender container, combine the sour cream, yogurt, and the remaining 2 tablespoons of the basil or parsley. Blend a few seconds or until the dressing is well incorporated; season to taste with salt and pepper.

5 Divide the chicken-vegetable mixture among the tortillas, leaving a 1- to 2-inch border. Drizzle 1 to 2 tablespoons of the sour cream-yogurt dressing over the filling. Transfer the remaining dressing to a small pitcher.

6 On 2 opposite sides of the tortilla, fold the tortilla ½ inch over the filling; then take one of the unfolded sides and start rolling to the end. Serve with the remaining sour cream-yogurt dressing.

(continued)

Any number of soups, including Fresh Tomato Gazpacho (see Chapter 9), Spring Vegetable Soup (see Chapter 16), or Black Bean Soup (see Chapter 9), would make a fine match to this chicken wrap.

Warming the tortillas in the microwave for about 30 seconds just before you use them makes the tortillas easier to work with.

You can make all kinds of wrap fillings based on ingredients in your refrigerator or pantry. Substitute any of these vegetables for the ones in our recipe: grilled portabello mushrooms (see recipe for Garlic-Grilled Mushrooms in Chapter 6), tomatoes, radicchio leaves, asparagus spears, sliced fennel, and more.

Before grilling onions, slice them thickly, ½ to ¾ inch, to keep them from falling apart and slipping between the grill grate and into the fire. Oil the grill and use a metal spatula to turn the slices only once, but wait until they've charred a bit on one side. Cooking time is about 4 minutes per side.

If you don't have an outdoor grill or the weather prevents you from using it, you can still grill with a stovetop grill pan, which looks like a frying pan but has ridges over the cooking surface that provide the great smoky flavor and sought-after marks of an outdoor grill. The pan comes in a variety of shapes and with nonstick or cast-iron surfaces.

More Pork

- ✔ Meal 1: Pork Tenderloins with Potatoes and Apples or Roasted Loin of Pork (see Chapter 6)
- ✔ Meal 2: Pork and Noodle Stir-Fry
- ✔ Meal 3: Pork Sandwiches with Assorted Dressings, Butters, and Condiments

After you make the Pork Tenderloins with Potatoes and Apples or Roasted Loin of Pork found in Chapter 6, you can use the leftovers to make a great stir-fry. Stir-frying is an easy technique to master and is the perfect way to use up leftover meat, poultry, or vegetables. When stir-frying, the oil in the wok or skillet should be very hot before adding the ingredients, but not so hot that it begins to smoke. You don't need a wok to stir-fry — a large skillet will do.

Before you start stir-frying, be sure to have all of your ingredients cleaned, chopped, and ready to go. Being prepared, with everything in its place, is called *mise en place* in French cooking. Measure and organize your ingredients, and set them up right next to the stove before you heat the cooking oil (as shown in Figure 17-2). Your aim is to place all the ingredients right at your fingertips for a quick and timely addition to the skillet.

Figure 17-2:
Have all of your ingredients ready to go before you start to stir-fry.

To make this dish you can use pork that is leftover from Pork Tenderloin with Potatoes and Apples (see Chapter 6) or Roast Loin of Pork (see Chapter 6). Or you can start with raw pork and stir-fry it separately before adding the vegetables to the skillet.

Pork and Noodle Stir-Fry

Tools: *Chef's knife, grater, vegetable peeler, large pot, colander, mixing bowl, wok or large skillet*

Preparation time: *About 15 minutes*

Cooking time: *About 15 minutes*

Yield: *4 servings*

½ pound dried Chinese noodles (available in Asian groceries), or thin spaghetti or linguini (broken in half)

2 teaspoons sesame oil

3 tablespoons light soy sauce

1 tablespoon dry or medium-dry sherry

2 teaspoons cornstarch

1 teaspoon packed brown sugar

2 cups thinly sliced cooked pork

2 tablespoons vegetable oil

(continued)

1 tablespoon peeled and grated ginger root

3 cups thinly sliced Napa cabbage, bok choy, or green cabbage

1 cup thinly sliced or shredded carrot

½ cup homemade or canned chicken stock

3 thinly sliced green onions (white and green parts)

1 large clove garlic, peeled and minced

½ jalapeño or red chili pepper, seeded and chopped (optional)

Salt and black pepper to taste

3 tablespoons chopped cilantro

1 Bring a large pot of lightly salted water to a boil; add the noodles and cook according to package directions. (Do not overcook, or the noodles will be mushy.) Drain and rinse the noodles under cold water; drain again. Transfer the noodles to a medium mixing bowl; toss them with the sesame oil to keep them from sticking together. Set aside.

2 In a medium mixing bowl, stir together 2 tablespoons of the soy sauce, the sherry, cornstarch, and brown sugar; add the pork and toss to mix well. Set aside.

3 Place a wok or large skillet over high heat. Add the vegetable oil and heat until the oil is hot but not yet smoking. Add the ginger and stir just a few seconds, or until it browns lightly. Add the cabbage, carrots, chicken stock, green onions, garlic, jalapeño pepper (if desired), and pork with all of the marinade. Cook, tossing the ingredients often, for 3 to 5 minutes, or until the vegetables are crisp-tender.

4 Remove the wok from the heat; add the noodles and toss thoroughly. Stir in the remaining tablespoon of soy sauce. Season to taste with salt and pepper. Sprinkle with the cilantro before serving.

Soup is a natural starter for this Asian-style dish. You could serve a light Carrot Soup with Dill (see Chapter 9), Spring Vegetable Soup (see Chapter 16), or Spinach Cloud Soup (see Chapter 9).

This stir-fry recipe can be divided in half to serve two instead of four. And you can substitute any number of ingredients. For example, you can use thinly sliced red peppers instead of the carrots. If you have leftover chicken instead of pork, you can use that instead. You could also substitute 2 to 3 cups of medium, shelled raw shrimp for the pork. Using light soy sauce, as the recipe calls for, adds a subtle salt flavor, but if you prefer a more intense flavor, use regular soy sauce instead. If you prefer, substitute 3 to 4 cups of cooked rice for the noodles. But don't toss the rice into the stir-fry; use it as a bed on which to place the pork and vegetable mixture.

Use two forks or two large wooden spoons to toss the shredded ingredients in the hot oil. The tossing doesn't have to be constant, but tossing thoroughly and often exposes all of the ingredients to the hot oil, and causes them to cook quickly.

To speed up the cooking you can cover the wok or skillet immediately after adding the vegetables and pork to the oil, but remove the cover after about 45 seconds so you can watch the mixture to keep it from scorching.

If the mixture in the wok gets dry, add a little more chicken stock and toss well. Always keep your eye on the wok to make sure there is a little liquid in the bottom.

Bok choy, with its long white stem and dark, ribbed leaves, resembles Romaine lettuce in its shape. Bok choy is a staple in Chinese cooking. It has a very mild flavor and comes in different sizes. The smaller bok choy is best for stir-frying, while the larger ones are best used in soups. Bok choy is available year-round in well-stocked groceries and Asian markets.

Napa cabbage is a laid-back term for common Chinese cabbage. It comes in two varieties. One variety is stout, with a thick core and wide leaves; the other is longer and narrower, with tall, clinging leaves. The flavor of both is more subtle than that of round cabbage, which makes it excellent for stir-frying. Napa cabbage is widely available in supermarkets.

Part V
Special Occasions

The 5th Wave   By Rich Tennant

"I'm creating a special birthday meal for a professor of ancient marine life, so give me the oldest fish you've got."

In this part . . .

The chapters in this part are the ones to turn to when you have a herd of people coming to your house in a few days and you need to figure out what to feed them. Whether you're planning a Super Bowl party for the whole gang, or you're hosting a traditional holiday meal, we provide the recipes you need in these chapters. Plus, we help you prepare for the party in advance, guiding you through the process of cooking ahead of time so that you can relax on the day of the party and enjoy yourself.

Chapter 18

Summertime Soiree

● ●

In This Chapter

▶ Planning a menu for a summertime party

▶ Making the perfect fried chicken

▶ Serving up summertime side dishes

▶ Making a dessert perfect for the patriotic

▶ Knowing how to make lemonade that's worth every nickel

● ●

> ### Recipes in This Chapter
>
> ▶ Fried Chicken for a Crowd
>
> ▶ Baked Beans
>
> ↻ Perfect Corn on the Cob
>
> ↻ All-American Coleslaw
>
> ↻ Macaroni and Ham Salad with Mustard Dressing
>
> ↻ Red, White, and Blue Berry Shortcake
>
> ↻ Strawberry Lemonade
>
> ↻ Watermelon Lemonade
>
>

Summer is filled with opportunities for outdoor gatherings. Whether you're celebrating a national holiday or simply surrounding yourself with family and friends, we provide the perfect menu for a summer soiree in this chapter. We even let you know what to make in advance and what to make the day of the party. So sit back and relax with a tall glass of lemonade (and if you don't have any on hand, we give you a couple great recipes at the end of this chapter). And leave the planning to us.

Planning the Menu

Planning a party can sometimes overwhelm even the most experience entertainer among us. But often, when you figure out what your menu will look like, the other things fall into place. The menu sets the tone for your entire party. And the one we provide here is the perfect one for summertime:

✔ Fried Chicken for a Crowd

✔ Baked Beans

✔ Perfect Corn on the Cob

✔ All-American Coleslaw

- Macaroni and Ham Salad with Mustard Dressing
- Red, White, and Blue Berry Shortcake
- Strawberry Lemonade
- Watermelon Lemonade

Planning ahead makes all the difference in cooking for large groups. Always make ahead of time the dishes that keep well.

For the menu in this chapter, you can do the following things the day before:

- Assemble the Baked Beans.
- Make the All-American Coleslaw.
- Make the Macaroni and Ham Salad with Mustard Dressing
- Make the Strawberry Lemonade and/or the Watermelon Lemonade
- Place the chicken pieces in the batter marinade (see the recipe for Fried Chicken for a Crowd).

The morning of your party, start your day off right by doing the following to get your Red, White, and Blue Berry Shortcake started.

- Make the biscuits.
- Hull and slice the strawberries; rinse, pick over, and drain the blueberries.

And you can finish off your cooking the day of the party with the following:

- Make the whipped cream for the Red, White, and Blue Berry Shortcake.
- Make the Fried Chicken for a Crowd and the Perfect Corn on the Cob, just before serving.
- Bake the Baked Beans.
- Assemble the Red, White, and Blue Berry Shortcake.

Now your party is off and running. Refer to the following sections for the recipes you need.

Making Fried Chicken to Please Any Crowd

Deep frying usually calls for cooking food in at least 2 inches of hot fat. However, in this next recipes, we reduce the fat to about ½ inch. With this method, less fat is absorbed by the chicken, less splattering of hot fat occurs, and, most importantly, the skin still develops that yummy, crispy crust.

Here are a few things to keep in mind when frying chicken:

- **Keep the oil in the pan hot enough (between 350 and 365 degrees) so that the chicken crust is not greasy.** A deep-frying thermometer, which comes with a clip that attaches to the side of the pot, is the best way to gauge the temperature. If you don't have such a thermometer, drop a small amount of batter into the hot oil; if it sizzles instantly, the oil has reached 365 degrees. If the batter burns in 5 seconds or so, the oil is too hot. Adjust the heat, as necessary, to raise or lower the temperature of the oil.

- **Use solid vegetable oil, like Crisco, when you're deep frying.** Solid vegetable shortening has just the right characteristics to make the chicken skin crispy and the meat moist. Vegetable oil works well, too.

- **When frying chicken, be sure the heat is even and doesn't fluctuate.** When the chicken first hits the oil, it causes the temperature to fall. So you need to raise the heat to offset this effect. Watch the temperature carefully; extreme heat causes the skin of the chicken to look like charred marshmallow.

- **Use a high-sided fry pan.** Cast-iron frying pans are best, because when they get hot they stay hot, even when you remove them from the heat.

- **If you have time, place the chicken pieces in the batter and let them sit overnight in the refrigerator.** This makes the batter cling more readily to the chicken during frying.

- **You can add all sorts of seasonings to the batter, including paprika, cayenne, nutmeg, cinnamon, garlic salt, garlic powder, and other spices.** Experiment with one or two of these spices at a time and see what you like best.

Fried chicken is sinfully rich, so one piece per person may be enough — especially if you are serving other entrees. To feed 4 or 5 people, just cut this recipe in half.

Fried Chicken for a Crowd

Tools: *2 large, deep skillets (preferably cast-iron), tongs, chef's knife, large bowl*

Preparation time: *15 minutes*

Cooking time: *About 20 minutes*

Yield: *8 to 10 servings*

7 to 8 pounds chicken parts (legs, wings, thighs, and breasts)

3½ cups buttermilk

1 tablespoon Tabasco sauce, or to taste

Salt and black pepper to taste

3 cups all-purpose flour

3 teaspoons salt, or to taste

Black pepper to taste

2 teaspoons garlic powder

1 teaspoon paprika

4 to 5 cups solid vegetable shortening (such as Crisco)

Parsley sprigs for garnish (optional)

1 Cut each whole breast in half by running a knife along the breastbone. Trim off any loose fat. Rinse the chicken pieces and pat dry with paper towels.

2 Pour the buttermilk into a large bowl. Stir in the Tabasco sauce, and add the salt and pepper. Add the chicken pieces and turn them to coat in the batter. If you have time, cover and refrigerate for 2 to 12 hours, turning occasionally.

3 In a large bowl or shallow baking dish, combine the flour and seasonings. Lift the chicken pieces out of the batter. Roll each piece in the seasoned flour several times, or until well coated all around. (Or place the seasoned flour in a 1-gallon resealable plastic bag, add the chicken pieces one at a time, and shake the bag until the chicken is well coated. Repeat with the remaining pieces.)

4 Set the coated chicken pieces on a dish for about 15 minutes to let the coating dry and adhere to the chicken.

5 Place two large and deep heavy skillets over medium-high heat; add enough of the Crisco or vegetable oil to each skillet to make a ½-inch layer of oil. Heat until the oil registers 350 degrees on a deep-frying thermometer or until a small amount of batter sizzles and bubbles when dropped into the pan.

6 Gently add the chicken pieces to the pan, skin side down, in a single layer. Do not crowd the pan. Cover and cook over medium heat for 10 minutes, checking after 5 minutes to see if the pieces are browning evenly. Move them around if necessary, and turn the heat down if they are browning too quickly.

7 Gently turn the pieces and cook, uncovered, another 10 to 12 minutes or until done. (The wings should be removed after about 7 minutes.) To test for doneness, remove a thigh or leg and carefully make a small incision in the center of each piece; the juices should run clear and the meat should be white with no trace of pink.

8 Drain the cooked pieces on a rack set over paper towels or on a baking sheet. If not serving immediately, the chicken may be kept warm by placing the rack on a baking sheet in a 200-degree oven. Chicken that is to be served from 30 minutes up to 1 hour later can be safely left on the rack at room temperature, loosely covered with wax paper, and reheated in a 350-degree oven. (It is also delicious cold.)

9 Serve the chicken on a large platter or in a basket lined with colorful napkins. Garnish with parsley sprigs, if you want.

When making fried chicken, be sure that all of your utensils are very dry; water and oil are not a good combination; together, they cause the hot oil to splatter and can give you a nasty burn. Use long tongs to turn the chicken pieces when cooking.

If you like hot, spicy flavors, push up the level of the Tabasco sauce in the batter. We used up to ¼ cup of Tabasco sauce with delicious results. Tabasco also makes a garlic pepper sauce that divinely accents the chicken.

Serving Up Side Dishes

Just as important as the main dish are the accompaniments.

Classic baked bean casseroles call for cooking dried beans for hours on end, as much as all day. If that isn't your idea of fun, we spare you that effort without sacrificing much flavor by using canned and frozen beans in the next recipe. This dish can be assembled and refrigerated a day or two ahead and then baked the day you serve it. Leftovers also are terrific. Just reheat the casserole, covered, in a 350-degree oven for about 15 minutes, or until warmed through. Add a little more water if the sauce needs to be thinned. You can use almost any precooked canned beans in this recipe.

Baked Beans

Tools: *Large skillet, saucepan, deep baking dish with cover, chef's knife*

Preparation time: *15 minutes*

Cooking time: *About 1 hour and 15 minutes*

Yield: *8 servings*

¼ pound thickly-sliced bacon (about 4 slices)

1 large onion, chopped

1 to 2 jalapeño peppers, or other hot chili peppers, seeded and chopped

1 large clove garlic, minced

½ cup molasses

½ cup chili sauce

½ cup ketchup

¼ cup water

1½ tablespoons cider vinegar

1½ tablespoons Worcestershire sauce

Black pepper to taste

1 10-ounce package frozen baby lima beans

1 16-ounce jar or can baked beans

1 16-ounce can red kidney beans, drained

1 Preheat the oven to 375 degrees.

2 In a large skillet, sauté the bacon over medium heat until lightly browned, turning occasionally. Drain on paper towels, reserving the bacon drippings in the pan. When the bacon is cool enough to handle, tear it into small pieces and set aside.

3 Add the onion, chili peppers, and garlic to the skillet and cook over medium heat until the onions are transparent, about 3 to 4 minutes, stirring often. Stir in the molasses, chili sauce, ketchup, water, vinegar, Worcestershire sauce, and black pepper. Bring to a boil, reduce heat, and simmer for 5 minutes, stirring occasionally.

4 Bring a medium saucepan of lightly salted water to a boil, add the lima beans, and cook for about 3 to 4 minutes, or until just tender, and then drain.

5 Place all of the beans in a large, deep baking dish. Add the molasses-onion mixture and stir well to combine. Sprinkle the reserved bacon pieces over the top. Cover and bake for 30 to 35 minutes or until bubbly; remove the cover and bake for about 25 minutes more to thicken the sauce slightly.

In addition to tasting great with fried chicken, baked beans go well with hamburgers. Check out Chapter 6 for our Perfect Hamburger recipe.

Americans in particular have always fancied themselves as corn connoisseurs. Every summer, on picnic tables across the land, culinary Olympic judges rate the current crop as if it were a high-dive competition. "This is pretty good — I give it an eight. But it's not like the ones we had last Labor Day." Soil, sun, and freshness are critical in producing superior corn. True corn-on-the-cob aficionados say that fresh corn should be picked as close to cooking time as possible. The sugar in corn quickly converts to starch after picking, making it lose its sweetness. However, the corn industry has made a lot of progress in recent years to develop strains of corn that hold their sweetness for several days.

Corn comes in colors ranging from almost white to deep yellow, and the ears and individual kernels can be big or small. Size and color have nothing to do with flavor. Corn in a store or market should look fresh. The husks should be green with no sign of dryness or splotching. The silk at the tip of the husk can be dark, but the silk inside should be moist.

Do not shuck the corn until cooking time. The silk and husk help keep the kernels moist. If you have to store corn, put it in a plastic bag and refrigerate.

The only way to ruin fresh corn is by overcooking it. About 5 to 6 minutes, just until the corn is heated through, is plenty for young, tender ears. Older ears may take up to 10 minutes.

Perfect Corn on the Cob

This recipe calls for one ear of corn per person, but if you have more guests or you think your guests may eat more than one ear each, just add more to the pot. The cooking time remains the same.

Tools: *Large pot, tongs*

Preparation time: *5 minutes*

Cooking time: *About 5 to 6 minutes*

Yield: *8 servings*

8 ears fresh sweet corn

Salt and black pepper to taste

½ cup (1 stick) butter

1 Bring a large pot of water to a boil. While waiting for the water to boil, husk the corn.

2 When the water boils, carefully drop the ears, one at a time, into the pot. Cover and boil for about 5 minutes, or until the corn is warmed through. Using tongs, remove the ears from the water and set them on a plate to drain. Serve immediately with salt, pepper, and 1 tablespoon of butter per ear.

For a change of pace, flavor the butter with assorted spices and herbs. For example, you can soften the butter to room temperature and mix in a little lemon or lime juice, chopped cilantro or chervil, or chopped fresh basil.

If you are accustomed to the gloppy, overly sweetened coleslaw served by many delicatessens, the following recipe will be a real treat. Our homemade coleslaw is not heavily coated with mayonnaise, which means that the flavors of the cabbage and other vegetables shine through.

All-American Coleslaw

Tools: *Chef's knife, grater (or food processor or mandoline), large bowl, small bowl, whisk*

Preparation time: *15 to 20 minutes*

Cooking time: *None (2 to 3 hours refrigeration)*

Yield: *10 servings*

1 medium head green cabbage (about 2 pounds), tough outer leaves removed

4 carrots, peeled and grated

2 red bell peppers, cored, seeded, and diced

1 medium onion, diced

1⅓ cups mayonnaise, or to taste

⅓ cup sugar

⅓ cup cider vinegar

Salt and black pepper to taste

1 Using a large chef's knife, halve the cabbage crosswise, cut out the hard, solid core, and then quarter the remaining chunks of leaves. Slice the cabbage, starting at one end, as thinly as possible. Then chop the slices crosswise to make short lengths. (You can do this quickly in a food processor using the shredding blade, or with a mandoline, as shown in Figure 18-1.) You should have about 16 cups of loosely packed cabbage. Place the cabbage, carrots, bell peppers, and onion in a large bowl.

2 In a small bowl, using a wire whisk or fork to blend, combine the remaining ingredients. Pour the dressing over the cabbage mixture and toss thoroughly to coat. Taste to see if it needs more salt and pepper. Cover the bowl with plastic wrap and refrigerate for at least 3 hours before serving to blend flavors, stirring occasionally.

If you like to make coleslaw, carrot salads, potato chips, sliced beets, and other such foods, you may want to invest in a tool called a *mandoline.* The classic French mandoline is an ungainly looking stainless steel device with various levers that allow you to make various cuts. You can buy a stainless steel mandoline or opt for the much less expensive plastic variety. Both are available at good kitchenware shops.

Figure 18-1:
How to
use a
mandoline.

How to Use a Mandoline

fancy!

faster, faster

okay, cut me down to size.

Place the mandoline on a cutting board. Choose a slicing blade and adjust it to a desired thickness...

..If your vegetable is too bulky to fit into the box under the handle, cut it down to size. Place the lid firmly down on the vegetable and run rapidly up and down over the slicing blade. The slices will fall onto the counter!

The ham in this salad adds a bit of distinctive saltiness and is a nice counterpoint to the cold macaroni.

Macaroni and Ham Salad with Mustard Dressing

Tools: *Chef's knife, citrus juicer, large pot, large bowl*

Preparation time: *15 to 20 minutes*

Cooking time: *None (2 hours refrigeration)*

Yield: *6 to 8 servings*

½ pound elbow macaroni

1 cup mayonnaise

1 cup diced (about ¼-inch cubes), fully cooked, smoked, or boiled ham

⅓ cup chopped fresh basil leaves

Juice of 1 lemon

2 tablespoons Dijon-style mustard

1 large clove garlic, minced

⅔ cup diced green or red bell pepper

⅔ cup diced fennel bulb or celery

¼ cup minced red onion

Salt and black pepper to taste

(continued)

1 Bring a large pot of salted water to a boil, add the macaroni, and cook until just tender, about 6 to 8 minutes. Drain, rinse under cold water, drain again, and place in a large bowl.

2 Add the remaining ingredients and toss well to combine. Refrigerate, covered, for at least 2 hours before serving.

This salad also goes well with Grilled Brochettes of Pork with Rosemary (see Chapter 6) or Mustard-Brushed Barbecue Chicken Breasts (see Chapter 6).

For a vegetarian version of this macaroni salad, omit the ham and add 2 chopped, hard-cooked eggs instead.

Made with strawberries, blueberries, and whipped cream, this patriotic cake is especially well-suited for a Fourth of July celebration. All the components of this cake — the berry mixture, the cream, and even the biscuits — can be made a few hours before serving and then assembled as the dinner dishes are being whisked off the table.

Red, White, and Blue Berry Shortcake

Tools: Paring knife, medium and large mixing bowls, electric mixer, spatula, baking sheet, serrated knife

Preparation time: 40 minutes

Cooking time: About 15 minutes

Yield: 8 servings

2 pints strawberries, rinsed and hulled

2 cups blueberries, rinsed and drained

⅓ cup (or more, to taste) plus 3½ tablespoons sugar

1 tablespoon Cointreau (optional)

1¼ cups heavy cream

2 tablespoons confectioners' sugar, or more, to taste

½ teaspoon vanilla extract

2⅔ cups self-rising cake flour

¼ teaspoon salt

10 tablespoons chilled butter, cut into small pieces

1 cup plus 1 to 2 tablespoons milk

1 Preheat the oven to 400 degrees.

2 Set aside 8 of the most perfect strawberries for a garnish. Crush half of the remaining strawberries using a fork or the back of a spoon; cut the rest in half.

3 In a medium mixing bowl, combine the sliced and crushed strawberries, blueberries, ⅓ cup sugar, and, if desired, the Cointreau. Taste the fruit mixture and add more sugar if necessary. Refrigerate until ready to assemble the shortcake.

4 In a bowl using an electric mixer, whip the cream with the confectioners' sugar and vanilla until stiff. Cover and refrigerate until you're ready to assemble the shortcake.

5 In a large mixing bowl, combine the flour, 3½ tablespoons sugar, and salt. Cut the chilled butter into the flour mixture using two knives, your fingertips, or a pastry blender, until the mixture resembles coarse breadcrumbs. Work quickly so as not to let the butter melt or form a paste.

6 Make a well in the center of the flour mixture and add 1 cup of the milk. Mix gently with a fork, rubber spatula, or wooden spoon just until most of the dry ingredients are moistened and a very soft dough is formed. Do not overmix.

7 Drop the dough, in eight equal portions 1 to 2 inches apart, onto an ungreased baking sheet. Lightly brush the tops of the rounds with the remaining 1 to 2 tablespoons of milk.

8 Bake the biscuits on the center rack of the oven for 15 to 17 minutes, or until golden brown. (Do not overbake, or the bottoms may darken or burn.) Transfer to a wire rack to cool. Finished shortcakes may be served warm or cold.

9 To assemble, using a serrated knife, carefully slice the shortcakes in half crosswise. Transfer each bottom half to an individual serving plate. Spread a generous dollop of whipped cream over the bottom of each biscuit; top with about ⅓ cup of the fruit mixture. Cover with the other half of the shortcakes. Spoon over more cream and berries, and drizzle with any berry juices that have accumulated. Garnish each serving with a reserved whole strawberry. Don't despair if berries fall around the cakes; it's part of the charm. Serve immediately.

If you like, make this recipe in the more traditional fashion using only strawberries, or substitute ½ pint each of raspberries and blackberries for the blueberries.

Mixing Lemonades with Flair

Classic lemonade becomes even more exciting when flavored with other fruit purees like strawberry and watermelon.

Strawberry Lemonade

Tools: *Strainer, blender or food processor, paring knife, large pitcher*

Preparation time: *10 to 15 minutes*

Cooking time: *None (2 hours chilling)*

Yield: *6 to 8 servings*

1½ cups fresh lemon juice, strained of pits (9 to 10 large lemons)

1½ cups sugar

6 cups water

1 pint strawberries, rinsed and hulled

Lemon slices for garnish (optional)

Mint sprigs for garnish (optional)

1 Combine the lemon juice, sugar, and water in a large pitcher. Stir well.

2 Place the hulled strawberries in a blender or food processor; add a little of the lemonade from the pitcher, and blend until smooth.

3 Pour the strawberries into the lemonade, stir, and chill for 2 hours. Stir well before serving. Pour into ice-filled glasses, garnishing each, if desired, with a lemon slice or a sprig of fresh mint.

To make classic lemonade, simply omit the strawberries.

The natural sweetness of watermelon allows you to minimize the amount of sugar used in this drink.

Watermelon Lemonade

Tools: *Strainer, blender or food processor, paring knife, large pitcher*

Preparation time: *About 15 minutes*

Cooking time: *None (2 hours chilling)*

Yield: *8 to 10 servings*

1½ cups fresh lemon juice, strained of pits
(9 to 10 large lemons)

1 cup plus 2 tablespoons sugar

6 cups water

3 cups watermelon chunks, seeds removed

Mint sprigs for garnish (optional)

1 Combine the lemon juice, sugar, and water in a large pitcher. Stir well.

2 Place the watermelon chunks in a blender or food processor; add a little of the lemonade from the pitcher, and blend until smooth.

3 Pour the watermelon mixture into the lemonade mixture, stir, and chill for 2 hours. Stir well before serving. Pour into ice-filled glasses, garnishing each, if desired, with a sprig of fresh mint.

When buying watermelons, ripeness is indicated by a pale yellow spot on its bottom; if both sides of the melon are totally green and show no sign of a pale yellow spot, the melon may not be mature enough to eat.

To cut a watermelon, take the largest knife you have and carefully thrust it into the top of the melon lengthwise. Then drag the knife all the way to one end, piercing the core; go back to the middle and drag it to the other end. The weight of the watermelon makes it easy to split the bottom by pulling apart the halves. See Figure 18-2 for an illustration.

Figure 18-2:
Cutting a watermelon.

How to Cut Open and Slice Watermelon

Use a long, sharp, chef's knife.

FIRST... Thrust the knife into the top of the melon, lengthwise. Then, drag the knife all the way to one end, piercing the core; go back to the middle and drag to the other end. The weight of the melon makes it easy to split the bottom by pulling apart the halves!

Cut across each half into half-moon-shape slices.

OR

picnic time!

Cut the halves in half to make smaller, wedge-shaped, slices!

Chapter 19

Super Bowl Buffet

- -

- -

*I*t has been scientifically proven that sitting in a reclining chair with a glass of beer or wine while watching football stirs the appetite as much as if you were playing on the field. In this chapter, we give you everything you need to keep your team going at full-force from the kickoff through the last seconds on the clock.

This menu is also ideal for any party or gathering where serving warm and hearty foods helps chase away the chills of winter.

Planning Your Super Bowl Menu

If you're not sure exactly what to serve when the crowd gathers for the big game, you can't go wrong with the following recipes:

- ✔ Crunchy Party Nibbles
- ✔ Spicy Chicken Wings with Blue Cheese Dressing
- ✔ Bean and Sausage Casserole
- ✔ Avocado and Pear Salad with Mixed Greens and Red Onion Vinaigrette
- ✔ Old-Fashioned Bread Pudding

To pull it all off, try doing these things the day before the party:

- ✔ Make the Crunchy Party Nibbles.
- ✔ Assemble the Bean and Sausage Casserole.
- ✔ Make the Blue Cheese Dressing.
- ✔ Rinse and dry the salad greens.
- ✔ Make the Warm Brandy Sauce.

A few hours before the big game, check these things off your list:

- ✔ Remove the tips from and season the chicken wings. Refrigerate about 2 hours before roasting.
- ✔ Make the Red Onion Vinaigrette.
- ✔ Toast the walnuts for the salad.
- ✔ Bake the Bean and Sausage Casserole.
- ✔ Assemble the Old-Fashioned Bread Pudding.

Just before the game starts and you're ready to eat, finish your preparations by doing the following:

- ✔ Prepare the Avocado and Pear Salad with Mixed Greens and serve with Red Onion Vinaigrette.
- ✔ Roast the Spicy Chicken Wings.
- ✔ Bake the Bread Pudding.
- ✔ Reheat the Warm Brandy Sauce.

Making Your Meal — From Appetizer to Dessert

The following recipe is a great snack to have with a couple beers, and it has two special advantages over other similar treats: First, it's better than the stuff you buy in the grocery store, and second, you can make it ahead of time.

Crunchy Party Nibbles

Tools: *Large roasting pan, large spoon or rubber spatula*

Preparation time: *About 20 minutes*

Cooking time: *35 to 40 minutes*

Yield: *About 5 cups*

2 tablespoons butter

1½ teaspoons vegetable oil

1 tablespoon Worcestershire sauce

½ teaspoon ground cumin

¼ teaspoon Tabasco sauce

¼ teaspoon paprika

¼ teaspoon garlic salt

¼ teaspoon garlic powder

¼ teaspoon salt or to taste

4 cups assorted bite-sized cereals (Shredded Wheat, Chex, and so on.)

1 cup mixed nuts (pecan halves, whole natural almonds, unsalted peanuts, and so on)

1 cup unsalted pretzel rounds

1 Preheat the oven to 300 degrees.

2 In a large roasting pan, heat the butter and oil in the oven (just long enough to melt the butter). Take the pan from the oven and add the Worcestershire sauce, cumin, Tabasco, paprika, garlic salt, garlic powder, and salt; stir well to combine. Add the cereal, nuts, and pretzels and toss thoroughly to coat.

3 Return the pan to the oven and bake for 30 to 35 minutes or until lightly toasted, stirring every 10 to 15 minutes. Let the mixture cool to room temperature. Store in an airtight container.

Here's another appetizer that's not only easy to make but is also easy on your pocketbook — a big plus when serving a crowd of ravenous football fans. Serve these zesty chicken wings informally, perhaps with Tabasco sauce on the side, and with the blue cheese dressing dip that follows. Stack an assortment of colorful raw vegetables (carrot sticks, bell peppers, celery, broccoli, and so on) alongside the wings.

Spicy Chicken Wings

Tools: *Chef's knife, citrus juicer, grater, large plastic bag or mixing bowl, large roasting pan*

Preparation time: *20 minutes (plus 2 hours chilling time before roasting)*

Cooking time: *About 45 minutes*

Yield: *8 appetizer servings*

3 pounds chicken wings	*2 teaspoons peeled, grated ginger*
3 tablespoons olive oil	*1½ teaspoons salt, or to taste*
3 tablespoons fresh lemon or lime juice	*Black pepper to taste*
4 large cloves garlic, minced	*1 teaspoon hot chili powder*
2 teaspoons ground cumin	*½ teaspoon cayenne pepper*
1 teaspoon dried oregano	*Tabasco sauce (optional)*
2 teaspoons paprika	

1 Preheat oven to 400 degrees.

2 Remove the tips of the chicken wings by laying the wing on a cutting board. With a heavy knife, locate the joint between the bony tip and the main part of the wing. Cut down firmly. Discard wing tips or freeze for later use in chicken broth. Rinse the chicken wings under cold tap water and pat them dry with paper towels.

3 Combine the remaining ingredients (except the Tabasco sauce) in a large, resealable plastic bag (or mixing bowl), shaking (or stirring) well to blend. Add the chicken wings; toss well to coat. Seal the bag (or cover the bowl) and refrigerate for about 2 hours.

4 Arrange the chicken legs in a single layer on a rack in a large roasting pan; roast in the oven for 40 to 45 minutes, or until sizzling, crispy, and browned. Turn them once after 20 to 25 minutes. If you want them spicier, serve the wings with Tabasco sauce on the side.

Hot chili powder is to regular chili powder what a bonfire is to a cigarette lighter, so use it sparingly. We suggest you add hot chili powder incrementally, stir it in well, and stand back. If nothing happens approach the bowl and continue cooking.

This dipping sauce recipe for Spicy Chicken Wings was inspired by The Anchor Bar, in Buffalo, New York, where the dish was invented.

Blue Cheese Dressing

Tools: *Chef's knife, food processor or blender.*

Preparation time: *5 to 10 minutes*

Cooking time: *None (chill about 2 hours before serving)*

Yield: *About 1½ cups*

⅔ cup mayonnaise

⅔ cup sour cream

2 tablespoons chopped onion

2 teaspoons red wine vinegar

1 clove garlic, minced

4 ounces (about 1 cup loosely packed) crumbled blue cheese

In a food processor or blender puree the mayonnaise, sour cream, onion, red wine vinegar, and garlic until smooth. Transfer to a small serving bowl; add the crumbled blue cheese and use a fork to mash the cheese into the mixture and break up any large clumps. Chill for at least 2 hours before serving.

The following hearty winter dish is ideal for casual or formal parties. It resembles the French culinary barbell called *cassoulet,* and it requires no fancy plating. It can be assembled and refrigerated the day before the game and then baked (and topped with bread crumbs) about 1 hour and 10 to 20 minutes before serving time.

Casseroles that are assembled and refrigerated the day before either need a little more baking time to remove the chill, or they need to be brought almost to room temperature before baking.

Bean and Sausage Casserole

Tools: *Chef's knife, vegetable peeler, large flameproof casserole (with lid)*

Preparation time: *15 to 20 minutes*

Cooking time: *About 1 hour and 20 minutes*

Yield: *8 servings*

(continued)

2 tablespoons olive oil

1 pound hot Italian pork sausage links, cut into 1- to 2-inch chunks

1 pound garlic-flavored or mild Italian sausage links, cut into 1- to 2-inch chunks

½ pound thickly-sliced bacon, cut into 1-inch pieces

2 large onions, chopped

2 15-ounce cans Great Northern or cannellini beans, drained

26-ounce can chopped tomatoes

1 large (Idaho) potato, peeled and cut into ½-inch cubes

1¼ cups homemade or canned chicken stock

½ cup dry white wine

¼ cup tomato paste

2 large cloves garlic, chopped

1 tablespoon fresh minced rosemary or 1½ teaspoons dried

Salt and black pepper to taste

2½ to 3 cups coarse white bread crumbs

1 Preheat oven to 350 degrees.

2 Heat the oil in a large, 3-quart, flame-proof casserole over medium-high heat; add the sausage in batches and cook, turning, for about 5 minutes, or until it is browned all over. Transfer the sausages to a large plate lined with paper towels. Let the sausages drain.

3 When all of the sausages are browned and removed from pan, pour off all the fat and discard. Add the bacon to the pan; cook for about 2 minutes, or until browned, stirring often. Remove the bacon to a plate with the sausage; pour off all but about 1 tablespoon of the fat in the pan. Add the onions and cook about 3 minutes, until soft but not browned, stirring and scraping the bottom of the pan occasionally to loosen the little browned bits.

4 Return the sausage and bacon to the pan; stir in the beans, tomatoes, potato, chicken stock, wine, tomato paste, garlic, rosemary, salt, and pepper; bring to a boil, uncovered, then remove from the heat and cover the casserole dish. (If desired, the casserole can be prepared up to this point, refrigerated, and then baked the next day as instructed in step 5.)

5 Bake the casserole for 50 minutes. Remove from the oven and sprinkle the top with the bread crumbs. (For a thick layer of crumbs use the full 3 cups.) Return the casserole to the oven and cook, uncovered, for 20 minutes, or until the top is golden brown.

This cool weather salad combines the different textures and flavors of red leaf lettuce, iceberg, and radicchio. Feel free to use your own favorite combination of salad greens as well.

Avocado and Pear Salad with Mixed Greens

Tools: *Chef's knife or paring knife, salad spinner (optional), wooden spoons, large salad bowl*

Preparation time: *About 20 minutes*

Cooking time: *About 2 to 3 minutes*

Yield: *10 servings*

12 to 14 cups mixed greens (red or green leaf lettuce, iceberg, radicchio, arugula, Boston, bibb, romaine, and so on), torn into bite-sized pieces, rinsed and dried

2 medium ripe avocados, peeled, pits removed, and cut into bite-sized chunks

2 medium-ripe Bosc (or other variety) pears, cored, and cut into ½-inch chunks

⅔ cup shelled, chopped walnuts, toasted

Salt and black pepper to taste

In a large salad bowl, toss together the greens; add the avocados, pears, and walnuts. Toss the salad lightly with salad dressing (use the following vinaigrette recipe if you like), using just enough to coat the greens without overdressing. Taste for seasonings.

Always be sure to rinse and thoroughly dry all salad greens. Also, be careful not to inundate the fragile greens with dressing. A salad should have just enough dressing to coat the greens when you toss it thoroughly.

You can rinse and dry salad greens ahead of time and chill them in a plastic bag. Pears and avocados, though, must be sliced and tossed into the greens just before serving to prevent them from discoloring.

No, don't try to toast walnuts by tossing them into your toaster — it would toast them just fine, but getting them out would be maddening. All you have to do is heat a pan (cast iron is great for this) over medium-high heat and put in the walnuts. Toast the walnuts while shaking the pan — it should take about 2 to 3 minutes to brown them slightly on the outside.

Red Onion Vinaigrette

Tools: *Chef's knife, whisk, bowl*

Preparation time: *5 minutes*

Cooking time: *None*

Yield: *About ¾ cup*

6 tablespoons extra-virgin olive oil

2½ tablespoons balsamic vinegar

¼ cup finely chopped red onion

1 large clove garlic, crushed

Salt and black pepper to taste

In a small bowl, whisk together the oil and vinegar; add the red onion, crushed garlic, salt, and pepper. Stir well to combine and let sit for 30 minutes to develop flavors. Remove the crushed garlic clove and taste for seasoning before tossing the salad with the dressing. The dressing should have just a little bite from the vinegar.

Bread puddings fall into two distinct categories. In the first version, bread is immersed in a custard mixture and baked over a pan of hot water. This "water bath" keeps the oven moist and prevents the custard from becoming grainy. In the second version (which uses more bread relative to custard), *all* of the custard is soaked up into the bread during baking; so, it doesn't need a water bath.

In the following recipe, we opt for the latter. This recipe is wonderfully rich, slightly dense, and has fewer than 50 calories per serving (okay, we're kidding about the calorie count). Serve it with the heady Warm Brandy Sauce. If you have any left over, it makes a great breakfast, with or without the booze.

Old Fashioned Bread Pudding with Warm Brandy Sauce

Tools: *Bread knife, whisk, mixing bowl, 9-x-13-inch baking pan, baking sheet, saucepan, whisk, small bowl*

Preparation time: *About 20 minutes*

Cooking time: *1 hour and 15 minutes for drying the bread and baking the custard, 5 minutes for cooking the brandy sauce*

Yield: *8 to 10 servings*

About 1 tablespoon butter for greasing the baking pan

1 loaf (16 to 18 ounces) of brioche, challah, or other egg bread

½ cup raisins

3 eggs

l cup sugar

2 tablespoons packed brown sugar

2½ cups milk

2 cups light cream or half-and-half

1 tablespoon vanilla extract

½ teaspoon grated orange peel

½ teaspoon ground cinnamon

¼ teaspoon ground nutmeg

1 Preheat the oven to 200 degrees. Butter a 9-x-13-inch baking pan.

2 Cut the bread into 1-inch-thick slices; place slices in a single layer on a baking sheet and dry them in the oven (about 15 minutes, turning once). Or lay the bread slices in one layer on a baking sheet and let them dry at room temperature overnight.

3 Preheat the oven to 325 degrees.

4 Tear the bread into 1½-inch pieces (you should have about 12 cups). Transfer the bread pieces to the buttered baking pan. Scatter the raisins over the bread.

5 In a large mixing bowl, whisk together the eggs and the sugars until well blended. Whisk in the milk, cream, vanilla extract, orange peel, cinnamon, and nutmeg. Pour this custard mixture over the bread. Press the bread with your fingers so it absorbs the liquid thoroughly; cover and refrigerate for about 1 hour before baking. Let stand at room temperature about 20 minutes to take off some of the chill.

6 Place the pudding, uncovered, on the center oven rack and bake until the surface is lightly browned and the custard is firm in the center (about 1 hour). Remove it from the oven and let it cool for 15 minutes before cutting into squares. Serve with Warm Brandy Sauce. Leftover pudding can be refrigerated and served cold or reheated. To reheat, cover with foil, and bake in a 325-degree oven for about 20 minutes.

Warm Brandy Sauce

¾ cup granulated sugar

¼ cup water

¼ cup butter

¼ cup brandy or Cognac

1 egg

⅛ teaspoon ground nutmeg

1 In a medium saucepan, combine the sugar, water, butter, and brandy. Simmer, whisking until the butter is melted and the sugar is dissolved. Remove from the heat.

2 In a small bowl, whisk the egg with the nutmeg until light and foamy, about 1 minute. Pour the egg mixture into the brandy mixture while whisking vigorously.

(continued)

3 Set the saucepan over low heat and bring to a simmer, stirring constantly. Cook until the sauce is thickened, about 1 minute. Do not allow it to boil rapidly or the egg may curdle. Spoon the sauce over individual portions of the bread pudding. (This sauce can be made ahead and refrigerated for up to two days. Reheat over low heat, stirring constantly).

This brandy sauce can be modified in many ways. If you like, substitute an equal amount of dark rum, Grand Marnier, or Kahlua.

Chapter 20

Thanksgiving Dinner

· ·

In This Chapter

▶ Ahead of the game

▶ Fowl play

▶ Okay, just a sliver: Pumpkin Pie

· ·

*T*he pilgrims had many things to be thankful for — and so do you. This chapter walks you through the annual ritual of Thanksgiving dinner. Along the way, we offer time-saving tips to make it a breeze (well, more like a draft).

Planning the Menu

For the perfect holiday meal, try the following menu:

↳ Creamy Horseradish and Fresh Tomato Dip

↳ Apple Curry Dip

↳ Roasted Turkey with Cornbread, Sausage, and Apple Stuffing

↳ Pan Gravy with Madeira

↳ Fresh Cranberry Relish

↳ Green Beans with Shallot Butter

↳ Mashed Sweet Potato Casserole

↳ Baked Sweet Potatoes

↳ Praline Pumpkin Pie

A huge holiday meal can seem overwhelming, but if you start cooking in advance, you can save yourself a lot of stress. One or two days before your meal, make the following:

- ✔ Praline Pumpkin Pie
- ✔ Rum-Baked Sweet Potatoes
- ✔ Fresh Cranberry Sauce
- ✔ Cornbread for the stuffing

The day before your big meal, remember to do the following:

- ✔ Trim the green beans and make the shallot butter.
- ✔ Make the Mashed Sweet Potato Casserole.
- ✔ Make and chill the vegetable dips.

The morning of your holiday meal, do the following:

- ✔ Whip the cream for the pie.
- ✔ Make the Cornbread, Sausage, and Apple Stuffing.

The afternoon of your meal, you can do the following:

- ✔ Roast the turkey.
- ✔ Make the Pan Gravy with Madeira.
- ✔ Cook the Green Beans with Shallots.
- ✔ Reheat the sweet potatoes.

Addictive Fresh Vegetable Dips

Serving substantial hors d'oeuvres, like aged cheeses or puff pastries filled with meat, is not a good idea. Cheese, in particular, sates the appetite quickly. We favor light, tasty starters like the fresh vegetables and assorted dips described below. The dips can be jazzed up in countless ways with dried or fresh herbs, hot sauces, and so on.

Creamy Horseradish and Fresh Tomato Dip

Tools: *Chef's knife, citrus juicer, mixing bowl, electric mixer*

Preparation time: *10 minutes*

Cooking time: *None*

Yield: *About 1½ cups*

½ cup mayonnaise

⅓ cup cream cheese (cool but not cold), cut into chunks (use reduced-fat cream cheese, if you prefer)

⅓ cup chili sauce

1 large ripe plum tomato, chopped

2 tablespoons finely chopped onion

2 tablespoons bottled horseradish, pressed to drain off liquid

Juice of 1 small lemon

1½ teaspoons Worcestershire sauce

Tabasco sauce to taste

Black pepper to taste

In a bowl, using an electric mixer, blend the mayonnaise, cream cheese, and chili sauce until creamy. Stir in the remaining ingredients, mixing well. Transfer to a serving bowl, cover, and chill until ready to serve.

Apple Curry Dip

Tools: *Paring knife, chef's knife, mixing bowl*

Preparation time: *10 minutes*

Cooking time: *None*

Yield: *About 1 cup*

1 Granny Smith apple, peeled, cored, and grated

½ cup mayonnaise

½ cup low-fat, plain yogurt

2 to 3 teaspoons curry powder, according to taste

Salt and black pepper to taste

2 tablespoons chopped parsley (as a garnish)

In a bowl, stir together all of the ingredients except the parsley; transfer the mixture to a small serving bowl and chill until served. Garnish with chopped parsley before serving.

The Main Course: Roasting a Turkey

Turkey is an ideal main course for entertaining a crowd — it's easy to cook, ranges in size, and looks great on the table. Most supermarket turkeys are frozen; fresh ones are better, so it's worth asking around to find one.

When a turkey is frozen its juices turn to ice crystals; when thawed, these crystals disrupt the protein cell membranes in the flesh and cause some of the juices to leak out — that's the reddish stuff you see in the packaging when you open it. A frozen turkey is never as moist as a fresh one.

If you buy a frozen turkey, let it defrost in the refrigerator (allow about two hours per pound).

Basting a turkey during roasting gives it a golden and crisp skin; however it does not penetrate the skin so it has no effect on the moisture of the meat.

If your turkey starts to get too brown during cooking, cover it loosely with aluminum foil.

In Table 20-1, we provide roasting times for a fresh or thawed turkey at 325 degrees. These times are approximate and should be used only as a guide; factors that could alter cooking time include the accuracy of your oven, the temperature of the bird when it goes into the oven, and the number of times the oven door is opened during roasting. Always use a meat thermometer to be sure of the temperature.

Table 20-1	Turkey Roasting Chart	
Weight	*Cooking Time (Unstuffed)*	*Cooking Time (Stuffed)*
8 to 12 pounds	2¾ to 3 hours	3 to 3½ hours
12 to 14 pounds	3 to 3¾ hours	3¼ to 4 hours
14 to 18 pounds	3¾ to 4¼ hours	4 to 4½ hours
20 to 24 pounds	4½ to 5 hours	4¾ to 5¼ hours

When you are trying to decide what size turkey to buy, consider that an 18- to 20-pound bird feeds 14 or more. A 25-pound bird could easily serve 20 or more. (One general guideline recommends 1 pound of turkey per person.) Also, be sure you know the dimensions of your oven and that the bird you buy will fit.

If you want to stuff the turkey (as opposed to cooking the stuffing in a separate casserole as our recipe instructs), here are a few things to keep in mind:

✔ Poultry of all kinds is particularly susceptible to salmonella bacteria, especially at lower temperatures. Keep the turkey well chilled before cooking.

✔ Just before cooking — *not* hours in advance! — stuff the turkey loosely; this way the stuffing cooks faster and more thoroughly than if you pack it in tightly.

✔ Always test the stuffing for doneness. It should register 160 degrees on an instant-read thermometer. If the bird is done, but your stuffing is not, remove the turkey from the oven, spoon the stuffing into a buttered casserole, and continue to bake it (as the bird rests).

In the following recipe, we do not stuff the turkey; the stuffing is baked separately. When you cook the stuffing separately, the turkey cooks faster and more evenly, and the risk of salmonella contamination is greatly reduced.

Roasted Turkey

Tools: Chef's knife, vegetable peeler, large roasting pan, roasting rack, meat thermometer (unless the turkey comes with one)

Preparation time: 15 minutes

Cooking time: 3 to 3½ hours (for a 10- to 12-pound turkey)

Yield: 10 to 12 servings

1 fresh or thawed frozen turkey (10 to 12 pounds)

1 onion, quartered

2 carrots, peeled and quartered

2 large cloves garlic, crushed

2 tablespoons vegetable oil

Salt and black pepper to taste

Madeira Pan Gravy (see recipe later in this section)

1 Preheat oven to 325 degrees with the oven rack on the lowest rung.

2 Set a wire roasting rack in a large roasting pan. Remove the giblets and neck from the turkey cavity and reserve for the stock; discard the liver. (While the turkey is roasting, you can prepare a quick turkey stock using the giblets and neck; this is used for the pan gravy recipe later in this chapter). Remove any excess fat from the turkey. Rinse the turkey inside and out with cold water and pat dry.

(continued)

3 Place in the turkey cavity the onion, carrots, and garlic. Tie the legs together with kitchen string. If desired, bend the wing tips back and fold them underneath the turkey.

4 Set the turkey, breast side up, on the roasting rack. Rub the turkey all over with 2 table-spoons of the oil. Season generously with salt and pepper. Add l cup of water to the roasting pan. If using a meat thermometer, insert it into the thickest part of the thigh, close to the body, without touching any bone.

5 Roast for about 3 to 3¼ hours, or until the thigh temperature registers 180 degrees. Add another ½ cup of water to the roasting pan if it gets dry. To brown the turkey evenly, turn the pan laterally about midway through the roasting. If the turkey turns brown before the roasting time is over, cover it loosely with aluminum foil to shield the skin. Start checking for doneness during the last 30 minutes of roasting, and baste with the pan drippings 2 to 3 times during the last hour.

6 Remove the turkey from the oven, transfer it to a carving board, and cover loosely with aluminum foil, letting it rest for 20 minutes while you make the gravy. Remove the veg-etables from the cavity and discard. Carve (see Figure 20-1). Serve with Madeira Pan Gravy (see recipe later in this section).

A turkey can be seasoned in all sorts of ways to add flavor and color to the skin. For example, mix 2 tablespoons of molasses or maple syrup with 2 table-spoons of reduced-sodium soy sauce; baste the turkey with this mixture, along with the pan juices, during the last hour of cooking.

Turkey roasting resources

The following organizations are available to pro-vide information about turkey roasting — in case you need a little help around the holidays:

✔ **The National Turkey Federation:** Visit www.eatturkey.com for over 600 recipes, as well as information about pur-chasing, storing, and cooking a turkey. They even give tips for using leftovers.

✔ **The USDA Meat and Poultry Hotline:** Visit them on the Web at www.fsis.usda.gov for food and safety tips about meat,

poultry, and eggs. You can also call them toll-free at 800-535-4555.

✔ **Butterball Turkey:** Between November 1 and December 23, you call 800-323-4848 for tips on roasting, storing, stuffing, and so on. Or, visit them online at www.butterball.com for recipes, tips, and a list of the ten most frequently asked ques-tions, along with their answers, of course!

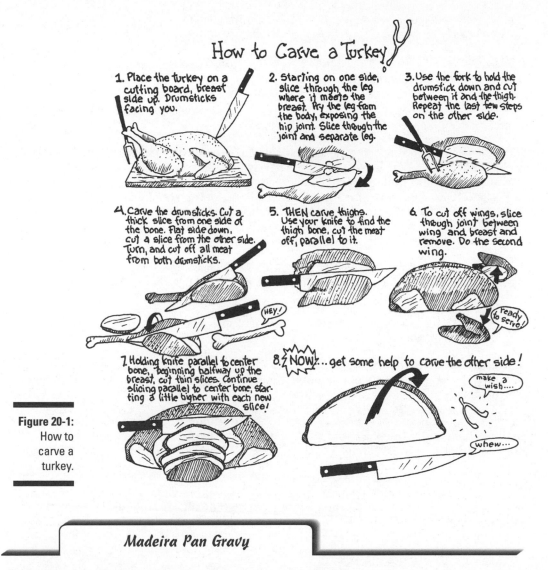

Figure 20-1: How to carve a turkey.

Madeira Pan Gravy

Tools: *Chef's knife, vegetable peeler, degreaser (optional), medium saucepan, roasting pan (from the turkey)*

Preparation time: *10 to 15 minutes*

Cooking time: *About 30 minutes*

Yield: *About 2 cups*

(continued)

4 cups homemade or canned (reduced-sodium) chicken stock

Turkey giblets (liver discarded) and neck

1 onion, peeled and quartered

2 carrots, quartered

2 stalks celery, quartered

1 bay leaf

½ cup Madeira

Turkey pan drippings

3 tablespoons flour

Salt and black pepper to taste (optional)

1 To make the turkey stock, in a medium saucepan, combine the chicken broth, turkey giblets and neck, onion, carrots, celery, and bay leaf. Cover and bring to a boil. Reduce the heat to low and simmer, partially covered, for 30 minutes. Strain the stock through cheesecloth or a fine sieve into a large measuring cup. (You should have between 1½ and 2 cups. If the stock has evaporated more than this, add water or additional chicken broth.) Refrigerate until ready to make the pan gravy. When the broth is chilled, skim off and discard any fat that rises to the surface. (Stock can be made several days ahead.)

2 Pour the drippings from the roasting pan into a 2-cup glass measuring cup or a degreaser. Spoon off and discard all but 3 tablespoons of fat from the drippings. Reserve the fat in a small cup.

3 Strain the skimmed drippings through a fine sieve into a second 2-cup glass measuring cup or bowl. Set aside.

4 Add the Madeira to the roasting pan and cook over medium-high heat, stirring and scraping the bottom for about 1 minute; strain this into the cup holding the skimmed pan drippings.

5 Add the 3 tablespoons of the reserved fat to the roasting pan. Set two burners to medium heat under the pan and heat the fat. Add the flour to the pan and stir constantly with a wire whisk, about 1 to 2 minutes, to blend the flour into the fat. The *roux* (a thickening paste of fat and flour) should turn golden brown.

6 Slowly whisk in the Madeira-pan drippings; whisk for about 1 minute, stirring and scraping the bottom of the pan. Continue whisking and gradually add the turkey stock, 1 cup at a time. Use only enough stock to reach a gravy consistency. Season to taste with salt and pepper.

Helpful Stuff about Stuffing

When most people think of roasted turkey, they think of stuffing as well. Take a look at the following tips about stuffing before you begin, and you'll be sure to leave your guests stuffed (pardon the pun!).

✔ **Whenever making stuffing for your roasted turkey (whether it is cooked in the bird or separately), make sure that the bread you use is very dry, even stale.** Two-day-old bread (left out uncovered) yields the best result; fresh, moist bread can leave it gummy. On the other hand, if the bread gets as hard as a Louisville Slugger, you may have a difficult time working with it.

To dry out fresh bread, place slices or cubes on a baking sheet and leave them uncovered a day or two, turning them now and then. Or dry out the bread on a baking sheet in a 200-degree oven, turning frequently.

✔ **As a general guideline, you need about ¾ to 1 cup of stuffing per pound of bird.** This amount also leaves you with delicious leftovers.

✔ **When making stuffing, over-mixing and packing it too densely into the bird's cavity can cause the stuffing to cook more slowly and crumble when served.** If not baking it inside the bird's cavity, bake your stuffing in a well-buttered, covered baking dish for about 45 minutes. Try to time the cooking so that the stuffing comes out of the oven as the bird is being carved.

✔ **Drizzle a little chicken stock, a little white wine, or some of the turkey pan drippings over it for extra flavor and moisture.**

In the following stuffing recipe, we use poultry seasoning, which is a commercial blend of ground sage, rosemary, thyme, marjoram, savory, and salt. However, you can experiment and substitute any of your favorite herbs. Be sure the poultry seasoning is not too old — one telltale sign is a faded, yellowish label with a promotional quote like "Eleanor Roosevelt's favorite!" Dried spices can lose potency within a year of opening.

Stuffing cooked separately from the turkey may need a little extra moisture. The stuffing in our recipe is kept moist with pork sausage, eggs, and an assortment of fruits and vegetables. However, if after 30 minutes in the oven, the stuffing becomes a little dry, simple add a little more chicken stock or warm water, then return it to the oven to finish baking.

Cornbread, Sausage, and Apple Stuffing

Tools: *Chef's knife, apple corer, large skillet, slotted spoon, whisk, ovenproof baking dish*

Preparation time: *20 minutes*

Cooking time: *About 1 hour*

Yield: *10 to 12 servings*

(continued)

About 7 to 8 tablespoons butter

1 pound bulk pork sausage (mild or hot, to taste)

1 large onion, diced

1 cup diced celery

1 large red bell pepper, cored, seeded, and diced

2 hot chili peppers or jalapeño peppers, seeded and diced (optional)

8 cups cornbread cubes (see Cornbread recipe later in this section)

4 cups stale French bread, cut into ⅓- to ½-inch cubes

2 Golden Delicious apples, peeled, cored, and cut into small cubes

⅓ cup chopped parsley

2 teaspoons poultry seasoning, or to taste

1 teaspoon sugar

Salt and black pepper to taste

1 14½-ounce can chicken stock, or 2 cups homemade

2 eggs, lightly beaten

1 In a large skillet, melt 2 tablespoons of the butter over medium-high heat. Add the sausage and cook until browned, about 5 minutes, stirring frequently to break it up. Using a slotted spoon, remove the sausage to a large mixing bowl.

2 Add to the skillet 4 more tablespoons of butter with the onion, celery, red bell pepper, and if desired, the hot peppers. Cook, stirring occasionally, about 4 to 5 minutes or until vegetables are cooked but still a little firm. Stir the vegetables into the sausage.

3 Add the cornbread and French bread cubes, apples, parsley, poultry seasoning, sugar, salt, and pepper; toss well.

4 In a small bowl, whisk together the chicken stock and eggs; add this to the stuffing, about 1 cup at a time, stirring well. Add enough egg-broth mixture to moisten the stuffing so that it holds together when lightly pressed between the palms of your hands.

5 Transfer the dressing into a well-buttered baking dish with a lid; dot with 1 to 2 tablespoons of butter. Cover and bake at 325 degrees for 45 to 55 minutes, or until heated through.

If you need a little more liquid to hold the stuffing together, use a little more stock or warm water. If you can't find bulk pork sausage, purchase sausage links and remove the casings.

You can substitute some white wine for some of the chicken stock to add more flavor. Instead of using poultry seasoning, substitute 2 to 3 tablespoons of fresh chopped herbs such as sage, marjoram, thyme, or any combination.

Cornbread mixes and cornbread muffins are often too moist and sweet to use as a base for stuffing. This cornbread recipe holds its shape when combined with the other stuffing ingredients. It can be made ahead of time and frozen, or wrapped and kept in the refrigerator for a few days. It's perfect for stuffing but too hard and dry to cut into squares and serve on its own.

Cornbread for Stuffing

Tools: *Measuring cup, large bowl, wire whisk, 8- or 9-inch square baking pan*

Preparation time: *5 minutes*

Cooking time: *20 minutes*

Yield: *About 8 cups cornbread cubes*

1 cup yellow cornmeal	*½ teaspoon salt*
1 cup flour	*l cup buttermilk*
1 tablespoon plus 1 teaspoon baking powder	*1 egg*
2 teaspoons sugar	*⅓ cup corn oil or vegetable oil*

1 Preheat the oven to 425 degrees.

2 In a large bowl, combine the cornmeal, flour, baking powder, sugar, and salt; stir to mix.

3 With a wire whisk, stir in the buttermilk, egg, and oil; beat just until the mixture is combined — do not over-mix. Spread the batter on a buttered 8- or 9-inch square baking pan. Bake for 20 minutes, or until the top of the bread springs back when touched. Cool in the pan on a wire rack. If you are not using the cornbread right away, cut the bread into big pieces, wrap tightly, and refrigerate until ready to make the stuffing. Slice the cornbread into ¼- to ½-inch cubes for turkey stuffing.

We dress up the following cranberry relish recipe by adding some brandy or Cointreau, but they're optional.

Fresh Cranberry Relish

Tools: *Paring knife, food processor*

Preparation time: *10 minutes*

Cooking time: *None (about 1 hour to chill)*

Yield: *About 3 cups*

1 navel orange

1 12-ounce package fresh or frozen cranberries

1 cup sugar

2 teaspoons brandy, Cointreau, or other orange liqueur (optional)

½ cup chopped walnuts (optional)

1 Starting at the stem end of the orange, remove the peel, working in a spiral fashion with a sharp paring knife; take care to leave behind the bitter white pith (the soft, white layer that lies beneath the orange peel). Set the orange peel aside.

2 Peel away and discard the layer of white pith from the orange; coarsely chop the fruit.

3 Put the orange pieces, the orange peel, and the cranberries into the bowl of a food processor. Pulse 4 or 5 times, or until the fruit is coarsely chopped. Transfer the cranberry-orange mixture to a bowl or a glass serving container. Stir in the sugar and, if desired, the brandy or orange liqueur and the walnuts. Chill until ready to serve.

Holiday Vegetables

The following recipe is simple and elegant; it also lends a nice green color to our menu that is dominated by shades of orange. And where many of the other side dishes are sweet, this bean dish is savory. You can make it at the last minute, although you can save time by trimming the beans and mincing the shallots ahead of time.

Green Beans with Shallots

Tools: *Chef's knife, large pot, large skillet*

Preparation time: *15 minutes*

Cooking time: *About 20 minutes*

Yield: *10 servings*

3 pounds fresh green beans, rinsed and trimmed

6 tablespoons butter

1 cup shallots, sliced crosswise into thin rounds

2 teaspoons fresh lemon juice (optional)

Salt and black pepper to taste

1 Place the beans in a large pot. Add cold salted water to cover. Cover the pot and bring to a boil over medium-high heat; cook until just tender but still firm, about 10 to 15 minutes. (Actual cooking time will depend on the tenderness and size of the beans.) Check for doneness after about 8 minutes.

2 As the beans cook, melt the butter in a large skillet. Add the shallots and cook over medium heat for 3 to 4 minutes, stirring often, until golden. Set aside.

3 Drain the beans well and add them to the skillet with the shallots. Stir to combine and heat briefly just before serving. If desired, stir in the lemon juice. Season to taste with salt and pepper.

An elegant alternative for this dish is thin, French string beans, also called *haricot verts*. If making this variation, reduce cooking time to 4 to 6 minutes or until tender.

Sweet potatoes are a traditional holiday favorite. Try one or both of our sweet potato recipes that follow.

Mashed Sweet Potatoes

Tools: *Large pot, potato masher or handheld electric mixer*

Preparation time: *15 minutes*

Cooking time: *20 minutes*

Yield: *10 servings*

5 pounds sweet potatoes, peeled and cut into large chunks

⅔ cup packed light brown sugar

½ cup light cream, half-and-half, or milk

6 tablespoons butter, softened

¾ teaspoon ground cinnamon

½ teaspoon ground allspice

¼ teaspoon ground nutmeg

Salt to taste

2 teaspoons maple or vanilla extract (optional)

(continued)

1 Place the potatoes in a pot with cold, lightly salted water to cover. Cover the pot and bring the water to a boil. Reduce the heat and simmer for about 20 minutes or until the potato chunks are very tender. Drain thoroughly and return the sweet potatoes to the same pot.

2 Add the brown sugar, cream, butter, spices, and salt. Place the pot over low heat and mash with a potato masher or beat with a handheld mixer on medium speed until smooth. Remove the mixture from the heat; if desired, stir in the maple or vanilla extract. When ready to serve, reheat over low heat, stirring often, until the potatoes are warmed through.

Remember that bottle of dark rum you bought impulsively at the duty free store in the airport? If you're like us, that bottle is sitting, unopened, in your kitchen. Well, get out the bottle . . . here's a great way to use it.

These terrific sweet potatoes can be baked very quickly — you can put them in the oven as you are removing the turkey to rest. The sweet potatoes are first parboiled (which softens them slightly and makes the second cooking much quicker) for about 15 minutes, then they bake for about 20 minutes to finish cooking.

Rum-Baked Sweet Potatoes

Tools: *Chef's knife, large pot, large skillet, baking dish*

Preparation time: *5 to 10 minutes*

Cooking time: *About 45 minutes*

Yield: *8 servings*

4 medium sweet potatoes (about 3½ pounds), peeled

¼ cup butter

1 cup packed dark brown sugar

⅓ cup dark rum

¼ cup fresh orange juice

½ teaspoon ground allspice

Salt and black pepper to taste

1 Preheat oven to 350 degrees.

2 Cut the potatoes in half lengthwise; place them in a large pot of lightly salted boiling water. Cover and boil for 15 to 20 minutes, or until still slightly firm when pierced with a fork. (Don't overcook, or they will fall apart. You want them slightly *under*cooked. Check for doneness after 10 minutes.) Drain and cut each sweet potato in half lengthwise and then widthwise into quarters. Place the potatoes in a single layer on a 9-x-13-inch baking pan (or a ceramic baking dish that can be brought right from the oven to the table). Set aside.

3 In a large skillet, melt the butter over medium heat; add the brown sugar, rum, and orange juice. Bring to a boil, stirring occasionally to break up any lumps of sugar. Reduce the heat and simmer for 7 to 8 minutes, stirring occasionally, until the sauce is thickened and slightly caramelized. Stir in the allspice.

4 Drizzle the rum mixture over sweet potatoes. Gently turn the potatoes in the glaze to coat all sides. Season the potatoes well with salt and pepper. Bake for 20 to 25 minutes or until the sauce is bubbly and the potatoes are heated through and tender.

This uncommon pumpkin pie uses a sweet, delicious, and thin bottom crust of crunchy pecans and brown sugar. The pecan layer is a nice contrast to the semisweet pumpkin filling. We give you the crust recipe using a food processor — the best and quickest way to make pie pastry. But of course you can use a pastry blender or two knives to work the butter and shortening into the flour and salt. (See Chapter 16 for complete instructions and illustrations).

Praline Pumpkin Pie

Tools: *Food processor, rolling pin, 9-inch pie pan, scissors (or sharp knife), aluminum foil, chef's knife, pan, saucepan, 2 medium mixing bowls, large mixing bowl, rubber spatula, handheld mixer (optional), wire cooling rack*

Preparation time: *5 to 10 minutes for the pastry crust (a little more if mixing by hand), 15 minutes for filling, 1 hour chilling*

Cooking time: *8 minutes for pastry crust, 1 hour for filling*

Yield: *8 servings*

3 tablespoons butter, chilled (for pastry)

3 tablespoons vegetable shortening (such as Crisco) or chilled margarine

1 cup flour

¼ teaspoon salt

2 to 3 tablespoons ice water

1 cup packed light brown sugar

3 tablespoons butter (for filling)

⅔ cup coarsely chopped, lightly toasted pecans

1½ cups canned pumpkin

3 eggs, lightly beaten

1 tablespoon granulated sugar

1 teaspoon ginger powder

1 teaspoon ground cinnamon

½ teaspoon ground nutmeg

1 5-ounce can evaporated milk

¼ cup whole milk

2 teaspoons vanilla extract

1 cup lightly sweetened whipped cream, optional

(continued)

Pastry Crust

1 In the bowl of a food processor, cream the butter and shortening. Stop the motor, if necessary, and use a rubber spatula to scrape the mixture toward the blade. Add the flour and salt and process just a few seconds until the dough resembles coarse cornmeal. (If you don't have a food processor, turn to Chapter 16 for instructions and illustrations on how to make pie dough by hand). Add the cold water a little at a time, pulsing just enough to bind the dry ingredients. The exact amount of water required depends on the humidity of your kitchen. *Do not overblend* or the dough will get tough. Shape the dough into a ball, wrap entirely with plastic wrap, and refrigerate for at least 1 hour.

2 Before baking the pie crust, preheat the oven to 450 degrees.

3 Lightly flour a large cutting board or counter and, with a rolling pin, roll out the dough into a circle that is about 12 inches in diameter. Loosely drape the dough around a rolling pin and position it over the pie pan. Unroll the dough onto the bottom of the pie plate and gently pat it flush against the sides. With scissors or a sharp knife, trim the overhanging pastry to ½ inch beyond the edge of the plate. Flute the crust by pinching the dough all around the edge. Do not prick the bottom. Line the bottom with a double thickness of aluminum foil. Bake for 8 minutes. Carefully remove the foil. Bake for 4 to 5 minutes more or until the bottom of the crust is set and dry. Let cool.

Filling

1 Preheat oven to 375 degrees.

2 In a small pan combine ⅓ cup of the brown sugar with the 3 tablespoons butter. Cook over medium heat for a few minutes, stirring constantly until the butter is melted and the brown sugar is dissolved. Stir in the pecans. With a spatula or spoon, spread this hot mixture over the bottom of the cooled pastry shell; set aside to cool to room temperature.

3 Meanwhile, in a large mixing bowl, combine the pumpkin with the remaining ⅔ cup of brown sugar; add the eggs, granulated sugar, and spices and beat lightly with a whisk or handheld mixer on low speed until well blended. Whisk or beat in the evaporated milk, whole milk, and vanilla extract, blending well. Pour the filling over the cooled pecan mixture in the pie shell.

4 Bake the pie for 45 to 50 minutes or until a knife inserted into the center comes out clean. Cool on a wire rack. Cover and refrigerate until ready to serve. If desired, spoon a heaping tablespoon of lightly sweetened whipped cream over each portion before serving (see Chapter 7 for a great whipped cream recipe).

Be sure to flute the pastry crust high over the edge of the plate; the filling of this pie comes all the way to the top.

Part VI
The Part of Tens

The 5th Wave — By Rich Tennant

COOKBOOKS TO AVOID

CLASSIC New England Boiled Desserts

PASTA ON THE GRILL WITH Rolf

HEADCHEESE HEADCHEESE and more HEADCHEESE at the Gilmore Inn

Technique de Manifold

Cooking on your engine block the French way!

In this part . . .

Think of this part as a cheat sheet to use after finishing the course. You can refer to these lists for specific reminders or just for fun. (We had fun writing them, anyway.)

Here, you'll find information about classic cookbooks that you may want around your kitchen. And you'll discover how to think like a chef.

Chapter 21

Ten Classic Cookbooks

*1*n America, cookbooks roll off assembly lines like Buicks. How can a shopper tell which books are good and which are better employed as trunk weights in a snowstorm?

For advice on sorting through the awesomely cluttered cookbook shelves in bookstores today, we talked to one of America's authorities, Nach Waxman, owner of Kitchen Arts & Letters (212-876-5550), a wonderful shop dedicated to food and wine books that has become a must-see for food lovers who visit New York City.

We asked Waxman: "How can browsers tell the difference between a mediocre cookbook and a great cookbook?" He said, "It may seem obvious at first, but a good cookbook had better be one that has food in it you like. Big-name authors, chic new ingredients, stylish color photographs — they all mean nothing if you don't see food that you really like. Flip through a book and see how many times in, say 20 pages, you find yourself saying, 'Wow, I'd really enjoy eating that.'

"Second, read a couple of recipes and make sure that you know what the authors are talking about. Do you speak their language?

"Third, make sure the book is not merely a collection of recipes — first do this, then do that — but a source of information and ideas that will let you make decisions on your own and will help your cooking grow. The idea is for you to be in control and not simply a rote follower of someone else's instructions."

This chapter lists ten wide-ranging cookbooks that have stood the test of time. Lots of great cookbooks are out there, but if you own the following books, you'll be set for years.

The Best of Craig Claiborne

Craig Claiborne with Pierre Franey (Times Books, 1999)

Hundreds of well written and reliable recipes from the famous culinary duo from *The New York Times.*

Better Homes and Gardens New Cookbook

Betters Homes and Gardens Editors (Better Homes and Gardens Books, 1999)

This is a great all-around book for home cooks. Most recipes are easy and well-suited for everyday cooking.

The Cake Bible

Rose Levy Beranbaum (Morrow, 1988)

An exhaustive, authoritative guide to baking any kind of cake imaginable.

Essentials of Classic Italian Cooking

Marcella Hazan (Knopf, 1992)

If you buy only one book on Italian cooking, you might well choose this one. Hazan, an easygoing and thorough teacher, covers all the techniques involved in Italian cuisine. The fresh pasta and gnocchi chapters are particularly well done.

How to Bake

Nick Malgieri (HarperCollins, 1995)

Nick Malgieri is a highly respected cooking instructor based in New York City. This book has an easygoing and authoritative approach to baking everything from baguettes to brownies.

James Beard's American Cookery

James Beard (Budget Book Service, 1996)

A broad look at American culinary styles through the impish personality of the larger-than-life James Beard. Recipes are traditional and solid.

The New Joy of Cooking

Irma S. Rombauer, Marion Rombauer Becker, and Ethan Becker (Scribner, 1997)

This best-selling classic is an excellent primer for beginning cooks, filled with lucid illustrations and instructions. This book tells you how to make the classic version of a dish — you take it from there.

Larousse Gastronomique: The New American Edition of the World's Greatest Culinary Encyclopedia

Edited by Jenifer Harvey Lang (Crown, 1988)

This book is more an encyclopedia of food than a cookbook. Filled with color photos and illustrations, it is the definitive resource for answers to cooking questions. The book does not give recipes per se but rather descriptions of how to make something as if you were telling a friend. Its historical notes are interesting, too.

Mastering the Art of French Cooking, Volumes I and II

Julia Child, Louisette Bertholle, and Simone Beck (Knopf, 1983 and 1991)

Not an everyday cookbook, this two-volume classic is where you go to learn how to do something the way it was originally intended. If you have a strong interest in French cuisine, this book is indispensable. Particularly interesting are the step-by-step instructions for making pastries, dough, bread, and cakes.

The New Doubleday Cookbook

Jean Anderson and Elaine Hanna (Doubleday, 1990)

This amazingly comprehensive book belongs in every cook's kitchen. For a tome of this size (967 pages), it is stylish and light on its feet. Instructions are well written, and illustrations are easy to follow. Every aspect of American and international cooking is covered. Whenever we couldn't find something in other references while researching this book, we found it in *The New Doubleday Cookbook*.

Buying cookbooks via the Internet

A lot of the fun of getting a cookbook is browsing through the books you don't buy. There are so many gorgeous books out there, full of pictures of glistening fruit pies and steaming loaves of bread, that were never meant to enter a real-life kitchen! But one great picture can get your taste buds working and your imagination off and running.

You also can buy the books you need to get started without ever leaving the comfort of your own home. One way is through the Internet. Here are some great Internet resources for buying books as well as all kinds of kitchen equipment:

✔ **www.epicurious.com:** Owned by Condé Nast publications, this is perhaps the most comprehensive food Web site around, combining 10,000 well-researched recipes from *Bon Appétit* and *Gourmet* magazines, and a giant library of cookbooks (including hard-to-find vintage books).

✔ **www.tavolo.com:** Affiliated with the Culinary Institute of America, this began as a recipe site but now sells a wide range of kitchen equipment, specialty foods, and cookbooks.

✔ **www.globalgourmet.com:** This offbeat and informative site is strong on food history and includes columns like "I Love Chocolate" and "Cooking with Kids." It also features a fine online cookbook store affiliated with the well-regarded bookseller Lisa Ekus Presents (lisaekus.com).

Chapter 22

Ten Ways to Think Like a Chef

*I*n observing and interviewing many chefs, we found a consensus among them about how to progress as a cook. The ten points in this chapter reflect their thoughts.

Know the Basic Techniques

Cooking is so much more fun — and successful — when you approach it with confidence. Chefs say that confidence arises from knowing your techniques so well that they are second nature.

Use Only the Freshest Ingredients

Use only the freshest ingredients and buy in-season fresh fruits and vegetables. Seasonal produce offers the highest quality and supply and the lowest price. Why make an apple pie in the summer from mealy apples held in storage all year when you can make one with fresh, ripe peaches or juicy plums? Let what's fresh and available at the market help you spontaneously decide what's for dinner.

Get It Together

So much of cooking, even for professionals, is preparation — slicing, peeling, dicing, and so on.

The French call this preparation *mise en place,* which translates to "everything in its place." Get the chopping, mincing, deboning, and washing chores out of the way in order to create an even, efficient flow of cooking steps.

That way, when the butter or oil is hot and sizzling in the skillet, you don't need to stop suddenly to peel and mince onions and garlic that are supposed to be sautéed in the hot fat.

With This Basil, I Thee Wed

Learn about herbs, both fresh and dried, so that you can season without always relying on a book or recipe. Chefs base some of the world's great cuisines on the combination of a few simple herbs and spices.

For example, Italian cooking relies heavily on the flavors of garlic, olive oil, tomatoes, Parmesan cheese, and basil. The French use a basic seasoning blend called *mirepoix* — a sautéed mixture of chopped onions, carrots, and celery. Many chefs begin their soups, stews, stuffings, and pan sauces with these simple, sautéed ingredients. Louisiana home cooks have their own version, which adds chopped bell pepper and garlic to the mix. You can vary this base by adding bacon, ham, fresh herbs, or even curry. In a perfectly made *mirepoix,* the vegetables cook slowly for a long time, causing them to caramelize slightly and sweeten.

All the Plate's a Stage

Think of the choreography of food on a plate. People eat with their eyes first. The food should be colorful and attractively arranged, with fresh herbs as a colorful garnish.

"Try to have an average of four components in every dish," says Frank Brigtsen, chef and owner of Brigtsen's restaurant in New Orleans. According to Brigtsen, four distinct components give a dish complexity without being too fussy. For example, Brigtsen serves at his restaurant a blackened tuna with a smoked corn sauce, a red bean salad, and avocado sour cream, which results in four distinct colors. "Dress up the main element of the dish, whether it's fish, meat, or poultry, with sauces, condiments, and garnishes that add a balance of interest and flavors," he says.

Plan Your Menus in Advance

Before cooking, think about contrasting flavors, textures, and colors. If the appetizer is a salad of grilled portobello mushrooms, then mushrooms in the entree is not an interesting choice. Keep the courses balanced and don't overload yourself. If you serve a time-consuming and complex appetizer, serve a simple entree or one that needs only reheating, like a tasty stew. If your appetizer is cold, be sure that the entree is hot.

Take a good look at the timing of the meal, too. Figure out how much cooking and preparation time are needed so that your diners don't feel they are getting the bum's rush or have to wait too long between courses.

Be Thrifty

Throw out nothing (unless, of course, it's spoiled). Every morsel of food is usable for soups, stocks, salads, and so on. You can sometimes make great meals from leftovers (see Chapter 17 for ideas for using leftovers).

Learn about different cuts of meat and how to cook them so that you don't have to rely on more expensive cuts. Hone your knife skills so that you can save money by purchasing whole chickens, ducks, fish, and so on and then cutting them up yourself.

Don't Be a Slave to Recipes

Use a good, basic recipe that you like as a starting point, but don't consider it written in stone. Say you have a recipe for basic stew. You make it once and decide that it could use more garlic, so the next time you double the amount. Or instead of turnips, you think that the sweet effect of chopped carrots would work, so you substitute one vegetable for the other. With experience and good technique, and by learning how ingredients work together, you can simply glance at a recipe and make adjustments to suit your taste.

Simplify, Simplify

"It's not what you decide to put into a dish that's important, it's what you decide to keep out," says Jan Birnbaum, owner and chef of The Catahoula Restaurant and Saloon in Calistoga, California. Start with a product that's fresh and flavorful and add only those seasonings that complement the food.

Above All, Have Fun

Take a cooking course, buy yourself a cookbook, or make a new dish that you've always wanted to try. Cooking, like golf, should be fun — something you look forward to. So what if you slam one into the rough every now and then? It's all part of the game.

As they say, a mistake is never a lost cause — it's a learning experience. And don't be afraid of cooking. "Cooking is about making decisions — not hesitant ones, but decisive ones. Figure out the results you want, give the situation serious, careful thought, and then go for it," says George Germon, chef and co-owner of Al Forno in Providence, Rhode Island.

Here's just one example of how you can start at the bottom and climb the learning tree. Cook spaghetti, drain, and toss with olive oil that has been used to cook a sliver of garlic (leave the garlic in the oil). Taste it. Now go one step up the flavor ladder by cooking another small batch of pasta. This time, cook onions with the garlic and olive oil. Taste the sweetness? Now do it again with dried oregano added to the other ingredients. See how the oregano adds a whole new flavor dimension? Now add crushed tomatoes. You have a completely different dish.

This little exercise, aside from producing a lot of leftover spaghetti, is a great exercise in taste discrimination. You can do it with other sauces, mousses, soups, and more. The more you learn about how different herbs and spices taste, the better cook you will be.

Part VII
Appendixes

The 5th Wave   By Rich Tennant

"Do I like arugula? I _love_ arugula!! Some of the best beaches in the world are there."

In this part . . .

As you're reading this book, you may want to flip back to the appendixes in this part to get a little extra information. If you've heard a cooking term, but you're not quite sure what it means, we have the definition for you. And if you need to make a substitution for a common ingredient, you've come to the right place. Equivalents, substitutions, abbreviations, definitions — they're all here at your fingertips.

Glossary of 100 (Plus) Common Cooking Terms

Cooking and recipe-writing have their own distinct language. Before you roast a chicken, for example, you need to know what *trussing* means. To make a soufflé that rises above the rim of the dish, you need to understand *whipping* and *folding* egg whites. This appendix gives you a list of basic terms. Most of them are thoroughly described and illustrated elsewhere in the book.

Adjust: To taste the dish before serving and add seasoning (such as salt and pepper), if necessary.

Al dente: An Italian phrase meaning "to the tooth" that describes the tender but still firm texture of perfectly cooked pasta. (See Chapter 11 for pasta recipes.)

Au gratin: A dish, usually topped with buttered bread crumbs, grated cheese, or both, that has been browned in the oven or under the broiler.

Bake: To cook in the dry heat of an oven. (See Chapter 13 for easy baking recipes.)

Barbecue: Any food cooked on a charcoal or gas grill. Also refers to the process of cooking foods in a pit or on a spit for a long time.

Baste: To add flavor and moisture by brushing food with pan drippings, fat, or a seasoned liquid as it cooks.

Batter: An uncooked, semiliquid mixture usually containing beaten eggs, flour, liquid, and a leavening ingredient, such as baking soda or baking powder, that makes the batter rise when cooked.

Beat: To mix ingredients briskly in a circular motion so that they become smooth and creamy. A hundred hand-beaten strokes generally equal one minute with an electric mixer, if you're the type who counts these things. (See Chapter 8 for information about beating egg whites.)

Beurre manié: A butter-flour paste used to thicken soups and stews. (Turn to Chapter 9 for instructions for making this paste.)

Bind: To bring together a liquid mixture, such as a sauce, with a thickening ingredient, such as cream or butter.

Blanch: To plunge vegetables or fruits into boiling water for a short time to loosen their skin or preserve their color. (See Chapter 3.)

Blend: To mix or combine two or more ingredients with a spoon, whisk, spatula, or electric mixer.

Boil: To bring the temperature of a liquid to 212 degrees for water at sea level, causing bubbles to break at the surface. (See Chapter 3.)

Bone (or debone): To remove the bones from meat, fish, or poultry.

Bouquet garni: A package of mixed herbs (often tied in cheesecloth) that is used to season stocks, soups, and stews to impart flavor. A typical combination is parsley, thyme, and bay leaf.

Braise: To brown meat or vegetables in fat and then cook, covered, in a small quantity of liquid over low heat, usually for a long time. The long, slow cooking both tenderizes and flavors the food, especially tough cuts of meat. Braising can take place either on the stovetop or in the oven. (See Chapter 5 for braising and stewing recipes.)

Bread: To coat a piece of food with crackers or bread crumbs to seal in moisture and give it a crisp crust. The piece of fish, poultry, meat, or vegetable is usually first dipped into a liquid, such as beaten egg or milk, to make the crumbs adhere.

Broil: To cook food under a hot oven coil, as opposed to grilling, in which the heat is underneath.

Brown: To cook food briefly over high heat, usually in fat and on top of the stove, to impart a rich brown color to its skin or surface. Food also may be browned in a very hot oven or under the broiler.

Brush: To coat the surface of food with a liquid ingredient such as melted butter, egg, or fruit glaze.

Butterfly: To split food down the center (removing bones if necessary), leaving the two halves joined at the seam so that the food opens flat to resemble a butterfly.

Caramelize: To heat sugar until it melts into a liquid, syrupy state that ranges from golden to dark brown in color (320 degrees to 350 degrees on a candy thermometer). See Chapter 7 for a recipe for Caramel Sauce. Also, to cook onions and other vegetables until they become soft and brown (the sugars they contain caramelize).

Chop: To cut food into small pieces by using a knife or food processor.

Clarify: To make a cloudy liquid clear by removing the impurities. For example, you can clarify a stock or broth by simmering raw egg whites or eggshells for 10 to 15 minutes to attract impurities. You then very gently strain the liquid through a sieve lined with cheesecloth.

Core: To cut out the core of a food, usually a fruit or vegetable such as an apple or pepper.

Cream: To beat one ingredient, such as butter, with another, such as sugar, until soft and smooth.

Crimp: To press together with your fingers or a fork and seal the rim of a double-crust pie to form a double thickness of dough that you can then shape into a decorative pattern. (See Chapter 16.)

Crumble: To break up or crush food, such as dried herbs or crackers, into small pieces with your fingers.

Cube: To cut food into ½-inch square pieces. Cubed food is larger than diced food. See also _dice_.

Cure: To preserve food such as meat or fish by salting, drying, and/or smoking.

Dash: See _pinch_.

Deglaze: To add liquid, usually wine or broth, to a hot skillet or roasting pan and scrape up the browned bits clinging to the bottom of the pan that pieces of sautéed meat, fish, or poultry left behind. You then reduce and season the pan sauce. See Chapter 7 for recipes that use this technique.

Degrease: To skim the fat off the surface of a soup or gravy with a spoon. Also done by chilling the mixture, turning the liquid fat into a solid, which you can then easily lift off the surface.

Demi-glace: A rich, brown sauce made by boiling down meat stock until it's reduced to a thick glaze that can coat a spoon. (See Chapter 7.)

Devein: To remove the vein from shrimp or other shellfish. (See Chapter 12 for illustrated instructions for cleaning shrimp.)

Devil: To season foods with hot and spicy ingredients such as Tabasco sauce, mustard, or red pepper flakes.

Dice: To cut into small (⅛-inch to ¼-inch) cubes.

Dilute: To thin a mixture by adding water or other liquid.

Disjoint: To sever a piece of meat at its joint, as when you separate a chicken leg from its thigh.

Dot: To distribute small portions or pieces of food (such as bits of butter) over the surface of another food.

Drain: To remove the liquid from a food, often in a colander. Also, to pour off liquid fat from a pan after you brown a food (such as bacon or ground meat).

Dredge: To coat the surface of a food by dragging it through flour, cornmeal, or crumbs.

Drizzle: To pour a liquid such as melted butter, sauce, or syrup over a food in a thin, slow stream.

Dust: To give the surface of food a thin coating of flour or confectioners' sugar.

Fillet: To cut the flesh away from the bones of a piece of meat or fish.

Flambé: To ignite food that is drenched in alcohol so that it bursts into a dramatic flame just before serving. (See Chapter 4 for a recipe for Sautéed Peppered Filet of Beef, which includes a flambé option.)

Fold: To combine a light mixture, such as beaten egg whites or whipped cream, with a heavier mixture, such as sugared egg yolks or melted chocolate, by using a gentle mixing motion. (See Chapter 8 for illustrated instructions.)

Fricassee: A white stew in which meat or poultry is not browned before cooking. (See Chapter 5.)

Fry: To cook or sauté food in fat over high heat. Deep-fried foods are submerged in hot fat and cooked until crisp.

Fumet: A concentrated fish stock that is used as a flavoring base for sauces.

Garnish: An edible plate adornment, ranging from a simple wedge of lemon to a fancy chocolate leaf. (See Chapter 9 for a list of soup garnishes.)

Glaze: To coat the surface of a food with syrup, melted jelly, an egg wash, or other thin, liquid mixture to give it a glossy shine.

Grate: To rub a large piece of food (such as a block of cheese) against the coarse, serrated holes of a grater.

Grease: To spread a thin layer of fat, usually butter, on the inside of a pan to prevent food from sticking as it cooks.

Grill: To cook food over a charcoal or gas grill, or to cook on an iron (or other) grill on the stovetop. (See Chapter 6.) Relatively high heat is used to sear food and add depth of flavor.

Hull: To trim strawberries by plucking out their green stems.

Julienne: To cut foods into thin (⅛ inch or less) strips.

Knead: The technique of pushing, folding, and pressing dough for yeast breads to give it a smooth, elastic texture. You can knead by hand or with an electric mixer equipped with a bread hook or a bread machine.

Marinate: To soak or steep a food such as meat, poultry, fish, or vegetables in a liquid mixture that may be seasoned with spices and herbs in order to impart flavor to the food before it is cooked. (See Chapter 6.) The steeping liquid is called the *marinade*.

Mash: To press food, usually with a potato masher or ricer, into a soft pulp. (See Chapter 3.)

Mince: To cut food into tiny pieces.

Mirepoix: A combination of finely chopped sautéed vegetables, usually carrots, onions, and celery, that is used as a seasoning base for soups, stews, stuffings, and other dishes. (See Chapter 22.)

Parboil: To partially cook foods, such as rice or dense vegetables like carrots and potatoes, by plunging them briefly into boiling water. (See Chapter 3.)

Pare: To remove the skin from fruits or vegetables.

Pickle: To preserve food in a salty brine or vinegar solution.

Pinch or dash: A small amount of any dry ingredient (between ¹⁄₁₆ and ⅛ teaspoon) that can be grasped between the tips of the thumb and forefinger.

Poach: To cook foods in a simmering, not boiling, liquid. (See Chapter 3.)

Pound: To flatten food, especially chicken breasts or meat, with a meat mallet or the flat side of a large knife (such as a cleaver) to make it uniform in thickness. Has some tenderizing effect.

Preheat: To turn on the oven, grill, or broiler before cooking food to set the temperature to the degree required by the recipe.

Puree: To mash or grind food into a paste by forcing through a food mill or sieve or by whirling in a food processor or blender. Finely mashed food also is called a puree.

Ream: To extract the juice from fruit, especially citrus.

Reconstitute: To bring dehydrated food, such as dried milk or juice, back to a liquid state by adding water.

Reduce: The technique of rapidly boiling a liquid mixture, such as wine, stock, or sauce, to decrease its original volume so that it thickens and concentrates in flavor.

Render: To cook a piece of meat over low heat so that its fat melts away.

Roast: To cook in the dry heat of an oven. (See Chapter 6.)

Roux: A cooked paste of flour and fat such as oil or butter that is used to thicken soups, stews, and gumbos. (See Chapter 7.)

Sauté: To cook food quickly in a small amount of fat, usually butter or oil, over very high heat. (See Chapter 4.)

Scald: To heat milk to just below the boiling point when making custards and dessert sauces to shorten the cooking time.

Score: To make shallow cuts (often in a crisscross pattern) on the exterior of a food (such as meat, fish, or bread) so that it cooks more evenly.

Sear: To brown quickly in a pan, under the broiler, or in a very hot oven. (See Chapter 4.)

Season: To flavor foods with herbs, spices, salt, pepper, and so on.

Shred: To reduce food to thin strips, usually by rubbing it against a grater.

Shuck: To remove shells from shellfish, such as clams (see Chapter 11 for illustrated instructions), oysters, and mussels or to remove husks from fresh corn.

Sift: To shake dry ingredients, such as flour or confectioners' sugar, through a fine mesh sifter to incorporate air and make them lighter.

Simmer: To gently cook food in a liquid just below the boiling point or just until tiny bubbles begin to break the surface (at about 185 degrees). (See Chapter 3.)

Skewer: To thread small pieces of food on long, thin rods made of bamboo or metal to hold meat, fish, or vegetables for grilling or broiling.

Skim: To remove the fat and bits of food that rise to the surface of a soup or stock with a spoon. (See Chapter 3.)

Steam: To cook over a small amount of simmering or boiling water in a covered pan so that the steam trapped in the pan cooks the food. (See Chapter 3.)

Stew: To simmer food for a long time in a tightly covered pot with just enough liquid to cover. The term *stew* also can describe a cooked dish. (See Chapter 5.)

Stir-fry: The Asian cooking technique of quickly frying small pieces of food in a wok with a small amount of fat over very high heat while constantly tossing and stirring the ingredients. The term *stir-fry* also can refer to a dish prepared this way.

Stock: The strained, flavorful liquid that is produced by cooking meat, fish, poultry, vegetables, seasonings, or other ingredients in water. (See Chapter 3.)

Strain: To separate liquids from solids by passing a mixture through a sieve.

Stuff: To fill a food cavity, such as the inside of chicken, turkey, or tomato, with various types of food.

Tenderize: To soften the connective tissue of meat by pounding or cooking very slowly for a long time. See also *braise*.

Toss: To turn over food a number of times to mix thoroughly, as when a green salad is mixed and coated with dressing.

Truss: To tie meat or poultry with string and/or skewers to maintain its shape during roasting. (See Chapter 6 for illustrated instructions for trussing a chicken.)

Whip: To beat air into ingredients such as eggs or cream with a whisk or electric beater to make them light and fluffy.

Whisk: A handheld wire kitchen utensil used to whip ingredients like eggs, cream, and sauces. When used as a verb, the term *whisk* describes the process of whipping or blending ingredients together with a wire whisk.

Zest: The colored, grated outer peel (the colored portion only) of citrus fruit that is used as a flavoring ingredient in dressings, stews, desserts, and so on.

Appendix B

Common Substitutions, Abbreviations, and Equivalents

· ·

*S*ay you're making a vinaigrette dressing for a salad and suddenly realize that you're out of vinegar. But you do have lemons, which are an acceptable substitute. How much lemon do you use? Or you may not have whole milk for a gratin dish, but you do have skim milk. Is skim milk okay? Situations like these are what this appendix is all about.

Some ingredients are almost always interchangeable: For example, you can substitute vegetable or olive oil in most cases for butter when sautéing or pan frying; lemon juice for vinegar in salad dressings and marinades; almonds for walnuts in baked breads and muffins; vegetable stock for beef or chicken stock in soups, stews, or sauces; and light cream for half-and-half.

But sometimes there is no acceptable substitution for an ingredient. Other times, the substitution is very exact and specific. This is most often the case for baked goods, where you need to follow a formula to produce a cake, soufflé, pastry, or bread with the perfect height, density, and texture.

Most of the following substitutions are for emergency situations only — when you have run out of an essential ingredient and need a very specific replacement.

For thickening soups, stews, and sauces:

- ✔ 1 tablespoon cornstarch or potato flour = 2 tablespoons all-purpose flour
- ✔ 1 tablespoon arrowroot = 2½ tablespoons all-purpose flour

For flour:

- ✔ 1 cup minus 2 tablespoons sifted all-purpose flour = 1 cup sifted cake flour

- ✔ 1 cup plus 2 tablespoons sifted cake flour = 1 cup sifted all-purpose flour

- ✔ 1 cup sifted self-rising flour = 1 cup sifted all-purpose flour plus 1¼ teaspoons baking powder and a pinch of salt

For leavening agents in baked goods:

- ✔ ¼ teaspoon baking soda plus ½ teaspoon cream of tartar = 1 teaspoon double-acting baking powder

- ✔ ¼ teaspoon baking soda plus ½ cup buttermilk or yogurt = 1 teaspoon double-acting baking powder in liquid mixtures only; reduce liquid in recipe by ½ cup

For dairy products:

- ✔ 1 cup whole milk = ½ cup unsweetened evaporated milk plus ½ cup water

  or 1 cup skim milk plus 2 teaspoons melted butter

  or 1 cup water plus ⅓ cup powdered milk

  or 1 cup soy milk

  or 1 cup buttermilk plus ½ teaspoon baking soda

- ✔ ¾ cup whole milk plus ⅓ cup melted butter = 1 cup heavy cream (but not for making whipped cream)

- ✔ 1 cup skim milk =1 cup water plus ¼ cup nonfat powdered milk, or ½ cup evaporated skim milk plus ½ cup water

- ✔ 1 cup sour milk = 1 cup buttermilk or plain yogurt or 1 cup minus 1 tablespoon milk, plus 1 tablespoon lemon juice or white vinegar after standing 5 to 10 minutes

- ✔ 1 cup sour cream = 1 cup plain yogurt

For eggs:

- ✔ 2 egg yolks = 1 egg for thickening sauces and custards
- ✔ 4 extra-large eggs = 5 large eggs or 6 small eggs

For sweetening:

- ✔ 1 cup sugar = 1 cup molasses (*or* honey) plus ½ teaspoon baking soda
- ✔ 1 cup brown sugar = 1 cup white sugar plus 1½ tablespoons molasses

Miscellaneous substitutions:

- ✔ 1 cup broth or stock = 1 bouillon cube dissolved in 1 cup boiling water
- ✔ 1 square (1 ounce) unsweetened chocolate = 3 tablespoons cocoa plus 1 tablespoon butter, margarine, or vegetable shortening
- ✔ 1 square (1 ounce) semisweet chocolate = 3 tablespoons cocoa plus 1 tablespoon butter, margarine, or vegetable shortening plus 2 tablespoons sugar
- ✔ 1 2- to 3-inch piece of vanilla bean = 1 teaspoon pure vanilla extract

Although we spell out measurements in this book, many cookbooks use abbreviations. Table B-1 lists common abbreviations and what they stand for.

Table B-1	Common Abbreviations
Abbreviation(s)	*What It Stands For*
C, c	cup
g	gram
kg	kilogram
L, l	liter
lb	pound
mL, ml	milliliter
oz	ounce
pt	pint
t, tsp	teaspoon
T, TB, Tbl, Tbsp	tablespoon

Cookbook writers have a penchant for practical jokes. Just when you are getting the hang of cups and tablespoons, they throw you a recipe in ounces and pounds. Tables B-2 and B-3 list common equivalent measures. All measurements are for level amounts. Note that some metric measurements are approximate.

Table B-2	Conversion Secrets	
This Measurement . . .	*. . . Equals This Measurement*	*. . . Equals This Metric Measurement*
Pinch or dash	less than ⅛ teaspoon	0.5 mL
3 teaspoons	1 tablespoon	15 mL
2 tablespoons	1 fluid ounce	30 mL
1 jigger	1½ fluid ounces	45 mL
4 tablespoons	¼ cup	50 mL
5 tablespoons plus 1 teaspoon	⅓ cup	75 mL
12 tablespoons	¾ cup	175 mL
16 tablespoons	1 cup	250 mL
1 cup	8 fluid ounces	250 mL
2 cups	1 pint or 16 fluid ounces	500 mL
2 pints	1 quart or 32 fluid ounces	1 L
4 quarts	1 gallon	4 L

Table B-3	Food Equivalents
This Measurement . . .	*. . . Equals This Measurement*
3 medium apples or bananas	about 1 pound
1 ounce baking chocolate	1 square
2 slices bread	about 1 cup fresh bread crumbs
1 pound brown sugar	2¼ cups packed
4 tablespoons butter	½ stick
8 tablespoons butter	1 stick
4 sticks butter	1 pound
8 ounces chocolate chips	about 1 cup
1 pound confectioners' sugar	about 4½ cups sifted

This Measurement . . .	*. . . Equals This Measurement*
1 pound granulated sugar	2 cups
½ pound hard cheese (such as cheddar)	about 2 cups grated
1 cup heavy whipping cream	2 cups whipped cream
1 medium lemon	3 tablespoons juice, 2 to 3 teaspoons grated zest
1 pound macaroni	4 cups raw, 8 cups cooked
4 ounces nuts	about ⅔ cup chopped
1 large onion	about 1 cup chopped
1 cup raw rice	4 cups cooked
1 pint strawberries	about 2 cups sliced
1 large tomato	about ¾ cup chopped
3 to 4 tomatoes	about 1 pound
1 pound all-purpose flour	about 4 cups sifted

Index

• *C* •

Dummies Books™
Bestsellers on Every Topic!

GENERAL INTEREST TITLES

BUSINESS & PERSONAL FINANCE

...counting For Dummies®	John A. Tracy, CPA	0-7645-5014-4	$19.99 US/$27.99 CAN
...siness Plans For Dummies®	Paul Tiffany, Ph.D. & Steven D. Peterson, Ph.D.	1-56884-868-4	$19.99 US/$27.99 CAN
...siness Writing For Dummies®	Sheryl Lindsell-Roberts	0-7645-5134-5	$16.99 US/$27.99 CAN
...nsulting For Dummies®	Bob Nelson & Peter Economy	0-7645-5034-9	$19.99 US/$27.99 CAN
...stomer Service For Dummies®, 2nd Edition	Karen Leland & Keith Bailey	0-7645-5209-0	$19.99 US/$27.99 CAN
...nchising For Dummies®	Dave Thomas & Michael Seid	0-7645-5160-4	$19.99 US/$27.99 CAN
...tting Results For Dummies®	Mark H. McCormack	0-7645-5205-8	$19.99 US/$27.99 CAN
...me Buying For Dummies®	Eric Tyson, MBA & Ray Brown	1-56884-385-2	$16.99 US/$24.99 CAN
...use Selling For Dummies®	Eric Tyson, MBA & Ray Brown	0-7645-5038-1	$16.99 US/$24.99 CAN
...man Resources Kit For Dummies®	Max Messmer	0-7645-5131-0	$19.99 US/$27.99 CAN
...esting For Dummies®, 2nd Edition	Eric Tyson, MBA	0-7645-5162-0	$19.99 US/$27.99 CAN
...w For Dummies®	John Ventura	1-56884-860-9	$19.99 US/$27.99 CAN
...dership For Dummies®	Marshall Loeb & Steven Kindel	0-7645-5176-0	$19.99 US/$27.99 CAN
...naging For Dummies®	Bob Nelson & Peter Economy	1-56884-858-7	$19.99 US/$27.99 CAN
...rketing For Dummies®	Alexander Hiam	1-56884-699-1	$19.99 US/$27.99 CAN
...tual Funds For Dummies®, 2nd Edition	Eric Tyson, MBA	0-7645-5112-4	$19.99 US/$27.99 CAN
...gotiating For Dummies®	Michael C. Donaldson & Mimi Donaldson	1-56884-867-6	$19.99 US/$27.99 CAN
...rsonal Finance For Dummies®, 3rd Edition	Eric Tyson, MBA	0-7645-5231-7	$19.99 US/$27.99 CAN
...rsonal Finance For Dummies® For Canadians, 2nd Edition	Eric Tyson, MBA & Tony Martin	0-7645-5123-X	$19.99 US/$27.99 CAN
...blic Speaking For Dummies®	Malcolm Kushner	0-7645-5159-0	$16.99 US/$24.99 CAN
...es Closing For Dummies®	Tom Hopkins	0-7645-5063-2	$14.99 US/$21.99 CAN
...es Prospecting For Dummies®	Tom Hopkins	0-7645-5066-7	$14.99 US/$21.99 CAN
...ling For Dummies®	Tom Hopkins	1-56884-389-5	$16.99 US/$24.99 CAN
...all Business For Dummies®	Eric Tyson, MBA & Jim Schell	0-7645-5094-2	$19.99 US/$27.99 CAN
...all Business Kit For Dummies®	Richard D. Harroch	0-7645-5093-4	$24.99 US/$34.99 CAN
...xes 2001 For Dummies®	Eric Tyson & David J. Silverman	0-7645-5306-2	$15.99 US/$23.99 CAN
...me Management For Dummies®, 2nd Edition	Jeffrey J. Mayer	0-7645-5145-0	$19.99 US/$27.99 CAN
...iting Business Letters For Dummies®	Sheryl Lindsell-Roberts	0-7645-5207-4	$16.99 US/$24.99 CAN

TECHNOLOGY TITLES

INTERNET/ONLINE

...erica Online® For Dummies®, 6th Edition	John Kaufeld	0-7645-0670-6	$19.99 US/$27.99 CAN
...nking Online Dummies®	Paul Murphy	0-7645-0458-4	$24.99 US/$34.99 CAN
...ay™ For Dummies®, 2nd Edition	Marcia Collier, Roland Woerner, & Stephanie Becker	0-7645-0761-3	$19.99 US/$27.99 CAN
...Mail For Dummies®, 2nd Edition	John R. Levine, Carol Baroudi, & Arnold Reinhold	0-7645-0131-3	$24.99 US/$34.99 CAN
...nealogy Online For Dummies®, 2nd Edition	Matthew L. Helm & April Leah Helm	0-7645-0543-2	$24.99 US/$34.99 CAN
...ernet Directory For Dummies®, 3rd Edition	Brad Hill	0-7645-0558-2	$24.99 US/$34.99 CAN
...ernet Auctions For Dummies®	Greg Holden	0-7645-0578-9	$24.99 US/$34.99 CAN
...ernet Explorer 5.5 For Windows® For Dummies®	Doug Lowe	0-7645-0738-9	$19.99 US/$28.99 CAN
...searching Online For Dummies®, 2nd Edition	Mary Ellen Bates & Reva Basch	0-7645-0546-7	$24.99 US/$34.99 CAN
... Searching Online For Dummies®	Pam Dixon	0-7645-0673-0	$24.99 US/$34.99 CAN
...esting Online For Dummies®, 3rd Edition	Kathleen Sindell, Ph.D.	0-7645-0725-7	$24.99 US/$34.99 CAN
...vel Planning Online For Dummies®, 2nd Edition	Noah Vadnai	0-7645-0438-X	$24.99 US/$34.99 CAN
...ernet Searching For Dummies®	Brad Hill	0-7645-0478-9	$24.99 US/$34.99 CAN
...oo!® For Dummies®, 2nd Edition	Brad Hill	0-7645-0762-1	$19.99 US/$27.99 CAN
...e Internet For Dummies®, 7th Edition	John R. Levine, Carol Baroudi, & Arnold Reinhold	0-7645-0674-9	$19.99 US/$27.99 CAN

OPERATING SYSTEMS

...S For Dummies®, 3rd Edition	Dan Gookin	0-7645-0361-8	$19.99 US/$27.99 CAN
...OME For Linux® For Dummies®	David B. Busch	0-7645-0650-1	$24.99 US/$37.99 CAN
...UX® For Dummies®, 2nd Edition	John Hall, Craig Witherspoon, & Coletta Witherspoon	0-7645-0421-5	$24.99 US/$34.99 CAN
...c® OS 9 For Dummies®	Bob LeVitus	0-7645-0652-8	$19.99 US/$28.99 CAN
...d Hat® Linux® For Dummies®	Jon "maddog" Hall, Paul Sery	0-7645-0663-3	$24.99 US/$37.99 CAN
...all Business Windows® 98 For Dummies®	Stephen Nelson	0-7645-0425-8	$24.99 US/$34.99 CAN
...IX® For Dummies®, 4th Edition	John R. Levine & Margaret Levine Young	0-7645-0419-3	$19.99 US/$27.99 CAN
...ndows® 95 For Dummies®, 2nd Edition	Andy Rathbone	0-7645-0180-1	$19.99 US/$27.99 CAN
...ndows® 98 For Dummies®	Andy Rathbone	0-7645-0261-1	$19.99 US/$27.99 CAN
...ndows® 2000 For Dummies®	Andy Rathbone	0-7645-0641-2	$19.99 US/$27.99 CAN
...ndows® 2000 Server For Dummies®	Ed Tittel	0-7645-0341-3	$24.99 US/$37.99 CAN
...ndows® ME Millennium Edition For Dummies®	Andy Rathbone	0-7645-0735-4	$19.99 US/$27.99 CAN

Dummies Books™
Bestsellers on Every Topic!

GENERAL INTEREST TITLES

FOOD & BEVERAGE/ENTERTAINING

Bartending For Dummies®	Ray Foley	0-7645-5051-9	$14.99 US/$21.99 CAN
Cooking For Dummies®, 2nd Edition	Bryan Miller & Marie Rama	0-7645-5250-3	$19.99 US/$27.99 CAN
Entertaining For Dummies®	Suzanne Williamson with Linda Smith	0-7645-5027-6	$19.99 US/$27.99 CAN
Gourmet Cooking For Dummies®	Charlie Trotter	0-7645-5029-2	$19.99 US/$27.99 CAN
Grilling For Dummies®	Marie Rama & John Mariani	0-7645-5076-4	$19.99 US/$27.99 CAN
Italian Cooking For Dummies®	Cesare Casella & Jack Bishop	0-7645-5098-5	$19.99 US/$27.99 CAN
Mexican Cooking For Dummies®	Mary Sue Miliken & Susan Feniger	0-7645-5169-8	$19.99 US/$27.99 CAN
Quick & Healthy Cooking For Dummies®	Lynn Fischer	0-7645-5214-7	$19.99 US/$27.99 CAN
Wine For Dummies®, 2nd Edition	Ed McCarthy & Mary Ewing-Mulligan	0-7645-5114-0	$19.99 US/$27.99 CAN
Chinese Cooking For Dummies®	Martin Yan	0-7645-5247-3	$19.99 US/$27.99 CAN
Etiquette For Dummies®	Sue Fox	0-7645-5170-1	$19.99 US/$27.99 CAN

SPORTS

Baseball For Dummies®, 2nd Edition	Joe Morgan with Richard Lally	0-7645-5234-1	$19.99 US/$27.99 CAN
Golf For Dummies®, 2nd Edition	Gary McCord	0-7645-5146-9	$19.99 US/$27.99 CAN
Fly Fishing For Dummies®	Peter Kaminsky	0-7645-5073-X	$19.99 US/$27.99 CAN
Football For Dummies®	Howie Long with John Czarnecki	0-7645-5054-3	$19.99 US/$27.99 CAN
Hockey For Dummies®	John Davidson with John Steinbreder	0-7645-5045-4	$19.99 US/$27.99 CAN
NASCAR For Dummies®	Mark Martin	0-7645-5219-8	$19.99 US/$27.99 CAN
Tennis For Dummies®	Patrick McEnroe with Peter Bodo	0-7645-5087-X	$19.99 US/$27.99 CAN
Soccer For Dummies®	U.S. Soccer Federation & Michael Lewiss	0-7645-5229-5	$19.99 US/$27.99 CAN

HOME & GARDEN

Annuals For Dummies®	Bill Marken & NGA	0-7645-5056-X	$16.99 US/$24.99 CAN
Container Gardening For Dummies®	Bill Marken & NGA	0-7645-5057-8	$16.99 US/$24.99 CAN
Decks & Patios For Dummies®	Robert J. Beckstrom & NGA	0-7645-5075-6	$16.99 US/$24.99 CAN
Flowering Bulbs For Dummies®	Judy Glattstein & NGA	0-7645-5103-5	$16.99 US/$24.99 CAN
Gardening For Dummies®, 2nd Edition	Michael MacCaskey & NGA	0-7645-5130-2	$16.99 US/$24.99 CAN
Herb Gardening For Dummies®	NGA	0-7645-5200-7	$16.99 US/$24.99 CAN
Home Improvement For Dummies®	Gene & Katie Hamilton & the Editors of HouseNet, Inc.	0-7645-5005-5	$19.99 US/$26.99 CAN
Houseplants For Dummies®	Larry Hodgson & NGA	0-7645-5102-7	$16.99 US/$24.99 CAN
Painting and Wallpapering For Dummies®	Gene Hamilton	0-7645-5150-7	$16.99 US/$24.99 CAN
Perennials For Dummies®	Marcia Tatroe & NGA	0-7645-5030-6	$16.99 US/$24.99 CAN
Roses For Dummies®, 2nd Edition	Lance Walheim	0-7645-5202-3	$16.99 US/$24.99 CAN
Trees and Shrubs For Dummies®	Ann Whitman & NGA	0-7645-5203-1	$16.99 US/$24.99 CAN
Vegetable Gardening For Dummies®	Charlie Nardozzi & NGA	0-7645-5129-9	$16.99 US/$24.99 CAN
Home Cooking For Dummies®	Patricia Hart McMillan & Katharine Kaye McMillan	0-7645-5107-8	$19.99 US/$27.99 CAN

TECHNOLOGY TITLES

WEB DESIGN & PUBLISHING

Active Server Pages For Dummies®, 2nd Edition	Bill Hatfield	0-7645-0603-X	$24.99 US/$37.99 CAN
Cold Fusion 4 For Dummies®	Alexis Gutzman	0-7645-0604-8	$24.99 US/$37.99 CAN
Creating Web Pages For Dummies®, 5th Edition	Bud Smith & Arthur Bebak	0-7645-0733-8	$24.99 US/$34.99 CAN
Dreamweaver™ 3 For Dummies®	Janine Warner & Paul Vachier	0-7645-0669-2	$24.99 US/$34.99 CAN
FrontPage® 2000 For Dummies®	Asha Dornfest	0-7645-0423-1	$24.99 US/$34.99 CAN
HTML 4 For Dummies®, 3rd Edition	Ed Tittel & Natanya Dits	0-7645-0572-6	$24.99 US/$34.99 CAN
Java™ For Dummies®, 3rd Edition	Aaron E. Walsh	0-7645-0417-7	$24.99 US/$34.99 CAN
PageMill™ 2 For Dummies®	Deke McClelland & John San Filippo	0-7645-0028-7	$24.99 US/$34.99 CAN
XML™ For Dummies®	Ed Tittel	0-7645-0692-7	$24.99 US/$37.99 CAN
Javascript For Dummies®, 3rd Edition	Emily Vander Veer	0-7645-0633-1	$24.99 US/$37.99 CAN

DESKTOP PUBLISHING GRAPHICS/MULTIMEDIA

Adobe® In Design™ For Dummies®	Deke McClelland	0-7645-0599-8	$19.99 US/$27.99 CAN
CorelDRAW™ 9 For Dummies®	Deke McClelland	0-7645-0523-8	$19.99 US/$27.99 CAN
Desktop Publishing and Design For Dummies®	Roger C. Parker	1-56884-234-1	$19.99 US/$27.99 CAN
Digital Photography For Dummies®, 3rd Edition	Julie Adair King	0-7645-0646-3	$24.99 US/$37.99 CAN
Microsoft® Publisher 98 For Dummies®	Jim McCarter	0-7645-0395-2	$19.99 US/$27.99 CAN
Visio 2000 For Dummies®	Debbie Walkowski	0-7645-0635-8	$19.99 US/$27.99 CAN
Microsoft® Publisher 2000 For Dummies®	Jim McCarter	0-7645-0525-4	$19.99 US/$27.99 CAN
Windows® Movie Maker For Dummies®	Keith Underdahl	0-7645-0749-1	$19.99 US/$27.99 CAN

Dummies Books™
Bestsellers on Every Topic!

GENERAL INTEREST TITLES

EDUCATION & TEST PREPARATION

ACT For Dummies®	Suzee Vlk	1-56884-387-9	$14.99 US/$21.99 CAN
College Financial Aid For Dummies®	Dr. Herm Davis & Joyce Lain Kennedy	0-7645-5049-7	$19.99 US/$27.99 CAN
College Planning For Dummies®, 2nd Edition	Pat Ordovensky	0-7645-5048-9	$19.99 US/$27.99 CAN
Everyday Math For Dummies®	Charles Seiter, Ph.D.	1-56884-248-1	$14.99 US/$21.99 CAN
The GMAT For Dummies®, 3rd Edition	Suzee Vlk	0-7645-5082-9	$16.99 US/$24.99 CAN
The GRE® For Dummies®, 3rd Edition	Suzee Vlk	0-7645-5083-7	$16.99 US/$24.99 CAN
Politics For Dummies®	Ann DeLaney	1-56884-381-X	$19.99 US/$27.99 CAN
The SAT I For Dummies®, 3rd Edition	Suzee Vlk	0-7645-5044-6	$14.99 US/$21.99 CAN

AUTOMOTIVE

Auto Repair For Dummies®	Deanna Sclar	0-7645-5089-6	$19.99 US/$27.99 CAN
Buying A Car For Dummies®	Deanna Sclar	0-7645-5091-8	$16.99 US/$24.99 CAN

LIFESTYLE/SELF-HELP

Dating For Dummies®	Dr. Joy Browne	0-7645-5072-1	$19.99 US/$27.99 CAN
Making Marriage Work For Dummies®	Steven Simring, M.D. & Sue Klavans Simring, D.S.W	0-7645-5173-6	$19.99 US/$27.99 CAN
Parenting For Dummies®	Sandra H. Gookin	1-56884-383-6	$16.99 US/$24.99 CAN
Success For Dummies®	Zig Ziglar	0-7645-5061-6	$19.99 US/$27.99 CAN
Weddings For Dummies®	Marcy Blum & Laura Fisher Kaiser	0-7645-5055-1	$19.99 US/$27.99 CAN

TECHNOLOGY TITLES

SUITES

Microsoft® Office 2000 For Windows® For Dummies®	Wallace Wang & Roger C. Parker	0-7645-0452-5	$19.99 US/$27.99 CAN
Microsoft® Office 2000 For Windows® For Dummies® Quick Reference	Doug Lowe & Bjoern Hartsfvang	0-7645-0453-3	$12.99 US/$17.99 CAN
Microsoft® Office 97 For Windows® For Dummies®	Wallace Wang & Roger C. Parker	0-7645-0050-3	$19.99 US/$27.99 CAN
Microsoft® Office 97 For Windows® For Dummies® Quick Reference	Doug Lowe	0-7645-0062-7	$12.99 US/$17.99 CAN
Microsoft® Office 98 For Macs® For Dummies®	Tom Negrino	0-7645-0229-8	$19.99 US/$27.99 CAN
Microsoft® Office X For Macs For Dummies®	Tom Negrino	0-7645-0702-8	$19.95 US/$27.99 CAN

WORD PROCESSING

Word 2000 For Windows® For Dummies® Quick Reference	Peter Weverka	0-7645-0449-5	$12.99 US/$19.99 CAN
Corel® WordPerfect® 8 For Windows® For Dummies®	Margaret Levine Young, David Kay & Jordan Young	0-7645-0186-0	$19.99 US/$27.99 CAN
Word 2000 For Windows® For Dummies®	Dan Gookin	0-7645-0448-7	$19.99 US/$27.99 CAN
Word For Windows® 95 For Dummies®	Dan Gookin	1-56884-932-X	$19.99 US/$27.99 CAN
Word 97 For Windows® For Dummies®	Dan Gookin	0-7645-0052-X	$19.99 US/$27.99 CAN
WordPerfect® 9 For Windows® For Dummies®	Margaret Levine Young	0-7645-0427-4	$19.99 US/$27.99 CAN
WordPerfect® 7 For Windows® 95 For Dummies®	Margaret Levine Young & David Kay	1-56884-949-4	$19.99 US/$27.99 CAN

SPREADSHEET/FINANCE/PROJECT MANAGEMENT

Excel For Windows® 95 For Dummies®	Greg Harvey	1-56884-930-3	$19.99 US/$27.99 CAN
Excel 2000 For Windows® For Dummies®	Greg Harvey	0-7645-0446-0	$19.99 US/$27.99 CAN
Excel 2000 For Windows® For Dummies® Quick Reference	John Walkenbach	0-7645-0447-9	$12.99 US/$17.99 CAN
Microsoft® Money 99 For Dummies®	Peter Weverka	0-7645-0433-9	$19.99 US/$27.99 CAN
Microsoft® Project 98 For Dummies®	Martin Doucette	0-7645-0321-9	$24.99 US/$34.99 CAN
Microsoft® Project 2000 For Dummies®	Martin Doucette	0-7645-0517-3	$24.99 US/$37.99 CAN
Microsoft® Money 2000 For Dummies®	Peter Weverka	0-7645-0579-3	$19.99 US/$27.99 CAN
MORE Excel 97 For Windows® For Dummies®	Greg Harvey	0-7645-0138-0	$22.99 US/$32.99 CAN
Quicken® 2000 For Dummies®	Stephen L . Nelson	0-7645-0607-2	$19.99 US/$27.99 CAN
Quicken® 2001 For Dummies®	Stephen L . Nelson	0-7645-0759-1	$19.99 US/$27.99 CAN
Quickbooks® 2000 For Dummies®	Stephen L . Nelson	0-7645-0665-x	$19.99 US/$27.99 CAN

Dummies Books™
Bestsellers on Every Topic!

GENERAL INTEREST TITLES

CAREERS

Title	Author	ISBN	Price
Cover Letters For Dummies®, 2nd Edition	Joyce Lain Kennedy	0-7645-5224-4	$12.99 US/$17.99 CAN
Cool Careers For Dummies®	Marty Nemko, Paul Edwards, & Sarah Edwards	0-7645-5095-0	$16.99 US/$24.99 CAN
Job Hunting For Dummies®, 2nd Edition	Max Messmer	0-7645-5163-9	$19.99 US/$26.99 CAN
Job Interviews For Dummies®, 2nd Edition	Joyce Lain Kennedy	0-7645-5225-2	$12.99 US/$17.99 CAN
Resumes For Dummies®, 2nd Edition	Joyce Lain Kennedy	0-7645-5113-2	$12.99 US/$17.99 CAN

FITNESS

Fitness Walking For Dummies®	Liz Neporent	0-7645-5192-2	$19.99 US/$27.99 CAN
Fitness For Dummies®, 2nd Edition	Suzanne Schlosberg & Liz Neporent	0-7645-5167-1	$19.99 US/$27.99 CAN
Nutrition For Dummies®, 2nd Edition	Carol Ann Rinzler	0-7645-5180-9	$19.99 US/$27.99 CAN
Running For Dummies®	Florence "Flo-Jo" Griffith Joyner & John Hanc	0-7645-5096-9	$19.99 US/$27.99 CAN

FOREIGN LANGUAGE

Spanish For Dummies®	Susana Wald	0-7645-5194-9	$24.99 US/$34.99 CAN
French For Dummies®	Dodi-Kartrin Schmidt & Michelle W. Willams	0-7645-5193-0	$24.99 US/$34.99 CAN

TECHNOLOGY TITLES

DATABASE

Title	Author	ISBN	Price
Access 2000 For Windows® For Dummies®	John Kaufeld	0-7645-0444-4	$19.99 US/$27.99 CAN
Access 97 For Windows® For Dummies®	John Kaufeld	0-7645-0048-1	$19.99 US/$27.99 CAN
Access 2000 For Windows For Dummies® Quick Reference	Alison Barrons	0-7645-0445-2	$12.99 US/$17.99 CAN
Approach® 97 For Windows® For Dummies®	Deborah S. Ray & Eric J. Ray	0-7645-0001-5	$19.99 US/$27.99 CAN
Crystal Reports 8 For Dummies®	Douglas J. Wolf	0-7645-0642-0	$24.99 US/$34.99 CAN
Data Warehousing For Dummies®	Alan R. Simon	0-7645-0170-4	$24.99 US/$34.99 CAN
FileMaker® Pro 4 For Dummies®	Tom Maremaa	0-7645-0210-7	$19.99 US/$27.99 CAN

NETWORKING/GROUPWARE

ATM For Dummies®	Cathy Gadecki & Christine Heckart	0-7645-0065-1	$24.99 US/$34.99 CAN
Client/Server Computing For Dummies®, 3rd Edition	Doug Lowe	0-7645-0476-2	$24.99 US/$34.99 CAN
DSL For Dummies®, 2nd Edition	David Angell	0-7645-0715-X	$24.99 US/$35.99 CAN
Lotus Notes® Release 4 For Dummies®	Stephen Londergan & Pat Freeland	1-56884-934-6	$19.99 US/$27.99 CAN
Microsoft® Outlook® 98 For Windows® For Dummies®	Bill Dyszel	0-7645-0393-6	$19.99 US/$28.99 CAN
Microsoft® Outlook® 2000 For Windows® For Dummies®	Bill Dyszel	0-7645-0471-1	$19.99 US/$27.99 CAN
Migrating to Windows® 2000 For Dummies®	Leonard Sterns	0-7645-0459-2	$24.99 US/$37.99 CAN
Networking For Dummies®, 4th Edition	Doug Lowe	0-7645-0498-3	$19.99 US/$27.99 CAN
Networking Home PCs For Dummies®	Kathy Ivens	0-7645-0491-6	$24.99 US/$35.99 CAN
Upgrading & Fixing Networks For Dummies®, 2nd Edition	Bill Camarda	0-7645-0542-4	$29.99 US/$42.99 CAN
TCP/IP For Dummies®, 4th Edition	Candace Leiden & Marshall Wilensky	0-7645-0726-5	$24.99 US/$35.99 CAN
Windows NT® Networking For Dummies®	Ed Tittel, Mary Madden, & Earl Follis	0-7645-0015-5	$24.99 US/$34.99 CAN

PROGRAMMING

Active Server Pages For Dummies®, 2nd Edition	Bill Hatfield	0-7645-0065-1	$24.99 US/$34.99 CAN
Beginning Programming For Dummies®	Wally Wang	0-7645-0596-0	$19.99 US/$29.99 CAN
C++ For Dummies® Quick Reference, 2nd Edition	Namir Shammas	0-7645-0390-1	$14.99 US/$21.99 CAN
Java™ Programming For Dummies®, 3rd Edition	David & Donald Koosis	0-7645-0388-X	$29.99 US/$42.99 CAN
JBuilder™ For Dummies®	Barry A. Burd	0-7645-0567-X	$24.99 US/$34.99 CAN
VBA For Dummies®, 2nd Edition	Steve Cummings	0-7645-0078-3	$24.99 US/$34.99 CAN
Windows® 2000 Programming For Dummies®	Richard Simon	0-7645-0469-X	$24.99 US/$37.99 CAN
XML For Dummies®, 2nd Edition	Ed Tittel	0-7645-0692-7	$24.99 US/$37.99 CAN

FOR DUMMIES
BOOK REGISTRATION

Register This Book and Win!

We want to hear from you!

Visit **dummies.com** to register this book and tell us how you liked it!

- ✔ Get entered in our monthly prize giveaway.

- ✔ Give us feedback about this book — tell us what you like best, what you like least, or maybe what you'd like to ask the author and us to change!

- ✔ Let us know any other *For Dummies* topics that interest you.

Your feedback helps us determine what books to publish, tells us what coverage to add as we revise our books, and lets us know whether we're meeting your needs as a *For Dummies* reader. You're our most valuable resource, and what you have to say is important to us!

Not on the Web yet? It's easy to get started with *Dummies 101®: The Internet For Windows® 98* or *The Internet For Dummies®* at local retailers everywhere.

Or let us know what you think by sending us a letter at the following address:

For Dummies Book Registration
Dummies Press
10475 Crosspoint Blvd.
Indianapolis, IN 46256

...FOR DUMMIES™

BESTSELLING BOOK SERIES